BEHAVIOUR DISORDERS IN CHILDREN

IDENTIFICATION, ASSESSMENT AND INTERVENTION STRATEGIES

SPECIAL EDUCATION SERIES

BEHAVIOUR DISORDERS IN CHILDREN

IDENTIFICATION, ASSESSMENT AND INTERVENTION STRATEGIES

Dr. G.Lokanadha Reddy
Professor
Department of Education
Alagappa University
Karaikudi–630 003

Dr. P. Santhakumari
P.G. Asst. in English
Govt. Hr. Sec. School
Matric Hr. Sec. School
Chatrapatti–626 102

&

Dr. A. Kusuma
Reader
Dept. of Human Development
and Family Studies
Sri Padmavathi Mahila
Visvavidhyalayam
Tirupati–517 502

Dr. V. Shyamala
Principal
Jay Hind Silver Jubilee
Matric Hr. Sec. School
Ayanavaram
Chennai–600 023

D P H

DISCOVERY PUBLISHING HOUSE
NEW DELHI-110002

Published by:

DISCOVERY PUBLISHING HOUSE PVT. LTD.
4383/4B, Ansari Road, Darya Ganj
New Delhi-110 002 (India)
Phone : +91-11-23279245; 23253475; 43596065
E-mail : discoverybooksindia@gmail.com
discoverypublishinghouse@gmail.com
namitwasan9@gmail.com
web : www.discoverypublishinggroup.com

First Published: **2005**
Reprinted: **2022**

ISBN: 978-81-7141-939-5

Behaviour Disorders in Children
Identification, Assessment and Intervention Strategies

Printed at:
Infinity Imaging Systems
Delhi

Foreword

Man is a social animal and his effective survival depends on how well he behaves in different social situations. In this context, any deviation from the accepted normal code of behaviour is considered a social stigma. As a result, the study on behaviour disorders or problem behaviours from childhood to adulthood has gained momentum globally. In India too, the subject of behaviour disorders in children and adolescents is widely drawing attention of the educationists, social workers, psychologists, criminologists and mental health professionals. Unfortunately, the literature available is very meagre in Indian context and such enriched literature is the need of the hour. Here is a book with a rare blend of theoretical and research frameworks leading to practical orientations for all those who are concerned with the field of behaviour disorders.

In this book, the authors have succeeded in delineating the concept of behaviour disorders, child development and models of development, and approaches to child behaviour disorders. The specific behaviour disorders such as anxiety, depression, conduct problems, ADHD, autism, schizophrenia, mental retardation and language and learning disabilities are discussed in terms of their definition, description, prevalence, developmental course, assessment and treatment. Eventhough the chapters are similar, they are not identical in their organisation, reflecting what is currently of most interest and what is best established. The authors' experiences and practices based on their research work are presented wherever there is a scope for such things.

On the whole, the authors made a tremendous effort to bring out the ways and means of changing problem behaviour by vividly presenting the different therapeutic measures with suitable illustrations. A chapter on research in behaviour disorders of this book gives impetus into the nature of research and ethical issues to be emphasized in research on behaviour disorders which leads the readers to comprehend the various aspects to be taken care of while conducting research on behaviour disorders.

It is my sincere hope that this book will receive a wide appreciation from readers and experts. This book will, no doubt be useful for students of B.Ed., M.Ed., and research courses in various Indian Universities in general and all categories of scholars in special education in particular. Also this book will serve as an excellent guide to general education teachers to tackle the problem behaviours in their classrooms. I hope this book will give teachers, parents and field practitioners the pertinent intellectual and practical skills needed to cope with children and adolescents of deviated behaviours.

Dr. P. Kanniappan
Vice Chancellor
Alagappa University
Karaikudi–630 003

Preface

In recent years, problem behaviour is the topic addressed by different people in different contexts. Behavioural disorders in children and adolescents is the area focussed by the teachers, psychologists, social workers, psychopathologists and parents. This concept among children and adolescents is widely prevalent not only in schools but also in home and community environments. But the literature available on behavioural disorders in Indian context is very scanty. Here is a book that deals in detail about the various internalizing and externalizing problem behaviours in children and adolescents, which gives an insight to the teachers about the different dimensions of human behaviour and its deviations. It is our earnest attempt to expound the essentials of the subject matter, which is a resultant of our own study and experiences in special as well as general education contexts.

The first chapter of this book deals with the concept, meaning and definition of behaviour disorders and stresses the need for interdisciplinary approach to tackle the problem. In the second and the third chapters, child development and models of development along with different approaches to child behaviour disorders are focussed. The procedure for identification and assessment of behaviour disorders are explained in the fourth chapter as it is vital for development of any remedial programme. Chapter five to nine present different types of disorders such as anxiety, depression, aggression, conduct disorder and ADHD in terms of their concept, causes, prevalence, factors, assessment and treatment. The concept of mental retardation, its characteristics, causes, assessment, treatment and educational provisions for mentally retarded children are explained in the tenth chapter.

As there is a close link between behavioural disorders and language learning, a chapter on language and learning disorders is exclusively dealt in this book. Likewise, autism and schizophrenia are the areas that are gaining importance in Indian scenario and hence a chapter is exclusively allotted for these disorders. The eating and sleeping disorders are common in childhood and adolescents stage causing great concern to parents. Teachers and parents should be aware of these disorders in terms of their causes, characteristics and treatment. A chapter on these aspects facilitates such awareness amidst teachers and parents. Behaviour therapy, behaviour modification therapy, cognition and metacognitive strategic orientation and the need for multidisciplinary concern for changing problem behaviour in children and adolescents are discussed in the fourteenth chapter. As behaviour disorders is a thriving area for research, the basic methods and types of research, and the ethical issues in research on behaviour disorders are emphasized in the last chapter.

This book has interesting features like chapter outlines that acquaint the readers with organisation and context of each chapter, chapter learning objectives, explanations of concepts supported with ample research bases, case histories, illustrations and finally chapter summary which recapitulates the main points. Each chapter is complemented with a list of references. We are confident that the readers will be able to perceive the concepts any constructive suggestion for the betterment of this book will be gratefully acknowledged.

I express my sincere gratitude to the Ministry of Social Justice and Empowerment, Government of India, New Delhi, for providing publication grant to publish this book. Without the Ministry's financial assistance, I might have not brought out this publication successfully.

Finally, we thank M/s Discovery Publishing House, New Delhi, for the great interest and promptness they have evinced in bringing out this book at an early date inspite of their many commitments in the publishing field.

—Authors

Contents

1

Concept of Behaviour Disorders

OBJECTIVES

This chapter defines the concept of behaviour disorders in children. It states the meaning and importance of the concept. It analyses the cultural and social perspectives of behavioural disorders in simple terms. It further enlightens the concept of acquiring behaviour and explains the influence of Sigmund Freud in understanding and treating childhood behaviour disorders. It further delineates the different theories on conditioning as well as social learning theory. It then analyses the mental hygiene and child guidance movements and stresses the need for inter-disciplinary approach to behavioural disorders. After reading this chapter, the readers must be able to:

(i) Define the concept of behaviour disorders;

(ii) State its meaning and importance;

(iii) Understand the cultural and social perspectives of behavioural disorders;

(iv) Know what is requiring behaviour;

(v) Explain the influence of Sigmund Freud on understanding and treating childhood behaviour disorders;

(vi) Delineate the different theories on conditioning;

(vii) Analyse the mental hygiene and child guidance movements; and

(viii) Realize the need for interdisciplinary approach to overcome behaviour disorders.

BEHAVIOUR DISORDERS: CONCEPT, MEANING AND IMPORTANCE

Of all living organisms in the world, humans have complex and diverse behaviour. Behaviour is simply what an organism does. Human behaviour is characterised by the complexity and diversity since it stems from multiple influences and their continuous interactions. Human behaviour is called 'normal', if it falls within the range of expected norms and 'abnormal', when it deviates from the set standard. Behaviour is often viewed as a parameter to assess one's personality. It is considered to be a manipulation of 'mental soundness'. It is therefore rightly said, "Behaviour is to personality what backbone is to body".

Behavioural problems or behavioural abnormalities are nothing but the manifestations of improper/abnormal cognitive and affective functioning. They are the result of interactions among variables such as biological structure and function, inheritance, cognition, social and emotional factors, family, peers, social class, culture and situational settings. Hence behavioural repertoires come in endless varieties and in consequence, behavioural disorders are examined, evaluated and treated from several perspectives. They are also referred to by various labels: behavioural disturbances, behavioural dysfunctions, behavioural problems, psychological problems, abnormal behaviour, maladaptive behaviour, impairments, deficiencies, deficits and psychopathology. Generally people think that behavioural problem (regardless of the label), like a medical disease, has a specific indicator. But this is not so. Instead, guidelines for identifying or diagnosing behavioural disorders are relatively based on making decisions of what or what is not problematic. There is, therefore, no concise and simple way to define and identify disorders functioning. At the same time, it is both possible and meaningful to draw the line between normal and abnormal behaviours based on some practical and ethical issues. Such differentiation is essential for offering appropriate interventional remedial services.

DEFINITION OF BEHAVIOUR DISORDERS

Behaviour disorder is often viewed as an 'abnormality'. 'Ab' means 'away' or 'from', whereas 'normal' means 'average or standard'. By definition, abnormality, means 'deviating from the norm or average'. Generally, it is assumed that any deviation of behaviour from the expected standard or norm is harmful in some way to the individual and results in disorder. The American Psychiatric Association (1994) defined a 'disorder' as an individual impairment of dysfunction that causes distress to the person or increased risk of death, pain, disability or loss of freedom.

Behavioural abnormality or disorder has also been defined as a failure of function adequately towards achieving some sense of personal well-being and making some contribution to larger social-group. Experiencing personal distress/discomfort (Miller and Morley, 1986), causing distress to others and behaving maladaptively, unexpectedly or bizarrely (Davison and Neale, 1994) are some of the 'practical' or 'clinical criteria' that assist to decide upon behavioural disorders. Along with the above criteria, age, as an index of development level, is always of consideration in judging behaviour.

Judgements about behaviour call forth developmental norms also. The typical rates and sequences of the growth of skills, knowledge and social-emotional behaviour serve as developmental standards to evaluate the possibility for behavioural abnormality or disorder. If a three-year-old baby is not able to walk or to sit without support, it normally gives rise to concern. Similarly, children sometimes 'act their age' but then fail to progress. This is known as 'regression'. Quite often, behaviour that meets the age may be judged disturbed, if it occurs too frequently or infrequently; if it is too intense or insufficiently intense; or if it is too long or too short a period of time. For instance, if a child displays fear, it is not unusual. On the other hand, if it displays fear in excessive number of situations and if it does not fade away with the passage of time, then 'fearfulness' becomes a problem. Unexpected changes in behaviour too may give rise to concern. Becoming too shy, nervous, cautious or turning to 'aloofness' are some examples for unexpected changes in behaviour.

In addition to delay, regression, atypical intensity or unexpected changes in behaviour, children very rarely exhibit behaviours that appear qualitatively deviant from the norms. For instance, usually normal children display socially responsible behaviour towards their parents, caretakers and peers, when they pass along the developmental stages. But the children diagnosed as autistic display atypical unresponsive behaviours. Such qualitatively different behaviours often indicate that there is a pervasive problem in development.

Mash and Dozois (1996) argued that a behavioural disorder should be viewed as a person's reactions to environmental circumstances rather than as a dysfunction within the individual. In other words, a behavioural standard must be established for what is acceptable or healthy and decision should be made about whether the behaviour concerned meets the standard or not.

Parker et al. (1995) followed a specific approach to behavioural disorder in which efforts were taken to identify the characteristics and abilities that people 'should' possess in order to be considered 'normal' and mentally healthy. According to them, abnormality is deviating from these characteristics either by not possessing them or by possessing characteristics that should not be possessed. In this approach, abnormal behaviour is viewed as "a deviation from ideal mental health". This definition relies on 'value judgements' about what constitutes an ideal mental health. But these value judgements differ from culture to culture or from age to age and hence they are said to be 'culture-bound' and 'era-dependent'. They are also limited by context in which, a behaviour occurs. In this regard, a behaviour disorder or abnormality is highly related to cultural and social stipulations and expectations. Hence it is imperative to know about the cultural and social perspectives on behaviour disorders.

CULTURAL AND SOCIAL PERSPECTIVES OF BEHAVIOUR DISORDERS

Cultural and societal standards/norms play an important role as the broadest basis for judging behaviour. As Ruth Benedict (1934b) proposed, each society selects certain behaviours that are of value to it and socializes its members to act accordingly.

Individuals who do not display these behaviours, for whatever reasons, are considered deviant by the society. For instance, in orthodox Hindu families, talkative girls who more freely with boys are viewed as deviant of behaviour, whereas in the American society, such behaviours are accepted as normal. Similarly, Benedict (1934a) noted that the Melanesians typically exhibited 'suspiciousness'. They would never leave their cooking pots for the fear of being poisoned by others. Virtues like 'helpfulness', 'kindness' and 'cheerfulness', which are generally viewed positively in any other culture, are considered abnormal by the Melanesians.

A study by Weisz et al. (1998) showed that culture might influence the degree to which childhood problems are considered serious. Parents and teachers in the United States and Thailand were asked to go through the descriptions of child problems and then answer the questions about them. The Thai adults were less worried than the United States adults. This is because of their deep faith in their Thai Buddhism that every condition changes and that behaviour does not reflect enduring personality. In yet another study, Weisz and his colleagues (1995) reported that teachers in Thailand were more concerned about conduct problems in students than teachers in the United States. This is because Thai teachers hold more demanding behavioural standards.

Culture can also influence how problem behaviours are explained. Stahl (1991) demonstrated this in a study. Mothers of North African and Middle Eastern background living in Israel were interviewed about their children who were retarded. Almost half of the mothers gave magic-religious causes for the condition. They believed in fate, demons entering the body, evil eye and punishment from God. They also relied on magic religious treatments such as burning the child's hands to drive out demons; burning a piece of cloth belonging to the person who cast the evil eye; praying or getting help from a rabbi. All these behaviours are consistent with their cultural beliefs.

Similarly all societies have standards or 'norms' for appropriate behaviours. When a person reveals abnormality of behaviour in terms of breaking his/her own society's standards or norms, he/she is considered to possess behaviour disorder. For instance, homosexuality is viewed as a serious abnormal behaviour that violates social norms in the Indian society. But in Britain, homosexuality is legal between consenting adults over the age of 18. Similarly in the Indian society, females are expected to be more passive, dependent, quiet, shy and sensitive whereas males are expected to be relatively more aggressive, dominant, active and adventurous.

It should also be noted that changes in social values from time to time can affect judgements of behaviour. For instance, a century ago, widow remarriage was intolerable whereas now it no more remains a cause for concern. On similar grounds, allowing inter caste marriages, accepting women in all positions on par with men, giving property rights to women, accepting women entrepreneurship are some of the global social standards blossoming with the change of era.

Behavioural disorders occur at all times during childhood and adolescence and no general age trend is established. But behavioural deviations in early childhood years may persist through adulthood and most often they predict future problems. Therefore, interest in behavioural disorders in children has evolved gradually and also gained momentum. The early decades of the twentieth century marked important influences: Freud's work, behaviourism and social learning theories, the mental hygiene and child guidance movements. These events and movements brought new knowledge and conceptualisations of childhood and adolescent disorders. Moreover such vistas of knowledge offer valuable assistance in effective treatments, prevention and advocacy to problem behaviours.

ACQUIRING BEHAVIOUR

Both animals and humans acquire most of their behaviour from the world around, in other words, 'social influences'. This is because of their ability to learn. Learning is nothing but an observable behaviour. Humans have a greater capacity to learn (i.e.,. To 'acquire') and to act/ behave on the results of that learning than any other animal on the earth. But Freud claimed that children's behaviours and personalities are partly formed through the process of 'identification' with their parents. He believed that deep instinctive urges direct much of human behaviour. He proposed a grand theory of universal principles known as psychoanalytic theory to explain both normal and abnormal behaviour. Through his psychoanalytic theory, he made the first modern systematic attempt to understand behavioural disorders in psychological terms.

INFLUENCE OF SIGMUND FREUD

Although Freud recognized the importance of social influences, he emphasized intra psychic or mental processes in behavioural development. Moreover, he proposed that critical mental process were unconscious, that is, inaccessible to rational awareness. According to him, the mind or personality consisted of three mental structures' – the id, the ego and the superego – and a fixed amount of psychological energy. His theory described a dynamic process of transfer of this energy among the structures of the mind.

The id, present at birth, is the source of all psychic energy. Operating entirely at an unconscious level, the id irrationally seeks immediate and unconditional gratification of all 'instinctual' urges. These 'instinctual' or biological impulses are sexual and aggressive in nature. The other psychic structures, the ego and the super ego, evolve from id and obtain their energy from it. The ego is primarily conscious, and its principal task is to mediate between instinctual urges and reality of the outside world. The nature ego employs its rational, cognitive, decision making functions to do so. The superego develops when the immature ego cannot handle all conflicts. The superego sets ideal standards for behavioural and it is the conscience or self-critical part of the individual. In trying to satisfy the id's instinctual urges, the ego must consider not only reality but also the ideals of the superego.

As the child develops, the focus of psychic energy passes from one bodily zone to the next, leading the individual through five fixed stages of psychosexual development. Each stage derives its name from the bodily zone that is the primary source of gratification during that period. The first stage is the oral stage and it extends from birth to roughly about the first year of life.

The centre of pleasure is mouth and the infant is dependent on the mother and thus the central themes of this stage are oral pleasures and interpersonal dependency. During the second stage, the locus of satisfaction shifts to the anal zone. This stage extends through second and third years of life. This period has several themes. The primary among them are holding back and giving things freely to others, which may be reflected in ungenerous or generous personalities in later life. The third stage is the phallic stage in which the genitals become the focus of pleasure. The chief conflict of this period is the desire to possess the opposite sex parent and the fear of retaliation from the same sex parent. For the boy, this conflict is called the Oedipus complex; for the girl, it is known as the Electra complex. The resolution of the Oedipus and Electra complex is central to both sex-role and moral and superego development. The child then enters into the next stage called the latency stage at about the age of six. In this stage, sexual and aggressive impulses are subdued. With puberty, these impulses are revived and the adolescent then enters the genital stage during which heterosexual interests predominate. This stage continues throughout the remaining part of the individual's life. The latency and genital stages are less important to the understanding of behavioural disorders because Freud suggested that the basic personality structure is totally carved by the end of the phallic stage. Painful experiences in anyone stage may cause conflicts between the three parts of personality (id, ego and superego). Conflict causes anxiety that threatens development. If the conflicts are repressed, some memory stays in the unconscious and may disrupt the personality and appear later as a symptom of neurosis or hysteria.

According to Freud (1949), the child is hindered in development and induced to develop problem behaviours, if it is unable to resolve crises or conflicts at anyone stage. Moreover, failure to reach clear cut resolution in anyone stage results in the individuals getting psychologically fixed at the stage. Fixation adversely affects or hinders development during the ensuring stages. From Freud's psychoanalytic perspective, the concept of anxiety is crucial to the development of disordered behaviour. Anxiety is the danger signal to the functions of ego and as a result some unacceptable id impulse is seeking to gain consciousness. By way of protecting itself from anxiety, the ego starts creating defence mechanisms such as repression, projection, displacement and reaction formation. These mechanisms mostly function to deny or distort unacceptable impulses. Though these mechanisms are adaptive, they tend to generate psychological symptoms.

Psychoanalytic theory remained dominant approach to childhood psychopathology during the first half of the twentieth century. Its influence has then started fading away. Eventhen, its contributions towards drawing attention to the importance of mental processes, anxiety and other emotions, infant and early childhood experiences and child-parent relationships have perennial value till-date in understanding and treating childhood behaviour disorders.

CONDITIONING

Conditioning is a process by which some learning takes place under certain conditions. According to this perspective, 'learning' has been defined as "a relative permanent change in behaviour that occurs as the result of previous experience". The position that believes in conditioning is known as behavioural social learning perspective. The central concept of this perspective is that childhood disorders are learnt in the same way that other behaviours are learnt. In 1913, J.B. Watson published an essay entitled, "Psychology as a Behaviourist Views It", which set in motion the behavioural perspective and it was a major rival to the psychoanalytic theory of Freud. Watson, unlike Freud, emphasized observable events rather than unconscious intrapsychic conflicts and also on objective empirical verification. Learning and the influence of environment were considered the major focus. In addition, development was viewed as a continuous process rather than as a fixed sequence of stages. The assumption behind it was the learning continues throughout the life span and therefore 'personality' is not set by a certain age.

There are three theories, which offer assistance to explain some of children's learning. They are:

1. Classical Conditioning;

2. Operant Conditioning; and
3. Social Learning theory.

1. Classical Conditioning

The founder of Classical Conditioning was Ivan Petrovich Pavlov, a dedicated Russian scientist. He studied how certain reflexes (such as salivation) could be triggered by things, which were associated with food. He taught some laboratory dogs to salivate when they heard a particular sound (for instance, bell). To prove that dogs could learn associations, he set up an experiment in which food was presented to dogs immediately after a particular sound was made. Two stimuli were 'paired'. Each pairing is called a 'trial'. The stimuli paired were 'unconditional stimulus' (food) and 'conditional stimulus' (bell). He also suggested that there are two responses respectively. The reflexive salivation caused by the food is unconditional response and salivating to the bell is conditional response. He drew 'the Learning Curve' placing the number of trials in the horizontal axis of the graph and the amount of salivation in the vertical axis to show the animal's progress in developing responses to conditional stimuli. A response to a given stimulus (ie. Salivation) may also occur to a different but similar stimulus. This is called 'stimulus generalization'. Pavlov conditioned his dogs to salivate to different sounds. At the same time, as they learned that some buzzers or bells did not mean that food was about to appear, they learned to discriminate between the bells that meant the appearance of food and those that did not. This principle was known as 'discrimination'. The learnt response of salivation extinguished when the animal heard the sound (the conditioned stimulus) and did not receive any food (unconditioned stimulus). This was called 'extinction'.

Following Pavlov's footsteps, two psychologists wanted to see whether young babies could be conditioned. They observed that infants of just a day or two old would begin to make sucking motions when they feel a nipple. The psychologists sounded a tone immediately before some two-and-three-day-old infants were breast-fed. After a very few trials, the infants started to make sucking motions when they heard the tone.

Similarly, Watson and Rayner (1920) experimented on an eleven-month-old boy called Albert to condition fear. Initially the boy showed no fear reactions to variety of objects, including a white rat. But he exhibited fear when a loud sound was produced along with the appearance of the white rat. After several of these pairings, he reacted with crying and avoidance when the rat was presented even without noise. Following this example, the behavioural researchers focussed their attention on applying classical conditioning principles to the treatment of behaviour disorders.

Subsequently, Mary Cove Jones (1924) made another landmark study to demonstrate how the principle of classical conditioning could be applied to the removal of fearful responses. Jone's contribution was important and stimulated the development of numerous treatments based on the principles of classical conditioning.

2. Operant Conditioning

The key feature of operant conditioning is that the subject behaves in some way, which is followed by some 'reward'. The subject may associate its behaviour with the reward and so learn to repeat it. The behaviour that the subject learns is called an 'operant'. Early this century, E.L. Thorndike (1905) made researches on operant conditioning. He assumed that the animals learned the association between the stimulus and response. He used several species of animals in various puzzle boxes and brought out observations in the form of 'Law of Effect'. The law states that a response will follow a stimulus, if it is associated in the animal's mind with 'a satisfying state of affairs'.

B.F. Skinner (1953), American psychologist, started to think about applying some of the principles of conditioning to human behaviour. He used the term 'reinforcer' to apply to anything which would make the animal (or human) repeat response. The main purpose of reinforcement is to shape and then maintain particular behaviour. He identified 'positive' and 'negative' reinforcers.

The approach to learning set forth in Thorndike's Law of Effect and in the work of B.F. Skinner and his followers is the behavioural perspective, which is most extensively applied to children's disorders. Operant conditioning emphasizes the consequences of behaviour. Behaviour is acquired or reduced and it is emitted in some circumstances but not in others, through reinforcement, extinction, punishment and other learning processes. The principles of operant conditioning have increasingly been applied to a broad range of difficult and complex problems. The applications share the assumption that problem behaviour can be changed through a learning process and that the focus of treatment should be on the consequences of behaviour. Central to this approach is the concept of functional assessment, which seeks to gain an understanding of what leads the behaviour and what contributed to its recurrence. This understanding provides insight into the function that behaviour problem is serving and suggests possible treatment interventions.

3. Social Learning Theory

Social Learning Theorists accept that children learn a great deal from reinforcement and punishment. But they claim that children also learn by observing and imitating social context and they see a child's personality being the result of its modelling its ideas as well as its behaviour on various adults, social learning is therefore called "observational learning". Social learning theory emphasizes how social forces act on the child, making it believe or think in one way or another. The investigator most widely associated with observational learning or modelling is Albert Bandura. He is a social psychologist who has conducted many studies that bear on the genesis and treatment of childhood disorders. He demonstrated that children can acquire a variety of behaviours (aggression, co-operation, sharing, gratification) by watching others perform them. His studies suggest how observational learning can lead to both the acquisition and the removal of problem behaviour.

Bandura and his colleagues conducted studies on children's imitation of aggressive behaviour and these studies illustrate how a problem behaviour may be acquired through the observation of a model. Bandura (1965) showed nursery school children a five-minute film in which an adult exhibited a number of unusual, aggressive behaviours toward a Bodo doll. The behaviours were accompanied by distinctive verbalizations. One group of children saw a final scene in which the model was rewarded for aggression; another group saw a final scene in which the model was punished; and the remaining group did not see any final scene. Later each child was left alone to play in a room containing the Bodo doll and other toys. The children who had seen the model punished exhibited fewer imitative aggressive responses in the playroom. The experimenter then re-entered the room and informed that for each aggressive behaviour (like the model) which any child could reproduce, a treat would be given. Now all the three groups showed the same high level of imitative aggression. The study thus clearly demonstrated that acquisition of the aggressive behaviour had occurred. It also revealed that its performance depended on certain environmental 'payoffs'.

The phenomenon of observational learning, though it seems simple, is actually quite complex. Numerous variables influence the imitative process. Hence, whether imitation is specific or generalized, complex processes are required for observational learning to occur (Bandura, 1977b). Such learning relies on the child's attending to the salient features of the model's behaviour. The social learning perspective has, therefore, placed increasing emphasis on the role of cognition and cognitive processes such as attention, memory and problem solving (Rosenthal, 1984; Grusec, 1992). When this social learning perspective is applied explicitly to the assessment and treatment of behaviour problems, it is often called behaviour modification or behaviour therapy.

HISTORY OF MENTAL HYGIENE AND THE CHILD GUIDANCE MOVEMENTS

Until the early part of twentieth century, the treatment to behaviour disorders often consisted of custodial hospital care. Then blossomed the mental hygiene movement in the United States. It aimed to increase understanding, improve treatment and prevent disorders from occurring at all. It recognized both psychological and behavioural causes of behaviour disorders. It nurtured th belief that the behaviour disorders stemmed from failure of th individual to adapt to life circumstances. It proposed a 'commonsense' approach to studying the patient's environment and to counselling. Cliffort Beers (1908), in his audio biographical account 'A Mind that Found Itself', talked of the 'insensitive and ineffective treatment' he had received as a mental patient. He also suggested for reform towards the approach to mental hygiene. His efforts led to the establishment of the National Committee for Mental Hygiene in America to study mental dysfunctions, support treatment and encourage prevention. Rie (1971) opined that children should become the focus of study and guidance because childhood experiences are influencing adult mental hygiene.

NEED FOR INTERDISCIPLINARY APPROACH

Achenbach (1974) insisted that those treat behavioural disorders should assume a new professional role that of a psychiatric social worker. Previously, in 1896, Lightner Witmer set up the first child psychology Clinic in the United States, which primarily assessed and treated children who had learning difficulties. He also founded the journal 'Psychological Clinic' and started a hospital school for long-term observation of children. He felt the need for interdisciplinary approach and related psychology to education, sociology and other disciplines.

The interdisciplinary approach was also taken up by William Healy, a Psychiatrist and Grace Fernald, a psychologist. They founded a Juvenile Psychopathic Institute in Chicago in 1909. Its focus was on delinquent children and its approach becomes the model for child guidance. Healy was quiet convinced that antisocial behaviour could be treated by psychological means by helping youngsters adjust to the circumstances in which they lived (Santostefano, 1978). This approach required understanding the whole personality and the multiple causes of behaviour. Freudian theory provided the central ideas for dealing with psychological conflicts and attempts were made to gather information about family and other important relationships. The psychiatrist, psychologist and social worker formed a collaborative team and discussed about the cases. In Boston, Healy and his wife Augusta Bronner, a psychologist opened the Judge Baker Guidance Centre in which they followed the interdisciplinary approach. Adopting the same approach, the National Committee for Mental Hygiene also established many child clinics. The cases who suffered from personality and emotional problems were also treated in these clinics. Such clinics flourished in the 1920s and 1930s. With the establishment of the American Orthopsychiatric Association (1924) with Healy as President, the child guidance movement was formally represented.

Systematic study of youth also becomes widespread during the early twentieth century. G. Stanley Hall was the principal figure in this endeavour. He collected questionnaire data about the youth's fears, dreams, preferences, play and other aspects of functioning. Some questionnaires focussed on the problems of youth with the goal of understanding mental disorder, crime, social disorder and the like (White, 1992). Hall also contributed much towards the establishment of the American Psychological Association of which he was the first president.

Simultaneously, in Europe, Alfred Binet and Theophil Simon stared designing a test to identify children who were in need of special education. They presented children of various ages with different tasks and problems, thereby establishing age norms by which intellectual performance could be evaluated. The Binet-Simon Test (1905) became the basis for the development of intelligence tests and also encouraged professionals to search for ways to measure other psychological attributes.

The essence of today's approach to child/adolescent psychopathology is multidisciplinary involving psychology, psychiatry, biology, neurobiology, medicine, education, sociology and anthropology, which contribute somewhat different but overlapping knowledge, understandings and interests. In short, the multidisciplinary approach emphasizes diversity and complexity.

SUMMARY

Behaviour is simply what a living organism does. Humans have complex and diverse behaviour. Human behaviour is called 'normal' if it falls within the range of expected norms and 'abnormal', when it deviates from the set standard. Behavioural problems are nothing but manifestations of improper/abnormal cognitive and affective functioning. They are referred to by various labels: behavioural disturbances, behavioural dysfunctions, psychological problems, abnormal behaviour, maladaptive behaviour, impairments, deficiencies, deficits and psychopathology.

Judgements about behaviour call forth developmental norms also. The typical rates and sequences of the growth of skills, knowledge and social-emotional behaviour serve as developmental standards to evaluate the possibility for behavioural abnormality. Mash and Dozois (1996) argued that a behavioural disorder should be viewed as a person's reactions to environmental circumstances rather than as a dysfunction within the individual. Parker et al. (1995) followed an approach in which abnormal behaviour is viewed as a deviation from ideal mental health and thus behaviour disorder is highly related to cultural and social stipulations.

Cultural and societal standards/norms play an important role as the broadest basis for judging behaviour.

Behavioural disorders occur at all times during childhood and adolescence and no general age trend is established. But behavioural deviations in early childhood years may persist through adulthood and most often they predict future problems. Therefore, interest in behavioural disorders in children has evolved gradually and gained momentum. The early decades of the twentieth century marked important influences: Freud's work, behaviourism and social learning theories, the mental hygiene and the child guidance movements. The knowledge about these aspects offers valuable assistance in effective treatments, prevention of and advocacy to problem behaviours.

Freud emphasised intrapsychic or mental processes in behavioural development. His psychoanalytic theory remained dominant approach to childhood psychopathology during the first half of the twentieth century.

On the contrary to psychoanalytic theory, the behavioural/ social learning perspective believes in 'conditioning'. The behaviourists view the development as a continuous process rather than as a fixed sequence of stages. The three theories—classical conditioning, operant conditioning and social learning theory—

offer assistance to explain children's learning. Operant conditioning perspective believes that behaviour is acquired or reduced through reinforcement, extinction, punishment and other learning processes whereas the social learning perspective emphasizes the importance of social forces and stresses the phenomenon of observational learning. In its extreme, the social learning theory places increasing emphasis on the role of cognition. Cognitive processes such as attention, memory and problem solving and thus gives rise to behaviour modification therapy.

The mental hygiene and child guidance movements that flourished during the later part of twentieth century nurtured the belief that the behaviour disorders stemmed from failure of the individual to adapt to life circumstances. They proposed a 'commonsense' approach to study the environment as well as to counselling. Then bloomed the realization of the need for interdisciplinary approach to behaviour disorders and this approach related psychology to education, sociology and other disciplines. The essence of today's approach to child/adolescent psychopathology is multidisciplinary involving psychology, psychiatry, biology, neurobiology, medicine, education, sociology and anthropology. In short, this approach emphasizes diversity and complexity.

REFERENCES

American Psychiatric Association (1994) *Diagnostic and Statistical Manual of Mental Disorders*. Washington D.C.: American Psychiatric Association.

Bandura, A., (1965) 'Influence of Models' Reinforcement Contingencies on the Acquisition of Imitative Responses'. *Journal of Personality and Social Psychology*, 1, 589-595.

Bandura, A., (1977b), *Social Learning Theory*. Englewood Cliffs, NJ: Prentice Hall.

Benedict, R., (1934a), 'Anthropology and the Abnormal'. *Journal of General Psychology*, 10, 59–82.

Benedict, R., (1934b), *Patterns of Culture*. Boston: Houghton–Mifflin.

Davison, G. and Neale, J.,(1994), *Abnormal Psychology*. (6th Edition). New York: Wiley.

Freud, S., (1949), *An Outline of Psycho-analysis*. Translated and Newly Edited by J.Stratchey. New York: W.W. Norton & Co.

Grusec, J.E., (1992), 'Social Learning Theory and Developmental Psychology: The Legacies of Robert Sears and Albert Bandura'. *Developmental Psychology*, 28, 776-786.

Jones, M.C., (1924), 'A Laboratory Study of Fear: The Case of Peter'. *Pedagogical Seminary*, 31, 308-315.

Mash, E.J. and Dozois, D.J.A., (1996), 'Child Psychopathology: A Developmental–systems Perspective'. In E.J. Mash & R.A. Barkley (Eds.), *Child Psychopathology*. New York: Guilford Press.

Miller, E. and Morley, S., (1986), *Investigating Abnormal Behaviour*. London: Erlbaum.

Parker, J.G., Rubin, K.H., Price, J.M. and De Rosier, M.E., (1995), 'Peer Relationship, Child Development and Adjusıment: A Developmental Psychopathology Perspective'. In D. Cicchetti & D. Cohen (Eds.), *Developmental Psychopathology (Vol. 2: Risk, Disorder and Adaptation)*. New York: Wiley.

Rosenthal, T.L., (1984), 'Some Organizing Hints for Communicating Applied Information'. In B. Gholson & T.L. Rosenthal (Eds.) *Applications of Cognitive–developmental Theory*. Orlando, F.L.: Academic Press.

Santostefano, S., (1978), *A Bio-developmental Approach to Clinical Child Psychology*. New York: Wiley-Inter Science.

Skinner, B.F., (1953), *Science and Human Behaviour*. New York: Macmillan.

Stahl, A., (1991), 'Beliefs of Jewish–Oriental Mothers Regarding Children Who are Mentally Retarded'. *Educational and Training in Mental Retardation*, 26, 361-369.

Thorndike, E.L., (1905), *The Elements of Psychology*. New York: Seiler.

Watson, J.B., (1913), 'Psychology as the Behaviourist Views It'. *Psychological Review*, 20, 158-177.

Watson, J.B. and Rayner, R., (1920), 'Conditioned Emotional Reactions'. *Journal of Experimental Psychology*, 3, 1-14.

Weisz, J.R., Chaiyasit, W., Weiss, B., Eastman, K.L. and Jackson, E.W., (1995), 'A Multimethod Study of Problem Behaviour Among Thai and American Children in School: Teacher Reports Versus Direct Observations'. *Child Development*, 66, 402–415.

Weisz, J.R., Suwanlet, S., Chaiyasit, W., Weiss, B., Walter, B.R. and Anderson, W.W., (1998), 'Thai and American Perspectives on Over-and Under Controlled Child Behaviour Problems: Exploring the Threshold Model Among Parents, Teachers and Psychologists'. *Journal of Counselling and Clinical Psychology*, 56, 601-609.

White, S.H., (1992), G. Stanley Hall: From Philosophy to Developmental Psychology. *Developmental Psychology*, 28, 25-34.

2

Child Development and Models of Development

OBJECTIVES

This chapter explains the concept of development and describes the developmental psychopathology. It analyses the contributions of genetics and also the role of physical and motor development in the build up of maladaptive behaviour. It shows how the physical disabilities influence the development. Further, development in relation to emotional and socio-cultural context is presented. This chapter also explains the models of development and conceptualises the developmental influences on behaviours. Finally it delves into the risk in indigenous populations. After reading this chapter, the readers must be able to:

(i) Define the concepts of development and developmental psychopathology;

(ii) Understand the contributions of genetics in behavioural developmental;

(iii) Know about the influence of physical disabilities on development;

(iv) Comprehend the concept of development in relation to emotional and socio-cultural context;

(v) Present the models of development;

(vi) Conceptualize developmental influences on behaviours;

(vii) Explain the timing of developmental influences; and

(viii) Define the risk in indigenous populations.

CONCEPT OF DEVELOPMENT

The relationship between normal and abnormal development is very important and this is universally acknowledged. Developmental psychology traditionally dealt with normal development as its subject matter until a few decades ago. Since then, developmental psychology and clinical child/adolescent psychology and psychiatry began to recognise that each had something to contribute as well as to gain from the other. Their cooperative efforts became meaningful after 1970s to warrant a recognizable new label called 'developmental psychopathology' (Cicchetti, 1984 and 1989). Developmental psychopathology is considered to be a general framework for understanding disordered behaviour in relation to normal development (Achenbach, 1990; Cicchetti and Cohen, 1995). As Sroufe (1986) remarked, this approach is interested not only in the origins and developmental course of disordered behaviour but also in individual adaptation and success.

The developmental approach contributed several specific issues to the study of problem behaviour of children and adolescents. The most important contribution is its descriptions of the usual course of growth. These descriptions are very helpful to judge problematic behaviour. The developmental research findings and developmental theories contribute facts, hypotheses and models pertaining to the processes responsible for development and thus they reveal obvious ways in which development might deviate. Numerous changes occur during one's lifetime. A single theory cannot explain all these changes. Hence diverse accounts of these developmental theories must be given enough consideration. The developmental approach is also focussing on specific issues that are relevant to child adolescent disorders. For instance, this approach is interested in conceptualizing the variables that either promote or hinder optimal development and in understanding the stability or continuity of behaviour over a period of time. Such issues are necessary for a thorough understanding of normal as well as abnormal development.

First of all, one should understand what development is. Generally it is treated as a synonym to 'growth' that occurs overtime. But development is much more complex. The developmental framework includes the following guidelines:

1. Development refers to change over the lifetime. This change may be either quantitative or qualitative or both;
2. There is a common, general course of early development of physical, cognitive, emotional and social systems. Within each system, early global structures and functions are finely differentiated and then integrated. Integration also occurs across systems;
3. Development, as some theorists emphasize, occurs in distinct qualitative stages that appear in he same order in all individuals. On the other hand, still some theorists believe that development is a gradual change, which may or may not have a fixed ordering and thus they negate the distinct stages of concept of development;
4. Development proceeds in a coherent pattern so that for each individual, present functioning is properly woven to the past as well as to the future;
5. Developmental change may take many forms during the lifespan. Particularly, these changes need not be positive always;
6. Human development is malleable but there are limitations on what can change and how much change is likely;
7. Above all, development is the result of interactions among biological, psychological and socio-cultural variables.

From the above guidelines, we come to a conclusion that normal development encompasses a wide array of complex influences and processes. We have to survey many aspects of early development, which serves as a broad context within which behavioural problems may occur.

GENETICS IN DEVELOPMENT

The contributions of 'genetics' to behavioural development operate in complex ways, both at species and at individual levels. The human beings are biologically tuned for common characteristics, through evolutionary processes, to adapt to environmental circumstances. Normal biological development ensures that children can physically manipulate the environment, take in and process information about the world around, communicate with others and form social and emotional bindings with others. However, some children do not adhere to this normal development pattern. This pattern deviates in their cases and as a result, problems ranging from negligible level to severity might occur. Further, when development is fundamentally sound also, the biological system provides ample scope for individuals to vary in characteristics. These variations are effected by many factors. One among these factors is genes.

The basic genetic material in the human cell consists of chromosomes. On these chromosomes, the hereditary units called genes occupy fixed places. Chromosomes are composed of deoxyribonucleic acid (DNA), the hereditary material that directs development and cell activity. Most cells have twenty-three pairs of chromosomes. One pair, the sex chromosomes, differs in females and males. Females have two X Chromosomes and males have an X and a Y chromosome. The Y chromosome has comparatively fewer genes and it is smaller as well as lighter.

In contrast to other cells, the ovum and sperm undergo a special maturation process called 'meiosis' which results in each having only twenty three single chromosomes, one from each of the original pairs. Thus at conception, each prospective parent contributes half of the chromosome complement to the offspring. Perspective mothers contribute an X chromosome, whereas perspecti fathers can contribute either an X or a Y chromosome.

The processes of meiosis and conception assure billions of possible chromosome combinations for anyone individual. Other genetic mechanisms result in even greater variability. For instance, chromosomes may exchange genes, break and reattach to each other and change by mutation, which is spontaneous alteration of the DNA molecule. Environmental interactions too contribute further to produce an infinite variety of humans.

Hereditary influences on behavioural characteristics are often misunderstood. Genes act only indirectly by guiding the biochemistry of cells. Some characteristics for which genetic influence has been established can substantially be modified by the environment. For instance, height is genetically influenced. But at the same time, it can be affected and modified by environmental conditions like diet and illness. Genes are therefore thought of as assisting to set a range within which characteristics develop. In addition, hereditary effects are often not set over time. In general, the path between genetic endowment (the 'genotype') and observable characteristics of the individual (the 'phenotype') is much more indirect and flexible than is often believed. Genetic influences on adaptive or maladaptive behaviour are crucial but they operate in conjunction with environmental influences.

PHYSICAL AND MOTOR DEVELOPMENT

Conception takes place in the fallopian tube. Within a few days of conception, the Zygote attaches itself to the wall of the uterus. The Zygote floats itself freely in the amniotic sac except for its attachment by the umbilical cord to the placenta of the mother. After conception, it takes about thirty-eight weeks for the zygote to develop into a full baby and subsequently birth occurs. These weeks of parental growth are very crucial in the sense that the organism is dramatically affected by biological and environmental factors. Adversities during pregnancy and birth are associated with numerous later behavioural difficulties.

Following some general principles, growth during the parental period occurs in a quite predictable manner. Growth takes place from the head to the tail regions (cephalo caudal) and so at birth, the head is dispropo.:tionately large. Growth also occurs from the centre of the body to the periphery. This process is illustrated in parental development by the growth of the chest and truck prior to that of the limbs, fingers and toes. With later development body proportion changes.

Throughout lifetime, different body parts develop at different rates (Tanner, 1970). For instance, during infancy and early childhood, the skeleton, muscles and internal organs grow rapidly. This growth slows down during middle childhood. again the rate of growth is accelerated in adolescence. On the contrary, the reproductive system, that shows slow process of development until adolescence, grows rapidly after adolescence. The sexual maturation is called 'puberty'. At the age of twenty or so, most of physical growth gets completed. Stability and aging characterize the physical systems during adulthood.

The nervous system begins to develop shortly after conception, when a group of cells called the neural plate thickens, folds forward and forms the neural tube. This tube differentiates into the nervous system and most brain cells are produced prenatally (Nowakowski, 1987). At birth the brain is about 25 per cent of its adult weight, making it proportionately larger than most other organs. Further growth occurs after birth. At about the fifth year, the brain reaches 95 per cent of its adult weight. The nerve cells (neurons) grow in size and in number of synaptic connections to the neurons. Myelin, a fatty cover, continues tc be laid down on the axons of some neurons; myelin speeds up nerve transmission. Different parts of the nervous system develop in spurts more rapidly than others, and this pattern is related to functioning (Greenough, Black and Wallace, 1987). The nerves that control reflexes are well developed at birth. But areas that control voluntary movement grow substantially during the first year of life and later. Brain development depends not only on biological programming but also on experience. Research findings of Hockfield and Lombroso (1998) revealed that animals, which have the opportunity to explore enriched environments, developed more neurons and synapses than animals reared in simple environment. Similarly, Casaer (1993) found out that experience also shapes early brain development by eliminating or pruning neurons that have few or redundant connections. Such brain changes are associated with behaviour such as increased capacity to learn and the ability to respond to specific sensory stimuli.

Motor development too is quite predictable like the physical development. Infants display many involuntary reflexes. Thelen (1986) found that some reflexes like blinking and sucking are related to vital bodily functioning whereas others are of questionable value and disappear early or get transformed into voluntary action. The absence of reflexes at birth and the persistence of specific reflexes beyond certain times are signs of nervous system dysfunction. Abnormal reflexes sound early warnings of developmental problems.

Voluntary movement also develops in a well known sequence. Generally it follows the head-to-tail principle. Babies gain control of their arms quickly than of their legs. Similarly, children are able to control the centre of the body before the extremities; they control large areas before small muscle groups. This is why, children find it difficult to hold the crayons or pencils at the early stage. Once when they gain control over specific muscle groups, they begin to integrate many motor operations into complex movements. Some motor milestones and the average age at which they are displayed are very useful to understand normal motor development.

Motor Milestones	Months
Rolls over	2 to 4
Sits without support	5 to 7
Stands holding on to furniture	8 to 9
Creeps on hands and knees	9 to 10
Stands without support	10 to 13
Walks alone	11 to 14
Walks upstairs alone, two feet per step	21 to 25

Deviations from the timing and patterning of these milestones indicate nervous system dysfunctioning and risk for developmental problems. Children's ability to jump rope, skate, climb, ride bicycles and the like increases noticeable between the age of six and twelve and these skills reach the maximum level of performance during teen age.

INFLUENCE OF PHYSICAL DISABILITIES ON DEVELOPMENT

The growth of motor and physical characteristics are of interest in themselves and also because they influence other aspects of development. For instance, if motor development is abnormal, the child may be considerably disadvantaged in manipulating and learning about the world. Jennings, Connors and Stegman (1988) have reported that motor handicaps and slow motor development can lessen motivation for mastering the environment and also they may influence how the child is perceived by others and the self. Similarly, physical abnormality may often be avoided/ neglected by others or reacted with a mix of sympathy, curiosity, disregard or embarrassment. Sometimes, people may be overly polite to physically abnormal individuals due to the fact that they are not sure about how to respond to physical abnormality. As a result, those with physical difficulties may further become disadvantaged, as they do not receive appropriate feed back about their behaviour. Sometimes, they may even be tempted to retort with aggression, frustration, anger and self-pity. Timing of puberty, as reported by Malo and Tremblay (1997), is yet another aspect of physical growth that can influence psychosocial functioning. Early maturing boys have been found as more popular, poised and attractive. But they also show problem behaviour. Later maturation in boys has been linked with anxiety, low self-esteem, and low social competence. In girls, early maturation is associated with depression, anxiety and troublesome behaviour. Due to early maturation, some girls select older peers, tend to break social norms, become involved in adolescent dating and drug use or drop out of school, as revealed by the study of Stattin and Magnusson (1990).

COGNITION AND COMMUNICATION

Infants, even from birth, are endowed with considerable capacity to sense their surroundings as well as to learn from them. Seeing, hearing, smelling, tasting and touching are the obvious examples. All the above activities develop rapidly during the first year of life and they provide a basis for experiencing the environment. Normally, a child with appropriate development perceives all sensory information accurately and processes it through learning and cognition. Children cognicize and conceptualize through many ways. The three basic and widely recognized learning processes are classical conditioning, operant conditioning and observational learning about which we have seen elaborately in the first chapter itself. These learning processes operate at or soon after birth. They enable the infant to associate events and to appropriately respond to them with increasing variability to events. The above basic processes of learning become more and more complex when the children are exposed to complex surroundings and events and inturn higher mental processes develop. The higher mental processes include the abilities to select and maintain attention to stimuli, form concepts, manipulate information and think about the surrounding world.

The most important approach that analyses the higher mental processes is widely known as the information processing approach. According to this approach, it is assumed that information is received by the sensory organs and encoded into the brain. There it is first received into short-term or working memory and then stored in long-term memory and used in thinking about or responding to the world. In this information-processing model, the cognitive processes like attention mechanisms and strategies to handle/ manipulate information are considered very crucial. Further, the information processing system of an individual operates executive functions, which permit the individual to plan, select, monitor, evaluate and revise strategies.

Jean Piaget's developmental theory is yet another influential view of cognition. In Piaget's view, the child is a biological organism that adopts to its environment by organizing and interpreting experiences actively (Flavell, 1963; Peterson, 1982). When the child is engaged in the above activities, the child's mind first constructs simple mental structures, otherwise called 'schemes' and then complex ones. Some of the child's experiences are interpreted by already existing schemes. This process is known as 'assimilation'. Still some of them require modification and growth of schemes. This process is called "accommodation". Both these processes (assimilation and accommodation) assist the child's mind to develop increasingly advanced schemas and to attain greater understanding of the world. This kind of cognitive development requires simultaneously biological maturation and experience. Hence Piaget hypothesized that cognitive growth occurs in four distinct periods/ stages which are roughly related with chronological age.

Piaget's Stages of Cognitive Development

Cognitive Development Stage	Corresponding Chronological age	Typical Behaviours
Sensorimotor stage	Birth to 2 years	Initially innate sensory motor reflexes; the behaviour becomes voluntary and integrated; mental ability develops to represent world in images and words.
Pre operational stage	2 to 7 years	Broadened view of the world is attained through concepts of space, number, colour etc.
Concrete operational stage	7 to 11 years	Able to see the world from other's point of view; increased understanding of relationships and events.
Formal operational stage	12 years onwards	Logical thinking develops; abstract thinking develops; able to form and evaluate hypotheses, deduce and induce principles.

Piaget's developmental theory assumed that the above four stages occur in a particular sequences and build on the preceding ones. This theory has valuable implications for how children perceive the world at any particular stage, what they are prepared to learn and how developmental problems might be interpreted.

Another important factor closely linked with cognitive development is the growth of communication skills such as language. To use language, a child needs the abilities such as distinguishing individual speech sounds, producing them correctly, to integrate them into words and words into grammatically correct sentences. Apart from these abilities, the child should be able to derive meaning from others' speech and to grasp the social context in which a message is being sent. To be an effective communicator, the child should both receive the message sent by others and send appropriate messages to others in accordance with the contextual needs/demands. Language acquisition is a time bound process that occurs simultaneously along with cognitive development and chronological ageing. By the time children begin elementary schooling, most of them master basic skills (Baker and Cantwell, 1991), communication continues to be perfected for many years, even though adulthood.

Language acquisition fascinates philosophers and scientists. Some of them insist on the focus of biological programming whereas some others insist on environmental input (Whitehurst and Valdez-Menchaca, 1988). No doubt, biological system is constructed in such a way to master language. At the same time, language development relies on social input. Social environment provides appropriate stimulation and facilitates early language acquisition. For instance, children brought up in big joint families quickly learn language than the ones growing in lonely surroundings. In addition, language is obviously related to intellectual functioning. Besides, it is a social activity. Impairments in language and communication can therefore, result in academic problems, social interactional problems, social isolation and low self-esteem.

DEVELOPMENT IN RELATION TO EMOTIONAL AND SOCIO-CULTURAL CONTEXT

There is no human experience on earth without emotional influence. Private experiences result either in outward expressions or emotions by smiles, frowns, scowls, drooping necks, murmurs and biting lips or personally experiencing the 'feelings' of sadness, happiness, anger, disgust, frustration and self-pity. The findings of Harris (1994) and Izard (1994) reveal that even very young infants show emotional outbursts and respond appropriately to the emotional expressions of their caretakers.

Often emotions are mistaken to be synonymous to temperament. Temperament, of course, includes emotion but it refers to basic disposition or makeup. The concept of temperament goes back to the classical Greek era. The temperament and problem behaviours are closely related. Chess and Thomas (1977) took interest in this aspect and they studied the New York city children. They were particularly interested in explaining how the problem behaviours develop. Environmental influences on the development of behaviour were duly recognized by these researchers. They were also struck by the individual differences in how infants behaved from the first day to life. On the basis of parental interviews and actual observations, they demonstrated that young babies had distinct individual differences in temperament that were somewhat stable over time. They also identified three basic temperamental styles: easy, slow-to-worm and difficult of which 'difficult temperament' is characterised by negative mood, intense reactions to stimuli, sleep irregularity and the like. Later researchers like Caspi, Elder & Bem (1988) and Gjone & Stevenson (1997a) associated this 'difficult temperament' with social and psychological disturbance.

Temperament is considered very important in development because the child's way of behaving enters immediately into social interactions that, in turn, influence the general environment and the child's behavioural tendencies. As Kagan, Arus and Sridman (1993) opined, temperament can be expected to be transformed and the individual's changing characteristic continue to play a role in his or her development.

Both emotions and temperament are having strong implications in a variety of behaviour disorders. Hence it is necessary that all children must learn to regulate or control their emotions. The acquisition of emoticnal regulation encompasses various capabilities such as learning to monitor, evaluate and modify the intensity as well as timing of emotional reactions. Weinberg et al. (1999) and Williams et al. (1999) found that emotional control is a major developmental task and it can be mastered gradually. They also arrived at the findings that some youngsters have more difficulty than others in regulating their emotional reactions. In addition, inadequate emotional control can cause anxiety and upset and can make it difficult for children to recover from stress to 'emotional calmness'. For some youngsters, regulating anger is very challenging. Thus the quality and the intensity of the emotions play an important role in behaviour disorders either as a central factor or as a side effect

Socio-cultural context also plays a crucial role in development. Development, whether it is adaptive or maladaptive occurs only in the socio-cultural context. Each child is typically viewed as embedded within family, community and cultural domains, which are not separate entities. All the three of them interact and overlap with each and the child. The variations in anyone domain cause variations in developmental level. According to Maccoby (1992), family is considered a major arena for socialization of children. Family influence is dominant during childhood when malleability is high and is pervasive throughout the entire life span. Early family attachments, family interactions, family roles and structure were broad aspects of the family context within which normal and disordered behaviour develop. Early child-parent interactions are the basis for the special social-emotional bond, which is called attachment. Researchers like Lyons-Ruth, Zeanah and Benoit (1996) identified four patterns of attachment: i) secure, ii) ambivalent, iii) avoidant and iv) disorganized/ disoriented. Of these, disorganized/ disoriented type of attachment is revealed by infants who have been exposed to pathological, abusive care taking. Such attachment leads to behaviour disorders like excessive social inhibition, excessive sociability or attachment to relative strangers. Similarly 'secure' attachment is associated with adaptive behaviour in childhood and adolescence such as competence and positive peer interactions. On the other hand, insecure attachment places children at risk for maladaptive behaviours and problems (Dunn and McGurie, 1992). Attachment experiences are hypnotized to become internalized. In other words, they become a basis for the child's construction of an internal working model for subsequent adaptation and relationships. Kerns et al. (1996) found that securely attached children have confidence in their caretakers and trust in others and this quality becomes a model for future relationships.

Family interactions exert direct influence on the behaviour of children. Dubow, Huesmann and Eron (1987) suggested the importance of parenting style. Maccoby and Martin (1983) found two dimensions to be central to how parents manage their children. Those two dimensions are degree of control and degree of acceptance. On the basis of these dimensions, they identified four types of parenting styles: authoritative, authoritarian, indulgent/ permissive and neglectful. Particular child characteristics are thought to be associated with each style. It is generally agreed that the authoritative style is related to most favourable attributes because such parents are warm, accepting and considerate. Their children in turn tend to become independent, socially responsible, pro social and self-confident. On the other hand, the authoritarian parents beget children with aggressive behaviour and low-esteem. Similarly children of indulgent or permissive parents tend to be impulsive, aggressive, dependent and irresponsible. Steinberg et al. (1994) arrived at the findings that neglectful parenting is associated with children's having difficulties in getting along with parents and peers, displaying antisocial behaviour and having school problems.

Family roles, family structure and peer relationships have a strong hold on the behavioural patterns of the children. Apart from the above, school remains the major context for moulding children's behaviour. Schools operate as social systems in and of themselves. Student-teacher relationships, classroom structure, pedagogy, rules, methods of discipline, standards and expectations all play a crucial role in shaping children's behaviour. Eccles et al. (1993) proved that certain qualities of school climate foster scholastic and positive social behaviours. Sylva (1994) also confirmed that schools exert sizable influence on academic achievement, social behaviour and later employment.

Social class or socio economic status (SES) which is determined by factors like family income, educational achievement and occupational level have a direct spell on children's behaviour. Almost all societies are stratified according to social class. Again social class is marked by differences due to environmental conditions, values, attitudes, expectations and opportunities. Investigations of Bradley and Whiteside-Mansell (1997) and McLoyd (1998) found that children of poor families are at risk for many adverse outcomes. They are more likely to die and to suffer from diseases and disabilities. Moreover, child-rearing practices do vary by social class.

The influences of social class operate within some broader cultural context of beliefs and values. Culture not only affects the goals toward which children are shaped but also influences how these goals are attained. The Indian culture expects the children to be passive, submissive, dependent on parents upto eighteen years or even more, very disciplined and to follow traditional role models. Similarly Mc Dermott (1991) observed that mothers and teachers in Japan and the United States interact differently with children (may be in accordance with the demands of their respective culture) and that this difference is linked to children's characteristics.

MODELS OF DEVELOPMENT

Developmentalists unanimously agree that growth is the result of numerous variables like biological, psychological and socio cultural. These variables continuously interact to bring about development. Different models of development are proposed the knowledge of which is a imperative for psychopathologists. These models of development describe and analyse in their own terms how development occurs.

Multifactor/Integrative Models

Multi factor or integrative models of development are otherwise known as interactional or transactional models. These models are based on the assumption that many factors interact to bring about developmental change and that interaction is ongoing or transactional and not static. This assumption appeals to common sense. The developmentalists who employ multi factor models try in different ways to explain behaviour. Two important examples of these models are the bio psychosocial model and the goodness-of-fit model both of which address behaviour problems (Compas, Hinden and Gerhardt, 1995).

The Bio Psycho-social Model

As it is implied by the name, the bio psycho-social model presumes that development is a function of interacting biological and psycho-social variables. The biological and the psycho-social (environmental) determinants of development were considered to be two entirely different groups in the past. That is, some argued that biological influences, especially genetic programming, primarily determined the development of children while others argued that environmental experiences and learning played the critical role in development. This is known as nature-nurture dichotomy. But now-a-days this dichotomy is rejected on the basis of empirical evidences. For instance, the findings of Aoki and Siekevitz (1988) showed that optimal development of brain and visual system depends on both genetic programming and stimulation from the environment. In this study, the researchers used only animals. The interplay of biology and environment in humans is provided by children born prematurely or suffering medical complications just before or after birth (Greenberg and Crinic, 1988; Sameroff, 1990). Generally, such individuals have more neurological and intellectual difficulties later in life than full-term infants. Still, it was discovered that many cases of premature infants do well and become indistinguishable from the full term infants, thanks to family and cultural factors. In such cases, social class/ home environment has become the important predictor of developmental outcome. Hence it is now commonly acknowledged that the development of children born with adverse medical experiences requires a multifactor explanation that considers both biological and psycho-social variables.

The Goodness-of-Fit Model

This model is based on the assumption that developmental outcome depends partly on how the children 'fit' or match their environments. In other words, development depends on how well the person and the environment fit each other. For instance, the conceptualization of match or mismatch is central in the work of Eccles and her colleagues (1993), which deals with adolescence. In the United States, the adolescent years are widely viewed as a time of biological and psychological transition, which is successfully negotiated by most individuals. However, 15 to 30 per cent of adolescents drop out of school, regularly consume alcohol and drugs, and get into legal trouble. Many of the problems begin in early adolescence. Eccles and her colleagues hypothesized that this situation results from a mismatch between the needs of developing adolescents and the opportunities provided by the school and the family. Their findings suggested that a mismatch between adolescent need for autonomy and the school environment might help explain the development of problems. In this developmental analysis, physical maturation interacts with the social environment to bring about a poor person-environment fit. Such a multi factor interactional analysis has much to offer when we seek better understanding about the development of behaviour problems.

CONCEPTUALIZING DEVELOPMENTAL INFLUENCES ON BEHAVIOURS

The above mentioned models conceptualize all the variables that underlie development simply as biological, psychological and socio-cultural. This is the usual and simple way of conceptualising the developmental influences. There are several other useful ways possible to view the developmental factors or influences. The developmental influences can be

(i) normative or non normative

(ii) necessary or sufficient

(iii) direct or indirect

(i) Normative or Non Normative Influences

Normative influences are influences, which happen to most people in predictable way. They are age graded and affect almost all individuals at similar times of life. For instance, puberty occurs for most people between the age of eleven and fourteen. Similarly, entrance into elementary education occurs between the age of five and seven years. On the other hand, non normative influences may occur only to certain persons, perhaps at unpredictable times and in a typical circumstances. For instance, severe illness or losing parents at young age occurs rarely in the life of individuals. Such non normative events are the chance events that affect development.

Both normative and non normative influences vary across cultures. Generally, non normative influences are more likely to result in heightened stress or challenge. For example, a child's severe illness presents challenges to adaptation.

(ii) Necessary or Sufficient Influences

Some developmental influences must 'necessarily' be present for the behaviour problem to occur. However, a necessary influence may or may not be sufficient to produce to the disorder. For instance, schizophrenia is a debilitating dysfunction, which affects youth. Many investigators believe that some genetic abnormality must exist and that is the necessary cause for the occurrence of the problem. But in some cases, the presence of genetic abnormality does not result in this disorder. That is, the genetic abnormality is sufficient to produce the disorder. The distinction between necessary and sufficient influences is essential to recognize the fact that many factors, which may play a role in development, do not necessarily play the same or equal roles. There are still some disorders for which one single factor is not clearly necessary. Different influences may add together and reach a threshold to produce an adverse outcome.

(iii) Direct or Indirect Influences

Influences on development may be direct or indirect. When direct influences operate, a particular variable (say X) directly leads to a particular outcome (say Y). In the case of indirect influences, the variable X influences one or more variables first, which, inturn, lead to Y. Usually it is more difficult to establish the indirect influences because a maze of complex influences exists in between cause and result.

THE TIMING OF DEVELOPMENTAL INFLUENCES

The time at which an influence occurs can make a difference in psychopathology. That is, events and experiences may have different influences, depending on the developmental level of the individual. For example, a child's separation from its mother due to death is probably less impact for a two-month-old child than at two-year-old baby because attachment is less at two months. Developmentalists have a special interest in the influence of early experience on the origin of problem behaviours. Researches on animals clearly indicate that early experiences are specifically having impact on the brain and behavioural development. Theoretical propositions also stress the importance of early influence. For instance, Freud (1949) considered the infant's love for its mother as the prototype for all later love relationships and thus crucial for social-personality development. Similarly, social learning theorists also suggested that early learning might be very important because it serves as basis for later learning.

RISK IN INDIGENOUS POPULATIONS

Risk is variable that increases the chance of behavioural difficulties or impairments. In the presence of risk, some individuals are vulnerable, that is, adversely affected, whereas others maintain healthy behavioural functioning, that is they are resilient. Resilience refers to protection from risk factors or the ability to bounce back in the face of life's adversities. Researchers have identified many risk factors of which culture is considered to be a major risk factor in certain situations. Culture is widely recognized as a determinant of standards for behaviour and as an influence on development. Kvernmo and Heyerdahl (1998) have come out with an important finding that children and adolescents belonging to indigenous or native cultural groups have higher rates of behavioural dysfunction than the youth of dominant populations. These indigenous groups included Dravidians in Indian, American Indians, Maori's in New Zeland, Inuits in Canada and Sami in Norway. Depression, anxiety, anger, enmity, jealousy, suppression due to exploitation and inferiority complex are the most common problems reported among indigenous populations. Research findings reveal that higher rates of behaviour disorder in indigenous populations are caused by 'acculturation'. Kvernmo and Heyerdahl (1998) defined acculturation as changes in culture resulting from different cultures coming into contact with each other. It is a dynamic process set into motion by voluntary actions like immigration, or by situations that force cultural change (that is, one cultural group forcing its dominance over another). Indigenous populations are though to be at risk for acculturative problems because the situation is often involuntary, the dominant group may try to change the culture of the indigenous group. As a result, the indigenous groups are forced to deal with prejudice and discrimination which inturn create practical hardships. In addition, indigenous populations are socially and economically downtrodden and disadvantaged. The tribal populations in the Indian States like Assam, Nagaland and Andra Pradesh have higher rates of birth, infant mortality, unemployment, illiteracy and poverty compared to the general population of India.

SUMMARY

Developmental psychopathology is considered to be a general framework for understanding disordered behaviour in relation to normal development. Development refers to change over the lifespan that proceeds in a coherent manner along various pathways. Developmental change is a product of transactions among biological, psychological and socio-cultural variables.

The genetic basis of development is the chromosomes, which direct the biochemistry of the baby. Hereditary influences, which are complex and indirect, set a range within which normal and dysfunctional behaviours develop. Genetic influences on adaptive and maladaptive behaviour are crucial but they operate in conjunction with environmental influences.

Early physical and motor growth occurs in universal and orderly sequences. The nervous system begins to develop after conception and it is relatively well developed at birth. Motor development too is quite predictable like physical development. Motor milestones are useful to understand normal motor development. Deviations from the timing and patterning of these milestones indicate nervous system dysfunctioning and risk for developmental problems. Motor handicaps and timing of puberty exert influence on psychosocial functioning.

Development of cognition and communication abilities occurs during the early childhood and they provide a basis for experiencing the environment. Children cognicize through ways. The three basic and widely recognized learning processes are classical conditioning, operant conditioning and observational learning. These basic learning processes operate at or soon after birth and they become more sophisticated as higher mental processes and thinking develop gradually. Jean Piaget's developmental theory proposed that children are biological organisms who adopt to their environments through assimilation and accommodation and develop increasingly sophisticated schemes of the world in four distinct stages which occur in a particular sequence. Growth of communication skills is another important factor closely linked with cognitive development. Communication is mainly made through language. Language acquisition is time-bound process, which relies on both sound biological system and social input. Impairments in language and communication can result in academic problems, social interactional problems, social isolation and low self-esteem.

Emotions and socio cultural context play a crucial role in development. It is necessary that all children must learn to regulate or control their emotions. The acquisition of emotional regulation encompasses various capabilities such as learning to monitor, evaluate and modify the intensity and timing of emotional reactions. The social context of development consists of overlapping, interacting domains of influences that include family, peers, school, social class and the broad culture.

The models of development describe and analyse how development occurs. The multifactor/ integrative models propose that many factors interact to bring about development. Two important examples of these models are the bio-psychosocial model and the goodness-of-fit model. The former presumes that development is a function of interacting biological and psychosocial (environmental) variables whereas the latter assumes that development depends on how well the person and the environment fit each other.

There are several other useful ways to conceptualize developmental influences. Development is influenced by normative or non normative factors which vary across cultures. Generally, non normative influences are more likely to result in heightened stress. It is also imperative to distinguish between 'necessary' and 'sufficient' influences and between 'direct' and 'indirect' factors. Similarly, the timing of developmental influences makes a difference in psychopathology.

Risk is an important variable that increases the chance of behavioural impairments. In the presence of risk, some individuals are vulnerable whereas some are resilient. Culture is considered to be major risk factor. Children and adolescents belonging to indigenous or native cultural groups have higher rates of behavioural dysfunction than the youth of dominant populations.

REFERENCES

Achenbach, T.M., (1990), 'Conceptualizations of Developmental Psychopathology'. In M. Lewis & S.M. Miller (Eds.) *Handbook of Developmental Psychopathology*. New York: Plenum.

Aoki, C. and Siekevitz, P., (1988), 'Plasticity in Brain Development'. *Scientific American*, 259, 56-64.

Baker, L. and Cantwell, D.P., (1991), 'The Development of Speech and Language'. In M. Lewis (Ed.), *Child and Adolescent Psychiatry: A Comprehensive Textbook*. Baltimore: Williams & Wilkins.

Bradley, R.H. and Whiteside-Mansell, L., (1997), 'Children in Poverty'. In R.T. Ammerman & M. Hersen (Eds.) *Handbook of Prevention and Treatment with Children and Adolescents*. New York: John Wiley.

Bubav, E.F., Huesmann, L.R. and Eron, R.D., (1987), 'Childhood Correlates of Adult Ego Development'. *Child Development*, 58, 859-869.

Casaer, P., (1993), 'Old and New Facts About Prenatal Brain Development'. *Journal of Child Psychology and Psychiatry*, 34, 101-109.

Caspi, A. Elder, G.H., Jr., and Bem, D.J., (1988), 'Moving Away from the World: Life-course Patterns of Shy Children'. *Developmental Psychology*, 24, 824-831.

Chess, S., and Thomas, A., (1972), 'Differences in Outcome with Early Intervention in Children with Behaviours Disorders'. In M. Roff, L. Robins & M. Pollock (Eds.) *Life History Research in Psychopathology*, Vol. 2, Minnepolis: University of Minnesota Press.

Cicchetti, D., (1984), 'The Emergence of Developmental Psychology'. *Child Development*, 55, 1-7.

Cicchetti, D., (1989), 'Developmental Psychology: Some Thoughts on its Evolution'. *Developmental and Psychopathology*, 1, 1-3.

Cicchetti, D. and Cohen, D.J., (1995), 'Perspectives on Developmental Psychopathology'. In D. Cichetti & D.J. Cohen (Eds.). *Developmental Psychopathology*, New York, John Wiley.

Compas, B.E., Hinden, B.R. and Gerhardt, C., (1995), 'Adolescent Development: Pathways and Processes of Risk and Resilience'. *Annual Review of Psychology*, 46, 265-295.

Dubow, E.F., Huesmann, L.R. and Eron, R.D., (1987), 'Childhood Correlates of Adult Ego Development'. *Child Development*, 58, 859-869.

Dunn, J. and McGurie, S., (1992), 'Sibling and Peer Relationships in Childhood'. *Journal of Child Psychology and Psychiatry*, 33, 67-105.

Eccles, J.S. Midgley, C., Wigfield, A., Buchaman, C.M., Reuman, D., Flanagan, C. and Macver, D., (1993), 'Development During Adolescence: The Impact of Stage Environment Fit on Young Adolescents' Experiences in Schools and in Families'. *American Psychologist*, 48, 0-101.

Flavell, J.H., (1963), 'The Developmental Psychology of Jean Piaget'. New York: Van Nostrand.

Freud, S., (1949), *An Outline of Psychoanalysis*. Translated and Newly Edited by J. Stratchey. New York: W.W. Norton and Co.

Gjone, H. and Stevenson, J., (1997a), 'A Longitudinal Twin Study of Temperament and Behaviour Problems: Common Genetic or Environmental Influence?' *Journal of the American Academy of Child and Adolescent Psychiatry*, 36, 1448-1456.

Greenberg, M.T. and Crinic, K.A., (1988), 'Longitudinal Predictions of Developmental Status and Social Interaction in Premature and Full-term Infants at Age Two'. *Child Development*, 59, 554-570.

Greenough, W.T., Black, J.E., and Wallace, C.S., (1987), 'Experience and Brain Development'. *Child Development*, 58, 539–559.

Harris, P.L., (1994), 'The Child's Understanding of Emotion: Developmental Change and the Family Environment'. *Journal of Child Psychology and Psychiatry*, 35, 3-28.

Hockfield, S., and Lombroso, P.J., (1998), 'Development of the Cerebral Cortex: IX. Cortical Development and Experience: I'. *Journal of the American Academy of Child and Adolescent Psychiatry*, 37, 992–993.

Izard, C.E., (1994), 'Innate and Universal Facial Expressions: Evidence from Developmental and Cross-cultural Research'. *Psychological Bulletin*, 115, 288-299.

Jennings, K.D., Connors, R.E., and Stegman, E.E., (1988), 'Does a Physical Handicap Alter the Development of Mastery Motivation During the Preschool Years?' *Journal of Child and Adolescent Psychiatry*, 27, 312-317.

Kagan, J., Arcus, D. and Sridman, N., (1993), 'The Idea of Temperament: Where Do We Go from Here?' In R.Plomin & G.E. McClean (Eds.), *Nature, Nature and Psychology*. Washington, DC: American Psychological Association.

Kenns, K.A., Klepac, L., and Cole, A.K., (1996), 'Peer Relationships and Preadolescents' Perceptions of Security in the Child-mother Relationship'. *Developmental Psychology*, 32, 457-466.

Kvernmo, S., and Heyerdahl, S., (1998), 'Influence of Ethnic Factors on Behaviour Problems in Indigenous Sami and Majority Norwegian Adolescents'. *Journal of the American Academy of Child and Adolescents Psychiatry*, 37, 745-751.

Lyons-Ruth, K., Zeanah, C.H., and Benoit, D., (1996), 'Disorder and Risk for Disorder During Infancy and Toddler Hood'. In E.J. Mash & R.A. Barkey (Eds.), *Child psychology*, New York: Guilford Press.

Maccoby, E.E., (1992), 'The Role of Parents in the Socialization of Children: An Historic Overview'. *Developmental Psychology*, 28, 1006-1017

Maccoby, E.E., and Martin, J.A., (1983), 'Socialization in the Context of the Family: Parent-child Interaction'. In P.H. Mussen (Ed.), *Handbook of Child Psychology*, Vol. IV, New York: Wiley.

Malo, J., and Tremblay, R.E., (1997), 'The Impact of Paternal Alcoholism and Maternal Social Position on Boys' School Adjustment, Pubertal Maturation and Sexual Behaviour: A Test of Two Competing Hypothesis'. *Journal of Child Psychology and Psychiatry*, 38, 187-197.

McDermott, J., (1991), 'The Effects of Ethnicity on Child and Adolescent Development'. In M. Lewis (Ed.), *Child and Adolescent Psychiatry*. A Comprehensive Textbook. Baltimore: Williams & Willkins.

McLyod, V.C., (1998), 'Socio-economic Disadvantages and Child Development'. *American Psychologist*, 53, 185-204.

Nowakowski, R.S., (1987), 'Basic Concepts of CNS Development'. *Child Development*, 58, 568-595.

Peterson, G.A., (1982), 'Cognitive Development in Infancy'. In B.B. Wolman (Ed.), *Handbook of Developmental Psychology*. Englewood Cliffs, NJ: Prentice Hall.

Sameroff, A.J., (1990), 'Neo-environmental Perspectives on Developmental Theory'. In R.M. Hodapp, J.A. Burack, & E. Zigler (Eds.), *Issues in the Developmental Approach to Mental Retardation*, New York: Cambridge University Press.

Sroufe, L.A., (1086), 'Appraisal: Bowlby's Contribution to Psycho Analytic Theory and Developmental Psychology; Attachment; Separation; Loss'. *Journal of Child Psychology and Psychiatry*. New York: Plenum.

Stattin, H., and Magunusson, D., (1990), *Paths Through Life: Vol. 2. Pubertal Maturation in Female Development*. Hillsdale, NJ: Erlbaum.

Steinberg, L., Lamborn S.D., Darling, N., Mounts, N.S., and Dornbusch, S.M., (1994), 'Over-time Changes in Adjustment and Competence Among Adolescents from Authoritative, Authorisation, Indulgent and Neglectful Families'. *Child Development*, 65, 754-770.

Tanner, J.M., (1970), 'Physical Growth'. In P.H. Mussen (Ed.), *Carmichael's Manual of Child Development*, Vol. I, New York: John Wiley.

Thalen, E., (1986), 'Treadmill-elicited Stepping in Seven Month Old Infants'. *Child Development*, 57, 1498–1506.

Weinberg, M.K., Tronick, E.Z., Cohn, J.F. and Olson, K.L., (1999), 'Gender Differences in Emotional Expressivity and Self-regulation During Early Infancy'. *Developmental Psychology*, 35, 175-188.

Whitehurst, G.J., and Valdez-Menchaca, M.C., (1988), 'What is the Role of Reinforcement in Early Language Acquisition?' *Child Development*, 59, 430-440.

Williams, B.R., Ponesse, J.S., Schachar, R.K., Logan, G.D., and Tannock, R., (1999), 'Development of Inhibitory Control Across the Life Span'. *Developmental Psychology*, 35, 205-213.

3

Approaches to Child Behaviour Disorders

OBJECTIVE

This chapter deals with various perspectives of behaviour disorders such as biological, psychodynamic, behavioural, social learning and cognitive perspectives. It also presents different models of treatment for behavioural disorders. After reading this chapter the readers must be able to:

(i) Distinguish different perspectives of behaviour disorders;

(ii) Understand the different aspects contributed by biological perspective;

(iii) Define psychodynamic perspective;

(iv) Say the views of behavioural perspective;

(v) Explain the social learning perspective;

(vi) Comprehend the cognitive perspective;

(vii) Analyze the different models of treatment for behavioural disorders.

PERSPECTIVES OF BEHAVIOUR DISORDERS

The figures of youngsters who are in dire need of mental health services have increased to gruesome proportions in the recent times. These youngsters display a variety of behavioural, emotional, social, learning and physical problems. Quite often, they have more than one difficulty. Our goal, therefore, extends to acquire an understanding of the various problems experienced by these youngsters, and of the variety of treatment approaches taken in to assist them. It is also necessary to be able to consider a variety of influences. In this chapter, we are going to examine several of the perspectives of behaviour disorders. Each one addresses a particular variety of influence that contributes to the complex interplay of influences that are the mosaic of child and adolescent behaviour disorders.

To study and understand a phenomenon, usually scientists make assumptions and form concepts. When a set of such assumptions is shared by a group of investigators, it is referred to as a paradigm. Usually the term 'perspective' is employed interchangeably with 'paradigm'. Perspectives help us make sense of puzzling and complex phenomena. The phenomena of childhood behavioural disorders is approached, investigated and interpreted by various perspectives like biological, psycho dynamic, behavioural/social learning and cognitive.

BIOLOGICAL PERSPECTIVE

Biological perspective insists that psychopathology is due to defective or malfunctioning biological system. This belief owes its origin to Greek culture. Hippocrates (460-370 B.C.) the father of medicine, advocated for somatogenesis. 'Soma' means 'body' and 'genesis' means 'origin'. He postulated that proper mental functioning relied on a healthy brain and that deviant thinking or behaviour was the result of brain pathology.

Following the tradition set by Hippocrates, the biological perspective assumed initially that biology causes abnormal behaviour directly. Originally Kraeplin in the late 1800s developed psychiatric classification system which was based on this assumption. Early discoveries confirmed the fact that certain behavioural problems are set in motion by particular biological causes. For example, it was discovered that a spirochete bacterium causes syphilis and the mental deterioration is the last stage of syphilis. This discovery led to the hope that similar causes would be found for all abnormal behaviours. But this proposition could not be proved in marry cases of behaviour abnormalities. Hence the predominant view, that biological influences are likely to be part of a complex transaction among biological and various psychological and socio-cultural influences, became prevalent now-a-days.

The biological influences on a child's behaviour can occur through a variety of processes and mechanisms. Particularly, the structure of the brain, the nervous system and its biochemical functioning and genetic influences are the important biological factors that exert direct influence on behaviour.

(i) Structure of the Brain

Nelson and Bloom (1997) and Rutter (1998) examined the structural integrity of the nervous system, particularly the brain, which is one of the biological influences. Human brain has three major subdivisions the hindbrain, midbrain and the forebrain. The hindbrain includes cerebellum pons and medulla. It regulates body functions such as sleeping, breathing, and heart beat rate and body moments. Similarly, the midbrain contains much of the reticular activating system, although this extends into the pons and medulla as well. The reticular activating system regulated sleep and waking. Further, the midbrain coordinates communication between the hindbrain and the forebrain. The forebrain consists of the two cerebral hemispheres connected by the corpus callosum. Each hemisphere has lobes or regions. The frontal lobes are near the front of the brain and the temporal lobes are near the temples on the side of the brain. The parietal lobes are situated near the top rear of the brain and the occipital lobes are located at the rear of head.

A wide variety of activities such as sensory processing, motor control and higher mental functioning like information processing, learning and memory are controlled by the cerebral hemispheres. The thalamus and hypothalamus are structures lying below the cerebral hemispheres between the forebrain and the midbrain. The thalamus is involved in processing and relaying information between the cerebral cortex and other parts of the central nervous system. The hypothalamus regulates basic urges such as hunger, thirst and sexual activity. The multi structured limbic system includes parts of the cerebral hemispheres, the thalamus, and the hypothalamus. This limbic system regulates the endocrine glands and the autonomic nervous system. It also plays a central role in the regulation of emotional and biological urges.

Abnormal development or any damage to the biological system can cause variety of intellectual and behavioural problems. Damages may occur during pregnancy (prenatal), at about the time of birth (perinatal) or during later development (postnatal). Prenatal damages are caused by toxic substances and drugs like thalidomide, alcohol, tobacco, cocaine, heroin and methadone. Radiation and environmental contaminants such as polychlorinated biphenyls (PCBS) also have negative effects. Further maternal diseases like rubella, syphilis and gonorrhea have harmful effects. Above all, Acquired Immune Deficiency Syndrome (AIDS) is a growing threat to newborn babies and this is the major current concern (Armistead et al., 1998).

Nervous system damage may also occur during or after birth. Excessive medication given to mother unusual delivery and lack of oxygen (anoxia) may result in damage to the newborn at birth. Liaw and Brooks-Gunn (1994) asserted that perinatal complications and SES factors have an interactive effect on the infant's subsequent development. Similarly, accidents, illness, malnutrition or accidental poisoning can cause postnatal damages. Tesman and Hills (1994) found that exposure of children to lead is one kind of accidental poisoning and this would have negative impact on processes such as attention and cognitive development.

(ii) Nervous System Functioning and Biochemistry

There is fairly broad agreement that biochemistry in some form contributes to disturbed behaviours. The biochemistry of neurotransmitters and central nervous system functioning has become important foci of biology's contribution to the study of behaviour disorders. The nervous system has billions of neurons. These neurons conduct the electrochemical impulses by which communication occurs. Neurons have three major parts: a cell body, dendrites and axons. Dendrites receive messages from other cells and axons transmit them to other cells. These messages must cross the synaptic gap (cleft) that lies between neurons. When an impulse reaches the end of an axon, neurotransmitters are released and they cross the synoptic gap and communicate with other cells through receptor sites on those cells. Defaults in neurotransmission may occur in many ways. For example, too much or too little of a particular neurotransmitter can be released. Problems may exist in the process (reuptake) by which the neuron reabsorbs the neurotransmitter for subsequent transmissions. In addition, the density and sensitivity of receptors to a particular neurotransmitter or the presence or absence of other chemicals (blocking agents) at the receptor sites may affect neurotransmissions. A number of different neurotransmitters have been identified as playing a role in various forms of abnormal behaviours, such as depression and attention deficit hyperactivity disorder (Emslie et al., 1994 and Pliszka et al., 1996). The major neurotransmitters that have been studied so far are norepinephrine, serotonin, dopamine, acetylcholine and gamma amibutyric acid (GABA).

How the biochemistry of the body reacts to various situations encountered by an individual is also part of the biological perspective on behaviours problems. The automatic nervous system helps to regulate one's emotional state. This system has two branches: the sympathetic and the parasympathetic nervous system. The former mediates increased arousal, preparing the body for action, whereas the latter works to slow down the arousal and to conserve the body's resources. One of the ways in which the automatic nervous system operates is through stimulation of the endocrine glands, which release hormones into the blood stream. Research on neuroendocrine functioning is an important part of the study of a variety of child and adolescent disorders. For example, recent research studies have revealed that differences in autonomic reactivity result in panic disorder; neurohormonal dysregulation results in obsessive-compulsive disorder; and growth hormone irregularities result in depression.

(iii) Genetic Influences

Genetic influences on human behaviour are extremely complex. The study of genetic influences is expanding in many directions. Genetic research tells us about etiology and also confirms the role of environment in causation. The patterns of genetic transmission are involved in the inheritance of many human attributes and disorders. Research findings reveal that inheritance of certain characteristics are influenced by either one gene pair or multiple genes transmissions. Gregor Mendel made the correct hypothesis for the first time that each parent carries two hereditary factors (that is, genes) but passes on only one to the offspring. He noted that one form of the factor is dominant, in that its transmission by either parent leads to the display of that form of the characteristic. The other recessive form displays itself only when both parents transmit it. Huntington's chorea is an example of a disease transmitted by a dominant gene. This disease causes death but does not show up until adulthood, when limb spasms, mental deterioration and dementia become evident. Similarly, 'Tay-Sachs' disease is an example of a disorder carried by one gene pair and transmitted recessively. This is a degenerative disease of the nervous system. It results in progressive deterioration of mental abilities, motor capacities and vision and then death by the age of one or three.

The sex-linked pattern of inheritance involves genes on the sex chromosomes. Of special interest is the situation in which the relevant gene is recessive and is carried on the X chromosome, such as in red-green colour blindness, hemophilia and Lesch-Nyhan Syndrome. The Lesch-Nyhan syndrome is a rare untreatable disorder. It results in unusual motor development, mental retardation and extreme self-mutilation in children. This disorder is found only in males, who die early and thus do not have offspring.

Researches are continuously emerging to explore the effects of genetic transmission on specific behaviour disorders. Molecular genetic methods are found to facilitate complex genetic inheritance. Molecular genetic is concerned with the search for the genes involved in the development of a disorder or of a characteristic that increases the risk for disorder.

In contrast to the effects due to a single gene pair, many child and adolescent behaviour disorders are also thought to involve many genes as well as environmental influences. Such multifactor inheritance is much more difficult to trace than single gene effects.

Accordingly, the study of genetic influences on human behaviour relies on a combination of evidence from a variety of research methods. The three major research strategies of behaviour genetics that have been applied to behaviour disorders are the family, twin and adoption methodologies (Plomin, 1994). Results from behaviour genetic research suggest that heritability estimates for behavioural dimensions or disorders rarely exceed 50 per cent (Plomin, 1994). This means that substantial variation in behaviour is attributable to non-genetic influences. Thus behaviour genetic research has provided evidence for the importance of environmental influence also.

(iv) Chromosome Abnormalities

Chromosomes that are aberrant in either number or structure are known to cause death or a variety of deficiencies. Approximately 40 per cent of spontaneously aborted foetus are said to have chromosomal abnormalities. Gath (1985) reported that among live births 3.52 infants per 1000 are born with an abnormal number of chromosomes and that 2.23 infants are born with structural abnormalities of the chromosomes. These 'accidents' are not inherited and hence they influence only the specific developing embryo. Simonoff et al. (1996) found mental retardation to be associated with such chromosomal anomalies. The most widely recognized disorder attributed to a chromosome aberration is Down Syndrome, which is characterized by mental deficiency. An # 21 chromosome causes it. A group of abnormalities resulting from sex chromosome aberrations has also been discovered. These disorders are often characterized by below average intelligence, atypical sexual development and other difficulties.

PSYCHODYNAMIC PERSPECTIVE

Psychoanalytic theory was the dominant perspective on childhood psychopathology during the first half of the twentieth centaury. The term 'Psychodynamic' denotes the active forces with in the personality that motivate behaviour and the inner causes of behaviour, in particular the unconscious conflict between the different structures that compose the whole personality. To put it in simple terms, psychological theories that attempt to explain how people change are called 'psychodynamic' theories. Freud's 'psychoanalytic theory' is psychodynamic. Freudian psychoanalytic theory proposed that human beings are born with two instinctive urges called 'libido' and 'death wish'. These urges provide psychic energy. Further, these urges are gratified by three parts of personality known as id, ego and superego, through four stages of development, which are oral, anal, phallic and genital. These four stages reflect the four sensitive parts otherwise known as 'erogenous zones' --mouth, anus, phallus and genitals and libido will seek expression through these zones. As children grow up, they pass through the above mentioned four stages one by one (A detailed account is given in first chapter). If too many painful experiences occur in any one stage, the child's personality will become 'fixated' in the stage the child is in at the time. For example, being 'fixated' in the first oral stage produces an aggressive, depressed and pessimistic personality, if the oral stimulation is insufficient. If the stimulation is too much, it will produce an over-optimistic, over-dependent and over-excitable personality. Fixation in the second (anal) stage can be caused by very strict or very easy-going potty training. This again leads to two types of adult personality. That is, the children may become over generous, very untidy and agree whatever anyone says. Or else they may become over-possessive, obsessive about things, sadistic and miserable. Fixation in the phallic (third) stage leads children to become unreasonable and to think a lot of themselves to be obsessed by power, particularly in relationships, and to become dominant and uncaring, big-headed and exhibitionists. They may have great pride and even great courage. They may also have sexual problems. Similarly, fixation in the genital stage will cause difficulties in relating to the opposite sex, to shyness and immaturity.

Painful experiences in anyone stage may also cause conflict between the three parts of personality. The conflicts produce anxiety which in turn causes neuroses. Freud said people use a lot of defence mechanisms to reduce anxiety. Defence mechanisms are mental processes, which are automatically triggered when anxiety occurs. Some of the important defence mechanisms are repression, projection, displacement, sublimation and rationalization. Psychodynamic perspective also suggests therapeutic psychoanalytic techniques like hypnosis, free association, dream analysis, transference and analysis of slips of the tongue to deal with the symptoms of neurosis. Brown and Zinkin (1994) devised two kinds of psycho-dynamic-oriented group therapy known as psychodrama and transactional analysis.

BEHAVIOURAL PERSPECTIVE

The behavioural perspective was set into motion by J.B. Watson (1913) the central concept of this perspective is that childhood disorders are learned in the same way that other behaviours are learned. Hence the behavioural perspective advocates the study of behaviour and emphasizes objective empirical verification. It also stresses the role of environmental factors influencing behaviour. This amounts essentially to a focus of learning. The key form of learning is conditioning, either classical (Pavlovian or respondent), which formed the basis of Watson's methodological behaviourisms, or operant (instrumental), which is at the centre of B.F. Skinner's radical behaviourism.

Behaviourism is often referred to as 'S–R' (Stimulus-Response) psychology. Both classical and operant conditioning account for observable behaviour (responses) in terms of environmental events (stimuli) but they view the stimulus-response relationship fundamentally in different ways. In classical conditioning, the stimulus is seen as triggering a response in a predictable, automatic way. But operant conditioning argues that most behaviour is not elicited by specific stimuli. Instead it is acquired or reduced and it is emitted in some circumstances but not in others, through reinforcement, extinction, punishment and other learning processes. The operant type of behavioural perspective is most extensively applied to children's disorders. The pivotal assumption of operant conditioning is that problem behaviour can be changed through a learning process and that the focus of treatment should be on the consequences of behaviour. The term 'behaviour therapy' has been used to describe any therapeutic approach deriving from the behavioural perspective based on classical conditioning where as 'behaviour modification therapy techniques' use operant conditioning.

Therapies based on classical conditioning concentrate on stimuli that elicit new responses, which are contrary to the old, maladaptive ones. Implosion therapy, flooding and systematic desensitization are the therapeutic approaches based on classical conditioning. Behaviourists interested in operant conditioning suggest therapies based on extinction, punishment and positive reinforcement.

SOCIAL LEARNING PERSPECTIVE

According to social learning perspective, humans and some non-humans can learn directly 'without' experiencing an event, and can acquire new forms of behaviour from others simply by observing them. This perspective is, therefore, known as observational learning. Moreover our observation of people being rewarded or punished can strengthen or reduce our own inhibitions against behaving in similar ways. If we see a positive outcome for a behaviour, our restraint against performing it is lowered. This is called 'response disinhibition'. However, if we see a negative outcome, our restraint is heightened, which is known as 'response inhibition'.

The investigation most widely associated with observational learning or modelling is Albert Bandura. He argues that maladaptive behaviours can be altered by exposing those, demonstrating them to appropriate aims to change thoughts and perceptions also. Modelling can either be participant modelling or symbolic modelling. The former involves the individual observing the therapist's behaviour and then imitating it, whereas the latter involves having people watch filmed or videotaped models. Participant modelling is proved to be more effective than the other one. Modelling has been successfully used with a variety of phobias and for eliminating undesirable behaviour. It has also been used to establish new and more appropriate behaviour and thus in assertive training and social skills training. Bandura (1977) believes that one reason for modelling's effectiveness is the development of self- efficacy.

Whether imitation is specific or generalized, complex processes are required for observational learning to occur (Bandura, 1977). That is, the individual must organize and encode the information presented through modelling and then remember it. The acquired behaviour must then be performed when it is anticipated that it will meet desired consequences. Hence more mimicking of behaviour is not enough for observational learning. In this aspect, the social learning perspective has placed much emphasis on cognitive processes such as memory, attention and problem-solving (Rosenthal, 1984).

COGNITIVE PERSPECTIVE

The cognitive perspective assumes that the cognitive processes are important to conceptualize the behaviour problems of children and adolescents, this perspective sees mental disorders as resulting from distortions in individual's cognitions. The tendencies to think negatively, misperceive social cues, make fault attributions regarding the causes of events and behaviour and fail to enact adequate problem solving are examples of cognitive processes hypothesized to be related to behavioural disorders. Cognitive perspective aims at the goal of changing maladaptive behaviour by changing the way the individual thinks. Cognitive therapies have therefore been viewed as a collection of techniques really belonging to the domain of the behavioural model and so they are called 'cognitive-behavioural therapies'.

Supporters of cognitive model, however, believe that behaviour change results from changes in cognitive processes, and hence cognitively based therapies can be separated from behavioural ones. Like psychodynamic therapy, the cognitive perspective aims to produce 'insight'. But, rather than focusing on the past, they try to produce insight into 'current cognitions'. Ellis' (1958) rational-emotive therapy. Beck's (1974) cognitive therapy for depression, attributional therapy and Meichenbaum's (1985) stress innoculation therapy are based on cognitive perspective. The therapy approach based on the cognitive perspective is helpful in treating several types of mental disorders, particularly depression and panic disorder.

MODELS OF TREATMENT FOR BEHAVIOURAL DISORDERS

The perspective that a psychopathologist adopts decides the style of the treatment offered. A professional with a behavioural or social-learning perspective is expected to offer treatments that are action oriented and he/she focuses on present problems, assuming that treatment is a learning process governed by principles common to all learning situations. In addition, based on the mode of treatment, there occur differences in the treatment services. The professionals who operate from a variety of theoretical perspectives advocate for the inclusion of the family in treatment. Similarly, if the concerned behaviour problem is thought to be arising out of a combination of influences, a professional tends to employ several different modes of treatment as Tuma and Pratt (1982) have done. Some of the most commonly used methods of treatment such as individual and group therapy, play therapy, parent training, treatment in residential settings and pharmacological treatment are dealt below one by one.

(i) Individual and Group Psychotherapy

Psychotherapy aims to offer a typical one-to-one verbal experience. This is the most common mode of treatment for adults. Treatment is also offered in groups. The same assumptions and methods which guide individual therapy may be applied, but in a group format. Although the group format may be selected in order to give service to larger number of children and adolescents, there are other rationales for this choice (Johnson, Rasbury and Siegel, 1977). Mainly, the groups offer the opportunity for socialization experiences, which are not found in the individual mode. Secondly, group treatment may be more appealing to the children or adolescents, in the sense, it is less threatening and offers an understanding to the children that they are not the only suffering lots and their peers are also having some difficulties. This gives mental courage to the children to face the treatment. Ultimately, group therapy includes such activities, which are not likely to occur in one-to-one verbal interchange sessions.

Whether the mode of treatment is in individual or in-group format, psychotherapy views verbal forms as an ideal form of intervention, particularly with older children and adolescents. It is generally agreed that the need to alter treatment procedures in accordance with the child's cognitive as well as emotional level of development should be realized. Realization of this need has given rise to non-verbal modes of treatment for very young children.

(ii) Play Therapy

A very common mode of behaviour therapy is play. Since play activities have much importance in the development of young children, as viewed by Rubin et al. (1983) and Smith (1998), play as a therapeutic vehicle has its own advantages. It remains a solution to deal with the children of lesser verbal abilities. In this play mode, the therapist uses some sort of play to concretize communications instead of relying exclusively on abstract verbal interactions. Most practitioners have accepted the play as a means of communications. The psychodynamic and the client-centered perspectives have led to two most well known perspectives on play therapy.

Two of the principal and early developers of child treatment from a psychoanalytic perspective have controversial views about play therapy. Early analysts felt the need for a change in analytic techniques in order to give effective treatments to children. This idea led to the use of play as a mechanism for children to express their thoughts and feelings. Verbal free association had been the central issue in adult treatment. But controversy arose over this issue as whether to view children's play as the equivalent to verbal free association. Further there was also controversy over the psychoanalytic interpretation of children's play.

Emphasis over the inclusion of play in the treatment of children was first made by the therapist, Melanie Klein (1932). Her idea gained a wide popularity. She used the term 'play therapy' to refer to the process whereby the child's play was used as the basis for psychoanalytic interpretation as if verbal tree association was used in the psychoanalysis of adults. But Anne Freud (1946) disagreed with this view. She viewed play as only one potential mode of expression. She was of the opinion that the child's expression of emotions and thoughts should not be equated with the purposeful production of free association of adults. Both of them disagreed on the issue of interpreting the material derived from play also Klein put a strong emphasis on symbolic interpretation pf play and hence she gave a pivotal role to play throughout the psychoanalytic process. On the other hand, Anne Freud allotted a meagre importance to play interpretation. Johnson et al. (1997) favour Anne Freud's position on play.

The work of Virginia Axline (1947) was another major influence on the evolution of play therapy. Her approach was client–centred play therapy. In this approach, the principles adopted for children of varying ages as well as adults remain the same. The therapist makes adjustments only in communication style so as to create the appropriate, accepting, and permissive and non-directive therapeutic environment. The use of play, no doubt, creates such an environment when the therapist deals with young children.

(iii) Parent Training

It is generally believed by the professionals that change in the child's behaviour may be effected by producing changes in the way that the parents manage the child. It is only the parent's perception, along with the child's actual behaviour, that has led the child being referred for treatment. Parent training modes have been applied to a wide variety of childhood behavioural problems. Social learning/behavioural perspective has contributed much to parent training procedures, in terms of systematic applications and research.

Initially, efforts were taken to concentrate on teaching parents to manage the consequences or contingencies applied to children's behaviour. Recent parent-training approaches include a wide vari[illegible] of skills, such as skills in verbal communication and expression of emotion. Moreover, investigators have reported that stressors such as socio-economic disadvantage, single parent status, social isolation, and maternal depression are related to poorer outcome of parent training (Forehand et al., 1984). Subsequently, parent training has been frequently employed as part of a multifaceted approach to treatment.

(iv) Treatment in Residential Settings

When the behavioural problems of the children become very severe, residential treatment is considered to be the best mode of intervention, as suggested by Johnson et al. (1997). There are many cases, with too difficult problems to treat that treatment on outpatient basis may not provide enough contact with and control over the patients. There may also be a concern that children with severe behavioural problems some times cause harm either to themselves or to others. In such cases, closer supervisory measures are necessary .It is unavoidable, therefore, to remove such cases from home where the circumstance may be highly problematic. Such environments suggest that effective interventions could not be given at home. When professionals nourish the opinion that alternative placements cannot be given in less restrictive environments, they go for the mode of institutionalising the children in foster homes. Further, in many cases, other modes of interventions would have become unsuccessful and ineffective. In those cases, residential treatment mode is ultimately resorted to.

Residential treatment may be offered in group homes, child psychiatry units in medical hospitals, units in non-medical settings, and juvenile homes, which are considered to be part of judicial system. Airwardi in Tamil Nadu State, India is well known for such residential treatment. Therapeutic, educational and vocational interventions are involved as treatment services given in the above monitored residential settings. But Johnson et al. (1997) consider that it is difficult to evaluate the effectiveness of these treatment services.

(v) Pharmacological Treatment

The interventions offered for a variety of childhood and adolescent behaviour disorders include pharmacological medications too (Werry and Aman, 1999). Medications that affect mood, thought processes or overt behaviour are called 'psychotropic' or 'psychoactive'. Treating behaviour disorders by prescribing such medications is often referred to as 'psychopharmacological treatment'. But the prescription of the psychopharmacological agents alone is not self-sufficient. Effective results are reported only when these agents are employed in combination with other modes of treatment. The pharmacological agents often employed in the treatment of children and adolescents include stimulants like methylphenidate, usually given to attention deficit hyperactivity disorder and antipsychotics like clozapine and risperidone given for schizophrenia and selective serotonin reuptake inhibitors like clomipramine which is used for obsessive-compulsive disorder.

Such psychotropic drugs exert their influence on the process of neurotransmission and hence they prove to be very effective. Poling, Gadow and Cleary (1991) clearly explained the different ways in which these drugs can affect neurotransmission. First of all, they alter the body's production of neurotransmitters. Secondly, they interfere with the storage of neurotransmitters. Thirdly, they alter the release of neurotransmitters. They also interfere with the inactivation or the reuptake of a neurotransmitter. Finally, they interact with receptors for a neurotransmitter. Poling et al. (1991) employed a lock-and-key analogy to describe how these drugs act by blocking receptors for the neurotransmitter dopamine. The molecules of the neuroleptic (antipsychotic) drug and dopamine act as similar keys but not identical. The receptor is the lock. The dopamine key fits the receptor lock perfectly and unlocks it and thus affects transmission to the neuron on which the receptor is located. On the contrary, the neuroleptic key will enter the dopamine receptor lock but will not unlock it. However, this imperfectly fitting key prevents dopamine from entering the receptor. Thus dopamine molecules are prevented from combining with receptors as well as from affecting neurotransmission. Blocking dopamine's functions is thus the mechanism by which certain antipsychotic agents are thought to have their therapeutic action.

SUMMARY

The investigators of behaviour disorders in children are guided by different major views or perspectives. Behaviour disorders are viewed as the resultant of the interplay of number influences. Each perspective addresses a particular variety of influence that contributes to the behaviour disorders in children and adolescents.

The biological perspective insists that psychopathology is due to defective or malfunctioning biological system. This perspective addresses a number of influences. The structural integrity of brain and nervous system, the biochemical functioning of the nervous system and genetic factors are the major ones. Damages of nervous system that occur during pregnancy (prenatal), at about the time of birth (perinatal) or during later development (postnatal) may give rise to behaviour disorders. Toxic substances and drugs, radiation and environmental contaminants, maternal diseases, excessive medications to mothers have negative effects. SES factors, accidents, illness, poisoning and malnutrition can cause damages. Neurotransmitters and neuroendocrine system are critical aspects of the role of nervous system functioning in the development of behaviour disorders. Similarly, hereditary influences on behaviour disorders are likely to involve multiple genes. Molecular genetics seeks to find specific genes that influence behaviour disorders. Chromosomal abnormalities also lead to a number of disorders.

The psychodynamic perspective believes that the active forces within the personality motivate behaviour. They insist that the unconscious conflict between the different structures that compose the whole personality causes behaviour problems. Freud's psychoanalytic theory is psychodynamic in nature. It proposes that human beings are born with two instinctive urges called 'libido' and 'death wish', which provide psychic energy. These urges are gratified by three parts of personality known as id, ego and superego, through four stages of development, namely, oral, anal, phallic and genital. Painful experiences in anyone stage may cause conflict between the three parts of personality as well as fixation.

Behavioural perspective assumes that childhood behaviour disorders are learnt in the same way that other behaviour is learnt. It stresses the need for empirical verification and the role of environmental factors in influencing behaviour. The role of learning is central to these perspectives and hence this approach involves a number of learning theories. The most important ones are classical conditioning and operant conditioning.

Social learning perspective, otherwise called observational learning, insists that humans can acquire new forms of behaviour from others simply by observing them. The cognitive perspective assumes that cognitive processes are important to conceptualize the behaviour problems of children and adolescents. This perspective aims to produce 'insight' into 'current cognitions'.

The perspective that the psychopathologist adopts decides the method of treatment to behaviour disorders. Various modes of treatment are available. Individual therapy, group therapy, play therapy, parent training, residential placement therapy and pharmacological treatment are the various modes of treatment that have been offered to a variety of childhood and adolescent behaviour problems.

REFERENCES

Axline, V.M., (1947), *Play Therapy*. Boston: Houghton Mifflin.

Bandura, A., (1977), *Social Learning Theory*. Englewood Cliffs, NJ: Prentice Hall.

Beck, A.T., (1974), 'The Development of Depression: A Cognitive Model'. In R.J. Friedman & M.M. Katz (Eds.), *The Psychology of Depression: Contemporary Theory and Research*. New York: Wiley.

Ellis, A., (1984), 'Rational-emotive Therapy'. In R. Corşini (Ed.). *Current Psychotherapies*. (3rd ed.) Itasca, 11: Peacock.

Emslie, G.J., Weinberg, W.A., Kennard, B.D. and Kowatch, R.A., (1994), 'Neurobiological Aspects of Depression in Children and Adolescents'. In W.M. Reynolds & H.F. Johnston (Eds.), *Handbook of Depression in Children and Adolescents*. New York: Plenum.

Forehand,R., Furey, W.M. and McMahon, R.J., (1984), 'The Role of Maternal Distress in a Parent Training Programme to Modify Child Non-compliance'. *Behavioural Psychotherapy*, 12, 93-108.

Freud, A., (1946), *The Psychoanalytical Treatment of Children*. London: Imago.

Gath, A., (1985), 'Chromosomal Abnormalities'. In M.Rulter & L. Hersov (Eds.), *Child and Adolescent Psychiatry: Modern Approaches*, 2nd Ed. Oxford: Blackwell Scientific Publications.

Johnson, J.H., Rebury, W.C. and Siegel, L.J., (1997), *Approaches to Child Treatment: Tntroduction to Theory, Research and Practice*. (2nd Ed.) Boston; Allyn and Bacon.

Klein, M., (1932), *The Psychoanalysis of Children*. London: Hogarth Press.

Liaw, F. and Brooks-Gunn, J., (1994), 'Cumulative Familial Risk and Low-Birth Weight Children's Cognitive and Behavioural Development'. *Journal of Clinical Child Psychology*, 23, 360-372.

Meichenbaum, D.H., (1985), *Stress Inoculation Training*. New York: Pergamon.

Nelson, C.A., & Bloom, F.E., (1997), 'Child Development and Neuroscience'. *Child Development*, 68, 970-987.

Plisztka, S,R., McCracken, J.T. and Maas, J.W., (1996), 'Catecholamines in Attention-deficit Hyperactivity Disorder: Current Perspectives'. *Journal of the American Academy of Child and Adolescent Psychiatry*, 35, 264-272.

Plomin, R., (1994), 'Genetic Research and Identification of Environmental Influences'. *Journal of Child Psychology and Psychiatry*, 35, 817-834.

Poling, A., Gadov, K.D. and Cleary, J., (1991), *'Drug Therapy for Behaviour Disorders: An Introduction*. New York: Pergamon.

Rosenthal, T.L., (1984), 'Some Organizing Hints for Communicating Applied Information'. In B. Gholson & T.L. Rosenthal (Eds.), *Application of Cognitive-developmental Theory*. Orlando, FL: Academic Press.

Rubin, K.H., Fein, G.G. and Landenberg, B., (1983), Play. In P.H. Mussen (Ed.), *Handbook of Child Psychology: Socialization, Personality and Social Behaviour*. Vol.4, New York, Wiley.

Rutter, M., (1998),. 'Routes from Research to Clinical Practice in Child Psychiatry: Retrospect and Prospect'. *Journal of Child Psychology and Psychiatry*, 39, 805-816.

Simonoff, E., Bolton, P. and Rutter, M., (1996), 'Mental Retardation: Genetic Findings, Clinical Implications and Research Agenda'. *Journal of Child Psychology and Psychiatry*, 37, 259-280.

Smith, P.K., (1988), 'Children's Play and Its Role in Early Development: A Re-evaluation of the "Play-ethos".' In A.D. Pellegrini (Ed.) *Psychological Bases for Early Education*. New York: Wiley.

Tesman, J.R. and Hills, A., (1994), 'Developmental Effects of Lead Exposure in Children'. *Social Policy Report Society for Research in Child Development*, VIII(3), 1-16.

Tuma, J.M. and Pratt, J.M., (1982), 'Clinical Child Psychology Practice and Training: A Survey'. *Journal of Clinical Child Psychology*, 11, 27-34.

Watson, J.B., (1913), 'Psychology as the Behaviourist Views It'. *Psychological Review*, 20, 158-177.

Werry, J.S. and Arman, M.G., (1999), *Practitioner's Guide to Psychoactive Drugs for Children and Adolescents* (2nd Ed). New York: Plenum Medical Book Company.

4

Identification and Assessment of Behavioural Disorders

OBJECTIVES

This chapter deals with identification and assessment of behavioural disorders. It elaborately describes the classification of behavioural disorders and stresses the need for a comprehensive assessment. It presents the different assessment methods such as interview, projective tests, observation, problem checklists and self-report instruments. It also analyses the intellectual/educational assessment as well as the assessment of physical functioning. After going through this chapter, this readers must be able to:

(i) Know the major categories or dimensions of behavioural disorders;

(ii) Understand the need for a comprehensive assessment;

(iii) Present the different methods of assessment;

(iv) Analyse the intellectual/educational assessment;

(v) Know about the various tools for educational assessment and finally; and

(vi) Realize the need for assessment of physical functioning.

To offer appropriate intervention services to the disordered population, accurate identification and assessment is a prerequisite. The terms identification refers to the process of assigning an individual to a categorical label. In this sense, it is synonymous to diagnosis. Assessment refers to an ongoing process of evaluating the youngsters possessing behavioural disorders. Both identification and assessment are entwined processes and they are intricately related to the scientific and clinical aspects of child and adolescent disorders.

CLASSIFICATION OF BEHAVIOURAL DISORDERS

By 'classification' we mean delineating major categories or dimensions of behavioural disorders. Sorting people into categories in order to predict their behaviour is not new. The first attempt at a unified classification of abnormal mental states was made by the Ancient Greek Physician Hippocrates who identified three categories of abnormal behaviour: mania (abnormal excitement), melancholia (abnormal dejection) and phrenitis (brain fever). Later, the Greek Physician Asclepiades described differences between hallucinations, delusions and illusions and explained how each could be used as a diagnostic sign.

Classification is done either for scientific or clinical purposes. Categorisation or a classification system is a simple way of systematically describing a phenomenon. As systems exist in all disciplines like biology, chemistry and physics to classify persons, things or events, systems also exist to classify behavioural disorders. These systems describe categories or dimensions of problem behaviours. A category is a discrete grouping. For instance, there are categories like anxiety disorder and conduct disorder. Similarly, the term 'dimension' means that behaviour is continuous and it can occur to varying degrees. For example, the behaviour 'anxiety' can be displayed by a child in varying levels, such as high, moderate and low. Any classification system must have clearly defined categories and dimensions. Further, a classification system must be reliable and valid. Reliability can be either interrater reliability or test-retest reliability. The former refers to whether different professional or diagnosticians use the same category to describe a person's disorder, whereas the latter refers to whether the use of a category is stable over some reasonable period of time. For example, a child, who was diagnosed as 'learning disabled' on the first evaluation, should also be diagnosed to have the same learning disability on the second evaluation.

Similarly to be valid, diagnostic categories must be clearly discriminable from one another.

Historically, the classification of abnormal behaviour focused primarily on adult disorders. Until recently, there was no extensive classification scheme for child and adolescent behaviour disorders. The clinical approach to classification relies on consensus among clinicians regarding disorders and their definitions. The first comprehensive attempt to classify abnormal behaviours clinically was developed by Kraepelin (1913), who proposed 18 distinct types of mental disorder, each with a characteristic pattern of symptoms (a syndrome), a distinct developmental course, particular underlying physical causes and a characteristic outcome. The most widely used classification system in the United States is the American Psychiatric Association's fourth revision of Diagnostic and Statistical Manual of Mental Disorders (DSM-IV). The other alternative system widely employed is the Tenth Revision of International Classification of Diseases (ICD) developed by world Health Organization (WHO, 1992). Its 'Diagnostic Classification: 0-3' (Zero to Three, 1995) is a system developed for classifying mental disorders of very young children.

ICD identified 11 major categories of mental disorder. They are:

1. Organic, including symptomatic, mental disorders (eg. dementia in Alzhemier's disease);
2. Mental and behavioural disorders due to psychoactive substance use (eg. alcohol, cocaine and hallucinogens);
3. Schizophrenia, schizotypal and delusional disorders;
4. Mood (affective) disorders;
5. Neurotic, stress-related and somatoform disorders;
6. Behavioural syndromes associated with physiological disturbances/factors;
7. Disorders of adult personality and behaviour;
8. Mental retardation;
9. Disorders of psychological development;

10. Behavioural and emotional disorders with onset usually occurring in childhood and adolescence;
11. Unspecified mental disorder.

DSM's system of classification is quite comprehensive. It is a categorical approach to classification. It views that the difference between normal and pathological is one of 'kind' rather than that of 'degree'. It also insists that distinctions should be made between 'qualitatively' different types of disorders. Major DSM- IV diagnostic categories described as "usually first diagnosed in infancy, childhood, or adolescence" are given below:

1. Mental Retardation;
2. Learning Disorders;
3. Motor skills Disorder;
4. Communication Disorder;
5. Pervasive Developmental Disorders (eg. Autism);
6. Attention Deficit and Disruptive Behaviour disorders;
7. Feeding and Eating Disorders of Infancy or Early Childhood;
8. Tic Disorder;
9. Elimination Disorders;
10. Other Disorders of Infancy, Childhood or Adolescence (eg. Separation Anxiety Disorder, Selective Mutism).

Sometimes, children and adolescents who are evaluated by professionals in clinic or school settings often present with a number of different problems. Having a number of different disorders is known as 'co-occurrence' or 'co-morbidity'. The case of Samuel (reported by Rapoport and Ismond, 1996) is an example of co-occurrence of behaviour disorders. Samuel, an 11-year old child, was referred to a clinic for attempted suicide after he had consumed a mixture of medicines prescribed to his mother, in an attempt to kill himself.

Samuel lived in an inner-city neighbourhood. Since second grade, he had been in repeated trouble for stealing and breaking into empty homes. He had academic difficulties and hence he was assigned to special reading class. He was a truant from school on a number of occasions. His mother has also experienced many depressive episodes: sometimes drank heavily; may have relied on prostitution for income; her husband had not been in contact with her since Samuel was born. At his interview, Samuel appeared sad and cried at one point. He reported having severe 'blue periods', the most recent of which had been continuous for the past month. During these periods he thought that he might be better off dead. He also reported that he had recently started to wake up in the middle of the night and had been avoiding his usual neighbourhood 'gang'.

Samuel was given a diagnosis and found to have co-occurrence of many disorders: major depressive disorders, dysthymia (a milder but chronic form of depression), conduct disorder, childhood onset type and reading disorder. At present solutions to such issues remain unsolved. Epidemiological research indicates that co-occurrence of child and adolescent disorders are quite high (Noltlemann and Jensen, 1995b).

Apart from the clinical approach to classification, there is another approach called the empirical approach. This approach employs statistical techniques to identify patterns of behaviour, which are interrelated. The respondent has to indicate the presence or absence of specific behaviours in the youngster. These responses are quantified in some way. For instance, if the child does not exhibit a certain characteristic '0' is given. If it is moderate degree, '1' is given and if the characteristic is clearly present, '2' is given. To develop taxonomy, such information is obtained for a large number of youngsters. Statistical techniques are then employed to indicate which behaviours tend to occur. Factor analysis and cluster analysis are the primary statistical techniques used in these studies. These procedures are based on correlations among items. The correlation of every item with the others is calculated, and groups of items that tend to occur together are thus identified (Achenbach, 1998). These groups are referred to as factors or clusters. The term 'syndrome' is also employed to describe behaviours that tend to occur together, whether identified by empirical or clinical judgement procedures. Thus the empirical and statistical procedures are employed as the basis for developing a classification scheme.

Multiple efforts have been undertaken to devèlop empirically defined syndromes. This kind of research involves different instruments, responded by different kinds of adult caregivers, evaluating different populations of youth, who are seen in different settings. The broad patterns were identified using such instruments. They are conduct disorder and anxiety- withdrawal. The first pattern has association with characteristics such as fighting, temper tantrums, disobedience and destructiveness. The second pattern is associated with anxious, shy, withdrawn and depressed behaviours. The instruments used to derive the above mentioned two brand-band clusters were Child Behaviour Checklist (CBCL), The Teacher Report Forms (TRF) and the Youth-Self-Report (YSR). The CBCL (Achenbach, 1991 b) can be completed by the parents of children between four to eighteen years of age. The TRF is a parallel instrument (Achenbach, 1991c) and it can be completed by teachers of children between five to eighteen years old. Similarly, the YSR (Achenbach, 1991d) is designed to be completed by youth from eleven to eighteen. Research with these instruments has also identified eight empirically defined syndromes. Of these, three syndromes fall within the broad category of Internalizing, two fall with the Externalizing group and three are neither clearly Internalizing nor clearly Externalizing (Achenbach, 1991a).

Eight syndromes.

Catcgory I: Internalizing syndromes

1. Withdrawn
2. Somatic complaints
3. Anxious/depressed.

Category II: Mixed syndromes

1. Social problems
2. Thought problems
3. Attention problems.

Category III: Externalizing syndromes

1. Delinquent behaviour
2. Aggressive behaviour.

Classification and diagnosis are intended to facilitate understanding and treatment of behaviour disorders. Although classification is intended as a scientific and clinical enterprise, it is also seen as a social process. That is, the diagnostic label becomes a social status, which carries implications for how people are thought of and treated. Many experts involved in the study and treatment of childhood behavioural problems advocate to be careful about the social values offered for labels and to reduce the possible harmful effects imparted by a diagnostic label on the social status.

A COMPREHENSIVE ASSESSMENT

Assessing child and adolescent behavioural problems is a complex process because behaviour disorders in youngsters are complex often containing a variety of components rather than a single problem behaviour. Moreover, these problems are thought of as arising out of and maintained by multiple influences which include biological features, various aspects of the child's behavioural, cognitive and social functioning and the impact of the family and other social systems like peers and school. Hence an assessment needs to be comprehensive in evaluating all potential influences causing the problem; in measuring a variety of aspects relating to the concerned child's biological, behavioural, cognitive and social functioning; and assessing various contexts and individuals with which whom the concerned child is expected to remain. Furthermore, information must be obtained from a variety of sources like the individual himself, his parents and teachers. Assessment, therefore, requires the use of multiple and varied methods as well as familiarity with assessment instruments meant for individuals of different ages. It needs multifaceted approach. The assessment process requires considerable skill and sensitivity. It should also be a continuous process so that new information can be collected carefully and as such the ongoing effects of treatment can be ascertained.

In addition, conducting a comprehensive assessment is necessary not only for planning and executing relevant intervention programmes. Different assessment methods offer assistance to the professionals and clinicians for cómprehensive assessment. These methods are dealt with in the remaining part of this chapter.

INTERVIEW

Interview is a face-to face verbal transaction. The most common form of assessment is the general clinical interview (Watkins et al., 1995). By interviewing the concerned youngster and various others in his social environment, information on all areas of functioning is obtained. Interviewing a variety of individuals (for example, parents, siblings, peers or teachers).who have contact with the disordered individual has strong rationale that behaviour is likely to vary according to the situation or to be viewed differently by various observers.

The question of whether to interview the affected person alone or in the presence of others has to be answered holding the age of the individual in mind. An old child is capable of giving enough information than a younger one. Yet professionals often prefer to interview even the very young child in order to obtain their own impressions. Bierman and Schwartz (1986) held the view that preschool and grade school children can provide valuable information, if appropriate developmental considerations are involved in tailoring the interview to the individual child. An advanced adult like, face-to-face interview may be threatening for a very young child and hence he may not come out freely with ample information. In such cases, interviews should be modelled after a familiar play activity or school task. Alternative assessment methods are also suggested by many professionals for the assessment of preadolescent children and they advocate to use more structured aspects of the evaluation (eg. rating scales and structured interviews) rather than the relatively unstructured general clinical interview (Kamphaus and Frick, 1996).

The general clinical interview is used not only to determine the nature of problem and perhaps to formulate a diagnosis but also to gather information that allows the clinician to conceptualize the case and to plan an appropriate therapeutic intervention. Hence many clinicians seek information regarding the nature of the problem, its past and recent history, present conditions feelings and perceptions of the individual, his attempts to solve the problem (if any) and his expectations with regard to treatment. The general clinical interview is, therefore, open-ended or unstructured. Such interviews are most often conducted in the context of a therapeutic interaction and are employed along with a variety of assessment instruments, it is always difficult to evaluate the reliability and validity of the interview itself. Hence, a recent development in the interviewing of children and adolescents is the use of structured interviews. Their reliability can easily be established. They have also been developed for a more limited purpose of deriving a diagnosis based on a particular classification scheme (such as DSM or ICD) or for use in screening larger populations for the prevalence of disorders. Some structural interviews used in diagnosing child and adolescent disorders are as follows:

1. Anxiety Disorders Interview for children (ADIS-C) developed by Silverman and Eisen (1992) for differential diagnosis of anxiety disorders in children;
2. Child Assessment Schedule (CAS) developed by Hodges et al. (1989) which is a conventional format modelled after traditional child clinical interview and relatively low in structure;
3. Diagnostic Interview for children and Adolescents (DICA) developed by Welner et al. (1987) which is a highly structured interview with separate versions for younger and older children;
4. Diagnostic Interview Schedule for Children (DISC) developed by Shaffer et al. (1996) which is a highly structured interview with questions organized diagnostically;
5. Interview Schedule for Children (ISC) developed by Kovacs (1985) which is low in structure with primary aim of assessing affective symptoms and associated problems.

6. Schedule for Affective Disorders and Schizophrenia in School Aged children (K-SADS) developed by Kaufman et al. (1997) which is intermediate in structure and assesses a wide range of childhood disorders.

In most of the structured interviews list of questions to be asked are preplanned and listed. In addition, rules are also provided to issue guidelines for conducting the interview as well as for recording and scoring the responses of the youngster. On the contrary, in the unstructured general clinical interview, there are no particular questions that the clinician must ask, no designated format and no stipulated method to record information. Anyway, there exists agree-on-procedure for conducting an effective interview. Indeed, there is an extensive literature on effective interviewing (Nietzel, Bernstein and Milich, 1994). However, unstructured interviews are intended to give great freedom to the clinicians.

PROJECTIVE TESTS

The most common form of psychological test employed to assess children was the projective test, in the past. Due to lack of empirical evidence regarding norms, reliability and validity, these tests are less commonly used now-a-days (Knoff, 1998). These tests were derived from the psychoanalytic notion of projection as a defence mechanism: one of the ways in which the ego deals with unacceptable impulses is to project them onto some external object. These tests are based on the assumption that the impulses cannot be expressed directly. Therefore, an ambiguous stimulus is presented, allowing the youngster to project on to the stimulus 'unacceptable' thoughts and impulses, as well as other defences against them.

Projective tests are also used by some clinicians in a manner that involves less psychodynamic inference. This type of analysis examines formal aspects of the test response. For instance, this type of test analyses the distance between human figures that the child draws. Interpretations are then made on the basis of the content of the response.

Rorschach test is the most common projective test. In this test, the youngster is asked what he/she sees in each of ten ink blots. The most commonly used methods for scoring and interpretation are based on the characteristics of the responses, such as the location of blot responded to, the determinants (eg. Colour and shading) and the content. (Exner and Weiner, 1995). The Human Figure Drawing (Koppitz, 1984) test requires the youngsters to draw a picture of a person and then a second person of the opposite sex. Similarly, the House-Tree-Person technique (Buck, 1992) expects the child to draw a house, a tree and a person. The Kinetic Family Drawing technique (Burns and Kaufman, 1970) asks the child to draw a picture of everyone in the family, including himself or herself, 'doing something'. The clinician then asks questions about the drawings.

There are still some projective tests, which ask the children to make up a story. Some common examples are Murray's (1943) Thematic Apperception Test (TAT), The Children's Apperception Test (CAT) of Bellak (1993) and the Roberts Apperception Test for children developed by McArthur and Roberts (1982).

OBSERVATION

Earlier, attempts were made to observe children's behaviour through diaries or continuous observations and narrations that were deliberately non-selective (Wright, 1960). Later, a more focused tradition of observation has evolved from the earlier one. Pinpointed set of behaviours that could be reliably coded by others, were observed (Bijou et al., 1969).

Recent observational methods have come from behavioural/ social learning perspective. The observations are most often made in the child's natural environment. For this purpose, planned situations are sometimes created in clinic or laboratory settings approximate naturally occurring interactions. Observations range from single, relatively simple and discrete behaviours of the child (eg. occurrence of toileting) to complex interactions are more difficult to observe and code than the behaviours of a single individual. Even then, they are theoretically and clinically relevant.

The behavioural observation system involves the following steps:

1. Explicitly pinpointing and defining behaviours to be observed;
2. Observing whether a particular behaviour or sequence of behaviours occurs;
3. Coding the behaviours;
4. Interpreting the behaviours observed.

Coding systems are subjected to the test of reliability. The behavioural/social learning studies commonly report on the reliability of the observations employed. The aspect of reliability most frequently reported is interrater reliability. Two or more observers independently observe the same behaviour and then the degree of agreement is calculated. A number of factors affect the reliability, the validity and the clinical utility of observations. (Hops, Davis and Longoria, 1995). The complexity of the observation system, and the changes in observer's use of the system are two most important factors that affect observation. Careful training as well as periodic monitoring of the observer's use of the system is suggested for increasing the effectiveness. Another impediment to the utility of direct observation is 'reactivity'. It refers to whether the knowledge of being observed changes one's behaviour. For instance, introduction of an observer into the situation and introduction of videotaping instrument may stimulate the person under observation to react in a novel manner than the usual way of behaviour. To reduce reactivity, the following measures can be taken: i) using somebody (like teachers), who is already known, as the observer, and ii) making the observers move freely and become familiar with the person concerned before the actual observation starts.

Behavioural perspective insists on behavioural observations, which are the most direct method of assessment. They require the least inference. They call forth reliable observers Training and maintaining reliable observers involve both difficulties and expenses, which remain a common obstacle to use behavioural observations. Attempts have been made to create systems that are amenable to widespread use of direct observation. Experienced observers are asked to make global ratings on the basis of observation of behaviour rather than recording those specific behaviours. Moreover, direct observation is just one aspect of a multi-method approach to behavioural assessment that can include self-monitoring of behaviour, interviews, ratings and checklists and self-report instruments.

PROBLEM CHECKLISTS

Problem checklist is a statistical technique to identify the presence of specific problem behaviours. The respondent has to indicate the presence or absence of the specific problem behaviour in the youngster by making scores that range from low to high. Problem checklists can be employed to sample a wide range of behaviour problems or those problems particular to specific disorder. There are thus a wide variety of Problem checklists. Some are for general use. Revised Behaviour Problem Checklist (Quay and Peterson, 1983) and Child Behaviour Checklist (Achenbach, 1991b) are examples for general-purpose problem checklists. Checklists can also be used with particular populations. The Revised Conners Parent Rating Scale (Conners et al., 1998b) is used when Attention Deficit Hyperactivity Disorder (ADHD) needs to be assessed. These instruments are valuable tools for clinicians and researchers.

Furthermore, problem checklists can be completed by different informants. This helps the clinicians gain a fuller appreciation of the clinical picture of the potential situational aspects of the child's problem. It is possible to compare multiple informants' reports about the child with respect to a common set of problem items and dimensions and thereby to arrive at a statistic indicating the degree of agreement. Thus these problem checklists enable to clinicians to compare a child to approximate norms and to examine issues such as situational aspects of a child's behaviour and the perceptions of various informants.

SELF REPORT INSTRUMENTS

Self-report Instruments can be used to assess constructs directly related to the presenting problem (eg. anxiety, depression) or related constructs of potential interest (eg. self-concept, control beliefs, parenting stress, family environment). Hence, like problem checklists, here too we have self-report Instruments for specific measures as well as self- report instruments for general measures (for example, the Youth Self Report of Achenbach, 1990).

Parents and other adults can also be asked to complete self-report instruments about themselves. These instruments may assess specific problems for these adults. For instance, a parent's own anxiety or depression might be assessed. Sometimes, a wide variety of aspects of these adults' functioning also becomes important and hence needs to be measured. For example, the feelings, attitudes and beliefs of the adults, particularly, with respect to the child or adolescent may pose a need to be assessed. Abidin's (1995) Parenting Stress Index is the best example for this. Similarly, the aspects of the family environment may have the necessity to be measured. Moos and Moos' (1986) Family Environment Scale is of this kind. Yet another example is Parent–Adolescent Relationship Questionnaire of Robin, Koepke and Moye (1990). Such assessments provide valuable information about the youngster's social environment and factors, which contribute to problem behaviours. Therefore, these assessments obtained through self-reporting instruments facilitate conceptualization of the whole problem behaviour and thereby lead to systematic planning of intervention services.

INTELLECTUAL/EDUCATIONAL ASSESSMENT

The assessment of intellectual-educational functioning plays a vital role in almost all clinical evaluations. This is because intellectual functioning is conceived to be the central defining feature for disorders such as mental retardation and learning disabilities.

Intellectual functioning either contributes to or it is affected by a wide variety of behavioural problems. The tests of intellectual functioning tend to have better established normative data, reliability and validity, when compared to most other assessment instruments. Intellectual functioning is assessed through a variety of instruments such as: i) intelligence tests; ii) developmental scales; and iii) ability and achievement tests.

(i) Intelligence Tests

Intelligence test is the most common assessment device for evaluating intellectual functioning. Next to interview, this is the most frequently employed assessment device. In clinical settings, the widely used intelligence tests are the Stanford-Binet—Fourth Edition (Thorndike, Hagen and Sattler, 1986), the Wechsler Preschool and Primary Scale of Intelligence—Revised (Wechsler, 1989), the Wechsler Intelligence Scale for Children—Third Edition (Wechsler, 1991) and Kaufman Assessment Battery for Children (Kaufman and Kaufman, 1983). These tests are administered individually and they yield an IQ score. The average score is 100. Thus the individual score can help to find out whether the particular person is above or below the average person of his/her age.

Intelligence tests are popular and very useful in predicting a variety of outcomes. Eventhen, these tests have long been the subject of controversy. Critics feel that the use of IQ scores has resulted in intelligence being viewed as a real thing rather than as a concept. Moreover, the IQ score has led to view the intelligence as a rigid and fixed attribute rather than as something complex and subtle. Another familiar criticism against intelligence tests is that they are culturally biased and hence they lead to social injustice (Kaplan, 1985). These criticisms along with the concern for legal, ethical and practical issues create a demand that the intelligence tests should be used cautiously. Kamphaus (1993), therefore, suggested that continued attention should be paid to test improvement and monitoring of appropriate usage.

(ii) Developmental Scales

A special kind of assessment instrument is required to assess the intellectual functioning of very young children, particularly, infants. A popular measure is the Bayley Scales of Infant Development (Bayley, 1969; 1993). Its original version extended from two to thirty months of age. The revised version expanded that range from one to forty-two months. The developmental tests yield a developmental index rather than an IQ score. An Intelligence test evaluates language and abstract reasoning abilities. But a developmental scale emphasizes sensorimotor skills and simple social skills. The Bayley Scale examines the ability to sit, walk, place objects, attend to visual and auditory stimuli, smile and imitate adults. The Bayley Scale includes a Motor Scale, a Mental Scale and a Behaviour Rating Scale that assesses aspects of the child's behavioural style, for instance attitude and interest. Sattler (1998) reported that there is only low correlation between performance on intelligence tests and performance on developmental scale because both of them tap different abilities.

(iii) *Ability and Achievement Tests*

Apart from assessing general intellectual functioning, it is also necessary to evaluate the functioning in a particular area. A variety of tests have been developed for this purpose. Further, some of these tests are administrated individually, whereas some of them are administered in groups. For example, the Wide Range Achievement Test (Jastak and Wilkinson, 1984) and the Woodcock Mastery Test (Woodcock, Mather and Barnes, 1987) are administered to individual youngsters to assess academic achievement. Similarly, the Iowa Test of Basic Skills (Hoover et al., 1996) and the Stanford Achievement Test (Harcourt Brace Education Measurement, 1997) are group-administered achievement tests employed in many school settings. These ability and achievement tests are particularly helpful when we are concerned about children with learning and school-related problems.

ASSESSMENT OF PHYSICAL FUNCTIONING

Understanding disordered behaviour also calls forth information about physical functioning. Physical examinations and assessments along with family and child histories bring to limelight the genetic problems, which are treatable by environmental manipulation. For instance, phenylketonuria is a recessive gene condition. Most of the cognitive problems usually associated with this condition can be prevented by avoiding phenyialanine in the child's diet. Similarly, the diseases and defects that effect import areas of functioning directly or indirectly can be diagnosed. Moreover, signs of atypical or lagging physical development are an early indication of developmental disorders that ultimately influence many aspects of behaviour.

Understanding a variety of problem behaviours especially mental retardation, autism, learning disabilities and attention deficit disorders necessitate the assessment of the nervous system

This is because brain and other neurological dysfunctions are thought to be associated with abnormal physical reflexes, motor coordination problems and sensory perceptual deficits. Assessment of neurological dysfunction in children involves both direct neurological assessment and indirect neuropsychological assessment. Such combined assessment requires the coordinated efforts of neurologists, psychologists and other professional workers.

There are a number of procedures that directly assess the integrity of the nervous system (Teodori, 1993). The computers have brought about many revolutions in neurological assessment. The electroencephalograph (EEG) and the Event-Related Potential (ERP) are the methods assisting neurological assessment. Both these methods require placing electrodes on the scalp and the electrodes record activity of the brain cortex in general or during a particular incident in which the individual is engaged in information processing. Dawson et al. (1997) arrived at individual differences in EEG activation patterns, when they studied about fearful and inhibited children and also about infants of depressed mothers. Nelson and Bloom (1997) have used ERP to study learning and language disorders.

New technologies and brain imaging techniques have also been evolved for neurological assessment. Some of them are CT scan (also referred to as Computerized Axial Tomography – CAT scan), Positron Emission Tomography (PET) scans and Functional Magnetic Resonance Imaging (FMRI). These new assessment tools are becoming increasingly important in individual neurological assessment and research.

Neuropsychological assessment employs tests that contain learning, sensorimotor, perceptual, verbal and memory tasks. From the individual's performance on these tasks, inferences are made about central nervous system functioning and thus it is an indirect means of assessing brain functions. The current interest in neuropsychological assessment is attributable to increased sensitivity to the needs and legal requirements of providing services to children with handicapping conditions, particularly to those who exhibit problems presumed to have a neurological etiology.

The most widely used neuropsychological assessment instruments are the Halstead–Reitan Neuropsychological Test Battery for children (Reitan and Wolfson, 1993) and the Luria–Nebraska Neuropsychological Battery-Children's Revision (Golden, Purisch and Hammeke, 1985). These tests are called 'batteries' since these instruments consist of several subtests or scales, each intended to assess one or more abilities. Neuropsychological assessment in children is still a young field and the development of instruments that derive from evolving research on cognitive development, neurological development and brain–behaviour relationship is ongoing. Researches are also ongoing to develop strategies that more clearly specify impairment and offer guidance for rehabilitation.

A common criticism levelled against neuropsychological assessments is that they are free from social and environmental influences. But Sameroff and Chandler (1975) are of the view that brain damage is correlated with social class and family variables, which are disadvantageous to social adjustment and physical health. Hence these socio-familial variables may themselves underlie both the brain damage and the observed behavioural/ learning problems. This issue should be given enough consideration.

SUMMARY

To offer appropriate intervention services to the disordered population, accurate identification and assessment is a prerequisite. Identification refers to the process of assigning a disordered individual to a categorical label. Assessment refers to an ongoing process of evaluating the youngsters possessing behavioural disorders. Both are entwined processes intricately related to the scientific and clinical aspects of child and adolescent disorders.

Two different approaches towards classification are prevalent: i) Clinical Approach and ii) Empirical Approach. Clinically derived classification relies on consensus among clinicians regarding disorders and their definitions. There was no extensive classification scheme for child and adolescent behaviour until recently. The first comprehensive attempt was made by Kraeplin (1913) who proposed 18 distinct types of disorder. The most widely used classification system in the United States is the American Psychiatric Association's Diagnostic and Statistical Manual of Mental disorders (DSM). The other alternative system widely employed is the Tenth Revision of International Classification of Diseases (ICD) developed by World Health Organisation. It identified 11 major categories of mental disorders whereas DSM identified 10 categories.

Quite often, children and adolescents present with a number of different problems. Having a number of different disorders is known as 'co-occurrence' or 'comorbidity'. Epidemiological research indicates that co-occurrence of child and adolescent disorders is quite high.

Apart from clinical approaches, there are empirical approaches to classification, which rely on behaviour checklists and statistical analyses and tend to be associated with dimensional rather than categorical means. Achenbach's Child Behaviour Checklist, Teacher Report Form and Youth Self-Report are examples of checklists employed in the empirical approach.

Conducting a comprehensive assessment is necessary not only for classification and diagnosis but also for planning and executing appropriate interventions. The complex process of assessment requires a multifaceted approach. Different assessment methods offer assistance to the professionals and clinicians for comprehensive assessment.

The general clinical interview is the most common form of assessment. It is open ended and unstructured. It is conducted in the context of a therapeutic interaction and employed with a variety of other assessment instruments. Its reliability cannot be established. Hence during recent times, structured interviews are developed. Their reliability can be established and they are developed for more limited purposes of deriving a diagnosis based on a particular classification scheme.

Projective Test was the most common form of psychological test employed in the past to assess children. Due to lack of empirical evidence regarding norms, reliability and validity they are less commonly used now-a-days.

Observation of behaviour is central to behavioural/social learning approach. It is a direct method of assessment. Observations range from single relatively simple and discrete behaviours of the child to complex interactions of family members. Though such on-going interactions are difficult to observe and code, they are theoretically and clinically relevant.

Problem checklists can be employed to sample a wide range of behaviour problems or those problems particular to a specific disorder. The problem checklists enable the clinicians to compare a child to appropriate norms and to examine issues such as situational aspects of child's behaviour and the perceptions of various informations. Self-report instruments can be used to assess constructs directly related to the presenting problem or related constructs of potential interest. Self-report measures are available for both the youngster and the relevant adults in the youngster's life. These instruments facilitate conceptualization of the whole problem behaviour and thereby lead to systematic planning of intervention services.

The assessment of intellectual-educational functioning plays a vital role in almost all clinical evaluations because intellectual functioning is conceived to be the central defining feature for certain disorders. Intellectual functioning is assessed through a variety of instruments such as intelligence tests, developmental scales and ability and achievement tests.

Understanding disordered behaviour also calls forth information about physical functioning. Assessment of physical functioning, especially of the nervous system, is important for many behaviour problems. Assessment of neurological dysfunction in children involves both direct neurological assessment and indirect neuropsychological assessment. Methods like EEG and ERP and brain imaging techniques like CT scan, PET scan and FMRI assist a lot in neurological assessment. Neuropsychological assessment employs tests that contain learning, sensorimotor, perceptual, verbal, and memory tasks. The most widely used neuropsychological assessment instruments are the Halstead–Reitan Neuropsychological Test Battery for Children and the Luria–Nebraska Neuropsychological Battery–Children's Revision.

REFERENCES

Abidin, R.R., (1995), *Parenting Stress Index: Professional Manual,* (3rd ed.). Odessa, FL: Psychological Assessment Resources.

Achenbach, T.M., (1998), 'Diagnosis, Assessment, Taxonomy and Case Formulations'. In T.H. Ollendick & Hersen, M. (Eds.), *Handbook of Child Psychopathology* (3rd ed.) . New York: Plenum Press.

Achenbach, T.M., (1991b), *Manual for the Child Behaviour Checklist/4-28 and 1991 Profile*. Burlington, VT: University of Vermont Department of Psychiatry.

Achenbach, T.M., (1991d), *Manual for the Youth Self-report and 1991 Profile.* Burlington, VT: University of Vermont Department of Psychiatry.

Achenbach, T.M., (1991c), *Manual for Teachers Report Form and 1991 Profile.* Burlington, VT: University of Vermont Department of Psychiatry.

Achenbach, T.M., (1991a), *Integrative Guide for the 1991 CBCL/4-18, YSR and TRF profiles.* Burlington, VT: University of Vermont Department of Psychiatry.

Bayley, N., (1969,1993), *Bayley Scales of Infant Development: Birth to Two Years.* San Antonio, TX: Psychological Corporation.

Bellak, L., (1993), *The T.A.T., C.A.T., and S.A.T. in Clinical Use* (5th Ed.). Boston: Allyn & Bacon.

Bijon, S.W., Pterson, R.F., Harris, F.R., Allen, K.E., and Johnson, M.S., (1969), 'Methodology for Experimental Studies of Young Children in Natural Settings'. *The Psychological Record*, 19, 177–210.

Buck, J.N., (1992), *House-Tree-Person Projective Drawing Technique (H-T-P): Manual and Interpretive Guide (Revised by W.L. Warren).* Los Angels: Western Psychological Services.

Burns, R.C. and Kaufman, S.H., (1970), *Kinetic Family Drawing (K-F-D) Research and Applications.* New York: Bruner/Mazel.

Conners, C.K., Sitarenios, G., Parker, J.D.A. and Epstein, J.N., (1998b), 'The Revised Conner's Parent Rating Scale (CPRS-R): Factor Structure,Reliability and Criterion Validity'. *Journal of Abnormal Child Psychology*, 26, 257–268.

Dawson, G., Frey, K., Panagiotides, H., Osterling, J. and Hessl, D., (1997), 'Infants of Depressed Mothers Exhibit a Typical Frontal Brain Activity: A Replication and Extension of Previous Findings'. *Journal of Child Psychology and Psychiatry,* 38,179–186.

Exner, J.E., Jr. and Weiner, I.B., (1995), *The Rorschach: A Comprehensive System* (Vol. 3) *Assessment of Children and Adolescents* (2nd Ed.). New York: Wiley.

Golden, C.J., Purisch, A.D. and Hammeke, T.A., (1985), *Luria-Nebraska Neuropsychological Battery: Forms I and II Manual.* Los Angels: Western Psychological Services

Harcourt Brace Education Measurement, (1997), *The Stanford Achievement Test,* Ninth Edition, San Antonio: Harcourt Brace Education Measurement.

Hodges, K., Cool, J. and McKnew, D., (1989), 'Test–retest reliability of a Clinical Research Interview for Children: The Child Assessment Schedule (CAS)'. *Psychological Assessment,* 1, 317-322.

Hoover, H.D., Heironymous, A.N., Frisbie, D.A. and Dunbar, S.B., (1996), *The Iowa Tests of Basic Skills,* Forms K, L and M. Itasca, IL: Riverside Publishing Company.

Hops, H., Davis. B. and Longoria, N., (1995), 'Methodological Issues in Direct Observation: Illustrations with the Living in Familial Environments (LIFE) Coding System'. *Journal of Clinical Child Psychology,* 24, 193–203.

Jastak, S. and Wilkinson, G.S., (1984), *Wide Range Achievement Test—Revised.* Wilmington, DE: Jastak Associates.

Kamphaus, R.W., (1993), *Clinical Assessment of Children's Intelligence.* Boston: Allyn and Bacon.

Kamphaus, R.W., and Frick, P.J., (1996), *Clinical Assessment of Child and Adolescent Personality and Behaviour.* Boston: Allyn and Bacon.

Kaplan, R.M., (1985), 'The Controversy Related to the Use of Psychological Tests'. In B. Wolman (Ed.), *Handbook of Intelligence.* New York: Wiley.

Kaufman, A.S., and Kaufman, N.L., (1983), *Administration and Scoring Manual for the Kaufman Assessment Battery for Children.* Circle Pines, M.N: American Guidance Service.

Kaufman, J., Birmaher, B., Brent, D., Rao, U., Flynn, C., Moreci, P., Williamson, D., and Ryan, N., (1997), 'Schedule for Affective Disorders and Schizophrenia for School–Age Children– Present and Lifetime Version (K-SDAS-PL): Initial Reliability and Validity Data'. *Journal of American Academy of Child and Adolescent Psychiatry.* 36, 980-988.

Knoff, H.M., (1998), 'Review of the Children's Apperception Test (1991 Revision)'. In J.C. Impara & B.S.Plake (Eds.), *The Thirteenth Mental Measurement Yearbook.* Lincoln: The University of Nebraska–Lincoln.

Kolko, D., (1987), 'Simplified Inpatient Treatment of Nocturnal Enuresis in Psychiatrically Disturbed Children'. *Behaviour Therapy,* 18, 99–112.

Koppitz, E.M., (1984), *Psychological Evaluation of Human Figure Drawings by Middle School Pupils.* Orlando, FL: Grune and Straton.

Kraepeline .E., (1913), *Clinical Psychiatry: A Text Book for Physicians* (Translated by A. Diffendoff) New York: Macmillan.

McArthur, D.S. and Roberts, G.E., (1982), *Roberts Apperception Test for Children: Manual.* Los Angels: Western Psychological Services.

Moos, R.H., and Moos, B.S., (1986), *Family Environment Scale Manual* (2nd Ed.). Palo Alto, CA: Consulting Psychologists Press.

Murray, H.A., (1943), *Thematic Apperception Test*. Cambridge, MA: Harvard University Press.

Nelson, C.A. and Bloom, F.E., (1997), 'Child Development and Neuroscience'. *Child Development*, 68, 970–987.

Nietzel, M.T., Bernstein, D.A., and Milich, R., (1994), *Introduction to Clinical Psychology* (4th Ed.), Englewood Cliffs, NJ: Prentice Hall.

Nottlemann, E.D, and Jenson, P.S., (1995b), 'Co-morbidity of Disorders in Children and Adolescents: Developmental Perspectives'. In T.H Ollendick, and R.J. Prinz (Eds.), *Advances in Clinical Child Psychology* (Vol.17), New York: Plenum Press.

Quay, H.C. and Peterson, D.R., (1983), *Interim Manual for the Revised Behaviour Problem Checklist*. Coral Gables, Fl: University of Miami.

Rapoport, J.L. and Ismond, D.R., (1996), *DSM–IV, Training Guide for Diagnosis of Childhood Disorders*. New York: Brunner/Mazel.

Reitan, R.M. and Wolfson, D., (1993), *The Halstead Rietan Neuropsychological Test Battery: Theory and Clinical Interpretation*, (2nd Ed.). Tucson: Neuropsychology Press.

Robin, A.L., Koepke, T., and Moye, A., (1990), 'Multidimensional Assessment of Parent-adolescent Relations'. *Psychological Assessment*, 2, 451–459.

Sameroff, A.J. and Chandler, M.J., (1975), 'Reproductive Risk and the Continuum of Caretaking Casualty'. In F.D. Horowitz (Ed.), *Review of Child Development Research*. Vol. 4, Chicago: University of Chicago Press.

Sattler, J.M., (1998), *Assessment of Children*, 3rd Ed. San Diego: Jerome M. Sattler, Publisher.

Shaffer, D., Fisher, P., Dulcan, M.K., Davies, M., Piacentini, J., Schwab-Stone, M.E., Lahey, B.B., Bourdon, K, Jenson, P.S., Bird, H.R., Camino, G., and Regier, D.A., (1996), 'The NIMH Diagnostic Interview Schedule for Children Version 2.3 (DISC-2.3): Description, Acceptability, Prevalence Rate, and Performance in the MECA Study'. *Journal of the American Academy of Child and Adolescent Psychiatry*, 35, 865-877.

Thorndike, R.L., Hagen, E.P. and Sattler, J.M., (1986), Stanford–Binet Intelligence Scale, 4th Ed. Chicago: Riverside.

Watkins, C.E., Campbell, V.L., Nieberding, R. and Hallmark, R., (1995), 'Contemporary Practice of Psychological Assessment by Clinical Psychologists'. *Professional Psychology: Research and Practice*, 26, 54-60.

Wechsler, D., (1989). *Wechsler Preschool and Primary Scale of Intelligence*—Revised (WPPSI-R). San Antonia, TX: The Psychological Corporation.

Wechsler, D., (1991), *Manual for the Wechsler Intelligence Scale for Children*–Third Edition (WISC–III). San Antonia, TX: The Psychological Corporation.

Woodcock, R.W., Mather, N. and Barnes. E.K., (1987), *Woodcock Mastery Tests-Revised: Examiner's Manual*, Forms G and H. Circle Pines, MN: American Guidance Service.

Wright, H.F., (1960), 'Observational Child Study'. In P.H. Mussen (Ed.), *Handbook of Research Methods in Child Development*. New York: John Wiley.

5

Anxiety Disorders

OBJECTIVES

This chapter defines anxiety disorder and describes its classification. It presents the different types of anxiety disorders, such as Panic Disorder (PD), Generalized Anxiety Disorder (GAD), Phobic disorders, Obsessive Compulsive Disorder (OCD) and Post-Traumatic Stress Disorder (PTSD). It also explains the separation Anxiety Disorder (SAD) and school refusal. It delves into the cause of anxiety disorders in children. It stresses the need for assessment of anxiety disorders and ultimately it analyses the different treatment produces. After going through this chapter, the readers must be able to:

(i) Define anxiety disorder and understand its classification;

(ii) Know about the different types of anxiety disorder;

(iii) Say what separation anxiety is and its consequences;

(iv) Analyse the causes of anxiety disorders;

(v) Differentiate biological and psychological influences;

(vi) Comprehend the assessment of anxiety disorder;

(vii) Delineate the different treatment measures to anxiety disorder such as pharmacological treatments and psychological interventions.

Children and adolescents are often described to have specific behaviour disorders. They are found to be anxious, fearful, withdrawn, timid, depressed and so on. Such youngsters are said to possess some kind of emotional difficulties, which are termed 'internalizing disorders'. Research evidences support that there exist empirically defined broadband internalizing syndromes. In the past, such broadband internalizing syndromes were broadly referred to as 'neuroses'. But now more specific terms such as anxiety disorders, phobias, obsessions and compulsions and depression are employed to indicate the 'internalizing' behaviour problems. In this chapter, we discuss the anxiety disorder.

DEFINITION AND CLASSIFICATION OF ANXIETY DISORDERS

Anxiety is a general feeling of dread of apprehensiveness typically accompanied by various psychological reactions, including increased heart rate, rapid and shallow breathing, sweating, muscle tension and dryness of the mouth. Often 'anxiety' is considered to be synonymous to fear. Barrios and O' Dell (1998) defined it as a complex pattern of three types of reactions to a perceived threat. This tripartite model describes overt behavioural responses (eg. running away, trembling voice, closing eyes), physiological responses (eg. Thoughts of being scared, self-deprecatory thought, images of bodily harm). It is generally agreed by researchers that some anxiety is biologically adaptive because it produces enhanced vigilance and a more realistic appraisal of a situation, allowing the person concerned to develop appropriate coping responses. Quite often, anxiety is experienced by many people and it interferes with normal every day functioning.

DSM-IV classification identifies 'anxiety' as one of the major categories of mental disorders. This classification is most commonly used in recent times. In ICD-10 classification, anxiety is subsumed by the major category 'Neurotic, stress-related and somatoform disorders'.

TYPES OF ANXIETY DISORDERS

DSM-IV recognizes four types of anxiety disorders. They are: i) Panic Disorders (PD) and General Anxiety Disorders (GAD); ii) Phobic disorders; iii) Obsessive-Compulsive disorders and iv) Post-traumatic stress disorder.

(i) Panic Disorders and Generalized Anxiety Disorders

Panic Disorder (PD) is characterised by sudden attacks of intense anxiety whereas Generalized Anxiety Disorder (GAD) is characterized by frequent and excessive anxiety or worry about a number of activities or events rather than anxiety being focused on particular objects or situations. The physical, cognitive and emotional problems caused by GAD lead people experiencing it to become tired, irritable, socially inept and to have difficulty in functioning effectively. GAD is relatively common problem in younger children, particularly in girls and the median age of onset is about 10 years. According to Clark et al. (1994). GAD is the most common anxiety disorder among adolescents.

In both these cases of PD and GAD, anxiety is 'free-floating' and occurs in the absense of any obvious anxiety-provoking object or situation. Thus, a person experiences anxiety but does not know why. The physiological reactions to these kinds of anxiety are chest pain and a tingling in the hands or the feet. Other symptoms include 'derealization' (the feeling that the world is not real) and 'depersonalization' (the loss of a sense of personal identity, manifested as a feeling of detachment from the body).

A distinction is made between panic attacks and panic Disorder. A panic attack is a discrete period of intense fear of terror that has a sudden onset and reaches a peak quickly (ten minutes or less) DSM-IV describes thirteen somatic or cognitive symptoms of a panic attack. The most important of them are palpitation, sweating, trembling, shortness of breath, chest pain, nausea, numbness and fear of dying. There are three different categories of panic attacks. They are: i) unexpected and uncued panic attacks which occur spontaneously without any apparent situational triggers; ii) situational bound or cued panic attacks which occur due to exposure to feared object or situation; and iii) situationally predisposed panic attacks which occur on exposure to a situational cue, but not all the time. If a child/person experiences recurrent unexpected panic attacks, if this recurrence leads to persistent concern and considerable change in behaviour, then it is called Panic Disorder. Panic attacks can last for a few minutes to several hours. Usually they occur during wakefulness. But Dilsaver (1989) found out that they can also occur during sleep.

The psychodynamic model sees GAD as the result of unacceptable unconscious conflicts blocked by the ego. These are powerful enough to produce constant tension and apprehension, but since they are unconscious, the person is unaware of the anxiety's source. Genetic component might also contribute to PD and GAD. Balon et al. (1989) reported that around 40 per cent of first-degree relatives of PD sufferers have the disorder themselves. Lesch et al. (cited in High field, 1996e) have shown that neuroticism levels are correlated with two versions of a gene responsible for transporting serotonin. One of these leads to more serotonin and neuroticism and the other to less of these. However, the gene accounts for only about four per cent of the total variation in anxiety, so other factors clearly cannot be ruled out. Papp et al. (1993) argued that PD is triggered by a dysfunction in receptors that monitor oxygen levels in the blood.

(ii) Phobic Disorders

Some children show strong, persistent and irrational fears of and desires to avoid particular objects, activities or situations. When such behaviour interferes with normal everyday functioning, then it is said that the person has a phobia. Normally, encountering the phobic stimulus results in intense anxiety which leads to feelings of tension, panic or even fear of death. Nausea, palpitations and difficultly in breathing may also occur. The psycho-dynamic model sees phobias as the surface expression of a much deeper conflict between id, ego and super ego which has its origin in childhood.

DSM-IV identified three categories of phobia. They are agoraphobia, social phobia and specific phobias.

(a) Agoraphobia

It is a fear of open spaces. It typically involves a fear of being in situations from which escape may be difficult or help is unavailable. In extreme cases, agoraphobics become 'prisoners' trapped in their own homes and dependent on others. It mostly occurs in women and it also typically occurs in early adulthood.

(b) Social Phobia

It is an intense and excessive fear of being in a situation in which being scrutinised by others is a possibility. This is otherwise known as Social Anxiety Disorder. DSM-IV describes social phobia as a marked and persistent fear of acting in an embarrassing or a humiliating way in social or performance situations. Youngsters with social phobia fear social situations. They are afraid to meet and talk with people and so it happens that they often miss school and are unwilling to participate in recreational activities. In children, social anxiety may be expressed by crying, tantrums, freezing or shrinking from social situations with unfamiliar people.

Adolescence is a developmental period during which social phobias are quite common. Kashani and Orvaschel (1990) estimated that social phobia occurs in approximately one per cent of children and adolescents. Beidel and Randall (1994) reported that children and adolescents with social phobias may experience distress in a variety of social situations. For youngsters in the eight to twelve years range, the most commonly identified situations are public speaking, reading aloud and giving a book report. Other situations identified are eating in public, writing in public, going to parties, using public rest rooms, speaking to authority personalities and informal interactions with peers, parents and friends. La Greca and Stone (1993) developed a Social Anxiety Scale for children. The scale suggests that social anxiety in elementary-school-age children can be grouped into three factors: i) fear of negative evaluation from peers; ii) social avoidance and distress in situations; and iii) generalized social avoidance and distress. Ginsburg, La Greca and Silverman (1998) reiterated that social anxiety is associated with less social acceptance, lesser feelings of self-worth and more negative interactions with peers.

In the recent times, selective mutism is conceptualised as a type of social phobia. Youngsters with selective mutism do not talk in 'select' or specific social situations like classrooms or play activities in which their talking is very important for their development. This behaviour occurs despite the fact that they do speak in other situations. For example, they may speak easily with family members. The onset of this disorder is usually occurring before age five. American Psychiatric Association (1994) describes the youngsters with selective mutism as shy, withdrawn, fearful and clinging.

(c) Specific Phobia

It is an extreme fear of a specific object (such as snake) or situation (such as being in the mid sea). Specific phobias usually develop in childhood but can occur at any time. Some of the common specific phobias are: aqua phobia (water), cynophobia (dogs), hematophobia (blood), monophobia (being alone), nycotophobia (death) and xenophobia (strangers). DSM-IV suggests that specific phobias can be subcategorised into five types: animal, natural environment, blood-injection-injury, situational and others.

Specific phobias are typically described as more prevalent in girls than boys (King et al., 1989). But this gender difference is not consistently reported (Silverman and Ginsberg, 1998). Usually children's phobias are relatively being. They will automatically diminish over time with or without treatment. Ollendick, King and Frary (1989) found that the number and intensity of phobias decreased with age. If phobias continue to persist over time and if they are unreasonable, then they should be given due consideration. Research reviews suggest that an average of about 5 per cent of the youngsters exhibit phobias.

Youngsters with specific phobias are also likely to meet the criteria for other diagnoses. Last, Strauss and Francis (1987) found that specific phobics had one or more other disorders like depression, mood disorders and externalising disorders such as Oppositional Defiant Disorder. Treatment studies of phobic children undertaken by King and Ollendick (1997) also suggest that many phobic children experience co-occurring disorders.

(iii) Obsessive-Compulsive Disorders (OCD)

In obsessive-compulsive disorder, the profound anxiety is reflected in obsessions and compulsions 'Obsessions' are recurrent thoughts or images and are experienced as senseless or repugnant. 'Compulsions' are irresistible urges to engage in repetitive behaviours performed according to rituals or rules as a way of reducing or preventing the discomfort associated with some future undesirable event. OCD was considered a rare neurosis in the past. But now it occupies a central position in clinical psychology and contemporary psychiatry. OCD is the fourth most common psychological problem in the United States whereas in Britain, it has been estimated that one and a half million people suffer from it. Females are often OCD sufferers and this disorder usually begins in young adulthood, and sometimes in childhood.

Quite often compulsions emerge from obsessions. Shakespeare's character Lady Macheth is the most famous fictional OCD sufferer. She acquires a hand-washing compulsion after helping her husband murder the King of Scotland. The billionaire Howard Hughes, Charles Darwin, Martin Luther and John Bunyan (Bennett, 1997) are the non-fictional sufferers OCD sufferers do recognize that their compulsive behaviours are meaningless. Even then, if they prevent themselves from engaging in these behaviours, they experience intense anxiety which is reduced only when the compulsive ritual is carried out (Hodgson and Rachman, 1972). According to psychodynamic model, obsessions are defence mechanisms which serve to occupy the mind and displace more threatening thoughts. The behavioural model too sees OCD as a way of reducing anxiety.

OCD is known to occur in children under the age of seven (Swedo et al., 1989c). The obsessions and compulsions among children are highly time-consuming and hence they result in interference with normal routines, academic functioning and social relationships (Rapoport, 1989). Flament et al. (1988) reported that the OCD prevalence rate is one per cent among adolescents and lifetime prevalence rate is 1.9 per cent in the general adolescent population. Swedo et al. (1989c) reported that the onset of obsessive-compulsive symptoms in boys tend to be prepubertal (mean age nine), whereas in girls, the average onset (mean age eleven years) was around puberty.

Generally OCD is described as following a course of the emergence and fading of various symptoms over time. Multiple obsessions and compulsions are usually present at any one time and then the symptoms change over time, though no clear progression is identified (Rettew et al., 1992). Hanna (1995) reported that most youngsters diagnosed with OCD also meet the criteria for least one other disorder. Multiple anxiety disorders, depression and eating disorders are commonly reported (Henin and Kendall, 1997). Leckman et al. (1997) found that OCD often occurs with Tourette's syndrome which is a chronic disorder with a genetic and neuro anatomical basis characterized by motor and vocal tics and related urges, and other tic disorders.

Comings and Comings (1987) found that OCD sufferers often have first-degree relatives with some sort of anxiety disorders. This suggests that there is genetic basis to OCD. But Tallis (1994) reported that in over half of the families of an OCD sufferer, members become actively involved in the rituals. This indicates the potential influence of 'learning'. That is why children with a parent who engages in ritualistic behaviour automatically develop such sort of behaviours. Further there is also evidence for the fact that OCD sufferers reveal a different pattern of brain activity compared to non OCD controls, in the form of increased metabolic activity in the left hemispheres frontal lobe. Mc Guire et al. (1994) found that when drugs are given to reduce the metabolic activity, the symptoms of OCD decline. The fact that OCD can be treated using drugs which increase serotonin's availability indicates that a deficiency of the neurotransmitter might be the reason for it.

(iv) Post-Traumatic Stress Disorder (PTSD)

PTSD is an anxiety disorder occurring in response to an extreme psychological or physical trauma outside the range of normal human experience (Thompson, 1997). Trauma is usually defined as an event outside everyday experience that would be distressing to almost anyone. Traumas include a physical threat to one's self or family, witnessing other people's death, and being involved in a natural or human-made disaster. PTSD may occur immediately following a traumatic experience or weeks, months and even years later. Yule (1993) reported the PTSD symptoms found among children are distressing recollections of the event, avoidance of remainders and signs of increased physiological arousal, manifested as sleep disturbances and poor concentration. Often, the children with PTSD do not confide their distress to parents or teachers for fear of upsetting them. As a result, their schoolwork is affected and they are often thrown off their educational career course. Many research findings have confirmed that children can experience PTSD. Pynoos et al. (1993) found a strong correlation between children's proximity to the epicentre of the 1988. American earthquake and the overall severity of the core components of PTSD, with girls reporting more persistent anxiety than boys.

The reactions of youngsters to traumatic events vary considerably. In general, symptoms of PTSD decline overtime but substantial numbers of youngsters continue to report symptoms. La Greca and her colleagues (1996) examined the symptoms of post-traumatic stress in third-through fifth-grade children, during the school year after the occurrence of a hurricane in Florida. They found that symptoms of avoidance and general numbing decreased over time. Ofcourse, the fading away of symptoms a varies from person to person. Similarly, not all children and adolescents experience the same pattern or intensity of symptoms and reactions too may vary in how long they persist and fluctuate over time. A number of factors seem to influence reactions. La Greca, Silverman and Wasserstein (1998) identified four factors that influence post-traumatic stress reactions. They are degree of exposure to trauma, child's characteristics, child's coping and access to social support.

SEPARATION ANXIETY AND SCHOOL REFUSAL

Anxiety concerning separation from primary caregiver is part of the normal development process in infants. Children, from the first year of life through the preschool years, exhibit periodic distress and worry when they are separated from their parents or other individuals to whom they have a major attachment. Expectations, beliefs and feelings of home sickness when separated from parents are quite common among almost all children. If the distress due to separation persists beyond the expected age or if it is in excess, then the separation anxiety is viewed as a problematic and disordered behaviour.

Usually the children with separation anxiety are clingy, following their parents around. They express general fear, experience nightmares, and complain of somatic symptoms such as dizziness, headaches, stomach aches, nausea etc. They imagine that some illness or tragedy might befall them or their caregivers and hence they become apathetic, depressed and reluctant to leave home or to participate in activities with their peers. They may even go to the extreme level of harming themselves so as avoid separation.

'School Phobic' was the term employed to describe the child who exhibits fear and anxiety regarding school attendance and school phobia is nothing but a manifestation of the fear of separation from the mother and home. Hersov (1960) suggested the more comprehensive term 'School refusal' instead of 'School Phobia'. The most common conceptualization of school refusal in children attributes the problem to separation anxiety. Psychodynamic model describes the child's insistence on remaining at home as satisfying both the child's and the mother's needs and conflicts concerning separation. Behavioural model explains the school refusal as the child's avoidance response due to the intense fear of losing the mother. Once avoidance behaviour develops, it may be reinforced by attention and other rewards such as toys and special food items which the child received when it is at home.

The DSM-IV describes eight symptoms of Separation Anxiety Disorder (SAD). They are:

(i) Recurrent and excessive worry about losing major attachment figures;

(ii) Persistent and excessive worry about losing them or about possible harm befalling them;

(iii) Persistent and excessive worry that an untoward event will lead to separation from a major attachment figure;

(iv) Persistent reluctance or refusal to go to school or elsewhere due to the fear of separation;

(v) Persistent fear to be alone or without major attachment figure at home or to be without them in other settings;

(vi) Persistent reluctance to sleep without the major attachment figure.

(vii) Repeated nightmares involving the theme of separation;

(viii) Repeated complaints of physical symptoms such as headaches, stomach aches, nausea or vomiting, when separated from major attachment figures.

The above symptoms and problems must be present prior to age eighteen and must result in significant distress or impairment in social, school or other areas of function. Only then, they are considered to be disordered behaviour.

SAD is probably one of the most common anxiety disorders in children. Research findings reveal that SAD is prevalent among 5 per cent of children. Clark et al. (1994) reported that this prevalence declines after early childhood and the disorder is probably uncommon among adolescents. School refusal is usually estimated to occur in 4 percent to 1.5 per cent of the general population (Ollendick and Mayer, 1984). School refusal, unlike SAD, can be found in children of all ages. In younger children, the problem of school refusal is likely to be related to separation anxiety. But children of middle-age groups and early adolescence, if they refuse schooling, are likely to have complex and mixed presentations of anxiety and depressive disorders. Hence Berg and Jackson (1985) & Blagg and Yule (1994) advocate for early prognosis before the age of ten because successful treatment is difficult with older children. If left untreated, serious long-term consequences are likely to arise. Further, to the extent that school refusal is related to a phobic reaction to some aspect of the school situation, the considerations regarding specific and social phobias would apply.

CAUSES OF ANXIETY DISORDERS IN CHILDREN

The causes of anxiety disorders in children and adolescents are by no means clear. Much of the information that is available represents a downward extension from the adult literature. It is probable that anxiety disorders are the resultant of multiple factors which interact with each other in complex ways. Different anxiety disorders result from different combinations of influences. The different factors are the biological and psychosocial in nature.

BIOLOGICAL INFLUENCES

Many research studies indicate that genetic contributions are the primary factors for anxiety disorders. The findings of Rutter et al. (1990b) & Silverman and Ginsburg (1998) ascertained that anxiety disorders occur in families. First of all, the family studies establish that children whose parents have anxiety disorder are at risk for developing an anxiety disorder. Beidel and Turner (1997) studied children of parents with anxiety disorders, depressive disorders, mixed anxiety/ depressive disorders and no disorder. They arrived at the findings that children of anxious parents primarily had anxiety disorders, whereas children of parents in the two other risk groups were more likely to have a variety of disorders. Last et al. (1991) found the family aggregation of anxiety disorders. That is, parents, whose children have anxiety disorders, had significantly higher rates of anxiety disorder. Similarly, Kendler et al. (1992b) and Torgesen (1993) specifically examined the influence of inheritance and suggested that genetic influences cause anxiety disorders. Particularly, Leonard et al. (1994) proved the genetic influences for obsessive Compulsive Disorder. There are also evidences to support the biological basis for OCD and they establish an association between OCD symptoms and certain known neurological disorders. Further, brain imaging studies produce evidences for the fact that OCD was linked to the anatomy of the basal ganglia, a group of brain structures lying under the cerebral cortex (Luxenberg et al., 1988).

PSYCHOSOCIAL INFLUENCES

Anxiety problems may develop either as a result of exposure to some traumatic event or through environmental paths. Rachman (1977) postulated three different environmental paths by which phobias might be acquired: i) direct experience/ conditioning (eg. a child is attacked by a dog); ii) indirect experience/ vicarious exposure modelling (eg. a child observes a fearful parent); and iii) transmission of information (eg. a child hears stories about traumatic experiences from others). In addition, Dadds and his colleagues (1996) proved that parents do influence the development of anxiety through their parenting styles. For instance, intrusive and over protective parenting styles contribute to the child's failure to develop a sense of control over evens. This failure, in turn, may contribute to a vulnerability to develop anxiety and other internalising disorders (Chorpita and Barlow, 1998). Similarly, insecure mother-child attachments have been shown to be a risk factor for the development of anxiety disorders (Bornstein, Borchardt and Perwein, 1996).

ASSESSMENT OF ANXIETY DISORDERS

A comprehensive assessment of a youngster with anxiety problems involves a variety of assessment needs. It should be sensitive to developmental issues. It should also differentiate normal fears and worries from the anxiety problems of clinical concern. The usual assessment procedures include general clinical interviews (which yield information that is valuable in formulating an understanding of the case and in planning intervention) and structured diagnostic interviews (both general and more specific to anxiety disorders).

Assessment of anxiety disorders is often guided by the tripartite model that will address one or more of the three response systems, namely, behavioural, physiological and subjective. In addition to diagnosis through three response system approach, assessment should also be guided by empirical findings of how anxiety problems in youngsters can be conceptualised. For instance, self-report instruments can be used for this purpose. The self-report instruments can be completed by the concerned youngster and parents. They offer scores on empirically defined factors such as physical symptoms, social anxiety, harm avoidance, separation anxiety and so on. This allows examination of the various aspects of anxiety presentation in a single instrument. March and his colleagues (1997) have developed one such multi dimensional anxiety self-report scale for children. Quite often, youngsters with anxiety disorders present with a variety of other problems. In such cases, more general empirically derived instruments may be employed and they are helpful in describing a range of behaviour problems and various people's perspectives. Achenbach's behaviour checklists are of this type.

Since aspects of environment also contribute to anxiety problems, the youngster's environment should also be assessed.

It is desirable to assess the specific environmental events that are associated with heightened anxiety, to evaluate the patterns of family interactions and communications, to study the reactions of adults or peers to the youngster's behaviour and ultimately to assess the existence of problems in other family members. Thus the assessments of multiple aspects of the problem as well as the use of multiple informants yield necessary information.

The overt behavioural aspects of children's and adolescents' fears and anxieties can be assessed through direct observation. The children can be asked to perform behavioural tasks in planned graduated steps and observations with regard to the children's approach can be made. Alternatively, observations can also be made in the natural environment where the fear or anxiety occurs. Trained observers may be called to serve the purpose. Checklists may be employed to check off the specific behaviours that are exhibited. Diaries to report daily observation can be maintained and they are helpful in both assessment and treatment efforts. Similarly, the subjective component of the youngster's anxiety can be evaluated by a variety of self-report measures such as the State-Trait Anxiety Inventory for children (Spielberger, 1973) and Revised Children's Manifest Anxiety Scale (Reynolds and Richmond, 1978). The psychological component of anxiety is assessed by measuring parameters such as heart rate, skin conductance and palmar sweat. Portable and inexpensive recording devices can be used for this purpose.

TREATMENT OF ANXIETY DISORDERS

The treatment of anxiety disorders involves both pharmacological and psychological measures. But compared to adult treatment, researches regarding effective treatment of anxiety in children and adolescents are less extensive.

Pharmacological Treatment

A variety of medications are used to treat anxiety disorders. Selective Serotonin Reuptake Inhibitors (SSRI), tricyclic anti-depressants and anxiolytics, particularly the benzodiazepines are often suggested for treating children and adolescent anxiety sufferers. Systematic study is needed to establish safe and effective medication. In practice, the use of medication for anxiety in youth is not the treatment of first choice. Only psychological interventions are employed first. Pharmacological medication is likely to be an adjunct to psychological interventions. Popper and Gherardi (1996) suggested that the relative contributions of these two components require investigation.

Psychological Interventions

Behavioural and cognitive-behavioural perspectives have contributed much to psychological interventions for treatment of fears and phobias. But investigations on effectiveness of treatment of severe anxiety problems are very limited.

(1) Behavioural Treatment Measures

Some of the behavioural procedures to treat anxiety disorders are: systematic desensitisation, modelling and contingency management.

(i) Systematic Desensitisation

This is one of the most widely used behavioural treatments. It has three variants, namely, imaginal desensitisation, 'in-vivo' desensitisation and emotive imagery. In imaginal desensitisation, a hierarchy of fear-provoking situations is constructed and the youngster is asked to visualize them. These visualizations are presented as the youngster is engaged in relaxation or some other response that is incompatible with fear. This process is repeated until the most anxiety-provoking scene is comfortably visualized. On the other hand, in 'in-vivo' desensitisation, the actual feared object or situation is employed rather than using visualizations. In emotive imagery, an exciting story involving the child's favourite hero, instead of relaxation, is presented as the anxiety inhibitor. The last two methods are proved to be effective in treating children's fears and phobias (Ollendick and King, 1998).

(ii) Modelling

This is a commonly employed behavioural procedure. In modelling therapy, the child observes another person interacting adaptively with the feared situation. The model can be live or symbolic (e.g. film or slides). The most effective method is participant modelling (Ollendick and King, 1998), in which observation is followed by the fearful child joining the model in making gradual approaches to the feared object. Lewis (1974) made use of participant modelling to treat fear of water and he is found it to be most effective.

(iii) Contingency Management

This procedure is based on operant principle. In this method, the child's avoidant/ anxious behaviour is addressed directly by altering the contingencies for such behaviour, ensuring that positive consequences follow exposure to the feared stimulus and assuring that positive consequences do not follow avoidance of the feared stimulus and that the child is rewarded for improvement. This procedure is otherwise called reinforced practice and this has been proved to be effective in treating children's fears and phobias (Ollendick and King, 1998).

(2) Cognitive-Behavioural Treatment

Cognitive-behavioural perspective has also contributed a variety of strategies designed to alter the thoughts, beliefs and perceptions of anxious children. Cognitive-behavioural procedures are based on the assumption that modifying the child's maladaptive cognitions will lead to changes in the child's anxious/ avoidant behaviour. Many research findings reveal that the self-management of children's beliefs or cognitions is one of the best treatment strategies. Children are taught to use positive statements through modelling, rehearsal and social reinforcement. The cognitive self-control approach to fear of dark was applied by Kanfer et al. (1975). Graziano's (Graziano and Mooney, 1982) home-based programme is another example of cognitive self-management strategy. Barrett, Dadds and Rapee (1996) have extended the cognitive behavioural approach by including a family involvement component. In this programme, in addition to the cognitive-behavioural procedures for the child's anxiety, the parents are given training in child-management, anxiety management, and communication and problem solving skills.

Treatment to OCD differs in number of ways from the other anxiety disorders. For OCD, two kinds of intervention (alone or in combination) are provided. Serotonin inhibitors have been proved effective pharmacological treatment for child and adolescent OCD sufferers. Clomipramine (an SRI) is yet another medication most extensively studied. The other treatment procedure recommended is cognitive-behavioural intervention therapy. This treatment includes education about OCD, training in modifying cognitions to resist obsessions and compulsions and to enhance change and contingency management and self-reinforcement. Psychopathologists often recommend for a combined cognitive-behavioural approach and pharmacological approach to treat children with OCD.

SUMMARY

Anxiety is a sort of emotional difficulty and it is one of the broadband internalising syndromes. It is defined as a general feeling of dread typically accompanied by various psychological reactions. It is generally a complex pattern of three response systems: overt behavioural, physiological and subjective responses. DSM-IV identifies it as one of the major categories of mental disorders and it recognises four types of anxiety disorders: Panic Disorder and General Anxiety Disorder (GAD), Phobic Disorder, Obsessive-Compulsive Disorder (OCD) and Post Traumatic Stress Disorder (PTSD).

Panic disorder is characterized by sudden attacks of intense anxiety whereas generalized anxiety disorder is characterized by frequent and excessive anxiety or worry about a number of activities or events. The psychodynamic model sees GAD as the result of unacceptable unconscious conflicts blocked by the ego. Genetic component might also contribute to PD and GAD.

Fears are quite common in children. It is the irrational nature of fear, together with its interference with normal functioning that makes a phobia a disorder. Three categories of phobias of agoraphobia, social phobia and specific phobia. Agoraphobia involves fear of being in situations from which escape may be difficult or help is unavailable. Social Phobia is an intense fear of being in a situation in which being scrutinized by others is a possibility. This is otherwise known as Social Anxiety Disorder. Specific Phobia is an extreme fear of a specific object or situation and it usually develops in childhood.

In Obsessive Compulsive Disorder (OCD), excessive anxiety is reflected in obsessions and compulsions. Obsessions are recurrent thoughts whereas compulsions are irresistible urges to engage in repetitive behaviours performed according to rituals. Research findings reveal that there is genetic basis to OCD. Compulsions can also be 'learnt'. Evidences are also there for the fact that deficiency of neurotransmitter might be one of the reasons for OCD.

Post Traumatic Stress Disorder (PTSD) is an anxiety disorder occurring in response to an extreme psychological or physical trauma outside the range of normal human experience. The reactions of youngsters to traumatic events vary considerably. Four factors seem to influence the post-traumatic stress reactions. They are the degree of exposure to the trauma, the child's characteristics, the child's coping and access to social support.

Anxiety concerning separation from primary care giver is part of the normal developmental process in infants. If this distress due to separation or fear of separation persists beyond the expected age or if it is in excess, then the distress becomes a disorder called separation anxiety disorder (SAD). School phobia or school refusal is the manifestation of some sort of separation anxiety from mother and home. SAD is probably one of the most common anxiety disorders in children.

Anxiety disorders are the resultant of multiple factors which interact with each other in complex ways. Evidences for biological influences are stronger, particularly in obsessive-compulsive disorder. Psychosocial factors also play an import role in the development of anxiety disorders. Most of the anxiety disorders are developed through environmental paths such as direct experience, indirect experience and transmission of information. Parenting style also influences the development of anxiety.

A comprehensive assessment of anxiety problems is guided by the three response systems: overt behaviour, subjective responses and physiological responses. Assessment should also be guided by empirical findings. An important method to assess the overt behavioural aspects of anxiety problems is direct observation. Self-report instruments and general behaviour checklists can be used to gather information about the subjective component of anxiety problems. The physiological component of anxiety may be assessed by the parameters such as heart rate, skin conductance and palmar sweat.

The treatment of anxiety disorders involves both pharmacological and psychological measures. Pharmacological treatment suggests for medications such as Serotonin Reuptake Inhibitors (SRI), tricyclic anti-depressants and anxiolytics. In practice, the use of medication is not the treatment of first choice. Only psychological interventions are tried first. Both behavioural and cognitive-behavioural perspectives have contributed to psychological interventions. Behavioural treatment measures are systematic desensitisation, modelling and contingency management. On the other hand, the cognitive-behavioural treatment resorts to a variety of strategies designed to alter the thoughts, beliefs, cognitions and perceptions of anxiety sufferers. In the recent times, cognitive self management strategies have been proved highly successful in offering remedial service to anxiety problems.

REFERENCES

American Psychiatric Association, (1994), *Diagnostic and Statistical Manual of Mental Disorders*. Washington D.C.: American Psychiatric Association.

Balon, R., Jordan, M., Phol, R. and Yeragni, N., (1989), 'Family History of Anxiety Disorders in Control Subjects with Lactate-induced Panic Attacks'. *American Journal of Psychiatry*, 146, 1304-1306.

Barrett, P.M., Dadds, M.R. and Rapee, R.M., (1996), 'Family Treatment of Childhood Anxiety: A Controlled Trial'. *Journal of Consulting Clinical Psychology*, 64, 333-342.

Barrios, B.A. and O'Dell, S.L., (1998), 'Fears and Anxieties'. In E.J. Mash & R.A. Barkley (Eds.), *Treatment of Childhood Disorders* (2nd Ed.). New York: Guilford Press.

Beidel, D.C. and Randall, J. , (1994), 'Social Phobia'. In T.H. Ollendick, N.J. King and W.Yule (Eds.), *International Handbook of Phobic and Anxiety Disorders in Children and Adolescents* (pp. 111-130). Yew York: Plenum Press.

Beidel, D.C. and Turner, S.M., (1997), 'At Risk for Anxiety: I. Psychopathology in the Offspring of Anxious Parents'. *Journal of American Academy of Child and Adolescent Psychiatry*, 36, 918-924.

Bennett, W., (1997), 'Daughter Dead After Living Like a Monk in a Room for 14 years'. *The Daily Telegraph*, 5, September, 3.

Berg, I. and Jackson, A., (1985), 'Teenage School Refusers Ten Years on Average After Inpatient Treatment. *British Journal of Psychiatry*, 147, 366-370.

Blagg, N. and Yule, W., (1994), School Refusal in T.H. Ollendick, N.J. King & W. Yale (Eds.), *International Handbook of Phobic and Anxiety Disorders in Children and Adolescents*. (pp. 169-186). New York: Plenum Press.

Chorpita, B.F. and Barlow, D.H., (1998), 'The Development of Anxiety: The Role of Control in the Early Environment'. *Psychological Bulletin*, 124, 3-21.

Clark, D.B., Smith. M.G., Neighbours, B.D., Skerlec, L.M. and Randall, J., (1994), 'Anxiety Disorders in Adolescence: Characteristics, Prevalence and Co morbidities'. *Clinical Psychology Review*, 14, 113-137.

Comings, D.E. and Comings, B.G., (1987), 'Hereditary Agrophobia and Obsessive–Compulsive Behaviour in Relatives of Patients with Gilles de la Tourette's Syndrome'. *British Journal of Psychiatry*, 151, 195-199.

Dads, M.R., Barrett, P.M., Rapee, R.M. and Ryan, S., (1996), 'Family Process and Child Anxiety and Aggression: An Observational Analysis'. *Journal of Abnormal Child Psychology*, 24, 715-734.

DSM-IV, (1994), 'Diagnostic and Statistical Manual of Mental Disorder', (4th Ed.), Washington: *American Psychiatric Association*.

Flament, M.F., Whitaker, A., Rapoport, J.L., Davies, M., Berg, C.Z., Kalikow, K., Sceery, W. and Shafer, D., (1988), 'Obsessive Compulsive Disorder in Adolescence: An Epidemiological Study'. *Journal of the American Academy of Child and Adolescent Psychiatry*, 27, 764-771.

Ginsburg, G.S., La Greca, A.M. and Silverman, W.K., (1998), 'Social Anxiety in Children with Anxiety Disorders: Relation with Social and Emotional Functioning'. *Journal of Abnormul Psychology*, 26, 175-185.

Graziano, A.M. and Mooney, K.C., (1982), 'Behavioural Treatment of "Might Fears" in Children: Maintenance of Improvement at 2½ to 3 year follow-up'. *Journal of Consulting and Clinical Psychology*, 50, 598-599.

Hanna, G.L., (1995), 'Demographic and Clinical Features of Obsessive-Compulsive Disorder in Children and Adolescents'. *Journal of the American Academy of Child and Adolescent Psychiatry*, 34, 19-27.

Henin, A., and Kendall, P.C., (1997), 'Obsessive-compulsive Disorder in Childhood and Adolescence'. In T.H. Ollendick & R.J. Prinz (Eds.), *Advances in Clinical Child Psychology*. (Vol. 19). New York: Plenum Press.

Hersov, L.A., (1960), 'Persistent Non-attendance at School'. *Journal of Child Psychology and Psychiatry*, 1, 130-136.

Highfield, R., (1996e), 'Don't Worry, It's Just in your Genes'. *The Daily Telegraph*, 20 November, 5.

Hodgson, R.J. and Rachman, S., (1972), 'The Effects of Contamination and Washing in Obsessional Patients'. *Behaviour Research and Therapy,* 10, 111-117.

ICD-10, (1992), The International Standard Classification of Diseases, Injuries and Causes of Death (ICD). Tenth Revision.

Kanfer, F.H., Kardy, P. and Newman, A., (1975), 'Reduction of Children's Fear of the Dark by Competence-related and Situational Threat-related Verbal Cues. *Journal of Consulting and Clinical Psychology,* 43, 251-258.

Kashani, J.H., and Orvaschel, H., (1990), 'A Community Study of Anxiety in Children and Adolescents'. *American Journal of Psychiatry,* 147, 313-318.

Kendler, K.S., Neale, M.C., Kessler, R.C., Heath, A.C. and Eaves, L.J., (1992b), 'The Genetic Epidemology of Phobias in Women: The Interrelationship of Agro Phobia, Social Phobia, Situational Phobia and Simple Phobia. *Archives of General Psychiatry,* 49, 273-281.

King, N.J., and Ollendick, T.H., (1997), 'Treatment of Childhood Phobias'. *Journal of Child Psychology and Psychiatry,* 38, 389-400.

King, N.J., Ollier, K., Iacuone, R., Schuster, S. Bays, K., Gullone, E. and Ollendick, T.H., (1989), 'Fears of Children and Adolescents: A Cross Sectional Australian Study Using the Revised Fear Survey Schedule for Children'. *Journal of Child Psychology and Psychiatry,* 30, 775-784.

La Greca, A.M. and Stone, W.L., (1993), 'Social Anxiety Scale for Children-Revised: Factor Structure and Concurrent Validity'. *Journal of Clinical Child Psychology,* 22, 17-27.

La Greca, A.M., Silverman, W.K. and Wasserstein, S.B., (1998), 'Children's Predisaster Functioning as a Predictor of Post-traumatic Stress Following Hurricane Andres. *Journal of Consulting and Clinical Psychology,* 66, 883-892.

La Greca, A.M., Silverman, W.K., Vernberg, E.M. and Prinstein, M.J., (1996), 'Symptoms of Post-traumatic Stress in Children after Hurricane Andrew: A Prospective Study'. *Journal of Consulting and Clinical Psychology,* 64, 712-723.

Last, C.G., Hersen, M., Kazdin, A.E., Orvaschel, H. and Perrin, S., (1991), 'Anxiety Disorders in Children and their Families'. *Archives of General Psychiatry,* 48, 928-934.

Last, C.G., Strauss, C.C. and Francis, G., (1987), 'Comorbidity Among Childhood Anxiety Disorders'. *Journal of Nervous and Mental Disease,* 175, 726-730.

Leckman, J.F., Peterson, B.S., Anderson, G.M., Arnsten, F.T., Paules, D.L. and Cohen, D.J., (1997), 'Pathogenesis of Tourette's Syndrome'. *Journal of Child Psychology and Psychiatry,* 38, 119-142.

Leonard, H.L., Swedo, S.E., Allen, A.J. and Rapoport, J.L., (1994), 'Obsessive-Compulsive Disorder'. In T.H. Ollendick, N.J. King and Yule, W. (Eds.), *International Handbook of Anxiety Disorders in Children and Adolescents*. New York: Plenum.

Lewis, S., (1974), 'A Comparison of Behaviour Therapy Techniques in the Reduction of Fearful Avoidance Behaviour'. *Behaviour Therapy*, 5, 648-655.

Luxenburg, J.S., Swedo, S.E., Flament, M.F., Friedland, R., Rapoport, J.L. and Rapoport, S.I., (1988), 'Neuroanatomical Abnormalities in Obsessive-Compulsive Disorder Detected with Quantitative X-ray Computed Tomography'. *American Journal of Psychiatry, 145, 1089-1093.*

March, J.S., Parker, J D.A., Sullivan, K., Stallings, P. and Conners, C.K., (1997), 'The Multidimensional Anxiety Scale for Children (MASC): Factor Structure, Reliability and Validity'. *Journal of the American Academy of Child and Adolescent Psychiatry*, 36, 554-565.

McGuire, P.K., Bench, C.J., Frith, C.D., Marks, I.M., Frackowiak, R.S.J. and Dolan, R.J., (1994), 'Functional Asymmetry of Obsessive–compulsive Phenomena'. *British Journal of Psychiatry*, 164, 459-468.

Ollendick, T.H. and King, N.J., (1998), 'Empirically Supported Treatments for Children with Phobic and Anxiety Disorders Current Status'. *Journal of Clinical Child Psychology*, 27, 156-167.

Ollendick, T.H. and Mayer, J.A., (1984), 'School Phobia'. In S.M. Turner (Ed.), *Behavioural Treatment of Anxiety Disorders*. New York: Plenum.

Ollendick, T.H., King, N.J. and Frary, R.B., (1989), 'Fears in Children and Adolescents: Reliability and Generalizability Across Gender, Age and Nationality'. *Behaviour Research and Therapy*, 27, 19-26.

Papp, L.A., Klein, D.F., Martinez, J., Schneier, F., Cole, R., Liebowitz, M.R., Hollander, E., Fyer, A.J., Jordan, F. and Gorman, J.M., (1993), 'Diagnostic and Substance Specificity of Recent Life-stress Experience'. *Journal of Consulting and Clinical Psychology*, 51, 467-469.

Popper, C.W. and Gherardi, P.C., (1996), 'Anxiety Disorders'. In J.M. Wiener (Ed.), *Diagnosis and Psychopharmacology of Childhood and Adolescent Disorders*. New York: John Wiley & Sons.

Pynoos, R.S., Goenijian, A., Tashjian, M., Karakashian, M., Manjikan, R., Manoukian, G., Steinberg, A.M. and Fairbanks, L.A., (1993), 'Post-traumatic Stress Reactions in Children After the 1988'. American Earthquake. *British Journal of Psychiatry*, 163, 239-247.

Rachman, S.J., (1977), 'The Conditioning Theory of Fear Acquisition: A Critical Examination'. *Behaviour Research and Therapy*, 15, 375-387.

Rapoport, J.L., (1989), 'The Biology of Obsessions and Compulsions'. *Scientific American*, 260, 83-89.

Rettew, D.C., Swedo. S.E., Leonard, H.L., Lenane, M.C. and Rapoport, J.L., (1992), 'Obsessions and Compulsions Across Time in 79 Children and Adolescents with Obsessive Compulsive Disorder'. *Journal of the American Academy of Child and Adolescent Psychology,* 31, 1050-1056.

Reynolds, C.R. and Richmond, B.O., (1978), 'What I Think and Feel: A Revised Measure of Children's Manifest Anxiety'. *Journal of Abnormal Child Psychology,* 6, 271-280.

Rutter, M., Macdonald, H., Le Counteur, A., Harrington, R., Bolton, P. and Baily, A., (1990b), 'Genetic Factors in Child Psychiatric Disorders –II. Empirical Findings'. *Journal Child Psychology and Psychiatry,* 31, 39-83.

Silverman, W.K. and Ginsburg, G.S., (1998), 'Anxiety Disorders'. In T.H. Ollendick & M. Hersen (Eds.), *Handbook of Child Psychopathology,* (3rd Ed.) New York: Plenum.

Spielberger, C.D., (1973), *Manual for the State-trait Anxiety Inventory for Children*. Palo Alto, CA: Consulting Psychologists Press.

Swedo, S.E., Rapoport, J.L., Leonard, H., Lenane, M. and Cheslow, D., (1989c), 'Obsessive –compulsive Disorder in Children and Adolescents: Clinical Phenomenology of 70 Consecutive Cases'. *Archives of General Psychiatry,* 46, 335-341.

Tallis, F., (1994), 'Obsessive-compulsive Disorder'. *The Psychologist,* 7, 312.

Thompson, S.B.N., (1997), 'War Experiences and Post-traumatic Stress Disorder'. *The Psychologist,* 10, 349-350.

Torgersen, S., (1993), 'Relationship Between Adult and Childhood Anxiety Disorders: Genetic Hypothesis'. In C.G. Last (Ed.), *Anxiety Across the Lifespan: A Developmental Perspective.* New York: Springer.

Yule, W., (1993), 'Children's Trauma from Transport Disasters'. *The Psychologist,* 7, 318-319.

6

Depression in Children and Adolescents

OBJECTIVES

This chapter defines depressive disorder and presents the classification of child and adolescent depression. It describes the prevalence of depressive disorder among child and adolescent population. It analyses the various influences on the development of depressive disorder. It delves into assessment and treatment practices. Finally, it presents the problems in peer relations as well as treatment for the same. After reading this chapter, the readers should be able to:

(i) Define depressive disorder;

(ii) Know the classification of child and adolescent depression;

(iii) Understand the prevalence of depression among the child and adolescent population;

(iv) Analyse the various influences on the development of depression in children and adolescents;

(v) Comprehend the assessment and the treatment practices for curing depression;

(vi) Describe the problems in peer relations; and

(vii) Know about the various treatment measures offered to set right the problems in peer relations.

Mood or affective disorders involve a prolonged and fundamental disturbance of mood and emotions. Mood is a pervasive and sustained emotional state that colours perceptions, thoughts and behaviours. At one extreme is 'manic disorder' or 'mania' characterized by wild, exuberant and unrealistic activity and a flight of ideas or distracting thoughts. At the other end is 'depressive disorder'. Mania usually occurs in conjunction with depression. In such cases, it is called 'bipolar disorder'. This chapter deals with depressive disorder in children and how it affects peer relations. Until recently, the problem of depression in children and adolescents had not received much attention. But now there has developed increased interest to examine the phenomenon in clinical and normal populations of youngsters. In addition, the new perspective of developmental psychopathology focused its attention on depression in children and adolescents.

DEFINITION AND CLASSIFICATION OF CHILD AND ADOLESCENT DEPRESSION

Generally the 'depression' refers to the experience of a pervasive unhappy mood. The clinical definition of depression also stresses this subjective experience of sadness or dysphoria as a central feature. The depressed youngsters experience a number of other problems as well. Irritability, loss of the experience of pleasure, social withdrawal, lowered self-esteem, inability to concentrate, poor school-work, alterations of biological functioning (sleeping, eating, elimination) and somatic complaints are often noted. The depressed youngsters also experience other psychological disorders. Both internalizing and externalizing difficulties are reported. Anxiety disorders, such as Separation Anxiety Disorder (SAD) are the most commonly noted additional disorders. Conduct disorder as well as Oppositional Defiant Disorder also co-occur among depressed youth. Among adolescents who have depressive problems, alcohol and substance abuse disorders are also common additional diagnoses. Compass's (1997) illustration of the case of a fifteen year old Nick has many of these features along with some of the other factors that contribute to the development and course of depression. Nick's father left before Nick was born. He lives with his mother. He was born with a curvature of the spine. As a result, he walks awkwardly and is limited in his physical abilities. Nick's mother reports that Nick is irritable and sullen much of the time. He is constantly fighting and arguing with his mother. Even the slightest thing seems to send him into a fit of anger. During such outbursts, he throws things and punched holes in walls and doors. His mother also reports that he seems unhappy and is withdrawn spending increasing amounts of time at home and alone. Over subsequent interviews, he reveals that he is very unhappy and feels helpless. He is self-conscious about his appearance; his peers tease him; he feels that he is disliked; and he hates himself. He is often absent from school. He spends much of the day at home alone playing video games or watching television. He refuses to go to bed before midnight.

The psychoanalytic perspective views depression as a phenomenon of the superego and of mature ego functioning (Kessler, 1988). In depression, the superego acts as a punisher of the ego. Since the child's superego is not sufficiently developed to play this role, it is impossible, within this perspective, for a depressive disorder to occur in children. Therefore, depression in children received little attention till recently.

Another major perspective explains the existence of depression in children through the concept of masked depression. This view believes that there is certainly a disorder of depression among children. But the usual dysphoric mood and other features considered essential to the diagnosis of depression are not present. Instead, the youngster's depression is 'masked' by other problems (depression equivalents) such as hyperactivity or delinquency. The 'underlying' depression itself is not directly displayed but is inferred by the clinician. Many researchers agree with this proposition that masked depressions are quite common among children and may have resulted in childhood depression being under diagnosed (Cytryn and Mcknew, 1974 & Malmquist,1977). Though the concept of masked depression is quite controversial, it is important in the sense it approves that depression is an important and prevalent childhood problem. The central notion of this concept is that depression in children does not exist visibly and the youngsters may display depression in a variety of age-related forms and in ways that may be different from adult depression. This concept that depression is manifested differently in child and adults contributed to the evolution of a developmental perspective. The developmental perspective believes that some of 'depressive' behaviours of a child may be viewed as typical of that developmental stage. It stresses that awareness of normative and developmental patterns is clearly important in the diagnostic practices. The developmental perspective has become an important element in the study of depression (Cicchetti and Toth, 1998; Schwartz, Gladstone and Kaslow, 1998).

As suggested above, understanding depression in children and adolescents is a complex task. Since there are various perspectives on depression in young people, a variety of definitions of depression is available. Carlson and Cantwell (1980) employed three different criteria to define depression. In the first criterion, the presence of depressive symptoms at intake was noted. Second criterion included the administration of a version of the Children's Depression Inventory. In the third criterion, separate interviews with youngsters and their parents were conducted. The implication is that the conclusions regarding correlates of depression may be affected by the criterion and informant employed to designate youngster as depressed. However, it is totally agreed that childhood depression is a syndrome or disorder.

DSM-IV classifies depression in the category of Mood Disorders. There are no separate diagnostic categories for mood disorders in children, or adolescents. The criteria employed to diagnose mood disorders are the same for children, adolescents and adults. Mood disorders may be sometimes unipolar (one mood, either depression or mania) and sometimes bipolar (involving both the moods of depression and mania). Major Depression Disorder (MDD) is the primary DSM category for defining depression. This disorder is described by the presence of one or more Major Depressive Episodes. The symptoms required for the presence of a Major Depressive Episode are the same for children, adolescents and adults with one exception. The one exception is that in children or adolescents, irritable mood can be substituted for depressed mood.

Symptoms used by DSM-IV to Diagnose a Major Depressive Episode

1. Depressed or irritable mood
2. Loss of interest or pleasure
3. Change in weight or appetite
4. Sleep problems
5. Motor agitation or retardation
6. Fatigue or loss of energy
7. Feelings of worthlessness or guilt
8. Difficultly in thinking; concentrating or making decisions
9. Thought of death or suicidal thoughts/ behaviour

The presence of five or more of the above symptoms is required to be diagnosed as disordered individual. The symptoms must be present for at least two weeks and must cause clinically significant distress or impairment in important areas of the youngster's functioning in school or social activities.

The other principal depressive disorder included in DSM-IV is dysthymic disorder. This is essentially a disorder in which many of the symptoms of Major Depressive Episode are present in less severe form but are more chronic in the sense they persist for a longer period of time. Again, the symptoms must cause clinically significant distress or impairment. The term 'double depression' is sometimes employed to describe instances in which both dysthymia and a major depressive episode are present. Dysthymia typically occurs prior to a major depressive episode.

Youngsters with depression disorder can also be given a diagnosis of Adjustment Disorder with Depressed Mood. The other mood disorders included in DSM-IV, Bipolar disorders and Cyclothymia, involve the presence of mania as well as depressive symptoms. In addition to the presence of mania, at least three or more other symptoms must be present in order to meet the criteria for Manic Episode.

Symptoms used by DSM-IV to Diagnose a Manic Episode

1. Persistent elevated expansive or irritable mood
2. Inflated self-esteem
3. Decreased need for sleep
4. Being more talkative than usual
5. Feeling of thoughts racing
6. Distractibility
7. Increased goal-directed activity or psychomotor agitation
8. Excessive pleasurable activity that can lead to negative consequences

Individuals diagnosed with bipolar and cyclothymic disorders experience both mania and depression. In comparison with depression, less is known about these disorders in children and adolescents (Nottlemann and Jensen,1995a).

The DSM approach follows the inherent view that mood disorders found in youngsters are the same as those found in adults. Many of the cognitive attributes, biological correlates and behaviours found in depressed adults have also been reported to occur in children and adolescents (Kaslow, Rehm and Seigel, 1984; Kazdin et al., 1985). Empirical approaches (for instance, researches employing Achenbach's instruments) too identify syndromes that involve depressive symptoms. Empirical research does not find a syndrome that includes symptoms of depression alone. The syndrome of mixed depression and anxiety features has emerged consistently in researches with children and adolescents.

PREVALENCE OF DEPRESSIVE DISORDER

Estimates of the prevalence of depression vary considerably. This is because there are differences in defining and diagnosing depression (Reynolds and Johnson, 1994; Schwartz et al., 1998). In addition, the developmental considerations complicate getting accurate estimates. The difficulty of administering similar assessments to youngsters of different ages is yet another consideration.

Research findings of Lewinsohn, Rhode and Seeley (1998) reveal that Major Depressive Disorder is the most prevalent form of affective disorder among children and adolescents. Bipolar disorders occur in less than one per cent of community samples of adolescents. Among youngsters of unipolar disorders, about 80 per cent experience MDD, and 10 per cent 'double depression'. The prevalence rate of MDD in children (in community surveys) range between 0.4 and 2.5 per cent and between 0.4 and 8.3 per cent in adolescents. The prevalence rate of dysthymic disorder among children range between 0.6 and 1.7 per cent, and among adolescents between 1.6 and 8.0 per cent (Birmaher et al., 1996a). The study of Lewinshon and his colleagues (1998) estimates that by age 19, approximately 28 per cent of adolescents will have experienced an episode of MDD. The findings of Lewinshon et al. (1993a) and Compas, Ey, & Grant (1993) suggest that about one out of four youngsters in the general population experiences a depressive disorder sometime during childhood or adolescence.

Usually no gender differences are reported for children aged six to twelve (Angold and Rutter,1992). When differences are reported, depression is more prevalent in boys than in girls during this age, that is, six to twelve (Anderson et al., 1987). Among adolescents, depression is more common in girls. For adults, female to male ratio is 2:1. In addition, several reports suggest that the rates of major depression may be increasing (Birmaher et al., 1996a). This trend has been reported for youngsters as well as adults.

Another aspect stressed by many research studies is that youngsters who are depressed typically experience other problems as well. The investigations examining DSM diagnoses indicate that 40 to 70 per cent of youngsters diagnosed with MDD also meet the criteria for another disorder and that 20 to 50 per cent have two or more additional disorders (Birmaher et al., 1996a). The most common additional non mood disorders are anxiety disorders, disruptive behaviour disorders and substance abuse disorders (Harrington, Rutter & Fombonne, 1996; Kovacs, 1996 and Lewinsohn et al., 1998).

The prevalence of depression at different developmental periods as well as how depression is manifested at different developmental stages is the focus of investigation for Schwartz, Gladstone and Kaslow (1998). They describe that infants and toddlers lack the cognitive and verbal abilities necessary to self-reflect and report depressive thoughts and problems. It is difficult, therefore, to know what the equivalent to adult depressive symptoms may be in this age group. It is likely that depressive behaviour in this age group may be quite different than in adults. But the description of deprivation reactions in infants separated from their primary caregivers in many ways seems similar to that of depression (Bowlby, 1960). These distressed infants and infants of depressed mothers have been observed to exhibit behaviours such as lethargy, feeding and sleep problems, irritability, sad facial expression, excessive crying and decreased responsivity behaviours often associated with depression.

Similarly, depression in preschoolers is also difficult to assess. Many of the symptoms associated with later depression have been noted in youngsters of this age group (e.g. irritability, sad facial expression, changes of mood, feeding and sleep problems, lethargy and excessive crying). For the period of middle childhood (six to twelve years), there is more evidence that a prolonged pattern of depressive symptoms may emerge. Younger children in this age group typically do not verbalize the hopelessness and self-depression associated with depression. Anyway, children between twelve years and mine who exhibit other symptoms of depression may verbalize feelings of hopelessness and low self-esteem. Still, in youngsters of this age group, depressive symptoms may not be a distinctive syndrome but may occur with a variety of symptoms usually associated with other disorders. In early adolescence, the manifestation of depression is in many ways similar to that of the childhood period. However, in relation to shifts in social and cognitive development overtime, the presentation of depression in older adolescents starts to resemble more closely the symptoms of adult depression. In their community sample of adolescents, Lewinsohn and his colleagues (1998) report a median age of onset for MDD at 15.5 years. Harrington and his colleagues (1997) report that the continuity to major depression in adulthood was lower among prepubertal onset youngsters than among those with post pubertal onset of depression. This finding is in consistent with depression with onset in adolescence as more similar to adult forms of the disorder and different from earlier onset depression. It is also noted that there is significant increase in the prevalence of depression in adolescence and prevalence may reach adult levels in the late adolescence.

There are studies on how long a major depression episode lasts and also on the recurrent nature of depression episode. In their Oregon Adolescent Depression Project (OADP), Lewinsohn et al. (1998) studied a community sample. The median duration of an episode of MDD was 8 weeks and the range was from 2 to 520 weeks. The recurrent nature of the depressive episodes is illustrated by the finding that among adolescents who recovered from their first episode, 5 per cent experienced another episode within six months, 12 per cent within a year and 33 per cent within four years. In addition, the follow-up studies suggest that some adolescents with MDD develop bipolar disorder within 5 years after the onset of depression (Lewinsohn et al., 1999). The youngsters with bipolar disorder also meet the criteria for other non affective disorders. The most common diagnoses are anxiety disorders (especially Separation Anxiety Disorder), disruptive disorders (especially Attention Deficit Hyperactivity Disorder) and substance abuse disorders. These youngsters also develop significant impairment in school, social and family functioning.

INFLUENCES ON THE DEVELOPMENT OF DEPRESSION

Many factors influence the development of depression. The major factors are biological influences and social-psychological influences.

(i) Biological Influences

Biological views of depression in children and adolescents focus on genetic and biochemical influences. Since there are limited data available on children and adolescents, the following data are derived from the adult literature (Emslie et al., 1994).

(a) Genetic Influences

Genetic influences play an important role in depression in children and adolescents. Number of research findings support hereditability component. Based on the observation that mood disorders tend to run in families, a genetic basis for them has been proposed. According to Weissman (1987), people with first-degree relations with whom an individual shares 50 per cent of his or her genes (e.g. parents and siblings) who have a mood disorder are ten times more likely to develop one than people with unaffected first-degree relatives. Allen (1976) has reported a higher average concordance rate for bipolar disorder in monozygots (72 per cent, the highest for any mental disorder) than in dizygots (14 per cent).

Similarly O'Connor and his colleagues (1998), using behavioural genetic methods, examined a sample of same-sex adolescent siblings between the ages of ten and eighteen years of age. The sample included monozygotic (MZ) and dizygotic (DZ) twins, full siblings, half siblings, and unrelated siblings. Results indicated an appreciable genetic component to depressive symptoms. However, there were significant influences of shared and non shared environment as well. For instance, Rende and his colleagues (1993) arrived at the finding that genetic influence operates on personality and temperamental factors, such as emotionality and sociability that affect the full range of depressive symptomatology. The expression of extreme depressive symptomatology, however, may result, against this background of moderate genetic influence, from environmental experiences that are shared by siblings in a family. Several psychological variables have been implicated in the development of depression that may operate in this manner. For example, being raised in a family in which a parent is depressed has received considerable attention.

DNA markers have been used to identify the gene or genes involved in mood disorders. This approach looks at the inheritance of mood disorders within high-risk families, and then searches for DNA segment that is inherited along with a predisposition to develop the disorder. Egeland et al. (1987) studied 81 people from four high-risk families, all of whom were members of the old order Amish community in Pennsylvania. Fourteen were diagnosed as having a bipolar disorder, and all had specific genetic markers at the tip of chromosome 11.

Ogilvie et al. (1996) have shown that cells use a gene called SERT to make a serotonin transporter protein, which plays an important role in the transmission of information between neurons. In most people, part of this gene contains ten or twelve repeating sections of DNA. However, in a significant number of people with depression, this part of gene has only nine repeating sequence. This offers one of the strongest hints that genes may be involved in depression.

(b) Biochemical Influences

Genes act by directing biochemical events. Researchers have looked at the biochemical processes, which may play a causal role in affective disorders. Research has linked these disorders to chemical imbalances in serotonin and nor-adrenaline. Schildkraut (1965) argued that too much nor-adrenaline at certain sites caused mania, whereas too little caused depression. Later research suggested that serotonin played a similar role.

Studies of the neuroendocrine systems (connections between the brain, hormones and various organs) reveal that deregulation of the neuro endocrine systems involving the hypothalamus, pituitary gland, and the adrenal and thyroid glands is thought of as a 'hallmark' of adult depression (Emslie et al., 1994). These systems are regulated by neurotransmitters.

Research on the biological aspects of depression suggests that during the earlier developmental periods of childhood and adolescence, the neuro-regulatory system is not equivalent to that in adulthood. Biological indicators later in development, for example in older adolescents who are more severely depressed, may be more similar to those for depressed adults.

Findings regarding biological correlates of depression in children and adolescents are limited and sometimes contradictory. For example, adults with major depression hyper secrete basal levels of cortisol, a stress hormone produced in the adrenal glands. Investigations of youngsters with major depression have failed to find cortisol hyper secretion. Indeed, the opposite, hypo secretion (less cortisol produced) has been found among depressed youngsters (Goenjian et al., 1996). Increased cortisol levels, similar to those for depressed adults, may occur among older and more severely depressed adolescents (Rao et al., 1996). In general, such differences in biological markers of depression might suggest that the child and the adults disorders are different. Alternatively, such differences to biological markers may represent age-related differences in the same disorder.

(ii) Social-Psychological Influences

The views regarding social and psychological influences on child and adolescent depression are based on theories derived from works with depressed adults.

It is quite often believed that depression results from separation and loss Psychoanalytic descriptions of depression enunciated by Freud emphasize the notion of object loss. The loss may be real (e.g. parental death or divorce) or symbolic. Identification with and ambivalent feelings toward the lost beloved object are thought to result in the persons directing hostile feelings concerning that love object toward the self. Psychologists believing in psychodynamic perspective emphasize loss of self-esteem and feelings of helplessness which result from object loss and they minimize the importance of aggression turned inward toward the self (Kessler,1998).

Behaviourally oriented descriptions too emphasize separation and loss. Ferster (1974) and Lewinsohn (1974) stressed the role of inadequate positive reinforcement in the development of depression. Separation from or loss of a loved one is likely to result in a decrease in the child's source of positive reinforcement.

A number of investigators (Bowlby, 1960 and Spitz, 1946) focused on the reactions of young children to prolonged separation from their parents. In such cases, the child initially goes through a period of 'protest' characterized by crying, asking for the parents, and restlessness. This is followed shortly by a period of depression and withdrawal. Some children begin to recover after several weeks. But most of them do not. High rates of early parental loss or separation among children referred for treatment of a variety of psychological problems have been cited in the past. Seligman et al. (1974) reported that among one hundred consecutive adolescent referrals, 36.4 per cent had experienced loss of one or both the parents. But the current view is that early loss is not in and of itself pathogenic. The link between such loss and later depression is not direct. Rather, it is hypothesized that such loss as well as other circumstances, can set in motion a chain of adverse circumstances such as lack of care, changes in family structure and socio-economic difficulties that put the individual at risk for later disorder (Bifulco, Harris & Brown, 1992; Saler & Skolnick, 1992).

Recently investigations of the impact of loss on children themselves have received attention (Tremblay & Israel, 1998). For instance, Sandler and his colleagues found support for a model consistent with the indirect effects of loss (West et al., 1991). Among a sample of ninety-two families who had lost a parent within the previous two years, depression in youngsters (aged eight to fifteen) was not directly linked to the loss. Rather, the level of parental demoralization, family warmth and stable positive evens following the loss mediated the effects of parental death on depression in their youngsters.

Behavioural, cognitive and cognitive-behavioural perspectives emphasize that influences such as interpersonal skills, cognitive distortions, views of self, control belief, self-regulation and stress are the focal factors of child and adolescent depression. For instance, Ferster (1978) and Lewinsohn (1974) suggested that a combination of lowered activity level and inadequate interpersonal skills plays a role in the development and maintenance of depression. There is evidence for the fact that depressed youths display deficits in social functioning and that they are viewed as less likable by others (Kaslow, Brown & Mee, 1994; Schwartz, Gladstone & Kaslow, 1998). Similarly, Bell- Dolan, Reaven & Peterson (1993) found that negative social behaviour (aggression and negative support seeking), social withdrawal, and low social competence were all related to higher ratings of depression.

Seligman and Peterson (1986) felt that learned helplessness is associated with the mood and behaviours characteristic of depression. The concept of helplessness as an element in depression is held by some psychodynamic workers as well. Helplessness conceptualizations emphasize how the person thinks about activity and outcome which is known as a person's attributional or explanatory style. An explanatory style in which one blames on self for 'negative events' (internal) views the cause of events as being stable (stable) over time and generalizable across situations (global) is thought to be characteristic of depressed individuals. The opposite style, that is, external-unstable-specific attributions for 'positive events' may also be viewed as part of this depressed style. In recent revisions of this perspective, the interaction of stressful life events with cognitive style is given greater emphasis (Abranson, Metalsky and Alloy, 1989). This revision is referred to as the hopelessness theory of depression. Attribution style (a diathesis) acts as a moderator between negative life events which the person sees as important (a stress) and hopelessness. Many studies have reported maladaptive attributional style in depressed youngsters (Gladstone and Kaslow, 1995).

The cognitive factors also play an important role in depression (Beck, 1976). He viewed that depression results from negative views of the self, others and future. He hypothesized that depressed individuals have developed certain errors in thinking which result in their distorting even mildly annoying events into opportunities for self-blame and failure. Many research studies found evidence in depressed youngsters for the cognitive distortions suggested by Beck's theory (Kendall, Stark & Adams, 1990; Leitenberg, Yost & Carroll-Wilson, 1986).

The dimension of control has also contributed to the development of depression. For example, deficits in one or more specific self-control behaviours (self-monitoring, self-evaluation, and self-reinforcement) are hypothesized to contribute to the development of depression. According to this self-control model (Rehm, 1977), depressed individuals selectively focus on negative rather than positive events and on immediate rather than delayed consequences of behaviour, set overly stringent self-evaluative criteria and provide themselves with little positive reinforcement and excessive punishment. Similarly, depressed children, despite similar performance, exhibit lower evaluations of their performance and punish themselves more than do non-depressed peers (Meyer, Dyck & Petrinack, 1989).

THE INFLUENCES OF PARENTAL DEPRESSION ON YOUNGSTERS

Many studies have found that youngsters from homes with a depressed parent are at increased risk for developing a psychological disorder. Hammen and her colleagues (1990) compared the long-term effects of maternal depression and maternal chronic medical illness. Over the course of a three-year period with evaluations at six-month intervals, children of both depressed mothers and medically ill mothers exhibited high rates of psychological disorder as compared with the children of non-ill mothers. Further rates of disorder were higher for children of depressed mothers than for those with medically ill mothers. Weissman and her colleagues (1997) too found that offspring of the depressed parents had increased rates of MDD, particularly before puberty. Beardslee and his colleagues (1998) also suggested that children with a depressed parent appear to be at risk for a variety of problems not just depression.

Parents can influence their children through variety non-biological pathways such as parent-child interactions, coaching and teaching practices and in arranging their child's social environment. In addition, the thinking and cognitive styles of parents also have strong impact on their children. Ineffective parenting, marital conflicts of parents and parental depression are the variables related to problematic outcomes in children (Cummings and Davies, 1994).

Finally, there is link between parent-child attachment and depression (Cicchetti & Toth, 1998). Attachment theory holds that children's internal working models or representations of the self and the social world are mainly influenced by early attachments. The child first experiences and learns to regulate intense emotions and arousal, experiences the social world, and develops a concept of self only through the early attachments. In short, working models that guide future experiences are first developed in the early attachment relationships. In children with insecure parent-child attachments, the cognitive and emotional contents of these working models are remarkably similar to the cognitive and emotional patterns characteristic of depression (Cumming and Davies, 1994).

SUICIDE AMONG CHILDREN AND ADOLESCENTS

Suicide is often thought of as a symptom of disorders such as depression. Many research findings confirmed that depression is related to suicide among children and adolescents (Flisher, 1999; Lewinsohn et al., 1996). Levy, Jurkovic and Spiro (1995) suggested that constructs such as hopelessness that are associated with depression have been found to be predictive of suicidal behaviour. The longitudinal study of Kovacs et al. (1993) reported that a significantly greater number of youngsters with depressive disorders attempted suicide than did youngsters with other disorders.

Compared to adults, the rate of completed suicide is relatively low among youngsters. Even then, the prevalence of completed suicide is increasing among young children. Suicidal behaviour includes not only completed suicide but also suicide attempts and suicidal ideation and this suicidal behaviour is a kind of psychopathology. This is prevalent among adolescents, and to a lesser extent among children. Lewinsohn and his colleagues (1996) found that a total of 19.4 per cent of adolescents involved in their longitudinal study had a history of suicidal ideation. Suicidal ideation was more prevalent in young women (23.7 per cent) than in young men (14.8 per cent).

Multiple factors contribute to an increased risk for suicide (Wagner, 1997). At the level of individual, risk factors include physical illness and psychological disorders, which involve attributes such as depression, hopelessness, impulsivity and aggression. Family factors and family disruption are also cited as risk factors. Other factors such as high levels of stress in school and social relations and socio-cultural influences are also thought to contribute to increased risk. Since the problem solving and self-regulatory skills and the ability to cope with stressful circumstances are limited in youngsters, they become vulnerable to suicidal behaviour.

Lewinshon et al. (1996) proposed a model of risk factors to suicidal behaviour. According to them, the contributors to suicidal risk are psychopathology, physical illness, environment and interpersonal problems. These four constructs are thought to have both a direct effect on suicidal behaviour and an indirect effect, which is mediated through the adolescents' cognitive/coping styles.

MODEL OF RISK FACTORS TO SUICIDAL BEHAVIOUR

(Lewinsohn et al., 1996)

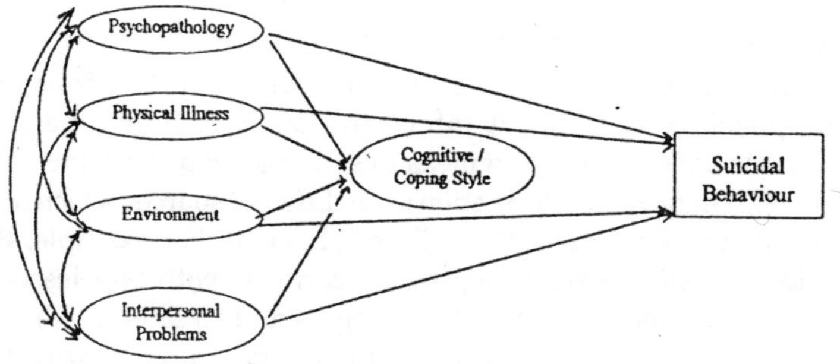

Suicidal behaviour is conceptualized as existing along a continuum

ASSESSMENT OF DEPRESSION

Since depression may manifest itself in a number of ways throughout development, the assessment of depression is likely to involve a number of strategies and to sample a broad spectrum of attributes. Further, youngsters who experience depression are also likely to experience a number of other difficulties. Since the variety of influences may contribute to the development of depression, assessing the parents, family and social environment as well as the individual characteristics of the youngster is informative and hence essential.

A general clinical interview and the use of a general dimensional instrument like the Child Behaviour Checklists are common tools. Interviews intended to yield a DSM diagnosis and a variety of measures that focus more specifically on depression and related constructs have been developed (Compass, 1997; Reynolds, 1994). These interviews and assessment devices have greatly facilitated research on depression in children and adolescents.

Self-report instruments are the most common measures of depression. The Children's Depression Inventory (CDI) (Kovacs, 1992) is an example for this. It is modeled on the Beck Depression Inventory, which is a commonly used inventory for adults. The other two self-report measures developed by Reynolds (1994) are said to have good psychometric properties. One is Reynolds Child Depression Scale for use with children eight to thirteen (Reynolds, 1989) and the other is Reynolds Adolescents Depression Scale for use with youngsters twelve to eighteen (Reynolds, 1987). Some self-report measures are worded in such a way that it can be completed by significant informants such as child's parents (Clarizio, 1994). Self-report measures completed by both the child and the parent yield information from different sources which may tap different aspects of the child's behaviour. For example, the children's self-reports of depression correlate with hopelessness and suicidal thoughts (Kazdin, Rodgers and Colbus, 1986) and parents' reports of depression in their child correlate with the child's mood- related expression and social behaviour (Kazdin et al., 1985).

Instruments can also be completed by other adults such as teachers and clinicians (Clarizio, 1994). Similarly, ratings by peers can also provide a unique perspective. Measures of characteristics that are related to depression have been developed. For instance, measures of attributes such as self-esteem (e.g. Harter, 1985) and provided control over events (e.g. Connell, 1985) are some of them. Further, assessing various cognitive processes such as hopelessness (Kazdin et al., 1986), attributional style (Seligman and Peterson, 1986) and cognitive distortions (e.g. Leitenberg et al., 1986) are helpful for both clinical and research purposes.

TREATMENT OF DEPRESSION

Treatments for depressed youngsters have been mostly adapted from the intervention to depressed adults. Treatment includes both pharmacological measures and cognitive-behavioural measures.

(i) Pharmacological Treatments

Since the effectiveness and safety of pharmacological medication for depressed youngsters remains unclear, the practice of prescribing anti depressant medicines for children and adolescents is still controversial (American Academy of Child and Adolescent Psychiatry, 1998). Tricyclic antidepressants such as imipramine, amitriptyline, nortriptyline and desipramine have been widely used. Selective serotonin reuptake inhibitors (SSRIs) such as fluoxetine (Prozac) and other compounds such as bupropion have also been employed with depressed children and adolescents. Since antidepressant medications are principally developed and marketed for adults, there are less well established guidelines for their administration and little systematic data on their safety.

(ii) Cognitive- Behavioural Treatments

Cognitive-behavioural perspective contributes to most of the psychological interventions for depression in children and adolescents. It focuses on educating and modifying the youngster's maladaptive cognitions like problematic attributions, excessively high standards, negative self- monitoring and so on. Behavioural aspects of treatments aim at increasing pleasurable experiences, social skills and improving communication, conflict resolution and social problem- solving skills.

Interventions suggested for youngsters have been based on downward extensions of interventions employed with adults. This approach has some limitations (Hammen et al., 1999) because the lives of depressed youngsters differ from those of adults on the basis of social contacts and skills. A better understanding of the social-psychological factors that contribute to depression in children and adolescents will lead to better treatment effects. The most effective treatment will result from the interventions addressing the relevant developmental experiences of depressed children and adolescents.

Butler et al. (1980) evaluated the relative effectiveness of role play, cognitive restructuring, and attention-placebo condition or no treatment. Fifth and sixth grade children were identified as depressed through self-report measures and teacher referral. The results favoured the role-play intervention. Weisz et al. (1997) compared a cognitive-behavioural intervention based on the relationship between perceived intervention based on the relationship between perceived control and depression to a no treatment control condition. The children with mild to moderate depressive symptoms in grades three to six were treated in small groups during school hours. Children's Depression Inventory (CDI) and the Revised Children's Depression Rating Scale were used. The results indicated that the treatment group showed significantly greater decrease in depressive symptoms. Similarly the findings of Lewinsohn et al. (1990) too confirm the effectiveness of the cognitive-behavioural treatment for depressed adolescents.

PEER RELATION AND DEVELOPMENT

Peer relations have become the focus of increasing attention (Putallaz and Dunn, 1990). Peers influence on immediate and long-term social and cognitive growth (Dunn, 1996). Simultaneously, there is a decline in the prevalence of Freudian theory, which had heavily emphasized parent-child relationships. This change allowed for the recognition of the importance of other socialization influences. Finally, a variety of social and economic conditions (e.g. increase in the number of employed parents) increased the opportunities for youngsters to interact with their peers.

Hart up (1989) suggested that two major kinds of relationships seem necessary to the child's development. The first one is vertical relationship to individuals (usually adults), who have greater knowledge and social power, provide the child with protection and security and they are the contexts within which basic social skills emerge. The second one is horizontal relationships with individuals such as peers and siblings, who have the same amount of social power as the children themselves. Some of the ways in which peer interactions may play a unique and essential role include the development of sociability and intimacy, elaboration of cooperation and reciprocity, negotiation of conflict and competition, control of aggression, socialization of sexuality and gender roles, moral development and development of empathy. These two relationships are necessary for optimum growth (Hartup, 1989).

PEER RELATIONS AND ADJUSTMENT

Peer relations potentially contribute to as youngster's adjustment. They are associated with later adjustment in life. Poor peer relations are associated with high rates of juvenile delinquency. (Roff, Sells and Golden, 1972), dropping out of school (Ullmann, 1957) and bad conduct discharges from the army (Roff, 1961). Cowen et al. (1973) found an association with later psychiatric referrals.

The association of peer status and later adjustment is clear for children with low peer acceptance and for those who exhibit aggression towards peers. The link between early shyness/ withdrawal and later maladjustment is not so clear, since this relationship has been less studied (Parker and Asher, 1987). Biederman et al. (1993) found evidence for the fact that the group of rejected children and other withdrawn and socially isolated children are at risk for later adjustment difficulties. Caspi et al. (1998) made an illustration of the developmental stability of a shy-withdrawn style and its long-term impact. They found significant correlation between shyness and excessive reserve when the children were eight or ten year old and teacher rating of withdrawal and related behaviours when the youngsters were preadolescents. Also, positive significant correlations were obtained between childhood shyness and shyness evaluated when the participants were about forty years old.

TREATMENT OF PROBLEMS IN PEER RELATIONS

Problems in peer relations are often reported for both children and adolescents in general population. Problems with peers are one of the most frequently mentioned problems in referrals to mental health centers. Problems in social relationships are also part of the diagnostic criteria for a wide variety of disorders such as autism, ADHD, conduct disorder and social phobia. Further, social relationship problems are associated with both externalizing and internalizing disorders in children (Parker et al., 1995). On the otherhand, successful peer relations may help to ensure the development of social competence in the face of multiple adverse factors. They may thereby serve a preventive function and reduce the likelihcod of disorder (Cicchetti, Toth and Bush, 1998). Therefore, the treatment of problems in peer relation is gaining momentum in the recent times.

Many programmes have been designed to improve the social skills and peer relations of children. The studies on such programmes reveal that the interventions to improve children's social competencies concentrate on the development of specific social skills and/or the cognitive process presumed to underlie the peer difficulties. Social skills approaches can be grouped as either molecular or molar in focus (La Greca, 1993). Molecular approaches emphasize the training of discrete skills such as eye contact, responding positively to peers, and initiating interactions. Molar approaches focus on training skills such as participation in group activities, cooperation, and sharing. On the other hand, social cognitive approaches stress training in social problem solving, taking another's perspective, self- control and the like. Increasingly, interventions have stressed more complex, multi model approaches (Beelman et al., 1994). Many interventions have been successful in producing long-term effects and generalization across time and setting. Such interventions have concentrated on reinforcing increase peer interaction (Allen et al., 1964 and Walker et al., 1979), imitation, coaching and instruction (e.g. exposure to filmed models) (O'Connor, 1972) and the use of peers in treatment (Odom and Strain, 1984).

Much of the research on interventions has occurred in a school context. Inclusion of teachers in intervention planning is important because of their potential role in monitoring peer behaviours and providing appropriate consequences. Teachers can also provide interventions such as peer pairing or cooperative group assignments that have the potential to foster the social integration of a child (La Greca, 1993). Parents too play an important role in a youngster's relation development. For instance, they arrange opportunities for peer interactions, monitor and supervise peer contacts. Vernberg et al. (1993) illustrated the role that parents can play in encouraging and enhancing their children's social skills. This type of multi componential interventional strategy involving parents is particularly effective for clinicians working with youngsters outside a school setting.

SUMMARY

Depression refers to the experience of pervasive unhappy mood. Irritability, loss of experience of pleasure, social withdrawal, lowered self-esteem, inability to concentrate, poor schoolwork, alterations of biological functioning and somatic complaints are often noted in depressed individuals. The psychoanalytic perspective views depression as a phenomenon of the superego and mature ego functioning. It suggests that the problem of depression would not exist in childhood. But the concept of masked depression believes that there is certainly a disorder of depression among children. It assumes that the youngster's depression is 'masked' by other problems, such as, hyperactivity or delinquency. It highlights developmental issues and stresses that some of depressive behaviours of a child may be viewed as typical of that developmental stage.

DSM-IV classifies depression in the category of Mood Disorders. The DSM approach holds the view that childhood depression is a disorder with the same essential features as its adult counterpart. Major Depressive Disorder (MDD) is the primary DSM category for defining depression. MDD is the most prevalent form of affective disorders among children and adolescents.

The other principal depressive disorder is dysthymic disorder, which is essentially a disorder in which many of the symptoms of Major Depressive Episode are present in less severe form but are more chronic and persist for a longer period. Bipolar disorders and cyclothymia involve the presence of mania as well as depressive symptoms.

MDD is the most prevalent form of affective disorder. Depression is more prevalent among adolescents than children. Between the age group of six to twelve, depression is more prevalent in boys than in girls. But among adolescents, depression is more common in girls. Youngsters with depression are likely to experience other problems as well.

Biological factors and social-psychological factors contribute to the development of depression. Biological factors include both genetic influences and bio-chemical-influences. The views regarding social and psychological influences on child and adolescent depression are based on theories derived from works with depressed adults. Separation/loss has been a major theme in many theories of depression. Behavioural, cognitive and cognitive behavioural perspectives emphasize the influences of interpersonal skills, cognitive distortions, control-beliefs, self-regulation and stress in the development of depression in children and adolescents. The influences of parental depression also increase the risk for developing a psychological disorder. Parents can exert influence on their children through a variety of non- biological pathways.

Suicidal ideation is often thought as a symptom of depression and other such disorders. Compared to adults, the rate of completed suicide is relatively low among youngsters. Eventhen, the prevalence of suicidal attempts is increasing to gruesome proportions in young children. Lewinshon et al. devised a model of risk factor contributing to suicidal behaviour.

Assessment of depression has been facilitated by the structured diagnostic interviews. Further self- report measures are frequently employed. Treatments for depressed youngsters have mostly been adapted from the intervention to depressed adults. Both pharmacological measures and cognitive behaviour measures are included in the treatment of depressed children and adolescents.

Problems with peers are one of the most frequently mentioned reasons for referrals for psychological services. Successful peer relations may protect the child from the impact of adverse factors and thereby decrease the likelihood of disorder. Many programmes have been designed to improve the social skills and peer relations of children. Inclusion of parents and teachers in the interventional services proves to be effective in eliminating the problems in peer relations.

REFERENCES

Abramson, L.Y., Metalsky, G.L. and Alloy, L.B., (1989), 'Hopelessness Depression: A Theory-based Subtype of Depression'. *Psychological Bulletin*, 96, 358-372.

Allen, K., Hart, B., Buell, J., Harris, F. and Wolf, M., (1964), 'Effects of Social Reinforcement on Isolated Behaviour of a Nursery School Child'. *Child Development*, 35, 511-518.

Allen, M., (1976), 'Twin Studies of Affective Illness'. *Archives of General Psychiatry,* 33, 1476-1478.

American Academy of Child and Adolescent Psychiatry , (1998), 'Practice Parameters for the Assessment and Treatment of Children and Adolescents with Depressive Disorders'. *Journal of the American Academy of Child and Adolescent Psychiatry,* 37, 63s-83s.

Anderson, J.C., Williams, S., McGee, R. and Silva, P.A., (1987), 'DSM-III Disorders in Preadolescent Children: Prevalence in a Large Sample from the General Population'. *Academy of General Psychiatry,* 44, 69-76.

Angold, A. and Rutter, M., (1992), 'Effects of Age and Pubertal Stratus on Depression in a Large Clinical Sample'. *Development and Psychopathology,* 4, 5-28.

Beardslee, W.R., Versage, E.M. and Gladstone, T.R.G., (1998), 'Children of Affectively Ill Parents: A Review of the Past 10 Years'. *Journal of the American Academy of Child and Adolescent Psychiatry,* 37, 1134-1141.

Beck, A.T., (1976), *Cognitive Theory and Emotional Disorders.* New York: International University Press.

Beelmann, A., Pfingsten, U. and Losel, F., (1994) 'Effects of Training Social Competence in Children: A Meta Analysis of Recent Evaluation Studies'. *Journal of Clinical Child Psychology,* 23, 260-271.

Bell- Donlan, D.J., Reaven, N.M. and Peterson, L., (1993), 'Depression and Social Functioning: A Multidimensional Study of the Linkages'. *Journal of Clinical Child Psychology,* 22,306-315.

Biederman, J., Rosenbaum, J.F., Bolduc-Murphy, E.A., Faraone, S.V., Chaloff, J., Hirshfield, D.R. and Kagan, J., (1993), 'A 3-year Follow-up of Children With and Without Behavioural Inhibition'. *Journal of the American Academy of Child and Adolescent Psychiatry,* 32, 814-821.

Bifulco, A., Harris, T. and Brown, G., (1992), 'Mourning or Early Inadequate Care? Re-examining the Relationship of Material Loss in Childhood with Adult Depression and Anxiety'. *Development and Psycho-pathology,* 4, 433–449.

Birmaher, B., Ryan, N.D., Willamson,D.E., Brent, D.A., Kaufman, J., Dahl, R.E., Perel, J. and Nelson, B., (1996a), 'Childhood and Adolescent Depression: A Review of the Past 10 Years'. Part I. *Journal of the American Academy of Child and Adolescent Psychiatry,* 35,1427-1439.

Bowlby, J.C., (1960), 'Grief and Mourning in Infancy and Early Childhood'. *Psychoanalytic Study of the Child,* 15, 9-52.

Butler, L., Miezitis, S., Friedman, R. and Cole, E., (1980), 'The Effect of Two School-based Intervention Programmes on Depressive Symptoms in Preadolescents'. *American Educational Research Journal,* 17, 111-119.

Carlson, G.A. and Cantwell, D.P., (1980), 'Unmasking Masked Depression in Children and Adolescents'. *American Journal of Psychiatry*, 137, 445-449.

Caspi, A., Elder, G.H., Jr. and Bem, D.J., (1988), 'Moving Away from the World: Life-course Patterns of Shy children'. *Developmental Psychology*, 24, 824-831.

Cicchetti, D. and Toth, S.L., (1998), 'The Development of Depression in Children and Adolescents'. *American Psychologist*, 53, 221-241.

Cicchetti, D., Toth, S. and Bush, M., (1988), 'Developmental Psychopathology and Incompetence in Childhood: Suggestions for Intervention'. In B.B. Lahey & A.E. Kazdin (Eds.), *Advances in Clinical Child Psychology*, Vol. 11, New York: Plenum.

Clarizio, H.F., (1994), 'Assessment of Depression in Children and Adolescents by Parents, Teachers, and Peers'. In W.M. Reynolds & H.F. Johnston (Eds.), *Handbook of Depression in Children and Adolescents*. New York: Plenum Press.

Compas, B.E., (1997), 'Depression in Children and Adolescents'. In E.J. Mash & L.G. Terdal (Eds.), *Assessment of Childhood Disorders* (3rd Ed.) New York: Guilford Press.

Compass, B.E., Ey, S. and Grant, K.E., (1993), 'Taxonomy, Assessment, and Diagnosis of Depression during Adolescence'. *Psychological Bulletin*, 14, 323-344.

Connell, J.P., (1985), 'A New Multidimensional Measure of Children's Perceptions of Control'. *Child Development*, 56, 1018-1041.

Cowen, E., Pederson, A., Babigian, H., Izo, L. and Trost, N., (1973), 'Long Term Follow-up of Early Detected Vulnerable Children'. *Journal of Consulting and Clinical Psychology*, 41,438-446.

Cummings, E.M. and Davies, P.T., (1994), 'Maternal Depression and Child Development'. *Journal of Child Psychology and Psychiatry*, 35, 73-112.

Cytryn, L. and McKnew, D., (1974), 'Factors Influencing the Changing Clinical Expression of the Depressive Process in Children'. *American Journal of Psychiatry*, 131, 879-881

Dunn, J., (1996), 'Children's Relationships: Bridging the Divide Between Cognitive and Social Development'. *Journal of Child Psychology and Psychiatry*, 37, 507-518.

Egeland, J., Gerhard, D., Pauls, D., Sussex, J., Kidd, K., Allen, C., Hostetter, A. and Houseman, D., (1987), 'Bipolar Affective Disorder Linked to DNA Markers on Chromosome', 11. *Nature*, 325, 783-787.

Emslie, G.J., Weinberg, W.A., Kennard, B.D. and Kowatch, R.A., (1994), 'Neurobiological Aspects of Depression in Children and Adolescents'. In W.M. Reynolds & H.F. Johnston (Eds.), *Handbook of Depression in children and adolescents*. New York: Plenum.

Ferster, C.B., (1974), 'Behavioural Approaches to Depression'. In R.J. Friedman & M.M. Katz (Eds.), *The Psychology of Depression: Contemporary Theory and Research*. Washington, DC: Winston.

Flisher, A.J., (1999), 'Mood Disorder in Suicidal Children and Adolescents: Recent Developments'. *Journal of Child Psychology and Psychiatry*, 40, 315-324.

Gladstone, T.R.G. and Kaslow, N.J., (1995), 'Depression and Attributions in Children and Adolescents: A Meta Analytic Review'. *Journal of Abnormal Child Psychology*, 23,597-606.

Goenjian, A.K., Yehuda, R., Pynoos, R.S., Steinberg, A.M., Tashjian, M., Yang. R.K., Najarian, L.M., Fairbanks, L.A., (1996), 'Basal cortisol, Dexamethasone Suppression of Cortisol, and MHPG in Adolescents After the 1988 Earthquake in Armenia'. *American Journal of Psychiatry*, 153, 929-934.

Hammen, C., Burge, D., Burney, E. and Adrian, C., (1990), 'Longitudinal Study of Diagnosis in Children of Women with Unipolar and Bipolar Affective Disorders'. *Archives of General Psychiatry*, 47, 1112-1117.

Hammen, C., Rudolph., K., Weisz, J., Rao, U. and Burge, D., (1999), 'The Context of Depression in Clinic Referred Youth: Neglected Areas in Treatment'. *Journal of the American Academy of Child and Adolescent Psychiatry*, 38, 64-71.

Harrington, R., Rutter, M. and Fombonne, E., (1996), 'Developmental Pathways in Depression: Multiple Meanings, Antecedents, and Endpoints'. *Development and Psychopathology*, 8, 601-616.

Harrington, R., Rutter, M., Weissman, M., Fudge, H., Groothues, C., Bredenkamp, D., Pickles, A., Rende, R. and Wickramaratne, P., (1997), 'Psychiatric Disorders in the Relatives of Depressed Probands: I. Comparison of Pre-pubertal, Adolescent and Early Adult Onset Cases'. *Journal of Affective Disorders*, 42, 9-22.

Harter, S., (1985), *Manual for the Self-perception Profile for Children*. Denver, CO: University of Denver.

Hartup, W.W., (1989), 'Social Relationships and Their Developmental Significance'. *American Psychologist*, 44, 120-126.

Kaslow, N.J., Brown, R.T. and Mee, L., (1994), 'Cognitive and Behavioural Correlates of Childhood Depression: A Developmental Perspective'. In W.M. Reynolds & H.F. Johnston (Eds.), *Handbook of Depression in Children and Adolescents*. New York: Plenum Press.

Kaslow, N.J., Rehm, L.P. and Siegel, A.W., (1984), 'Social Cognitive and Cognitive Correlates of Depression in Children'. *Journal of Abnormal Child Psychology*, 12, 605-620.

Kazdin, A.E., Esveldt- Dawson, K., Sherick, R.B. and Colbus, D., (1985), 'Assessment of Overt Behaviour and Childhood Depression Among Psychiatrically Disturbed Children'. *Journal of Consulting and Clinical Psychology,* 53, 201- 210.

Kazdin, A.E., Rogers, A. and Colbus, D., (1986), 'The Hopelessness Scale for Children: Psychometric Characteristics and Concurrent Validity'. *Journal of Consulting and Clinical Psychology,* 54, 241-245.

Kendall, P.C., Stark, K.D. and Adams, T., (1990), 'Cognitive Deficit or Cognitive Distortion in Childhood Depression'. *Journal of Abnormal Child Psychology,* 18, 255-270.

Kessler, J.W., (1988), *Psychopathology of Childhood.* Englewood Cliffs, N.J: Prentice Hall.

Kovacs, M., (1992), *Children's Depressive Inventory.* North Tonawanda, NY: Multi–Health System.

Kovacs, M., Goldston, D. and Gatsonis, C., (1993), 'Suicidal Behaviour and Childhood-onset Depressive Disorders: A Longitudinal Investigation'. *Journal of the American Academy of Child Adolescent Psychiatry,* 32, 8-20.

La Greca, A.M., (1993), 'Social Skills Training with Children: Where Do We Go From Here'. Journal of Clinical Child Psychology, 22, 288-298.

Leitenberg, H., Yost, L.W. and Carroll-Wilson, M., (1986), 'Negative Cognitive Errors in Children: Questionnaire Development, Normative Data, and Comparisons Between Children With and Without Self-reported Symptoms of Depression, Low Self-esteem and Evaluation Anxiety'. *Journal of Consulting and Clinical Psychology,* 54, 58- 536.

Levy, S.R., Jurkovic, G.L. and Spiro, A., (1995), 'A Multisystems Analysis of Adolescent Suicide Attempters'. *Journal of Abnormal Child Psychology,* 23, 221-234.

Lewinsohn, P. , (1974), 'A Behavioural Approach to Depression'. In R.J. Friedman & M.M. Katz (Eds.), *The Psychology of Depression: Contemporary Theory and Research.* Washington, DC: Winston.

Lewinsohn, P.M., Clarke, G.N., Hops, H. and Andrews, J., (1990), 'Cognitive Behaviour Treatment for Depressed Adolescents'. *Behaviour Therapy,* 21, 385-402.

Lewinsohn, P.M., Hops, H., Roberts, R.E., Seeley , J.R. and Andrews, J.A., (1993a), 'Adolescent Psychopathology: I Prevalence and Incidence of Depression and other DSM-III- R. Disorders in High School Students'. *Journal of Abnormal Psychology,* 102, 133-144.

Lewinsohn, P.M., Rohde, D. and Seeley, J.R., (1996), 'Adolescents Suicidal Ideation and Attempts: Prevalence, Risk Factors, and Clinical Implications'. *Clinical Psychology: Science and Practice,* 3, 25-46.

Lewinsohn, P.M., Rohde, P. and Seeley, J.R., (1998), 'Major Depressive Disorder in Older Adolescents: Prevalence, Risk Factors, and Clinical Implications'. *Clinical Psychology Review,* 18, 765-794.

Lewinsohn, P.M., Rohde, P., Klein, D.N. and Seeley, J.R., (1999), 'Natural Course of Adolescent Major Depressive Disorders: I Continuity onto Young Adulthood'. *Journal of the American Academy of Child and Adolescent Psychiatry,* 38, 5663.

Malmquist, C.P., (1997). 'Childhood Depression: A Clinical and Behaviour Perspective'. In J.G. Schulterbrandt & A. Raskin (Eds.), *Depression in Childhood: Diagnosis, Treatment, and Conceptual Models.* New York: Raven Press.

Meyer, N.E., Dyck, D.G. and Petrinack, R.J., (1989), 'Cognitive Appraisal and Attributional Correlates of Depressive Symptoms in Children'. *Journal of Abnormal Child Psychology,* 17, 325-336.

Nottlemann, F.D. and Jensen, P.S., (1995a), 'Bipolar Affective Disorders in Children and Adolescents: Introduction'. *Journal of the American Acrdemy of Child and Adolescent Psychiatry,* 34, 705- 708.

O'Connor, R.D., (1972), 'The Relative Efficacy of Modelling, Shaping and Combined Procedures'. *Journal of Abnormal Psychology,* 79, 327-334.

O'Connor, T.G., McGuire, S., Reiss, D., Hetherington, E.M. and Plomin, R., (1998), 'Co-occurrence of Depressive Symptoms and Antisocial Behaviour in Adolescence: A Common Genetic Liability'. *Journal of Abnormal Psychology,* 107, 27-37.

Odom, S.L. and Strain, P.S., (1984), 'Peer-mediated Approaches to Promoting Children's Social Interaction: A Review'. *American Journal of Orthopsychiatry,* 54, 544-557.

Ogilvie, A.D., Battersby, S., Bubb, V.J., Fink, G., Harmar, A.J., Goowin, G.M. and Smith , C.A.D. , (1996), 'Polymorphism in the Serotonin Transporter Gene Associated with Susceptibility to Major Depression'. *The Lancet,* 347, 731-733.

Parker, J.G. and Asher, S.R., (1987). 'Peer Relations and Later Personal Adjustment: Are Low-accepted Children at Risk?' *Psychological Bulletin,* 102, 357-389.

Parker, J.G., Rubin, K.H., Price, J.M. and De Rosier, M., (1995), 'Peer Relationships, Child Development and Adjustment: A Developmental Psychopathology Perspective'. In D. Cicchetti & D. Cohen (Eds.) *Developmental Psychopathology,* (Vol.2: Risk, Disorder and Adaptation). New York: Wiley.

Putallaz, M. and Dunn, S.E., (1990), 'The Importance of Peer Relations'. In M. Lewis & S.M. Miller, *Handbook of Developmental Psychopathology,* New York: Plenum.

Rao, U., Dahl, D., Ryan, N.D. Birmaher, B., Williamson, D.E., Giles, D.E., Rao, R., Kaufmam, J. and Nelson, B., (1996), 'The Relationship Between Longitudinal Clinical Course and Sleep and Cortisol Changes in Adolescent Depression'. *Biological Psychiatry*, 40, 474-483.

Rehm, L.P., (1977), 'A self-control Model of Depression'. *Behaviour Therapy*, 8, 787-804.

Rende, R.D., Plomin, R., Reiss, D. and Hetherington, E.M. , (1993), 'Genetic and Environmental Influences on Depressive Symptomology in Adolescence: Individual Differences and Extreme Scores. *Journal of Child Psychology and Psychiatry*, 34, 1387–1398.

Reynold, W.M., (1987), *Reynolds Adolescent Depression Scale: Professional Manual*. Odessa, FL: Psychological Assessment Resources.

Reynolds, W.M., (1994), 'Assessment of Depression in Children and Adolescents by Self-report Questionnaires'. In W.M. Reynolds & H.F. Johnston (Eds.), *Handbook of Depression in Children and Adolescents*. New York: Plenum Press.

Reynolds, W.M., (1989), *Reynolds Child Depression Scale: Professional Manual*. Odessa, FL: Psychological Assessment Resources.

Reynolds, W.M. and Johnston, H.F., (1994), 'The Nature and Study of Depression in Children and Adolescents'. In W.M. Reynolds & H.F. Johnston (Eds.), *Handbook of Depression in Children and Adolescents*. New York: Plenum Press.

Roff, M., (1961), 'Childhood Social Interactions and Young Adult Bad Conduct'. *Journal of Abnormal and Social Psychology*, 63, 33-337.

Roff, M., Sells, S. and Golden, M., (1972), *Social Adjustment and Personality Development in Children*. Minneapolis: University of Minnesota Press.

Saler, L. and Skolnick, N., (1992), 'Childhood Parental Death and Depression in Adulthood: Roles of Surviving Parent and Family Environment'. *American Journal of Orthopsychiatry*, 62, 504-516.

Schildcraut, J., (1965), 'The Catecholamine Hypothesis of Affective Disorders: A Review of Supporting Evidence'. *American Journal of Psychiatry*, 122, 509-522.

Schwartz, J.A.J., Gladstone, T.R.G. and Kaslow, N.J., (1998), 'Depressive Disorders'. In T.H. Ollendick & M. Hersen (Eds.), *Handbook of Child Psychopathology* (3rd Ed.) New York: Plenum Press.

Seligman, M.P. and Peterson, C., (1986), 'A Learned Helplessness Perspective on Childhood Depression: Theory and Research'. In M.Rutter, C.E. Hazard, & P.B. Read (Eds.), *Depression in Young People: Developmental and Clinical Perspective*. New York: Guilford.

Seligman, R., Gleser, G., Rauh, J. and Harris, L. , (1974), 'The Effect of Earlier Parental Loss in Adolescence'. *Archives of General Psychiatry*, 31, 475-479.

Spitz, R.A., (1946), 'Anaclitic Depression'. *In the Psychoanalytic Study of the Child,* Vol. 2, New York: International Universities Press.

Tremblay, G.C. and Israel, A.C., (1998), 'Children's Adjustment to Parental Death'. *Clinical Psychology: Science and Practice,* 5, 424-438.

Ullmann, C.A., (1957), 'Teachers, Peers, and Tests as Predictors of Adjustment'. *Journal of Educational Psychology,* 48, 257-267.

Vernberg, E., Beery, S.H.., Ewell, K.K. and Absender, D.A., (1993), 'Parents' Use of Friendship Facilitation Strategies and the Formation of Friendships in Early Adolescence: A Prospective Study'. *Journal of Family Psychology,* 7, 356-369.

Wagner, B.M., (1997), 'Family Risk Factors for Child and Adolescent Suicidal Behaviour'. *Psychological Bulletin,* 121, 246-298.

Walker, H., Greenwocd, C., Hops, H. and Todd, N., (1979), 'Differential Effects of Reinforcing Topographic Components of Social Interaction'. *Behaviour Modification,* 3, 291-321.

Weissmam, M., (1987), 'Advances in Psychiatric Epidemiology: Rates and Risks for Major Depression'. *American Journal of Public Health,* 77, 445-451.

Weissman, M.M., Warner, V., Wickramarante, P., Moreau, D. and Olfson, M., (1997), 'Offspring of Depressed Parents: 10 Years Later'. *Archives of General Psychiatry,* 54, 932-940.

Weisz, J.R., Thurber, C.A., Sweeney, L., Proffitt, V.D. and LeGagnoux, G.L., (1997), 'Brief Treatment of Mild-to-moderate Child Depression Using Primary and Secondary Control Enhancement Training'. *Journal of Consulting and Clinical Psychology,* 65, 703-707.

West, S.G., Sandler, I., Pillow, D.R., Baca, L. and Gersten, J.C., (1991), 'The Use of Structural Equation Modelling in Generative Research: Toward the Design of a Preventative Intervention for Bereaved Children'. *American Journal of Community Psychology,* 19, 459-480.

7

Aggression in Children and Adolescents

OBJECTIVES

This chapter defines aggression and describes the general pattern of aggressive behaviour. It presents both biological and social learning explanations of aggression. It also explains other factors such as frustration, child-rearing styles, peer group and media, which contribute to the development of aggression. It also lists out the socio-psychological characteristics of aggressiveness. Ultimately, it describes the various measures to reduction and control of aggressive behaviour. After reading this chapter, the readers should be able to:

(i) Define aggression;

(ii) Describe the general pattern of aggressive behaviour;

(iii) Present both biological and social explanations of aggression;

(iv) Know about the various factors contributing to aggressive behaviour;

(v) Delineate the various socio-psychological characteristics of aggressiveness; and

(vi) Explain various measures to the reduction and control of aggressive behaviour.

INTRODUCTION

Behaviours, which show a lack of feeling and concern for the welfare of others are known as anti-social behaviours. Once such antisocial behaviour is aggression. Used as a noun, 'aggression' usually refers to some behaviour intended to harm or destroy another person who is motivated to avoid such treatment. Penrod calls this 'antisocial aggression' to distinguish it from those instances when a person defends himself from attack (sanctioned aggression) or when an aircraft hijacker is shot and killed by security agents (prosocial aggression). When used as an adjective, 'aggressive' sometimes conveys an action carried out with energy and persistence, and may even be regarded as socially desirable (Lloyd et al., 1984). Moyer (1976) and Berkowitz (1993) view aggression as always involving behaviour, either physical or symbolic, performed with the intention of harming some one. All children are occasionally aggressive and some are more aggressive than others. Children's aggressive behaviours range from the least harmful kind of aggression (e.g. Calling some one a name for psychologically upsetting) to the more serious ones to inflict physical injury on another person or damage property. Psychologists, therefore, tend to use a number of distinctions. When aggressive behaviour is intended to hurt someone or damage some one through verbal or physical or both means, they say it is 'hostile aggression'. On the other hand, the behaviour, which uses aggression in order to achieve a particular end, including self-defence, involves 'instrumental aggression'. An extreme form of aggression is described as violence.

THE PATTERN OF AGGRESSIVE BEHAVIOUR

Usually children start being physically aggressive towards things rather than people, from around two or four years of age. After four, many children are more likely to use verbal rather than psychical aggression. This is intended to hurt someone's feelings. From about six or seven, many children channel their energies more into competition and sport. Outbursts of aggression are increasingly likely to be controlled as the child grows.

ORIGINS OF AGGRESSION

Social and developmental psychologists have studied the origins of aggression and have found links with both biology and the environment. Those supporting the view that aggression is caused by biological forces show how changing hormones and metabolic levels will alter aggressive behaviour and have conducted animal experiments to discover the hormones, which are involved in aggressive behaviour. On the other hand, social learning theorists have shown that genetic forces can be overcome by social ones. For instance, they insist that aggressive behaviour can be reduced by using a combination of reinforcement and punishments.

BIOLOGICAL EXPLANATIONS OF AGGRESSION

There are many evidences for the fact that aggression is genetically transmitted. It can be seen in animals and humans, at quite young ages, and it has been shown to be affected by hormone levels. Evidence to support the biological explanation comes from those theories which see instinctive forces governing the aspects of behaviour, and from experiments using animal subjects. The main theories, which concentrate on biological factors: are (i) Freud's psychoanalytic theory; and ii) Lorenz's ethological theory.

(i) Sigmund Freud's Psychoanalytic Theory

Freud's (1949) theory argues that people are born with aggressive impulses including the death instinct. These urges are thought to be a part of the id. They are irrational and demanding. They try to make the child expose itself to danger and this conflicts with the life preservation instincts within the libido. From when the child is about three years old, these aggressive instincts must be kept under control by the superego. When the child has not been socialized to think that aggression is wrong, its superego may not be strong enough to resist the aggressive instincts and they may break-through into consciousness as aggression. Unpleasant feelings, which have been repressed into the unconscious mind may also be released through aggression. Freud called this release of repressed feelings anxieties and memories (from the unconscious into conscious) 'catharsis'. Freud insisted that human beings will always be aggressive since they have instinctive urges. He thought that aggressive urges could be channeled into aggressive sports, work, other aspects of one's own life, or even to watching others behave aggressively. According to Freud, the superego is a major factor in controlling human aggression.

(ii) Konrad Loren's Ethological Theory

Konrad believed that human beings have evolved an instinct or innate drive to be violent. He defined aggression as the "fighting instinct in beast and man which is directed against members of the same species". Humans have a need to be aggressive in order to catch and kill animals for food, to defend themselves against attackers, etc. Usually, this urge is stronger in the male than in the female. This is because the male in most of the animal species does most of the hunting of prey, defending himself and his territory and challenging others. Sometimes aggression gets off automatically and sometimes it occurs for no apparent reason. According to Lorenz, our instinctive energy boils over and as a result, we behave aggressively.

Apart from these theoretical evidences, we have experimental evidences too to prove that the biological factors influence behaviour. The two areas of study are hormone influence and brain centres. W.C. Young gave a pregnant monkey a large amount of the male hormone testosterone, when its baby was developing in its womb. The female infant, when it was born, behaved in a more assertive way. It joined in rough games and challenged the males for a higher status in the group. Other similar experiments have shown that monkeys injected with testosterone between birth and puberty developed similar assertive behaviour.

Experiments on various animals have shown that some particular brain centres are involved in aggression. Particularly, the part of the brain called 'limbic system' is closely concerned with aggression. Laboratory experiments with numerous animals show that aggressive responses can be deliberately triggered by electrical or chemical stimulation of this part of the brain.

Through selective breeding, laboratory researchers have produced rats and cats that are extremely placid. However, when their aggression centres are stimulated electrically, they even strike at and pounce on things around them. It has also been found that those people with brain disorders involving the part of the human brain, which controls aggression are more likely to be aggressive than others.

SOCIAL LEARNING EXPLANATIONS FOR AGGRESSION

The rules we apply in deciding whether to be aggressive are mostly socially learned. We learn how to be aggressive, with whom to be aggressive, when to be or when not to be aggressive—through reinforcement and imitation of aggressive models we see around us in the social environment. Because human beings have consciousness, they develop an awareness of themselves. Part of what we know about ourselves comes from seeing how others treat us. Our behaviour is constantly changing to adapt to changing circumstances around us. If others behave aggressively towards us, we may learn that aggressive behaviour is an appropriate response. Social learning theorists like Bandura (1973), Walters, Ross and Mischel (1974) therefore, say that many aspects of aggression can be explained by social influences. They explain that human beings learn about aggression through a mixture of tuition, observation, imitation, modelling, reinforcement and punishment.

Bandura and his colleagues (1961, 1963) have demonstrated how a child's aggressive tendencies can be strengthened through vicarious reinforcement (seeing others being rewarded for behaving aggressively). They have conducted many experiments to show the effect of observation and modelling on many aspects of behaviour, including aggression. When a sample of pre-school children saw an adult behaving aggressively towards the Bobo doll, they were more aggressive towards it. Bandura and Walters (1959) also asked a group of nursery school children to call their dolls bad and wicked. They gave them small presents as reinforcements. A control group was reinforced for not verbally abusing their dolls. The two groups were then observed playing with various toys. The children who were reinforced for verbally abusing their doll's were more verbally abusive towards their toys as well as more aggressive in other ways too. They were more likely to hit, kick or throw their toys down. It seems that reinforcing aggressive behaviour increased the likelihood of a child's being more aggressive in the future. Observation, imitation and reward are apparently powerful influences on the likelihood of children behaving aggressively.

FRUSTRATION AND AGGRESSION

Dollard et al. (1939) intended to translate Freudian psychoanalytic concepts into learning theory terms. Theirs is known as frustration-aggression-hypothesis which proposes that: "aggression is always a consequence of frustration and contrariwise... The existence of frustration, always leads to some from of aggression". 'Frustration' refers to an unpleasant feeling produced by an unfulfilled desire.

Whilst Dollard et al. agreed that aggression was an innate response, they agreed that it would only be elicited in specific situations. Thus, whenever an important need was thwarted, the resulting frustration would produce an aggressive response. Barker et al. (1941) too produced consistent evidence with Dollard et al. Young children were shown an attractive set of toys but prevented from playing with them. When the children were eventually allowed access to the toys, they threw them, stamped on them and smashed them. These behaviours did not occur in a comparison group of children who were not frustrated.

A modification of frustration-aggression-hypothesis says that frustration can lead to anger and anger, inturn, can lead to aggression. This is true, but not all aggression is the result of anger either, nor does everyone behave aggressively when they are angry. This modified theory was known as cue-arousal or aggressive cue theory. This theory was proposed by Berkowitz (1968). According to Berkowitz, two conditions act together to produce aggression when frustration occurs. The first is a 'readiness' to act aggressively. The second is the presence of 'environmental cues' associated either with aggressive behaviour or with the frustrating person or object. For Berkowitz then, when we might become angry as a response to frustration, aggressive behaviour will be elicited only when certain environmental cues are present.

CHILD REARING STYLES AND AGGRESSION

The family is usually the first, most important and most long term influence on the child. The ways in which parents bring up their children are called child-rearing styles and they reflect the importance of parental models. The parental models can differ greatly. Some of the child-rearing styles are authoritarian, permissive, authoritative and democratic. Children who are raised by aggressive and physically abusive parents often behave in the same way (Kaufman and Zigler, 1987). McCord, McCord and Howard (1961) found that aggressive boys were likely to have punitive, rejecting parents. Straus et al. (1980) correctly stated that each generation learns to be violent by being a participant in a violent family. Further, Eron, Walder, Toigo and Lefkowitz (1963) found that the aggressiveness of the children was related to the severity of the punishment imposed by the parents.

Robert Sears, Eleanor Maccoby and Harry Levin (1957) conducted one of the most famous studies on aggressive behaviour in children. They interviewed 379 American mothers of five-year-olds to study the relationship between the two variables: i) child-rearing style and ii) parents' reports of their children's aggressive behaviour. The researchers asked parents what kind of things they punished their children for. They found the following relationships. Permissive parents used very little discipline and were very inconsistent in the way they used punishment. The children of these parents were highly aggressive. Sears et al. identified another group of parents who seemed just the opposite. They used excessive discipline, and punished their children for relatively minor faults. Their children were almost as aggressive as those of the permissive parents. These children would feel frustrated at their treatment and since their parents modelled aggressive behaviour towards their children, the children learned that aggression was an appropriate way to achieve what they wanted. A third group of parents seemed to take a more reasonable attitude towards discipline and punished their children's occasional outbursts of aggression. They explained to their children what was expected of them and explained why they expected children's co-operation. Their children were more in control, and were least aggressive. Six years later, Sears revisited the children. The children of permissive parents continued to be aggressive while the children whose parents punished them excessively had become less aggressive than they had been, but they had also become more anxious and nervous. The children of the disciplined group still showed the least aggression.

ROLE OF THE PEER GROUP IN AGGRESSION

Peers too influence the aggressive behaviour of a child. Gerald Patterson and his colleagues (1972) found that one child's behaviour can act as a model and reinforcer for another child's behaviour. They studied a four-year-old Susan who gave in and cried. Her submissive behaviour gave some satisfaction to Christopher. Satisfaction acted as a reinforcer that increased the likelihood of Christopher hitting a third child. Also by showing other children that she gave in, Susan was likely to be attacked even more. If, on the other hand, Susan fought back when Christopher hit her, then Christopher was more likely to back off and found someone else to hit. Patterson's conclusion is that 'victims' who find that fighting back can be rewarding may well become aggressors themselves who then go on to attack other children.

THE RELATIONSHIP BETWEEN AGGRESSION AND THE MEDIA

The impact of the media on the behaviour of the young children is increasing. There has been an increase in the number people who watch television, an increase in the number of hours of television broadcast, an increase in the number of hours watched and an increase in the amount of violence shown on it. The positive correlation between the media programmes and aggressive behaviour had been ascertained by many research findings. For example, Stein and Friedrich (1972) found that those children who had seen the programmes containing aggression did behave aggressively. Similarly, Eron and his colleagues (1985) too found evidence in a large sample of 800 children (8½ years old) for the fact that those children who watch a great amount of violence on television behave most aggressively themselves. Eron's study also found a positive correlation between the amount of television violence watched by young boys (8 or 9 years of age) and how aggressive they were as young adults (at 18 or 19). Parke et al. (1977) too agreed that the children who watch violent television are more aggressive than those who do not.

Indeed, the American National Institute of Mental Health's (1982) review of 2500 studies led it to conclude that: "the consensus amongst most of the research community is that violence on television does lead to aggressive behaviour by children and teenagers who watch the programmes. This conclusion is based on laboratory experiments and field studies. Not all children become aggressive, of course, but the correlations between violence and aggression are positive. In magnitude, television violence is as strongly correlated with aggressive behaviour as any other behavioural variable that has been measured".

In Britain, the link between media violence and aggression was brought to the spotlight following two-year-old James Bulger's murder by two teenage boys in February, 1993. At their trial, Mr. Justice Moreland said: "It is not for me to pass judgment on their upbringing, but I suspect that exposure to violent video films may, in part, be an explanation" (cited in Cumberbatch, 1997). However many researchers like Cumberbatch believe that the link between media violence and aggressive behaviour to be over stated. They also believe that it is difficult to justify the overall conclusion that viewing television at an early age predicts later aggression.

SOCIOPSYCHOLOGICAL CHARACTERISTICS OF AGGRESSIVENESS

Achenbach (1993) listed a set of aggressive behaviours. These behaviours can be taken as characteristics of aggressiveness.

1. argues;
2. brags;
3. mean to others;
4. demands attention;
5. destroys others' things;
6. destroys own things;

7. disobedient at school;
8. jealous;
9. fights;
10. attacks people;
11. shows off;
12. stubborn mood changes;
13. sudden mood changes;
14. talks too much;
15. teases;
16. temper tantrums;
17. threatens;
18. loud;
19. disobedient at home;
20. defiant;
21. disturbs others;
22. talks out of turn;
23. disrupts class;
24. explosive; and
25. easily frustrated.

THE REDUCTION AND CONTROL OF AGGRESSIVE BEHAVIOUR

(i) Catharsis

Both the Freudian and Ethological approaches to aggression propose that the most effective way of reducing it is through 'catharsis'. But this view of giving youngsters the opportunity to 'let off steam' through arousing is not strongly supported by experimental evidences.

(ii) Punishment

Punishment can be effective in deterring aggressive behaviour provided that it is prompt, of sufficient magnitude to be aversive, and highly probable following the aggressive behaviour (Bower and Hilgard, 1981). But psychological research suggests that punishment may also be ineffective because the recipient sees it as being unjustified, particularly, if it is not applied in the same way to others. If this is the case, aggressive behaviour may be more likely to occur because of the recipient's desire for revenge (Baron and Byrne, 1994). That is, the recipient of punishment views the persons who deliver punishment as aggressive models and, no doubt, starts following him.

(iii) *Exposure to Non-aggressive Models*

It is possible to reduce aggression by adding more non-aggressive models to the environment. A number of studies have shown that seeing other people behaving non-aggressively can reduce aggression (Donnerstein and Donnersein, 1976).

GENERAL APPROACHES TO THE REDUCTION OF AGGRESSION

Baron and Byrne (1994) suggested three other approaches that might be effective in reducing aggression. They were social skills training, cognitive interventions and incompatible responses.

(a) *Social Skill Training*

People who lack the ability to communicate their wishes to others often suffer repeated frustration and this can lead them to behave aggressively (Hollin and Howells, 1997). Those lacking essential social skills evidently account for a high proportion of the violence occurring in any given society (Toch, 1980). Toch, therefore, suggested the solution to train people in the essential social skills. Researchers like Goldstein et al. (1981) and Schneider (1991) reiterated that such training can be effective in reducing the likelihood of a person being either the source or a target of aggressive behaviour.

(b) *Cognitive Interventions*

If our attributions for a person's behaviour determine the likelihood of us behaving aggressively, it seems reasonable to propose that changing our attributions for a particular behaviour might be effective in reducing aggression. Kremer and Stephens (1983) have found that when people are made aware of the mitigating circumstances for a person's potentially aggression-inducing behaviour, they are less likely to behave aggressively, provided that the information about the mitigating circumstances is given early enough and is believable.

(c) Incompatible Response

According to the principle of 'reciprocal inhibition' (Wolpe, 1958), it is impossible to experience two incompatible emotional responses simultaneously. Researchers like Barron (1983) have applied this principle to the reduction of aggressive behaviour and shown that when emotional states incompatible with anger or actual aggression are induced, the tendency to react aggressively is reduced.

CLINICAL APPROACHES TO THE REDUCTION OF AGGRESSION

A variety of techniques drawn from mainstream clinical psychology may be used to reduce aggression (Hollin and Howells, 1997). Some of those techniques are desensitization, active challenging, environmental control and rehearsal and practice.

SUMMARY

Behaviours, which show a lack of feeling and concern for the welfare of others are known as antisocial behaviours. One such antisocial behaviour is aggression. Psychologists view aggression as the behaviour, either physical or symbolic performed with the intention of harming someone. Children's aggressive behaviours range from the least harmful kind of aggression to the more serious ones to inflict physical injury on another person or damage property. An extreme form of aggression is described as violence.

Social and developmental psychologists have studied the origins of aggression and found links with both biology and the environment. Biological explanations show how changing hormones and metabolic levels cause the aggressive behaviour. The main theories like Freud's psychoanalytic theory as well as Lorenz's ethological theory contribute to biological explanations. The psychoanalytic theory argues that people are born with aggressive impulses/urges. Similarly, Lorenz's ethological theory too views aggression as an 'innate drive'. Both Freud and Lorenz believed that aggression occurs spontaneously when aggressive energy builds up. Experimental evidences too prove that the biological factors contribute to aggression. Experiments with regard to particular hormones and brain centres shows that aggressive behaviour can be stimulated.

Social learning theory sees aggressive behaviours as being learning through reinforcement, modelling and imitation. Bandura et al. showed that children's aggressive tendencies can be strengthened by vicarious reinforcement.

Dollard et al.'s frustration-aggression-hypothesis proposes that aggression is always a consequence of frustration. On the other hand, Berkowitz's cue-arousal theory insisted that when we become angry as a response to frustration, aggressive behaviours will be elicited, when certain environmental cues are present.

The child-rearing styles exert influence on the behaviour of the children. They reflect the importance of parental models. Many research findings suggest that children who are raised by aggressive and physically abusive parents express aggressive behaviour.

Peers too influence the aggressive behaviour of a child. Patterson et al. found that one child's behaviour can act as a model or reinforcer for another child's behaviour. The impact of media on the behaviour of the young children is also increasing. There is a consensus among most of the research community that violence on television does lead to aggressive behaviour. Many laboratory experiments and field studies confirm the positive correlation between television violence and aggression.

Catharsis and punishment are suggested as measures to the reduction and control of aggressive behaviour. Aggressiveness can also be reduced by offering exposure to non-aggressive models. Baron and Byrn suggested that social-skill training, cognitive interventions and incompatible responses are the effective approaches in reducing aggression. A variety of techniques like desensitization, active challenging, environmental control and rehearsal and practice, drawn from mainstream clinical psychology, can also be used to reduce aggression.

REFERENCES

Achenbach, T.M., (1993), 'Empirically Based Taxonomy: How to Use Syndromes and Profile Types Derived from the CBCL/4-18, TRF, and YSR. Burlington, VT: University of Vermont Department of Psychiatry.

Bandura, A., (1973), *Aggression: A Social Learning Analysis*. London, Prentice Hall.

Bandura, A. and Walters, R.H., (1959), *Adolescent Aggression*. New York, Ronald Press.

Bandura, A., Ross, D. and Ross, S.A., (1963), 'Initiation of Film-mediated Aggression Models'. *Journal of Abnormal and Social Psychology*, 66, 3-11.

Bandura, A., Ross, D. and Ross, S.A., (1961), 'Transmission of Aggression Through Imitation of Aggressive Models'. *Journal of Abnormal and Social Psychology*, 63, 575-582.

Barker, R., Dembo, T. and Lewin, K., (1941), 'Frustration and Regression: An Experiment with Young Children'. *University of Iowa Studies in Child Welfare*, 18 , 1-314.

Baron, R.A., (1983), 'The Reduction of Human Aggression: An Incompatible Response Strategy'. In R.G. Geen & E. Donnerstein (Eds.). *Aggression: Theoretical and Empirical Reviews*. New York: Academic Press.

Barron, R.A. and Byrne, D.S., (1994), *Social Psychology: Understanding Human Interaction*. (7th Edition). London: Allyn & Bacon

Berkowitz, L., (1993), *Aggression: Its Causes, Consequences and Control*. New York: McGraw–Hill.

Berkowitz, L., (1968), 'Impulse, Aggression and the Gun'. *Psychology Today*. September, 18-22.

Bower, G.H. and Hilgard, E.R., (1981), *Theories of Learning*. Englewood Cliffs, NJ: Prentice Hall.

Cumberbatch, G., (1997), 'Media Violence: Science and Common Sense'. Psychology Review, 3, 2-7.

Dollard, J., Doob, L.W., Mower, O.H. and Sears, R.R., (1939), *Frustration and Aggression*. New Haven, CT: Harvard University Press.

Donnerstein, E. and Donnerstein, M., (1976), 'Research in the Control of Interracial Aggression'. In R.G. Geen & E. O'Neil (Eds.) *Perspectives on Aggression*, New York: Academic Press.

Eron, L.D. and Huesmann, L.R., (1985), 'The Role of Television in the Development of Pro-social and Anti-social Behaviour'. In D. Olweus, M. Radke-Yarrow, and J. Block (Eds.) *Development of Anti-social and Pro-Social Behaviour*. Orlando, FL: Academic Press.

Eron, L.D., Walder, L.O., Toigo, R. and Lefkowitz, M.M., (1963), 'Social Class, Parental Punishment for Aggression and Child Aggression'. *Child Development*, 34, 849-867.

Freud, S., (1949), *An Outline of Psychoanalysis*. London: Hogarth Press.

Goldstein, A.P., Carr, E.D., Davidson, W.S. and Wehr, P., (1981), *In Response to Aggression: Methods of Control and Prosocial Alternatives*. New York: Pergamon.

Hollin, C. and Howells, K., (1997), 'Controlling Violent Behaviour'. *Psychology Review*, 3, 10-14.

Kaufman, J. and Zigler, E., (1987), 'Do Abused Children Become Abused Parents?' *American Journal of Orthopsychiatry*, 57, 186-192.

Kremer, J.F. and Stephens, L., (1983), 'Attributions and Arousal as Mediators of Mitigation's Effect on Retardation'. *Journal of Personality and Social Psychology*, 45, 335-343.

Lloyd, P., Mayes, A., Manstead, A.S.R., Mendell, P.R. and Wagner, H.L., (1984), *Introduction to Psychology–An Integrated Approach*. London: Fontana.

McCord, W., MCCord, J. and Howard, A., (1961), 'Familial Correlates of Aggression in Non-delinquent Male Children'. *Journal of Abnormal Social Psychology*, 62, 79-93.

Moyer, K.E., (1976), *The Psychobiology of Aggression*. New York: John Wiley.

Parke, R.D., Berkowitz, L., Leyens, J.P., West, S.G. and Sebastian, R.J., (1977), 'Some Effects of Violent and Non-violent Movies on the Behaviour of Juvenile Delinquents'. In L. Berkowitz (Ed.) *Advances in Experimental Social Psychology*, Vol. 10, New York: Academic Press.

Patterson, G.R., Cobb, J.A. and Ray, R.S., (1972), 'Direct Intervention in the Classroom: A Set of Procedures for the Aggressive Child'. In F. Clark, D. Evans and L. Hamerlynck (Eds.), *Implementing Behavioural Programmes for Schools and Clinics*, Champaign, III, Research Press.

Ross, A.O., (1974), *Psychological Disorders of Children: A Behavioural Approach to Theory, Research and Therapy*. New York, McGraw-Hill.

Schneider, B.H., (1991), 'A Comparison of Skill Building and Desensitisation Strategies for Intervention with Aggressive Children'. *Aggressive Behaviour*, 17, 301-311.

Sears, R.R., Maccoby, E.E. and Levin, H., (1957), *Patterns of Child Rearing*. Evanston, Illinois, Row, Peterson.

Straus, M., Gelles, R. and Steinmetz, S., (1980), *Behind Closed Doors: Violence in the American Family*. Garden City, NY: Anchor Press.

Toch, H., (1980), *Violent Men* (Revised Edition). Cambridge, MA: Schenkman.

Wolpe, J., (1958), *Psychotherapy by Reciprocal Inhibition*. Stanford, CA: Stanford University Press.

8

Conduct Disorders

OBJECTIVES

This chapter describes conduct disorders and presents the classification of conduct behaviour problems. The prevalence and pattern of conduct disorders, their stability over time, their developmental aspects and various influences on the development of conduct disordered behaviours are analysed clearly. Finally, this chapter delves into assessment as well as treatment of conduct disorders. After reading this chapter, this readers should be able to:

(i) Define conduct disorders;

(ii) Analyse their classification;

(iii) Present the prevalence, pattern and stability of conduct problems;

(iv) Comprehend the developmental pathways to conduct disorder behaviour;

(v) Describe the various influences on the development of conduct problems;

(vi) Know about the various assessment procedures of conduct disorders; and

(vii) List out the treatment measures for conduct problems.

INTRODUCTION

Quite often most parents, teachers, other adults and peers express deep concern over youngsters, problematic behaviours such as fighting, lying, stealing or destroying property or repeatedly failing to follow directions and the persistence of these behaviours over time create a socially handicapping conditions and serious disturbances in personal relationships. These problem behaviours are labelled as conduct disorders. The various terms employed to describe these deviant behaviours (e.g. acting out, disruptive, externalising, under controlled, oppositional, antisocial or delinquent) reflect the wide range of the broad category as well as its complexity and heterogeneity. Generally, the term 'conduct disorder' is used to describe severe levels of the general group of aggressive-antisocial behaviours.

DESCRIPTION AND CLASSIFICATION OF CONDUCT DISORDERS

An empirically derived syndrome involving aggressive, oppositional, destructive and antisocial behaviour has been identified in a wide variety of studies. This syndrome has been given a wide variety of names, such as under controlled, externalizing or conduct disorder. There have also been efforts to distinguish narrower groupings within this broad externalizing conduct disorder syndrome. For instance, Achenbach (1993) described two syndromes: i) aggressive behaviour (fighting, destroying things and being explosive); and ii) delinquent behaviour (lying, stealing and being truant), within the broader externalizing syndrome. The validity of this distinction is supported by many research findings. For example, Edelbrock et al. (1995) suggested a higher degree of heritability for the aggressive than the delinquent syndromes. In addition, Stanger, Achenbach and Verhulst (1997) found that the average scores in the population of the two syndromes declined between ages four and ten. After age ten, the scores on the aggressive syndrome continued to decline, whereas scores on the delinquent syndrome increased. They also found that the stability (the similarity of a particular individual's behaviour at two points in time) was higher for the aggressive than for the delinquent syndrome. The above findings suggest that it is important to distinguish between types of externalizing/conduct disorder problems.

Another approach suggests a distinction based on age of onset (Hinshaw, Lahey and Hart, 1993): i) a later or adolescent-onset category consisting principally of non-aggressive and delinquent behaviours; and ii) an early-onset category that includes these behaviours as well as aggressive behaviours.

Two other approaches to sub categorizing are 'salient symptom approach' and 'the overt-covert dimension' (Kazdin, 1989a). The salient symptom approach is based on the primary behaviour problem being displayed. For example antisocial children, whose primary problem is aggression, are distinguished from those whose primary problem is stealing. The second, approach is based on distinction between 'overt' conformation antisocial behaviours (e.g. arguing, fighting, temper tantrums) and 'covert' or concealed antisocial behaviours (e.g. fire setting, lying, stealing, truancy).

A further expansion of this distinction suggests grouping conduct problems by employing two dimensions: an overt-covert distinction and destructive–nondestructive dimension of behaviour (Frick, 1998). This approach and the clusters of behaviours based on it are illustrated in the following figure:

Clusters of Conduct Disorder Behaviour Defined by the Two Dimensions of Overt-to-Covert and Destructive-to-Nondestructive (Frick, 1998)

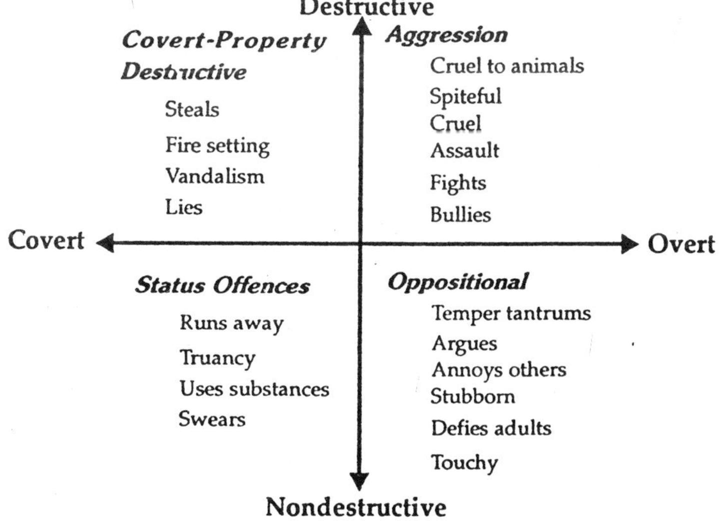

The DSM approach includes the diagnostic categories of Attention Deficit Hyperactivity Disorder and two other diagnosis, namely, Oppositional Defiant Disorder (ODD) and Conduct Disorder (CD) under the broad category of Attention Deficit and Disruptive Behaviour Disorders. ODD is described as a pattern of negativistic, hostile and defiant behaviour lasting at least six months. On the other hand, the essential feature of the diagnosis of Conduct Disorder (CD) is a repetitive and persistent pattern of behaviour that violates the basic rights of others as well as the major age-appropriate societal norms. The list of symptoms for conduct disorder as suggested by DSM-IV are presented below.

Behaviours Used by DSM-IV in Diagnosing Conduct Disorder

Aggression toward People/Animals

Bullies, threatens, or intimidates

Initiates physical fights

Has used a weapon

Is physically cruel to people

Is physically cruel to animals

Has stolen while confronting a victim

Has forced someone into sexual activity

Destruction of Property

Has deliberately engaged in fire setting with the intention of causing serious damage

Has deliberately destroyed others' property (other than fire setting)

Deceitfulness or Theft

Has broken into house, building or car

Often lies to obtain goods or favours or to avoid obligations

Has stolen items of nontrivial value without confronting a victim

Serious Violation of Rules

Stays out at night despite parental prohibitions, beginning before age thirteen

Has runway from home overnight at least twice (or once without returning for a lengthy period)

Is often truant from school, beginning before age thirteen

CONDUCT DISORDER AND CO-OCCURRENCE

Youngsters who receive one of the disruptive disorder diagnoses also frequently experience other difficulties and receive other diagnoses. For example, most youngsters who receive the diagnosis of CD also meet the criteria for ODD. The reported average are of onset was about six years for ODD and about nine years for CD. This suggests that the boys having behaviours characteristic pf ODD may develop into conduct disordered boys. That is the behaviours of ODD are 'retained' as additional antisocial behaviours emerge. At the same time, ODD does not always result in CD. Hinshaw, Lahey and Hart (1993) correctly said that although most cases of CD meet the criteria for ODD, most youngsters with ODD do not progress to a conduct disorder. In addition, there is considerable co-occurrence of ODD and CD with Attention Deficit Hyperactivity Disorder (ADHD).

Youngsters with CD commonly experience a variety of other difficulties too. They are frequently rejected by their peers (Nowcomb et al., 1993). Youngsters with CD are also frequently described as having certain cognitive impairments and lower school achievement (Caspi & Moffitt, 1995 and Maughan & Rutter, 1998). Internalizing disorders, such as anxiety and depression also occur at higher than expected rates among youngsters with CD (Loeber and Keenan, 1994). Similarly, the youngsters with conduct disordered behaviours may turn into 'delinquents' or 'juveniles'. The term 'delinquency' is a legal term rather than a psychological one. As a legal term, it refers to a juvenile (under eighteen) who has committed an index crime or a status offence. In addition, conduct disordered youngsters may even use illicit substances like alcohol and other drugs.

PREVALENCE AND PATTERN OF CONDUCT DISORDER

Prior to preschool, boys and girls do not differ in the level of conduct problems displayed, but by about age four, boys exhibit greater physical aggression and other externalising behaviour problems than the girls do (Keenan and Shaw, 1997). Kazdin (1995a) felt that conduct problems are also one of the most frequent reasons for referral to child and adolescent treatment services. The prevalence rate in community samples is between 2 and 10 per cent, with estimates of 6 to 10 pe rcent for ODD and 2 to 9 per cent for CD (Earls, 1994). Conduct disorders are more prevalent among boys than in girls; a ratio of about 4:1 is typically cited (Earls, 1994).

STABILITY OF CONDUCT DISORDERS

Fergusson, Lynskey and Horwood (1996) considered the stability of conduct disorders over time as an important aspect. Early presence of CD appears to be related to later aggressive and antisocial behaviour and to a range of psychological and social-emotional difficulties in later life (Farrington, 1995). The findings of Stagner et al. (1996) and Olweus (1979) established a substantial correlation for the stability of aggressive, externalising behaviour from preschool into adolescence. This does not mean that all individuals who exhibit early conduct disordered behaviour continue to do so. Only some portion of youngsters continues to exhibit antisocial behaviour whereas others desist externalising problems. Loeber and Stouthamer-Leober (1998) reported that among a community sample of inner-city boys, the prevalence of physical fighting started to decrease by age fifteen.

DEVELOPMENTAL ASPECTS OF CONDUCT DISORDERS

Two distinct developmental pathways leading to antisocial behaviour have been proposed. One is childhood onset and other is adolescent onset. The childhood-onset developmental pathways fits with the notion of the stability of conduct disordered behaviour. Moffitt (1993a) terms this pattern "life-course persistent antisocial behaviour". The early-onset pathway is less common than the adolescent-onset pattern. Youngsters following this pattern are also more likely to exhibit other problems such as ADHD, learning disabilities, and academic difficulties. The adolescent onset pattern is the more common developmental pathway. In this pattern, little oppositional or antisocial behaviour is exhibited during childhood. Only in adolescence many youngsters begin to engage in illegal activities to qualify for a diagnosis of conduct disorder. Youngsters following this pathway tend to exhibit less severe antisocial behaviour and to be less aggressive. They are also less likely to persist in their antisocial behaviours beyond adolescence. Hence Moffitt (1993a) called this pattern "adolescent-limited antisocial behaviour".

VARIOUS INFLUENCES OF CONDUCT DISORDERS

The development of conduct-disordered and antisocial behaviour may be affected by a variety of influences. Dishion, French and Patterson (1995) proposed a hypothetical ecological model to illustrate how antisocial behaviour may be influenced by a variety of factors.

Various Factors Influencing Antisocial Behaviour

(From Dishion, French & Patterson, 1995)

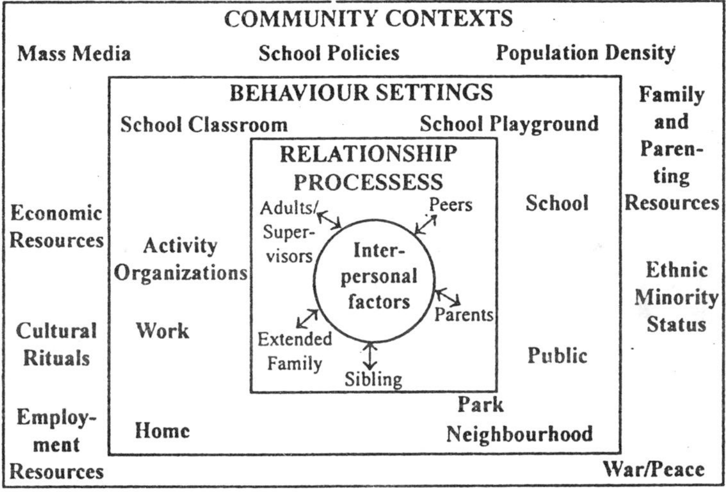

Intra personal factors are characteristics of individuals that interact with the environment in the development of antisocial behaviour. Relationship process is the immediate context in which this development occurs. Behaviour settings are the physical settings in which these relationships occur, and community contexts are larger social influences. Each system directly or indirectly affects the development of antisocial behaviour.

Conduct disordered behaviour is likely to develop through a complex interaction of influences. Most of the children learn and imitate such disordered behaviours from their parents, siblings, grand parents or peers. Such deviant behaviours are ubiquitous in television programmes and in other media. In most cases, family influences play an important role in the genesis of various conduct disorders. As Frick (1994), Patterson, Reid and Dishion (1992) viewed, conduct disordered children may be part of a deviant family system. Numerous family variables have been implicated, including family socio-economic status, family size, marital disruption, poor-quality parenting, parental neglect and parental psychopathology. Further, Patterson, De Barysh and Ramsey (1989) considered that the disruptors of effective parenting such as income, unemployment, parental education, marital conflict and divorce, neighbourhood ethnic group may lead a child to antisocial behaviour.

Youngsters' peer affiliations too exert influence on the antisocial behaviour. Patterson and his colleagues (1992) have found that aggressive boys often experience rejection by their peers and this rejection, in combination with other influences, leads to a drift into deviant peer groups. Difficulties in interpersonal relations have repeatedly been found among conduct disordered youths. The findings of Coie, Belding and Underwood (1988) indicate that aggressive children are often rejected by their peers. These rejected aggressive children suffer immediate social consequences, and they are also at risk for negative long-term outcomes such as delinquency, adult criminality, educational failure and a variety of indices of adult psychological maladjustment (Parker and Asher, 1987). Similarly, Fergussion and Horwood (1996) found that the deviant peer associations play a role in the imitation and maintenance of antisocial behaviour.

Social-cognitive factors too contribute to antisocial behaviour. For example, inability to use another person's perspective, inability to use social problem-solving skills, not thinking before the act or inability to use self-verbalizations to control their behaviour may operate on the youngsters' behaviour. Reactively, conduct disordered youngsters display deficiencies in early stages of the social cognitive process. For instance, they under utilize social cues and misattribute hostile intent to their peers' neutral actions.

Research findings reveal that antisocial and criminal behaviour has strong biological roots too. Rutter et al. (1999) hypothesized that genetic component contributes to antisocial behaviour that persists from childhood into adult life. A number of longitudinal behaviour genetic studies of children and adolescents (for e.g. Hewitt et al., 1997) suggest a genetic component to conduct disordered /externalising behaviour. There is also support for the effects of shared environment in the findings. That is, although genetic influences may play some role, they inevitably interact in complex ways with environmental influences, such as social conditions, family variables and certain social learning experiments that are major factors in determining the etiology of conduct disorders (Rutter et al., 1990).

It has also been hypothesized that neurophysiological variables are related to antisocial behaviour. Raine and Venable's (1984) review of the literature found support for the existence of lower resting heart rate among antisocial youths. Quay (1993) too hypothesized a biological foundation for aggressive, life-course persistent conduct disorders. He suggested that an imbalance between the Behavioural Inhibition System (BIS) and Behavioural Activation System (BAS) of the brain creates a predisposition that in combination with adverse environmental circumstances produces behaviour problems. According to Quay, for example, an overactive behavioural activation system (reflected in heart rate) combined with an underactive behavioural inhibition system (reflected in skin conductance response) may be implicated in the genesis of persistent aggressive conduct disorders.

Deficits in neuropsychological functioning are also found to contribute to the development of conduct disorders. Neurological damage may directly produce conduct disordered behaviour. In addition, Moffitt's (1993b) review suggested that deficits in neuropsychological variables, such as sustaining attention, abstract reasoning, goal formation, planning and self-awareness are related to the onset of conduct disorder, its stability overtime, aggressiveness and the presence of ADHD symptoms.

ASSESSMENT PROCEDURES OF CONDUCT DISORDERS

Assessment of conduct disordered behaviour is likely to be a complex and multifaceted process. Valuable information may be obtained from multiple informants, including the youth, parents, other family members, teachers and peers. The various manifestations of conduct disordered behaviour need to be evaluated. Various assessment procedures, such as interviews, behavioural rating scales and behavioural observations are used in addressing conduct and other problem behaviours.

(a) Interviews

The parents, the older children and adolescents may provide information through a general clinical interview. But with very young children, an interview may not be easily conducted to obtain reliable information. However, the opportunity to interact with the young child may be helpful to the clinician for formulating hypotheses and in establishing rapport. An interview with the entire family may also provide valuable information. Moreover, an interview with the teacher or school personnel is frequently part of the assessment process and it can provide valuable information with regard to certain social shares of functioning. Structured interviews with the youngster and parents are also conducted for the purpose of diagnosis.

(b) Behavioural Rating Scales

Youngsters' behaviours are assessed through a number of behavioural rating scales, which are normally completed by adults or by the youngster. Several behavioural rating scales are recommended for use with youngsters with conduct problems. For instance, the Achenbach (1991a) instruments like child behaviour checklists, youth self-report and teacher report form, provide valuable information about a broad array of problem areas, including those of an externalising nature. The rating scale system of Reynolds and Kamphaus (1992) known as "The Behavioural Assessment System for Children" (BASC) allows assessment of the broad array of problems through the reports of multiple informants.

The Eyeberg Child Behavioural Inventory (ECBI) and the Sutter-Eyeberg Students Behaviour Inventory (SESBI) of Eyberg (1992) focus more specifically on conduct and can be used for youngsters of age two to sixteen, whereas the SESBI items sampling the range of "disruptive behaviour" problems that correspond to DSM disagnoses of ODD and Attention Deficit Disorder as well as Conduct Disorder. Majority of the items address conduct problems.

The most widely used youth self-report measure of conduct problem is "The Self-Report Delinquency Scale" (SRD) developed by Elliott et al. (1985). It consists of items derived form the Uniform Crime Reports and includes index offences (e.g. theft and aggravated assault), other delinquent behaviours, and drug use. It is intended for use with youngsters of age eleven to nineteen. Self-report measures are less commonly used with very young children because of concern with their ability to accurately report conduct problems.

(c) Behavioural Observations

Since the reports based on interviews and questionnaires are potentially biased in nature, behavioural observation systems have long been a part of the assessment of conduct problems. A large number of systems are designed for use in clinic, home and school settings. Some observational systems have been employed in more than one setting. The behavioural coding system developed by Forehand et al. (1991) and the Dyadic Parent-Child Interaction Coding System II developed by Eyberg et al. (1994) are two observational systems for assessing parent-child interactions in the clinic. Similarly, "The Interpersonal Process Code" developed by Rusby et al. (1991) is designed for clinic use and it is developed in such a way to be used in a variety of settings (e.g. home, school) and with various participants (eg. peers, teachers).

Observation in natural settings is desirable because only in natural settings many conduct problem behaviours and interactions occur. Such systems are very rare since they are complex and require extensive periods of training and the use of trained observers. An alternative to using trained observers in home and other natural settings is to train adults in the child's environment (e.g. parents) to record and observe certain behaviours. The Parent Daily Report (PDR) developed by Chamberlain and Reid (1987) is of this kind. During brief telephone interviews, the parent is asked whether any of the targeted behaviours occurred during the past twenty-four hours. The Daily Telephone Discipline Interview developed by Webster, Stratton and Spitzer (1991) was an extension to the PDR to provide more information about parental interventions surrounding child behaviours reported on the PDR. Most of the above mentioned observational systems are targeted for children, their parents, teachers and peers. Similarly, observational systems are also available for coding parent-adolescent conflict, problem solving and communication (Foster and Robin, 1997).

TREATMENT MEASURES FOR CONDUCT DISORDERS

Many different treatment measures have been attempted with conduct disordered youth. Some of the treatment measures which have been proved effective and promising are: i) parent-training programmes; ii) cognitive problem-solving skills training; iii) functional family therapy; iv) community-based programmes and v) multi-systematic therapy.

(i) Parent-Training Programmes

Parent-training is the most successful approach to reducing conduct disorders and antisocial behaviours in youth (Kazdin, 1997). The common features of parent-training programmes are: i) Treatments are conducted primarily with the parents. In other words, the therapist teaches the parents to alter interactions with their child so as to increase prosocial behaviour and to reduce deviant behaviour, ii) New ways of identifying, defining and observing behaviour problems are taught, iii) Social learning principles and procedures that follow from them are taught; iv) Behaviour change programmes and techniques are reviewed; v) The child's functioning in school is usually incorporated into treatment in which parent-managed reinforcement programmes for school and school-related behaviour and also teacher-managed monitoring and feedback are incorporated. Forehand and his colleagues (1980), for example, developed one such parent-management training programmes to treat non-compliant children and they found it to be successfully reducing not only the non compliance but also other problem behaviours, such as tantrums, aggression and crying. Webster-Stratton and her colleagues (1984) developed a videotape group discussion programme for young children of age three to eight years with conduct disordered behaviour. A standard package of videotaped programmes of modelled parenting skills has been developed. The package contained 250 vignettes of about two minutes each, including examples of parents interacting with their children in both appropriate and inappropriate ways. They are shown to group of parents, and following each vignette, there is a therapist-led discussion of the relevant interactions. The parents are also given homework assignments that allow them to practise parenting skills at home with their children. The researchers found this programme very successful in reducing the problem behaviour of children and the parents too were found to have developed better parenting-skills. Further, these improvements were maintained at the follow-up evaluations over many years.

(ii) Cognitive Problem-Solving Skills Training

The parent-training approaches focus on family aspects of conduct disordered behaviour, whereas the cognitive problem-solving skill training approach concentrates specifically on aspects of the child's functioning and addressed social-cognitive deficiencies and distortions among conduct disordered youngsters (Kazdin, 1993c). The common features of the problem solving skill training programmes are: 1) the emphasis is on the thought processes involved in the child's approach to interpersonal situations: 2) prosocial behaviours are fostered through modelling, role playing and direct reinforcement; 3) cognitive-problem-solving skills are taught through structured tasks, such as games, academic activities and stories; 4) therapists play an active role by being a model of cognitive processes, making verbal self-statements, providing cues to prompt appropriate skills and applying feedback.

It has been suggested that problem solving approaches are more effective with older youngsters because they have fully developed cognitive abilities. Kazdin, Siegel and Bass (1992) compared three different interventions applied to youngsters of age 7 to 13 who were referred for severe antisocial behaviour. The companions were on problem solving skill training (PSST), parent-management training (PMT) and a combined PSST plus PMT condition. They found that the combined condition had significantly greater therapeutic effect than either of the treatments alone and resulted in a greater proportion of the youngsters' falling within normative levels of cognitive functioning.

(iii) Functional Family Therapy

The Functional Family Therapy (FFT) is a treatment programme for delinquents. FFT programmes integrate behavioural-social learning, cognitive-behavioural and family systems perspectives (Alexander, Holtzworth-Munroe and Jameson, 1994). The goals of this therapy are to improve the communication skills of families; modify cognitive sets, expectations, attitudes and affective reactions; and establish new interpretations and meanings of behaviour. Treatment sessions directly focus on altering communication patterns of the family. The therapists employ a variety of techniques like modelling, prompting, shaping and rehearsing effective communication skills and feedback and reinforcement for positive changes.

(iv) Community Based Programmes

A traditional approach to intervention with delinquents is institutionalization. Reform schools, training schools and detention centres implement therapeutic, educational or rehabilitative programming. Most of such schools provide custodial care alone. The Teaching Family Model (TFM) developed at Achievement Place is an often-recommended example of a community based programme for delinquent youth and an example of many behaviourally based interventions. Achievement place is a home-style residential treatment programme in which adolescents, who have legally been declared delinquent, live in a house with two trained teaching parents. The youths attend school during day and also have regular work responsibilities. The academic problems, aggression and other non-violating behaviours exhibited by these adolescents are viewed as an expression of failures of past environments to teach appropriate behaviours. Accordingly, these deficits are corrected through modelling, practice instruction and feedback. The programme centres on a token economy in which points and praise are gained for appropriate behaviours and lost for inappropriate behaviours. If a resident meets a certain level of performance, the right to go on a merit system is offered. The goal is gradually to transfer a youngster who is able to perform adequately on merit to his or her natural home. Teaching-parents help the actual parents or guardians to structure a programme to maintain gains made at Achievement Place.

(v) Multi Systemic Therapy

Multi Systemic Therapy (MST) is a family-systems-based approach. Here the child is considered to exist in a number of systems, including family, peers, school, neighbourhood and community. MST uses treatment strategies derived from family-systems-therapy and from behaviour therapy to treat serious juvenile offenders and their families. It seeks to preserve the family and to maintain the youths in their homes. It addresses not only the family system but also skills of the offender and extra familiar influences such as peers, school and neighbourhood. Henggeler, Melton and Smith (1992) found that MST was significantly more effective than the usual services.

A change in the way in which conduct disorders are conceptualized as well as in treating adolescents with serious and persistent conduct disorders is suggested. Wolf et al. (1987) suggested to view CD as "social disability". Kazdin (1987) suggested viewing it as analogous to a chronic physical disease, such as diabetes. The implication behind such suggestion is that single and short-term treatments to conduct disorders should be avoided. Instead, multiple interventions throughout the youngster's life into early adulthood should be offered. The multidimensional nature of antisocial behaviour and the potential stability of conduct disordered behaviour call forth early, multifaceted, flexible and ongoing interventions.

SUMMARY

Conduct disordered behaviours are described as acting out, disruptive, externalising, under controlled, oppositional, antisocial or delinquent behaviour and they create socially handicapping conditions and serious disturbances in personal relationships.

The DSM approach includes the diagnostic categories of ADHD and two other diagnosis, namely, ODD and CD under the broad category of Attention – Deficit and Disruptive Behaviour Disorders. ODD is described as a pattern of negativistic, hostile and defiant behaviour lasting at least for six months. CD is a repetitive and persistent pattern of behaviour that violates the basic rights of others as well as the major age appropriate societal norms.

Youngsters who receive one of the disruptive disorder diagnosis also frequently experience other difficulties such as cognitive impairments, lower school achievement, anxiety or depression. They may even turn into delinquents or juveniles. In addition, conduct disordered youngsters may even use illicit abusive substances like alcohol and other drugs.

Prior to preschool, boys and girls do not differ in the level of conduct problems displayed but by about age four, boys exhibit greater physical aggression and other externalising behaviour problems than the girls. The stability of CD over time is an important aspect. Research findings establish that aggressive, externalising behaviours remain stable from preschool into adolescence. But some youngsters are able to desist externalising problems.

Two district developmental pathways leading to antisocial behaviour have been proposed. One is childhood onset and the other is adolescent onset. The adolescent pathway is more common developmental pathway but does not persist beyond adolescence in many cases.

The development CD may be influenced by a variety of factors. Dishion et al.'s ecological model proposes that intra personal factors, relationship processes, behaviour settings and community context have either direct or indirect influence on the development of antisocial behaviour. Peer affiliations and social cognitive factors (e.g. lack of social problem solving skills) also have an impact on the deviant behaviour. Antisocial and criminal behaviours have strong biological roots too. Research findings reveal that genetic components contribute to conduct disordered behaviour. Neurophysiological as well as neuropsychological variables are also found to have their own contributions to the development of antisocial behaviour.

Assessment of conduct disordered behaviour is likely to be a complex and multifaceted process. Various assessment procedures such as interviews, behaviour rating scales and behavioural observations are normally used to address conduct and antisocial behaviours'. Observation in natural settings is desirable because only in natural settings many conduct problem behaviours occur. But such observation systems are rare.

Different treatment measures have been attempted with conduct disordered youth. Some of the effective treatment measures are parent management training programmes, cognitive problem-solving skills training, functional family therapy, community-based programmes and Multi Systemic Therapy. Suggestions for viewing conduct disorders as a 'social disability' and as analogous to chronic physical disease like diabetes are gaining momentum at present. The implication behind such suggestion is that long-term and multiple interventions should be offered to the conduct disordered youth throughout the youngster's life into early adulthood.

REFERENCES

Achenbach, T.M., (1993), 'Empirically Based Taxonomy: How to Use Syndromes and Profile Types Derived from the CBCL/4-18, TRF and YSR'. Burlington, VT: University of Vermont Department of Psychiatry.

Achenbach, T.M., (1991a), *'Integrative Guide for the 1991* CBCL/4-18, *YSR and TRF profiles'*. Burlington, VT: University of Vermont, Department of Psychiatry.

Alexander, J.F., Holtzworth-Munroe, A. and Jameson, P.B., (1994), 'The Process and Outcome of Martial and Family Therapy Research: Review and Evaluation'. In A.E. Bergin & S.L. Garfield (Eds.), *Hundbook of Psychotherapy and Behaviour Change,* (4th Ed.). New York: John Wiley & Sons.

Caspi, A. and Moffitt, T.E., (1995), 'The Continuity of Maladaptive Behaviour: From Description to Understanding in the Study of Antisocial Behaviour'. In D. Cicchetti & D.J. Cohen (Eds.), *Developmental Psychopathology. (Vol. 2: Risk, Disorder and Adaptation).* New York: John Wiley & Sons.

Chamberlain, P. and Reid, J.B., (1987), 'Parent Observation and Report of Child Symptoms'. *Behavioural Assessment,* 9, 97-109.

Coie, J.D., Belding, M. and Underwood, M., (1988), 'Aggression and Peer Rejection in Childhood'. In B.B. Lahey & A.E. Kazdin (Eds.), *Advances in Clinical Child Psychology,* Vol. 11, New York: Plenum Press.

Dishion, T.J., French, D.C. and Patterson, G.R., (1995), 'The Development and Ecology of Antisocial Behaviour'. In D. Cicchetti & D.J. Cohen (Eds.), *Developmental Psychopathology,* (Vol. 2: *Risk, Disorder and Adaptation).* New york: John Wiley & Sons.

Earls, F., (1994), 'Oppositional-defiant and Conduct Disorders'. In M. Rutter, E. Taylor & L. Hersov (Eds.), *Child and Adolescence Psychiatry: Modern Approaches.* 3rd Ed. London: Blackwell Scientific Publications.

Edelbrock, C., Rende, R., Plomin, R. and Thompson, L.A., (1995), 'A Twin Study of Competence and Problem Behaviour in Childhood and Early Adolescence'. *Journal of Child Psychology and Psychiatry,* 36, 775-785.

Elliot, D.S., Huizings, D. and Ageton, S.S., (1985),„*Explaining Delinquency and Drug Use.* Beverly Hills, CA: Sage.

Eyberg, S.M., (1992), 'Parent and Teacher Behaviour Inventories for the Assessment of Conduct Problem Behaviours in Children'. In L. Vandecreek, S Knapp & T.L. Jackson (Eds.). *Innovation in Clinical Practice: A Source Book (Vol. III).* Sarasota, FL: Professional Resource Exchange.

Farrington, D.P., (1995), 'The Development of Offending and Antisocial Behaviour from Childhood: Key Findings from the Cambridge Study in Delinquent Development'. *Journal of Child Psychology and Psychiatry,* 36, 929-964.

Fergussion, D.M., Lynskey, M.T. and Horwood, L.J., (1997), Attentional Difficulties in Middle Childhood and Psychosocial Outcomes in Young Adulthood'. *Journal of Child Psychology and Psychiatry,* 38, 633-644.

Fergusson, D.M. and Harwood, L.J., (1996), 'The Role of Adolescent Peer Affiliations in the Continuity Between Childhood Behavioural Adjustment and Juvenile Offending'. *Journal of Abnormal Child Psychology,* 24, 205-221.

Forehand, R., Wells, K.C. and Griest, D.L., (1980), 'An Examination of the Social Validity of a Parents Training Programme'. *Behaviour Therapy,* II, 488-502.

Forehand, R., Wierson, M., Frame, C.L., Kemptom, T. and Armistead, L., (1991), Juvenile Fire Setting: A Unique Syndrome or an Advanced Level of Antisocial Behaviour?' *Behaviour Research and Therapy,* 29, 125-128.

Foster, S.L. and Robin, A.L., (1997), 'Family Conflicts and Communication in Adolescence'. In E.J. Mash & L.G. Terdal (Eds.). *Assessment cf Childhood Disorders,* (3rd Ed.), New York: Guilford Press.

Frick, P.J., (1998), 'Conduct Disorders'. In T.H. Ollendick & Hersen, M. (Eds.), *Handbook of Child Psychopathology,* (3rd Ed.). New York: Plenum Press.

Frick, P.J., (1994), 'Family Dysfunction and the Disruptive Disorders: A Review of Recent Empirical Findings'. In T.H. Ollendick & Prinz, R.J. (Eds.), *Advances in Clinical Child Psychology.* Vol. 16, New York: Plenum Press.

Henggeler, S.W., Melton, G.B. and Smith, L.A., (1992), 'Family Preservation Using Multi Systemic Therapy: An Effective Alternative to Incarcerating Serious Juvenile Offenders'. *Journal of Counselling and Clinical Psychology,* 60, 953-961.

Hewitt, J.K., Silberg, J.L., Rutter, M., Simoff, E., Mayer, J.M., Maes, H., pickles, A., Neale, M.C., Loeber, R., Erickson, M.T., Kendler, C.A. and Eaves, L.J., (1997), 'Genetics and Developmental Psychopathology: I. Phenotypic Assessment in Virginia Twin Study of Adolescent Behavioural Development'. *Journal of Child Psychology and Psychiatry,* 38, 943-963.

Hinshaw, S.P., Lahey, B.B. and Hart, E.L., (1993), 'Issues of Taxonomy and Co Morbidity in the Development of Conduct Disorder'. *Development and Psychopathology,* 5, 31-49.

Kazdin, A.E., (1989a), 'Conduct and Oppositional Disorders'. In C.G. Last & M. Hersen (Eds.), *Handbook of Psychiatric Diagnosis.* New York: Wiley.

Kazdin, A.E., (1995a), *Conduct Disorders in Childhood and Adolescence* (2nd Ed.). Thousand Oaks, CA: Sage.

Kazdin, A.E., (1997), 'Practitioner Review: Psychosocial Treatments for Conduct Disorder in Children'. *Journal of Child Psychology and Psychiatry,* 38, 161-178.

Kazdin, A.E., (1993c), 'Treatment of Conduct Disorder: Progress and Directions in Psychotherapy Research'. *Developmental and Psychopathology,* 5, 277-310.

Kazdin, A.E., (1987), 'Treatment of Antisocial Behaviour in Children: Current Status and Future Directions'. *Psychological Bulletin,* 102, 187-203.

Kazdin, A.E., Siegal, T.C. and Bass, D., (1992), 'Cognitive Problem-solving Skills Training and Parent Management Training in the Treatment of Antisocial Behaviour in Children'. *Journal of Counselling and Clinical Psychology,* 60, 733-747.

Keenan, K. and Shaw, D., (1997), 'Developmental and Social Influences on Young Girls' Early Problem Behaviour'. *Psychological Bulletin,* 121, 95-113.

Loeber, R. and Keenan, K., (1994), 'Interaction Between Conduct Disorder and its Comorbid Conditions: Effects of Age and Gender'. *Clinical Psychology Review,*14, 497-523.

Loeber, R. and Stouthamer-Loeber, M., (1998), 'Development of Juvenile Aggression and Violence: Some Common Misconceptions and Controversies'. *American Psychologist,* 53, 242-259.

Maughan, B. and Rutter, M., (1998), 'Continuities and Discontinuities in Antisocial Behaviour from Childhood to Adulthood Life'. In T.H. Ollendick & R.J. Prinz (Eds.), *Advances in Clinical Child Psychology,* (Vol. 20). New York: Plenum Press.

Moffitt, T.E., (1993a), 'Adolescence-limited and Lifecourse-persistent Antisocial Behaviour: A Developmental Taxonomy'. *Psychological Review,* 100, 674-701.

Moffitt, T.E., (1993b), 'The Neuropsychology of Conduct Disorder'. *Development and Psychopathology,* 5, 135-152.

Newcomb, A.F., Bukowski, W.M. and Pattee, L., (1993), 'Children's Peer Relations: A Meta-analysis Review of Popular, Rejected, Neglected, Controversial and Average Sociometric Status'. *Psychological Bulletin,* 113, 99-128.

Olweus, D., (1979), 'Stability of Aggressive Reaction Patterns in Males: A Review'. *Psychological Bulletin,* 86, 852-875.

Parker, J.G. and Asher, S.R., (1987), 'Peer Relations and Later Personal Adjustment: Are Low-accepted Children at Risk?' *Psychological Bulletin,* 102, 357-389.

Patterson, G.R., De Baryshe, B.D. and Ramsey, E., (1989), 'A Developmental Perspective on Antisocial Behaviour'. *American Psychologist,* **44,** 329-335.

Patterson, G.R., Reid, J.B. and Dishion, T.J., (1992), 'Antisocial boys'. Eugene, OR: Castalia Publishing Company.

Quay, H.C., (1993), 'The Psychobiology of under Socialized Aggressive Conduct Disorder'. *A Theoretical Perspective Developmental and Psychopathology,* 5, 165-180.

Raine, A. and Venables, P.H., (1984), 'Tonic Heart Rate Level, Social Class and Antisocial Behaviour in Adolescents'. *Biological Psychology,* 18, 123-132.

Reynolds, C.R. and Kamphaus, R.W., (1992), *The Behaviour Assessment System for Children.* Circle Pines. MN: American Guidance Service.

Rusby, J.C., Esters, A. and Dishion T., (1991), *The Interpersonal Process Code* (IPC). Unpublished Manuscript, Oregon Social Learning Centre, Eugene.

Rutter, M., Silberg, J., O'Connor, T. and Simonoff, E., (1999), 'Genetics and Child Psychiatry: II Empirical Research Findings'. *Journal of Child Psychology and Psychiatry,* 40, 19-55.

Stanger, C., Achenbach, T.M. and Verhulst, F.C., (1997), 'Accelerated Longitudinal Comparisons of Aggressive Versus Delinquent Syndromes'. *Development and Psychopathology,* 9, 43-58.

Stanger, C., MacDonald, V.V., McConaughy, S.H. and Achenbach, T.M., (1996), 'Predictors of Cross Informant Syndromes Among Children and Youths Refereed for Mental Health Services'. *Journal of Abnormal Child Psychology,* 24, 597-614.

Webster-Stratton, C. and Spitzer, A., (1991), 'Development, Reliability and Validity of the Daily Telephone Discipline Interview'. *Behavioural Assessment*, 13, 221-239.

Wolf, L., Braukmann, C.J. and Ramp, K.A., (1987), 'Serious Delinquent Behaviour as Part of a Significantly Handicapping Condition: Cures and Supportive Environments'. *Journal of Applied behaviour Analysis*, 20, 347-359.

9

Attention Deficit Hyperactivity Disorder

OBJECTIVES

This chapter delves into the historical background of Attention Deficit Hyperactivity Disorder. It presents the classification and diagnosis of ADHD. It analyses the clinical as well as associated characteristics of ADHD. Theoretical perspectives on ADHD are presented. The co-occurring disorders of ADHD are explained. Further, different factors associated with ADHD are described. Early assessment procedures along with treatment measures are analysed. Finally, the chapter stresses the need for multimodal treatment. After reading this chapter, the readers must be able to:

(i) Give the historical background of ADHD;

(ii) Present the classification of ADHD;

(iii) Define the clinical and associated characteristics of ADHD;

(iv) Understand the various theoretical perspectives on ADHD;

(v) Know about the co-occurring disorders of ADHD;

(vi) Explain the different factors causing ADHD;

(vii) Present the different assessment of procedures;

(viii) Describe the treatment measures for ADHD; and

(ix) Realise the need for multimodel treatments.

INTRODUCTION

There are children who never sit still. They are always into something or the other but they never prolong in a task. They don't pay attention to what others say. They never think before they act. In school, they are often up and out of their seats in a fraction of a second. They do not do well in school and often lag behind their peers. Such problems give concern for parents and teachers. The children who exhibit these symptoms of inattention and impulsivity are diagnosed as Attention Deficit Hyperactivity Disordered (ADHD) children. Earlier, it was widely referred to as 'hyperactivity' or 'attention deficit disorder'. These terms reflect the changing conceptualizations of the disorder.

HISTORICAL BACKGROUND OF ADHD

The deviance of behaviour, which is at present termed 'Attention Deficit Hyperactivity Disorder', has travelled a long road of conceptualization (Barkley, 1996). In the distant past, an English physician called George Still described a group of boys with a 'defect in moral control' as inattentive, impulsive, overactive, lawless and aggressive. In the United States, between 1917 and 1918, an encephalitis epidemic aroused interest in the individuals who suffered a sort of brain infection and were left with similar attributes. Similar clinical picture was also noted in children who had suffered head injury, birth trauma, and exposure to excessive infections and toxins.

Earlier conceptualizations gave emphasis to the over activity or motor restlessness of these children. Hence the terms 'hyperkinesis' and 'hyperkinetic syndrome' were variously applied (Barkley, 1989). At present we use the term 'hyperactivity' to denote the excessive motor activity. Yet several other behavioural problems were recognized as being associated with hyperactivity. They are attention deficit and impulsivity. Gradually, attention deficits took central role and hyperactivity was downgraded in importance. This shift in conceptualization was reflected in DSM–III (1980) classification, which recognized attention deficit disorder with hyperactivity (ADDH) or without hyperactivity. In DSM-III-R (1987), the disorder was relabelled 'Attention Deficit Hyperactive Disorder' (ADHD). The category of attention deficit with out hyperactivity was dropped. Children were diagnosed on the basis of displaying eight of fourteen behaviours, which could be different mixes of inattention, hyperactivity and impulsivity. That is, ADHD was viewed as unidimensional, so that any mix of symptoms met the criteria. Along with the changing criteria, ideas about etiology also shifted and included brain damage, minimal brain damage and to a lesser extent, environmental influences.

CLASSIFICATION AND DIAGNOSIS OF ADHD

Due to the problem in defining the relationship among inattention, hyperactivity and impulsivity as to whether view them as part of a single dimension or co-occurring independent dimensions, DSM–IV (1994) reconceptualized the disorder. According to the DSM – IV classification, ADHD is now viewed as having two factors, inattention and hyperactivity/impulsivity. These two factors compose three subtypes: (i) Prodominantly Inattentive, (ii) Predominantly Hyperactive/Impulsive and (iii) a Combined Type. The major symptoms for ADHD and the subtypes as derived by DSM–IV are given below:

DSM–IV Symptoms of ADHD

(A) Symptoms of Inattention

- Fails to attend to details or makes careless mistakes in schoolwork or other activities
- Has difficulty in sustaining attention
- Does not seem to listen when spoken to
- Does not follow through on instructions or duties
- Has difficulty organizing tasks and activities
- Avoids, dislikes tasks requiring sustained mental effort
- Often loses things necessary for tasks or activities
- Is distracted by extraneous stimuli
- Is forgetful in daily activities

(B) Symptoms of Hyperactivity–Impulsivity, Hyperactivity

- Fidgets with hands or feet squirm
- Leaves seat appropriately
- Runs about or claims inappropriately (in adolescents or adults, may only be feelings of restlessness)
- Has difficulty playing quietly or in quiet activities
- Is often 'on the go' as if 'driven by motor'
- Talks incessantly

(C) Impulsivity

- Blurts out answers before questions are completed
- Has difficulty awaiting turn
- Interrupts or intrudes on others

Requirements for Diagnosis

ADHD Predominantly Inattentive Type: Six or more symptoms of A

ADHD Predominantly Hyperactive–Impulsive Type: more symptoms of B

ADHD Combined Type: Six or more symptoms of both A and B

Diagnosis of ADHD demands onset before age seven and the display of symptoms for at least six months. Since the criterion behaviours appear to some degree in normal children also and may vary with developmental level, a diagnosis is given only when symptoms are at odds with developmental level. In addition, symptoms must be pervasive, in the sense, they must occur at least in two settings (for example, home and school).

CLINICAL CHARACTERISTICS OF ADHD

Children with ADHD are often said to exhibit the characteristics, such as in attentiveness, distraction, lack of sustained attention, hyperactivity and impulsivity.

Inattentiveness

Attention problems are noted in various ways among children with ADHD. Compared with most of their peers, the ADHD children skip rapidly from one activity to another. They do not pay attention to what is said to them. They are easily distracted because they do not concentrate. They do not stick to a given task. They often daydream and lose things. Research findings of Barkley (1998a) reveal that they pay less attention to their work than learning disabled children. There are also reports about their behaviour that they appear to be unable to concentrate in certain situations but in some other situations they are sitting for hours together playing a game, drawing or building with blocks. This implies that their attention can be focused or sustained when they are interested or motivated.

The children with ADHD were tested on two other elements of attention: selective attention and sustained attention. 'Selective attention' refers to the ability to attend to relevant environmental stimuli or not to be distracted by irrelevant stimuli. The findings of Leung and Connolly (1996) indicate that the introduction of irrelevant stimuli does distract children with ADHD. For example, Milich and Lorch (1994) found that the boys with ADHD were more distracted from television watching by the presence of toys than the normal boys. In addition, Douglas (1983) reported that distraction is more likely when the tasks are boring, distasteful or difficult and when the irrelevant stimuli are novel or salient.

Similarly, 'sustained attention' refers to paying attention to a task over a period of time. The findings of Losier, McGrath and Klien (1996) and that of Taylor (1995) reveal that the children with ADHD are deficient in sustained attention. When the length of the given task increases, a deficit in sustained attention would lead to a worsening of performance.

Hyperactivity

Children with ADHD are described as always on the run, restless, fidgety and unable to sit still. They squirm, wiggle, tap their fingers and elbow their classmates (Greehill, 1991). Very often, they have minor mishaps, such as spilling drinks, knocking over objects as well as more serious accidents that result in bodily harm. They are excessively energetic, haphazard, disorganized and lacking in goals. They also appear to have difficulty in regulating their actions according to the wishes of others or to the demands of the particular situation. The devices, such as actometers and pedometers are helpful in measuring movement, can be used to demonstrating the excessive movement of children with ADHD.

Impulsivity

Impulsivity refers to the deficiency in inhibiting behaviour, which appears as 'acting without thinking'. The children with ADHD may jump in and try to solve a problem before figuring out the first step, heedlessly engage in dangerous behaviours, cut in line in front of others or take shortcuts when performing a task. Games that require patience or restraint are not well negotiated and they may also interrupt others or blurt out socially inappropriate or hurtful verbalizations. In short, they are unable to hold back, inhibit and control behaviour and their behaviours often lead others to judge them as careless, irresponsible, immature, lazy or rude. The findings of Oosterlaan, Logan and Sergeant (1998) reveal that inhibition of motor response is an important characteristic of children with ADHD. Although the children diagnosed as ADHD are heterogeneous with regard to symptoms, the most frequently seen type is combination of inattention, hyperactivity and impulsiveness.

ASSOCIATED CHARACTERISTICS OF ADHD

In addition to the above mentioned clinical characteristics, the children with ADHD are also exhibiting their difficulties in diverse areas of functioning and such behaviours are known as 'associated characteristics'. Particularly, the children with ADHD are said to have intellectual impairment, academic problems, cognitive deficits and social and conduct problems.

(i) Intellectual Impairment

The children with ADHD perform slightly lower on general intelligence tests than normal children (Anastopoulos and Barkley, 1992). Sonuga-Barke et al. (1994) found that intellectual impairment has been linked to hyperactivity in children as young as three years of age. It is also established that the children with ADHD are at risk for specific learning disabilities. They have impairments specifically in reading, mathematics, spelling and other academic areas, which are due to lowered general intelligence.

(ii) Academic Problems

Children with ADHD often do not appear to achieve what they seem capable of learning. Academic failure is also striking among youth with ADHD. It is evidenced by low achievement test scores, school grades, failure to get promoted in school and placement in special education classes (Dulcan, 1989). Lahey et al. (1998) reported that academic problems may be obvious in the first few years of schooling.

(iii) Deficit Cognitive Executive Functioning

Various basic cognitive deficits are always associated with ADHD. For example, the children with ADHD were deficit in verbal memory and visual-spatial abilities. Tannock (1998) also found evidence for deficits in executive functions that involve planning, organizing actions, inhibiting responses, mentally representing a task, switching strategies and self-regulation.

(iv) Social and Conduct Problems

A high percentage of cases of ADHD is reported to have social difficulties. They are talkative and socially busy; they often initiate social exchanges; they tend to be louder, faster and more forceful than their peers. Their vigour, intensity and emotionality is out of keeping with the social situation. Their behaviour is intractable, disruptive, noncompliant and disagreeable. Their annoying actions, though they may seem unintentional, get into trouble and disrupt the normal flow of social interaction. Some children with ADHD are highly aggressive. Sometime they have social goals that could be expected to create problems. For example, as reported by Melnick and Hinshaw (1996), they may prefer fun and trouble even at the expense of breaking rules.

Children with ADHD have trouble in making and keeping friends. They are often judged negatively. Their peers tend to dislike and reject them (Flicek, 1992). Rejection and dislike apply mostly to the children who are impulsive and hyperactive, whereas, the children with attention problems tend to be ignored or neglected (Hinshaw, 1998). Teachers associate all types of the children with ADHD with lowered prosocial and cooperative behaviours. They associate hyperactivity or impulsivity with disruptive and less self-controlled behaviours (Lahey et al., 1998). Hence they tend to become more directive and controlling towards the children with ADHD.

ADHD also takes a toll on family well being and interaction. The parents of children with ADHD become excessively directive and intrusive (Barkley, 1998a). Particularly, mothers become negative, quarrelsome, and unrewarding. Broader indices of family malfunctioning are also associated with ADHD. Excessive parenting stress, lowered sense of parenting competence, increased alcohol use, increase marital conflict and separation and divorce are the resultant problems especially when the child is associated with oppositional and serious conduct problems.

The children with ADHD, due to the hyperactivity/ impulsivity, suffer more accidental injury (Szartmari et al., 1989). Among individuals who experience accidents such as bicycle misfortunes, a greater number appears to be hyperactive, impulsive or defiant. Older youth with ADHD are at greater risk for automobile accidents and for driving offences such as speeding, overtaking and so on.

Hinshaw (1998) studied ADHD in terms of general adaptiveness. He found deficiencies in self-care and independence in children with ADHD, though they have normal intelligence. The implication behind this finding is that many children with ADHD seem capable of more mature behaviour but they do not enact it. Hence they require greater monitoring from parents and others.

THEORETICAL PERSPECTIVES ON ADHD

Many theoretical propositions try to conceptualize the problem of ADHD. The most important ones are motivational theories and theories of self-regulation and inhibition.

Motivational Theories

These theories emphasize that children with ADHD require especially strong or salient reinforcers. The children with ADHD seem to prefer immediate small reward to delayed larger reward. It has been suggested that ADHD involves lowered sensitivity to reinforcement, so that rewards must be increased or made more salient in some way to control the child's behaviour (Barkley, 1990). This leads to the reasoning that weak or inconsistent reinforcement could be the basis for the child's failure to pay attention, persist on tasks or comply with others' requests or directives. Similarly, Sonuga-Barke (1994) suggested that motivation regarding delay might explain many behaviours that characterize ADHD. According to him, the child has an aversion to delay and thus acts rapidly to avoid delay in specific situations and hence adopts an impulsive style of behaviour.

Theories of Self-Regulation and Inhibition

Douglas (1998) used theory of self-regulation, which is a concept that encompasses higher-order information processing, to explain facets of the hyperactivity, impulsivity and inattention of ADHD. She proposed that central to self-regulation are deficits in inhibition, problems in modulating arousal, and atypical responses to the consequences of behaviour. These aspects of behaviour appear in many accounts of ADHD.

Quay based his conceptualization of ADHD on Gray's neurobiological model of brain functioning (Oosterlaan et al., 1998). This model proposes that two brains systems (Behavioural Inhibition System – BIS and Behavioural Activation System – BAS) work in opposition to each other. The BIS is related to anxiety and tends to inhibit behaviour in situations that are novel, fear eliciting or characterized by punishment or non-reward. On the other hand, BAS is sensitive to rewards and activates responding in the presence of reinforcement. Quay hypothesized that Behavioural Activation System is under active in ADHD children and as a result they are deficient in behavioural inhibition.

Barkley's (1998 a) model of ADHD broadly links behavioural inhibition to executive functions of self-regulation.

Barkley's Model of ADHD

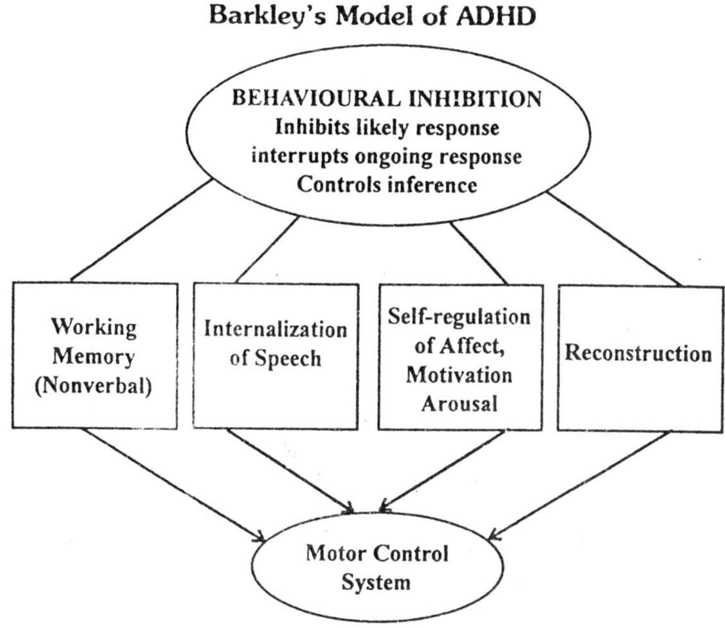

According to Barkley, behavioural inhibition is central and it is critical to the performance of other executive functions. These other executive functions, in turn, influence the motor control of behaviour. Behavioural inhibition consists of three abilities, namely, ability to inhibit likely responses from occurring in the situation, the ability to inhibit on going responses and the ability to protect the executive functions against interference from other events so that they can operate. In these ways, behavioural inhibition facilitates the workings of the executive functions. Barkley also proposes four executive functions (working memory, internalization of speech, self-regulation of affect and motivation and reconstitution), which provide the means for the individual to self-regulate his/her behaviour. When inhibition is disordered, self-regulation is adversely affected.

ADHD AND CO-OCCURRING DISORDERS

ADHD coexists with other diagnosable behaviour disorders. Co-occurrence of ADHD and LD is widely reported (Faraone, Biedernian and Kiely, 1996). From clinical point of view, it is important to know whether early ADHD leads to LD or vice versa, since such knowledge could lead to better prevention or intervention.

Children with ADHD frequently have difficulties in social interaction. They are frequently reported as noncompliant, oppositional, annoying and argumentative, in short, the behaviours diagnosed as Oppositional Defiant Disorder (ODD). Further, ODD may lead to conduct disorder (CD), which involves aggression, deceit and violations of rules.

ADHD is more strongly associated with cognitive impairment and neuro developmental abnormalities. Children with ADHD, with the co-occurrence of ODD and CD problems, show greater levels of aggression, lying, cheating and stealing (Jensen, Martin and Cantwell, 1997). Loeber et al. (1995) also suggested that hyperactivity and impulsivity of ADHD precede and predict conduct disorder symptoms but that the opposite is not true. Barkley (1998a) also reported that about 25 per cent of youth with ADHD also have anxiety disorders. Along with the disruptions of ADHD, they experience the fears, worries and other internalizing problems of anxiety. The Co-occurrence of ADHD and depression was also reported by Biederman et al. (1996)

FACTORS ASSOCIATED WITH ADHD

Several factors are reported to be contributing to ADHD. The most important factors are brain dysfunction and brain damage, the biochemistry of the brain, genetic factors, prenatal and postnatal birth complications, diet, environmental factors and psychosocial factors.

(i) Brain Dysfunction and Brain Damage

In a small percentage of cases, (perhaps 5 per cent), brain damage from vehicle accidents, falls and other trauma is related to symptoms of ADHD (Max et al., 1998). Semrud-Clikeman et al. (1994) reported that damage to the frontal lobe has associations with the symptoms of ADHD. Further, various measures point to brain abnormalities in ADHD. Although obvious structural damage is usually not evident, more subtle anamolies have emerged. For example, the corpus callosum (fibers by which the two hemispheres communicate with each other) and the cerebellum (involved in motor coordination and certain kinds of memory) are sometimes smaller than average (Tannock, 1998). The most consistent abnormality is the smaller than average size of the right frontal area, the caudate nucleus and the globus pallidus. In some cases, these areas are equal in size on both sides of the brain, in contrast to the normal brain, which is asymmetrical, the right side being somewhat larger than the left. Moreover, abnormality of these brain areas is associated with poor response inhibition in children with ADHD (Casey et al., 1997).

Brain scans show that children with ADHD have decreased blood flow and decreased glucose utilization, which are signs of underactivity. In addition, children with hyperactivity show abnormal electrophysiological responding (Hechtman, 1991). Measures of electrical activity such as heart rate and skin conductance indicate under arousal (Barkley, 1998a).

(ii) The Biochemistry of the Brain

The biochemistry of the brain also plays a role in ADHD. Most emphasis has been given to nor-epinephrine, dopamine and serotonin (Taylor, 1994). Particularly the neurotransmitters dopamine and nor epinephrine are considered important in the functioning of the frontal- striatal and related areas of the brain (Anastopoulos and Barkley, 1992). Pliszka, McCracken and Mass (1996) suggested that dopamine, nor-epinephrine and epinephrine all play an intricate role in ADHD, which is hypothesized to involve the frontal and parietal lobes and several other brain structures.

(iii) Genetic Factors

Numerous studies have shown that the families of children with ADHD have higher rates of psychopathology, including ADHD (Barkley, 1998 and Tannock, 1998). Many studies also provide evidence of inheritance and suggest that both inattention and hyperactivity/ impulsivity are heritable. The mode of inheritance is not established (Neuman et al., 1999). Some evidence exists for a single gene with complex dominant transmission.

(iv) Prenatal and Post-natal Complications

There is supportive evidence for the idea that ADHD is traceable to pregnancy and birth complications. Studies on children born prematurely and of very low birth weight indicate risk for attention problems and hyperactivity/ impulsiveness (Sykes et al., 1997). Prenatal maternal alcohol use was linked to attention deficits and difficulties in organizing tasks (Streissguth et al., 1995). Evidences also occur to prove that pregnancy and birth complications do account for some cases of ADHD.

(v) Dietary Effects on ADHD

A common belief that diet causes hyperactivity is prevalent among the general public. Anecdotal reports of the parents of clinic and non-clinic children indicate their belief that sugar intake causes their offspring to become hyperactive and disorganized. Correlational studies like that of Prinz and Riddle (1986) have shown a link between sugar consumption and behaviours that characterize ADHD. In 1975, Feingold, a physician researcher interested in allergies, published a book "Why your child is hyperactive?" which inspired investigation into dietary effects on hyperactivity. He asserted that food containing artificial dyes and flavours, certain preservatives and naturally occurring salicylates (eg. in apricots, prunes, tomatoes, cucumbers) was related to hyperactivity. He claimed that 25 to 50 per cent of hyperactive-learning disabled children responded favourably to diet that eliminated these substances (Harley and Matthews, 1980). On the other hand, it was claimed that when children on diet ingested a prohibited food, hyperactivity occurred dramatically and persisted for two or three days. Feingold's claims were also challenged and refused by many researchers like Conners (1980). The overall evidence suggests that diet does not play a strong role in the etiology of ADHD but may affect a small number of children, most likely those who are intolerant to certain foods (Richters et al., 1995 and Taylor, 1994).

(vi) Environmental Factors

Many environmental factors aggravate the symptoms of ADHD. Of these, exposure to lead is dangerous to humans and high levels of lead have been associated with serious deficits in biological functioning, cognition and behaviour (Tesman and Hills, 1994). Furthermore, low- levels of exposure over long periods of time have also adverse effects on children. Exposure to lead can come from lead-based paints, automobile emissions, leaded crystal, ceramic dishes and solder on old copper pipes. Many studies have found significant but small links between lead levels and attention and activity levels (Fergusson, Horwood and Lynskey, 1989). Barkley (1998a) reported that no more than 4 per cent of the variance in ADHD symptoms can be attributed to lead in children with high lead levels and most children with ADHD do not have high levels of lead.

(vii) Psychosocial Factors

Though the psychosocial factors are not considered primary in he eticlogy of ADHD, they do play a role. An association of ADHD behaviours with adverse family variables, such as parental malaise, marital discord, coldness to the child and criticism of the child, was established by Goodman and Stevenson (1989). Similarly Stormont-Spurgin and Zentall (1995) found a link with family adversities, such as family dysfunction, single parenting and urban status. An unfavourable mother-child relationship also predicted stability of the problems. Hechtman (1991) suggested that the controlling, intrusive parental style that is associated with ADHD may worsen the child's behaviour.

It is also possible that teacher behaviours might play a role by influencing a child's attentiveness and reflectivity. Classroom organization and the structuring of activities do have influence on attentiveness, especially for children predisposed to ADHD behaviours. Teacher's perception and tolerance of student behaviour may influence daily social interactions. Many researchers believe that parents or teachers are a primary cause of ADHD. In the opinion of Barkley (1996) psychosocial variables, particularly family factors, provide the critical context within which the disorder develops. The psychosocial variables, no doubt, shape the nature and the severity of the disorders as well as maintain them over a period of time. This is particularly true for cases that involve the combination of ADHD and oppositional/ conduct disorders.

ASSESSMENT OF ADHD

ADHD is conceptualized as a bio psychosocial disorder and hence assessment of ADHD must be broad based and include various procedures that are capable of evaluating the primary and secondary manifestations of the disorder, family functioning and biological functioning. Moreover, ADHD is situationally specific in nature at times, evaluation should include different settings, such as home and school. In furtherance, ADHD has high rates of co-occurrence with other behavioural disorders, assessment requires careful distinctions. The widely used assessment tools for ADHD are interviews, rating scales, direct observation and other procedures.

(i) Interviews

In most case of ADHD, parents are the chief source of information. Hence, standard, structured or semi-structured interviews can be used. Information with regard to the child's as well as the family's history, the school, the child's behavioural problems and strengths should be obtained through interviews. Details about the situations identified as troublesome should also be obtained through interviews.

The nature and length of the interview depend on the age and the ability of the person. With younger children, the interview may simply be a time for getting acquainted, establishing rapport and observing the child's appearance and behaviour. Observations of behaviour must be interpreted cautiously; because children with ADHD are known to act more appropriately during office visits than they are reported to act in other settings.

Next to parent, children spend most of the time with teachers and hence teachers can directly address difficulties in the school setting. Teacher interviews are of much value and the focus of teacher interview should be on learning and academic problems as well as on peer interactions. In addition, information can be obtained about parent- school interaction and cooperation as well as school services.[4]

(ii) Rating Scales

Parent and teacher rating scales and checklists are other popular tools assessing ADHD and they provide much information with relatively little time and effort. Rating scales are useful not only to identify ADHD but also its co-occurrence with other disorders. Both broadband and narrow band-rating scales are available. The broadband scales are helpful in determining whether the behaviour is deviant from the norm and different from behaviours displayed by other diagnostic groups. The narrowband scales are useful in assessing specific aspects of ADHD, such as school behaviour. For several of the instruments, both parent and teacher versions are available. There are also self-report versions, which are particularly useful for adolescents.

The Conners parent and teacher scales (Conners et al., 1998a) are widely employed for initial screening. They are easy to use and there is good evidence for their validity (Edolbrock and Rancurello, 1985). Moreover, both scales have been revised recently.

(iii) Direct Observations

Direct observations are extremely useful in assessing ADHD. But they are time-consuming and expensive. Observations need to focus on interpersonal and school functioning (Rapport, 1993). In home, compliance and stimulus-consequence patterns are important. In the school, social interaction is equally important, along with behaviours such as 'out of seat', aggression, disruption and inattention.

(iv) Other Procedures

Additional assessment methods are also necessary. They include standardized tests of intelligence, academic achievement and adaptive behaviour. Procedures to evaluate inattention and impulsivity have also been developed. Continuous performances Test (CPT) to assess inattention and Matching Familiar Figure Test (MFFT) and Stop-Signal task (Schachar and Logan, 1990) to assess impulsivity are the best examples. However, as Barkley (1998a) commented, their use in assessment is limited.

Since the family plays a role in the developmental course and maintenance of ADHD, questionnaires that describe family functioning are of immense value. Measures of peer relations are also useful.

In some cases, biological assessment is also needed. It includes a medical/developmental history and a medical examination that encompasses an EEG or brain scan. Medical evaluation does not help to identify ADHD. But is worthwhile when biological factors are highly suspected. In such cases, it provides information potentially useful in understanding the disorder and also for offering treatment.

TREATMENT OF ADHD

Various treatments have been applied to ADHD. They are individual counselling, parent training, academic remediation, cognitive therapy, social skills training and insight therapies (Whalen and Henker, 1998). Pharmacological medication and behavioural interventions are the best choice.

(i) Pharmacological Treatment

Many pharmacological agents like stimulant, antidepressant and anticonvulsant drugs have been used for ADHD. The most commonly used medications are given below:

Most Common Medication for ADHD

Stimulants: Medications of first choice

- Ritalin (Methylphenidate)
- Dexedrin (Dextroamphetamine)
- Cylert (Pemoline)
- Adderall (combined Amphetamine and Dextroamphetamine)

Antidepressants: First Alternative Choice

- Tricyclics (eg. Desipramine, Imipramine)
- Other antidepressants

Less-Used Medications

- Anticonvulsants
- Antihypertensives
- Antipsychotics.

An estimated 75 per cent of stimulant medicated children show increased attention and reduced impulsivity and activity level, both in the laboratory and in the structured, natural environments that elicit ADHD behaviours (Whalen and Henker, 1998). Stimulant medications can also reduce co-occurring aggressive, noncompliant, oppositional behaviours (Hinshaw et al., 1989). In addition, parents and teachers must interact more positively and use fewer controlling behaviours with ADHD children, who are benefiting from medications (Gadow and Pomeroy, 1991).

Despite the benefits of stimulant medication, several concerns have been expressed. Children under the age of four years may benefit the least and also suffer more adverse side effects (Barkley, 1990). When ADHD combines with significant problems in anxiety or depression, response to stimulant medication is likely to be poor, and response to antidepressants to be more favourable. Even with children who benefit, evidence is lacking for long-lasting efficacy (DuPaul et al., 1998). Moreover, many stimulants induce adverse biological side effects. Most common side effects are insomnia, anorexia, stomach pain, headache, irritability, rashes and involuntary muscle movement (DuPaul et al., 1998). Suppression of growth is also reported. Monitoring is always essential, as a minority of children cannot tolerate stimulants at all. Professionals who recognize the benefits of stimulants also sound cautions against the misuse or overuse of stimulants.

(ii) Behavioural Interventions

Since the pharmacological treatments have short-term success and cause intolerable side effects, behavioural interventions are often recommended to treat ADHD. Behavioural interventions are applied to a wide range of problems. They emphasize the behaviour modification towards controlling attention and impulsivity, rule adherence, enhanced academic effort and improved social interaction. Powerful salient external reinforcers are often needed over long periods of time, as suggested by Barkley (1998b). Reinforcement should either be positive or negative in accordance with the occurring behaviour.

Behavioural interventions are generally conducted in special settings, such as special classrooms or in the clinic. More benefit is expected from interventions that are offered in 'real world' settings. Since the treatments that are conducted in the child's natural environments proved to be effective, efforts should be taken to offer behavioural interventions in the home or school, or with parents or teachers who work directly with the child.

Dealing with a child with ADHD is stressful for families. Parents tend to become worn down and overly directive. They may even view themselves as lacking in normal skills of parenting (Anastopoulos, Smith and Wien, 1998). Further, parents have obvious influence on their children. These aspects make families a natural focus of interventions and parent training a major goal of interventions. Since ADHD involves a deficit in self-regulation and frequently oppositional defiant behaviour, the parent-training programmes should emphasize the management non-compliance and defiance in children. Research data produced by Anastopoulos et al. (1998) suggest that parent interventions can result in improvement of children's functioning of self-esteem with regard to parenting.

School-based behavioural intervention programmes are effective in producing improvements with regard to attention, disruptive behaviour, and academic performance. Generally, the teacher administers the school-based interventions. The procedures include token reinforcement, punishment and contingency contracting. In the last procedure, the child and the teacher sign a written agreement specifying how the child will behave and the contingencies that will accrue. Teachers are given training and consultation to conduct these programmes. In furtherance, parents and teachers can work together to improve the child's behaviour in the classroom.

Interventions aiming at cognitive-behavioural treatment have also been successful. They focus on enhancing self-control and self-regulation, which would seem a natural target in treating ADHD. Self-Control can also increase generalization and maintenance of appropriate behaviour. Several techniques have been employed to enhance self-regulation. Some of them are self- monitoring, self-instruction, self-statements and self-guidance. Social- skill training is another cognitive- behavioural intervention. It is highly effective, when it is combined with intensive behaviour treatments.

NEED FOR MULTIMODEL TREATMENTS

Pharmacological medications are effective in bringing about short-term improvements in ADHD. They have their own drawbacks. Similarly, behavioural interventions, though they are successful, pose an intense demand for caretakers. No one approach offers long-term effects or complete in itself. Hence the at least thrive is for the combination of the two treatments as well as for multimodal interventions that would include a wider range of therapies. Ialongo and colleagues (1993) indicated that a combined approach was important in maintaining treatment benefits over time. Similarly Statterfield (1994) reported the supremacy of multimodal treatment employed for serious antisocial behaviour in boys with ADHD.

SUMMARY

The children who exhibit the symptoms of inattention and impulsivity are diagnosed as Attention Deficit Hyperactivity Disordered children. ADHD has travelled a long road of conceptualization. Earlier conceptualization gave emphasis to the over activity and hence the terms 'hyperkinesis' and 'hyper kinetic syndrome' were used. Later, the focus was shifted to inattention. DSM-IV views ADHD as having two factors: inattention and hyperactivity or impulsivity. According DSM-IV classification, there are three subtypes of ADHD: (i) Predominantly Inattentive; (ii) Predominantly Hyperactive/ Impulsive and (iii) a Combined Type.

Children with ADHD are said to exhibit the characteristics, such as inattentiveness, distraction, lack of sustained attention, hyperactivity and impulsivity. Other associated characteristics of ADHD children are intellectual impairment, academic problems, deficit cognitive executive functioning, and social and conduct problems.

Many theoretical propositions try to conceptualize the problem of ADHD. Of which, motivational theories and theories of self-regulation and inhibition are very important. The motivational theories emphasize that children with ADHD require especially strong reinforcers. Theories of self-regulation and inhibition lay emphasis on behavioural inhibition to executive functions of self-regulation.

ADHD coexists with other diagnosable behaviour disorders such as learning difficulties, non-compliance, ODD and CD. It is also associated with cognitive impairment and neuro-developmental abnormalities. Co morbid conditions of anxiety disorder and depression with ADHD are also reported.

Several factors are said to contribute to ADHD. They are brain dysfunction and brain damage, the biochemistry of the brain, genetic factors, prenatal and post-natal complications, diet, environment and psychosocial factors.

ADHD is conceptualized as a bio-psychosocial disorder and hence assessment of ADHD must be broad based and include various procedures that are capable of evaluating the primary and secondary manifestations of the disorder. The widely used assessment tools for ADHD are interviews, rating scales, direct observation and other procedures such as standardized tests of intelligence, Continuous Performance Test, Matching Familiar Figure Test and Stop-signal task. In some cases, biological assessment is also needed.

Various treatments have been applied to ADHD. Individual counselling, parent training, academic remediation, cognitive therapy, social skills training and insight therapies are often recommended for treating ADHD. In practice, pharmacological medication and behavioural interventions are the best choice.

Pharmacological treatment includes the use of stimulations, antidepressants and anti-convulsants. Pharmacological medication has many adverse biological side effects and they are effective in bringing about only short-term improvements in ADHD. Hence Behavioural Interventions are used alternatively to treat ADHD. They emphasize behaviour modification towards controlling attention, impulsivity and improved social interaction. They are generally conducted in special settings. More benefits are expected from interventions that are offered in 'real world' settings. Further, they should also aim at modifying the behaviour of parents, peers and other adults who are interested in the child. The latest thrive is for the combination of the two treatments as well as for multimodal interventions that would include a wide range of therapies.

REFERENCES

Anastopoulos, A.D. and Barkley, R.A., (1992), 'Attention Deficit Hyperactivity Disorder'. In C.E. Walker & M.C. Roberts (Eds.), *Handbook of Clinical Child Psychopathology,* NY: John Wiley.

Anastopoulos, A.D., Smith, J.M. and Wein, E.E., (1998), 'Counselling and Training Parents'. In R.A.Barkley, *Attention Deficit Hyperactivity Disorder,* New York :Guilford Press.

Barkley, R.A., (1996), 'Attention-deficit/Hyperactivity Disorder'. In E.J. Mash & R.A. Barkley (Eds.), *Child Psychopathology,* New York: Guilford Press.

Barkley, R.A., (1989), 'Attention-deficit/Hyperactivity Disorder'. In E.J. Mash & R.A. Barkley (Eds.), *Treatment of Childhood Disorders,* New York: Guilford Press.

Barkley, R.A., (1998a), *Attention-deficit/Hyperactivity Disorder.* New York: Guilford Press.

Barkley, R.A., (1990), 'Attention-deficit Hyperactivity Disorder'. New York: Guilford.

Biederman, J., Faraone, S.V., Milberger, S., Jetton, J.G., Chen, L., Mick. E., Greene, R.W. and Russell, R.L., (1996), 'Is Childhood Oppositional Defiant Disorder a Precursor to Adolescent Conduct Disorder? Findings from a Four-year Follow-up Study of Children with ADHD'. *Journal of the American Academy of Child and Adolescent Psychiatry,* 35, 1193-1204.

Casey, B.J., Castellanos, F.X., Giedd, J.N., Marsh, W.L., Hamburger, S.D., Schubert, A.B., Vauss, Y.C., Vaituzis, A.C., Dickstein, D.P., Sarfatti. S.E. and Rapport, J.L., (1997), 'Implication of Right Frontostriatal Circuitry in Response Inhibition and Attention-deficit/Hyperactivity Disorder'. *Journal of the American Academy of Child and Adolescent Psychiatry,* 36, 374-383.

Conners, C.K., (1980), 'Artificial Colours in the Diet and Disruptive Behaviour'. In R.M. Knights & D.J. Bakker (Eds.), *Treatment of Hyperactivity and Learning Disabled Children.* Baltimore: University Park Press.

Conners, C.K., Siltarenios, G., Parker, J.D.A. and Epstein, J.N., (1998a), 'Revision and Restandardization of the Conners Teacher Rating Scale (CTRS-R): Factor Structure, Reliability, and Criterion Validity'. *Journal of Abnormal Child Psychology,* 26, 279-291.

Douglas, V.I., (1983), 'Attentional and Cognitive Problems'. In M. Rutter (Ed.), *Developmental Neuropsychiatry.* New York: Guilford.

Douglas, V.I., (1988), 'Cognitive Deficits in Children with Attention Deficit Disorder with Hyperactivity'. In L.M. Bloomingdale & J. Sergeant (Eds.), Attention Deficit Disorder: Criteria, Cognition, Intervention. Elmsford, New York: Pergamon Press.

DSM-III, (1980), *Diagnostic and Statistical Manual of Mental Disorders* (3rd Edition). Washington, D.C. American Psychiatric Association.

DSM-III R, (1987), *Diagnostic and Statistical Manual of Mental Disorders* (3rd Edition, Revised). Washington, D.C. American Psychiatric Association.

DSM-IV, (1994), *Diagnostic and Statistical Manual of Mental Disorders* (4th Edition). Washington, D.C. American Psychiatric Association.

Du Paul, G.J., Barkley, R.A. and Connor, D.F., (1998), 'Stimulants'. In R.A. Barkley (Ed.), *Attention Deficit Hyperactivity Disorder.* Guilford Press.

Dulcan, M.K., (1989), 'Attention Deficit Disorders'. In C.G. Last & M. Hersen (Eds.), *Handbook of Child Psychiatric Diagnosis,* New York: Wiley.

Edelbrock, C. and Rancurello, M.D., (1985), 'Childhood Hyperactivity: An Overview of Rating Scales and their Applications'. *Clinical Psychology Review, 5, 429-445.*

Faraone, S.V., Biederman, J. and Kiely, K., (1996), 'Cognitive Functioning, Learning Disability and School Failure in Attention Deficit Hyperactivity Disorder: A Family Study Perspective'. In J.H. Beitchman, J. Cohen, M.M. Konstantareas & R. Tannock (Eds.), *Language, Learning and Behaviour Disorders.* New York: Cambridge University Press.

Feingold, B.F., (1975), 'Interdependence as a Working Concept'. In D. Mpoxon (Ed.), *Managing Criminal Justice,* pp. 8-17, London: HMSO.

Fergusson, D.M., Horwood, L.J. and Lynskey, M.T., (1993), 'Early Dentine Lead Levels and Subsequent Cognitive and Behavioural Development'. *Journal of Child Psychology and Psychiatry,* 34, 215-227.

Flicek, M., (1992), 'Social Status of Boys with both Academic Problems and Attention-deficit Hyperactivity Disorder'. *Journal of Abnormal Child Psychology,* 20, 353-366.

Gadow, K.D. and Pomeroy, J.C., (1991), 'An Overview of Psychopharmacotherapy for Children and Adolescents'. In T.R. Kratochwill & R.J. Morris (Eds.), *The Practice of Child Therapy.* Boston: Allyn and Bacon.

Goodman, R. and Stevenson, J., (1989), 'A Twin Study of Hyperactivity-II: The Actiological Role of Genes, Family Relationships and Perinatal Adversity'. *Journal of Child Psychology and Psychiatry,* 30, 691-709.

Greenhill, L.L., (1991), 'Attention-deficit Hyperactivity Disorder'. In J.M. Weiner (Ed.), *Textbook of Child and Adolescent Psychiatry.* Washington, DC: American Psychiatric Press.

Harley, J.P. and Matthews, C.G., (1980), 'Food Additives and Hyperactivity in Children: Experimental Investigations'. In R.M. Knights and D.J. Bakker (Eds.), *Treatment of Hyperactive and Learning Disordered Children.* Baltimore: University Park Press.

Hechtman, L., (1991), 'Developmental, Neurological and Psychosocial Aspects of Hyperactivity, Impulsivity and Inattention'. In M. Lewis (Ed.), *Child and Adolescent Psychiatry, A Comprehensive Textbook.* Baltimore: Williams & Wilkins.

Hinshaw, S.P., (1998), 'Is ADHD An Impairing Condition in Childhood and Adolescence?' Chapters Prepared for NIH Consensus Development Conference on Attention Deficit Hyperactivity Disorder.

Hinshaw, S.P., Hanker, B., Whalen, C.K., Erhardt, D. and Dunnington, R.E., (1989), 'Aggressive, Prosocial and Non Social Behaviour in Naturalistic Settings'. *Journal of Consulting and Clinical Psychology,* 57, 636-643.

Ialango, N.S., Horn, W.F., Pascoe, J.M., Greenberg, G., Packard, T., Lopez, M., Wagner, A. and Pultler, L., (1993), 'The Effects of a Multimodal Intervention with Attention-deficit Hyperactivity Disorder Children: A 9-month Follow-up'. *Journal of the American Academy of Child and Adolescent Psychiatry,* 32, 182-189.

Jensen, P.S., Martin, B.A. and Cantwell, D.P., (1997), 'Comorbidity in ADHD: Implications for Research, Practice and DSM-IV'. *Journal of the Academy of Child and Adolescent Psychiatry,* 36 1065-1075.

Lahey, B.B., Pelham, W.E., Stein, M.A., Loney, J., Trapani, C., Nugent, K., Kipp, H., Schmidt, E., Lee, S., Cale, M., Gold, E., Hartung, C.M., Willcutt, E. and Baumann, B., (1998), 'Validity of DSM-IV Attention–deficit/ Hyperactivity Disorder for Younger Children'. *Journal of the American Academy of Child and Adolescent Psychiatry,* 37, 695-702.

Leung, P.W.L. and Connolly, K.J., (1996), 'Distractibility in Hyperactive and Conduct–disordered Children'. *Journal of Child Psychology and Psychiatry,* 37, 305-312.

Loeber, R., Green, S.M., Keenan, K. and Lahey, B., (1995), 'Which Boys will Fare Worse? Early Predictors of the Onset of Conduct Disorder in a Six-Year Longitudinal Study'. *Journal of the American Academy of Childhood Adolescent Psychiatry,* 34, 499-509.

Losier, B.J., Mc Grath, P.J. and Klein, R., (1996), 'Error Patterns on the Continuous Performance Test in Non-medicated and Medicated Samples of Children With and Without ADHD: A Meta-analytic Review'. *Journal of Child Psychology and Psychiatry,* 37, 971-987.

Max, J.E., Arndt, S., Castillo, C.S., Bukura, H., Robin, D.A., Lindgren, S.D., Smith, W.L., Sato, Y. and Mattheis, P.J., (1998), 'Attention-deficit Hyperactivity Symptomatology After Traumatic Brain Injury: A Prospective Study'. *Journal of the American Academy of Child and Adolescent Psychiatry,* 37, 841-847.

Melnick, S.M. and Hinshaw, S.P., (1996), 'What They Want and What They Get: The Social Goals of Boys with ADHD and Comparison Boys'. *Journal of Abnormal Child Psychology,* 24, 169-185.

Milich, R. and Lorch, E.P., (1994), 'Television Viewing Methodology to Understand Cognitive Processing of ADHD Children'. In T.H. Ollendick & R.J. Prinz (Eds.), *Advances in Clinical Child Psychology*. New York: Plenum Press.

Neuman, R.J., Todd, R.D., Heath, A.C., Reich, W., Hudzick, J.J., Bucholz, K.K., Madden, P.A.F., Begleiter, H., Porjesz, B., Kuperman, S., Hesselbruck, V. and Reitch, T., (1999), 'Evaluation of ADHD Typology in Three Contrasting Samples: A Latent Class Approach'. *Journal of the American Academy of Child and Adolescent Psychiatry*, 38, 25-33.

Oosterlaan, J., Logan, G.D. and Sergeant, J.A., (1998), 'Response Inhibition in AD/HD, CD, Comorbid AD/HD + CD, Anxious and Control Children: A Meta Analysis of Studies with the Stop Task'. *Journal of Child Psychology and Psychiatry*, 39, 411-425.

Pliszka, S.R., McCracken, J.T. and Maas, J.W., (1996), 'Catecholamines in Attention-deficit Hyperactivity Disorder: Current Perspectives'. *Journal of the American Academy of Child and Adolescent Psychiatry*, 35, 264-272.

Prinz, R.J. and Riddle, D.B., (1986), 'Associations Between Nutrition and Behaviour in Five-year-old Children'. *Nutrition Reviews*, 44 (Suppl.), 151-157.

Rapport, M.D., (1993), 'Attention Deficit Hyperactivity Disorder'. In T.H. Ollendick & M. Hersen (Eds.). *Handbook of Child and Adolescent Assessment*, Boston: Allyn and Bacon.

Richters, J.E. and Colleagues, (1995), 'NIMH Collaborative Multisite Multimodal Treatment Study of Children with ADHD: I Background and Rationale'. *Journal of the American Academy of Child and Adolescent Psychiatry*, 34, 987-1000.

Satterfield, J.H., (1994), 'Prediction of Antisocial Behaviour in ADHD: Letters to the Editor'. *Journal of the American of Child and Adolescent Psychiatry*, 34, 398-400.

Schachar, R. and Logan, D.L., (1990), 'Impulsivity and Inhibitory Control in Normal Development and Childhood Psychopathology'. *Developmental Psychology*, 26, 710-720.

Semrud-Clikeman, M., Filipek, P.A., Biederman, J., Steingard, R., Kennedy, D., Renshaw, P. and Bekken, K., (1994), 'Attention-deficit Hyperactivity Disorder: Magnetic Resource Imaging Morphometric Analysis of the Corpus Callosum'. *Journal of the American Academy of Child and Adolescent Psychiatry*, 33, 875-881.

Sonuga-Barke, E.J.S., (1994), 'On Dysfunction and Function in Psychological Theories of Childhood Disorder'. *Journal of Child Psychology and Psychiatry*, 35, 801-815.

Sonuga-Barke, E.J.S., Houlberg, K. and Hall, M., (1994), 'When is "Impulsiveness" not Impulsive? The Case of Hyperactive Children's Cognitive Style'. *Journal of Child Psychology and Psychiatry*, 35, 1247-1253.

Stormont-Spurgin, M. and Zentall, S.S., (1995), 'Contributing Factors in the Manifestation of Aggression in Preschoolers with Hyperactivity'. *Journal of Child Psychology and Psychiatry*, 36, 491-509.

Streissguth, A.P., Bookstein, F.L., Sampson, P.D. and Barr, H.M., (1995), 'Attention: Prenatal Alcohol and Continuities of Vigilance and Attentional Problems from 4 Through 14 years'. *Development and Psychopathology*, 7, 419-446.

Sykes, D.H., Hoy, E.A., Bill, J.M., McClure, B.G., Holliday, H.L. and Reid, M.M., (1997), 'Behavioural Adjustment in School of Very Low Birth Weight Children'. *Journal of Child Psychology and Psychiatry*, 38, 315-325.

Szatmari, P., Offord, D.R. and Boyle, M.H., (1989), 'Correlates, Associated Impairments and Patterns of Service Utilization of Children with Attention Deficit Disorders: Findings from the Ontario Child Health Study'. *Journal of Child Psychology and Psychiatry*, 30, 205-217.

Tannock, R., (1998), 'Attention Deficit Hyperactivity Disorder: Advances in Cognitive, Neurological and Genetic Research'. *Journal of Child Psychology and Psychiatry*, 39, 65-99.

Taylor, E., (1995), 'Dysfunctions of Attention'. In D. Cicchetti & D.J. Cohen (Eds.), *Developmental Psychopathology*, New York: John Wiley.

Taylor, E., (1994), 'Syndromes of Attention Deficit and Hyperactivity'. In M. Rutter, E. Taylor and L. Hersov (Eds.), *Child and Adolescents Psychiatry: Modern Approaches*, New York: Blackwell Scientific.

Tessman, J.R. and Hills, A., (1994), 'Developmental Effects of the Lead Exposure in Children'. *Social Policy Report, Society for Research in Child Development*, VIII (3), 1-16.

Whalen, C.K. and Hanker, B., (1998), 'Attention-deficit/Hyperactivity Disorders'. In T.H. Ollendick & M. Hersen (Eds.), *Handbook of Child Psychopathology*, New York Plenum Press.

10

Mental Retardation

OBJECTIVES

This chapter on 'Mental Retardation' offers the definition and classification. It explains the prevalence of mental retardation. It describes the cognitive as well as the social characteristics of the mentally retarded children. It delves into the various causal factors that contribute to mental retardation. It presents the assessment of intelligence and adaptive behaviour. Ultimately, it outlines the treatment for MR and also the educational provisions for the children with mental retardation. After reading this chapter, the readers must be able to:

(i) Define 'mental retardation';

(ii) Know about its classification;

(iii) Chart out the characteristics of the children with MR;

(iv) Describe the various assessment measures of MR;

(v) Present the different treatment practices; and

(vi) Understand the educational provisions for the children with MR.

It is quite common we often come across some children who are socially incapable and intellectually disabled. They have deficient mental functioning and hence they become handicaps in the daily tasks of living. These children belong to the category of mentally retarded. The concept of mental retardation was little understood until seventeenth century. In the early part of the nineteenth century, this concept took root to develop into 'mental handicap'. The most familiar terms 'idiot', 'imbecile' and 'moron' were once employed in the professional literature to denote the mental retardation. Since these terms have negative connotations, attempts were made to arrive at different terminology by substituting more positive labels such as 'intellectually challenged'. The current trend is to view mental retardation as a trait of the individual, perhaps more strongly than most other behavioural disorders. Further, mental retardation is recognized as a socially constructed condition. The socialist Jane Mercer (1973) held that it is the individual's social system that determines whether he/she is retarded or not. She asserted that many of the mentally retarded children, particularly those who are of higher functioning, do not 'officially' become retarded until they enter school. The school as a social system has a certain set of expectations which some children do not meet.

DEFINING MENTAL RETARDATION

All major classification systems recognize mental retardation. The American Association on Mental Retardation (AAMR) had taken much efforts to define MR. The currently offered definition of MR by AAMR is as follows:

"Mental retardation refers to substantial limitations in present functioning. It is characterized by significantly sub-average intellectual functioning, existing concurrently with related limitations in two or more of the following applicable adaptive skill areas: communication, self-care, home living, social skills, community use, self-direction, health and safety, functional academics, leisure and work. Mental retardation manifests before age 18".

Sub average intellectual functioning refers to an approximate I.Q. score of 70 to 75 or below in a general test of intelligence. Limitations in adoptive skills are viewed as related to intellectual limitations rather than to circumstances like cultural background. Finally, the age criterion implies that mental retardation is seen as a developmental disorder. It is usually considered that from the age eighteen onwards many individuals assume adult roles because only at that time the crucial psychosocial development as well as brain development might have typically occurred.

The current definition of mental retardation reflects the paradigm shift in the conceptualization and identification. Earlier, MR was considered a mental disorder and it was diagnosed on the basis of physical examinations and ill-defined global judgements of every competence. Then the emphasis was focused on intelligence test performance through construction of more objective, general tests of intelligence. Due to the limitations and abuse of these tests, the emphasis was shifted to adoptive behaviour. Thus the individuals who fall into the retarded range on intelligence tests but otherwise get along adequately at home, school, or work are not judged as MR now. Similarly, deficits in adaptive behaviour without poor performance on intelligence tests also do not warrant the diagnosis of retardation.

AAMR proposed a model of MR to show how the individual is viewed as functioning in complex ways in a sociocultural context. The diagnosis of MR depends on how the individual is actually functioning in the environment, if functioning changes, so might the diagnosis. In turn, the functioning is related to capabilities, which interact with the environments in which individuals live, learn, play, work and socialize.

AAMR's Model of Mental Retardation

(Luckasson et al., 1992)

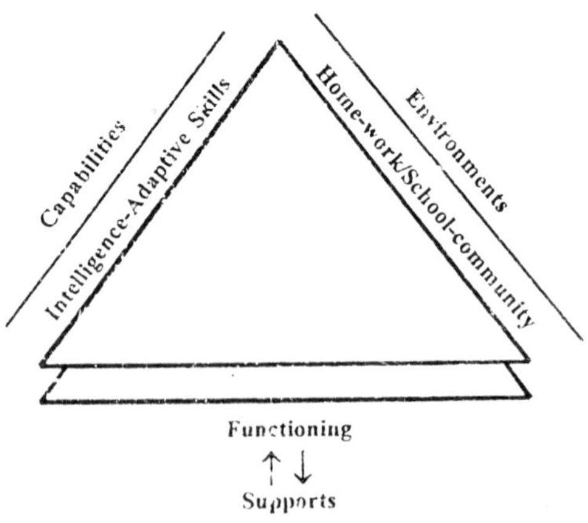

This model also reveals that functioning and supports provided to the individual are reciprocally related. That is, the personal strengths exist along with deficits and that functioning will generally improve with appropriate supports.

CLASSIFICATION OF MENTAL RETARDATION

Earlier AAMR classified MR on the basis of variability that exists in abilities and behaviours of individuals with mental retardation. Based on this reasoning, AAMR once employed four levels of retardation: mild, moderate, severe and profound. Individuals were assigned to a level according to their intelligence test scores.

AAMR's new model avoided the classification of MR on the basis of IQ levels. Instead, the recent classification of AAMR relies more on the needed environmental supports. For each person, descriptions are to be given of strengths and weakness with regard to four aspects: i) intellectual functioning and adaptive skills; ii) psychological and emotional functioning; iii) physical functioning and health; and iv) the person's current environment and the environment that would be optimal for continued growth.

Based on the needed supports across these four aspects, a profile is developed. The profile should stipulate for each aspect whether the level of support required is intermittent, limited, extensive or pervasive. Thus instead of a broad diagnosis based on IQ such as 'severe mental retardation', the diagnosis might be "a person with mental retardation with extensive supports needed in the areas of social skills and self-direction". (Luckasson et al., 1992). This approach assumes that needs for support might be different in one area of functioning from another. It further reveals that AAMR's conceptualization of MR is linked dynamically to the environment rather than being viewed as a static quality of the individual. It also calls forth a clear understanding of the four levels of needed support in simple terms, which is given below:

AAMR's Levels of Needed Support

(Luckasson et al., 1992)

Intermittent	:	Support on 'as needed' basis. Person needs sporadic supports or short term supports during life–span transitions or crisis (e.g. during job loss or acute medical crisis). Supports may be of high or low intensity.
Limited	:	High or low intensity supports are needed consistently for only a limited time (e.g. time limited employment training).
Extensive	:	Supports characterized by regular involvement (e.g. daily) in at least some environments (e.g. work or home) and are not time-limited (e.g. long-term home living supports.)
Pervasive	:	Supports characterized by constancy and high intensity across environments. Potentially life sustaining in nature. Typically involves more staff members and intrusiveness.

Many professionals criticize the classification of MR by levels of support because there is no reliable method for measuring levels of support at present. Hence classification by levels is perceived to be faulty. Particularly DSM-IV (1994) is at odds with AAMR in the aspect that it continues to classify MR by intelligence levels. DSM-IV identifies four levels of MR and it offers a general description of function for each level.

DSM – IV Classification of Levels of MR

Level	IQ Range	Functioning
1	2	3
Mild (Educable)	50 – 55 to about 70	Social and communication skills usually develop in preschool years. Have minimal sensor motor deficits. Can acquire about sixth grade academic skills by late teens. Usually achieve adult vocational and social–skills for self-support. Many need guidance, assistance, supervised living, but often live successfully in the community.

(Contd...)

1	2	3
Moderate (Trainable)	35–40 to 50–55	Communication skills usually develop in early childhood.
		Attend to personal care, with support.
		Are unlikely to progress beyond second-grade academic skills.
		Can benefit from social and occupation skills training and do supervised unskilled or semiskilled work.
		Adapt well to supervised community living.
Severe (Severely or Profoundly handicapped)	20–25 to 35–40	May learn to talk and minimally care for self at school age.
		Have limited ability to profit from pre academic training.
		In adulthood, may perform simple tasks with supervision.
		In most cases, adapt well to community living with family or in group homes.
Profound (Severely or Profoundly handicapped)	Below 20–25	In most cases, have a neurological condition.
		Have sensorimotor impairments in childhood.
		With training, may show improvements in motor, self–care, communication skills.
		May do simple supervised tasks.
		For optimal development, require structure, constant supervision with individual caretaker.

The DSM-IV (1994) classification also coincides with the classification used by educators in the United States, which consists of three subgroups based on expectations for learning: educable, trainable and severely/profoundly handicapped.

PREVALENCE OF MENTAL RETARDATION

Singh, Oswald and Ellis (1998) estimated that the prevalence of mental retardation is about 2 to 3 per cent of the general population, when IQ is taken as the criterion. But prevalence drops to under 1 per cent (Scott, 1994), when IQ and adaptive behaviours are taken into consideration. This implies the fact that about half of those with mild retardation are not identified because their behaviour is sufficiently adaptive in their environments.

The variables such as socio-economic groups, gender, environment and physical disorders are to be considered, when prevalence is examined. Low socio- economic groups account for a disproportionate number of cases of mild retardation and MR is also more prevalent in some minority groups. Further, it is prevalent more among males than females. In addition, MR is associated with a high prevalence of physical disorders (Singh et al., 1998). Impairments tend to rise with increasing severity of retardation.

CHARACTERISTICS OF CHILDREN WITH MENTAL RETARDATION

There is a great deal of variability in the behaviour of retarded students. We must, therefore, consider each retarded person as a unique and separate individual. The most obvious characteristics of MR children are discussed hereunder.

(a) Cognitive Characteristics

Retarded children exhibit cognitive problems. Research has documented that retarded children are likely to have difficulties in the areas related to cognition, namely, attention, memory, language and academics. Many of the cognitive problems of retarded individuals are due to attentional problems (Brooks and McCauley, 1984). Many MR children often attend to wrong things. They have difficulty in allocating their attention properly. Attention is crucial at various stages of information processing in the brain. The MR children have revealed many deficiencies in properly processing the information. For example, at the sensory register stage of information processing, the MR persons are less able to orient and select stimuli (Tomporowski and Tinsley, 1997). Similarly, many authorities have conceptualized that mentally retarded children will have greater memory problems. (Schultz, 1983) than their non retarded peers. In other words, the more complicated the memory task, the more likely it is that a retarded individual will have difficulties with it.

One of the primary reasons for retarded children finding problems on more complicated memory tasks is that they have difficulty using efficient learning strategies such as mediation and organization (Borkowski and Wanschura, 1974). Rehearsal is a mediation strategy. Borkowski and Cavanaugh (1979) found that retarded children generally do not use rehearsal spontaneously. They are inefficient in clustering, which is an important organizing strategy. Researchers like Brown (1974) have attributed retarded children's ineffective use of learning strategies such as rehearsal and clustering to the fact that their executive control processes are less well developed. In other words, mentally retarded children are deficient in executive control processes, which are also called meta cognitive processes. Research evidences demonstrate that when confronted with learning problems, retarded individuals frequently have trouble in picking the best strategies to use, monitoring the use of the strategies (i.e. keeping track of their own performance) and evaluating the use of strategies. McMillan et al. (1986) also reported that the MR children inadequately select, and monitor strategies and they develop metamemory more slowly than normal children. At the same time, Glidden (1985) has shown that the mentally retarded children, though deficient in the spontaneous use of learning strategies and executive control processes, can be taught to use such processes successfully.

Many of the retarded children have language and speech problems, particularly, articulation errors. Normally, their language development progresses at a slower rate. When the degree of retardation is greater, the language and speech difficulties are more severe.

It is an established fact that there is a strong relationship between intelligence and achievement. Therefore, the retarded children naturally lag behind their non retarded peers in all areas of achievement. MacMillan (1982) ascertained that they tend to be underachievers in relation to expectations based on their intellectual level.

Piagetians believed that retarded children follow the same universal sequence of stages as other children but that they advance more slowly and fall short of full mental growth. Piaget's colleague,

Inhelder was the first to study retardation from this perspective (Woodword, 1979). She found evidence that is profound retardation, development reaches only the sensorimotor stage; in moderate retardation, only the beginning of preoperations; in mild retardation no more than concrete operations. Following her footsteps, Hodapp and Zigler (1997) ascertained that mental retardation is best characterized as quantitatively different from development. This view was referred to as the 'developmental position'. On the contrary, the 'deficit position' argued that mental retardation involved deficits or defects, that is, qualitative differences.

(b) Social Characteristics

Mentally retarded individuals are candidates for a variety of social and emotional problems. Luftig (1998) reported that MR individuals have problems in making friends. Leahy et al. (1982) found them to be poor in self-concepts. Since most of them have speech problems, they find it difficult to communicate with others properly. Mildly retarded individuals often avoid associating with other retarded persons for fear of emphasizing their own stigma.

In addition to social-emotional problems, many MR children have motivational problems (Zigler and Balla, 1982). They tend to lack confidence in their own abilities. They strongly believe that they have little control over what happens to them and that they are primarily controlled by other people or events. Therefore they have a tendency to give up easily when faced with challenging tasks.

MR children often show deficits in social skills crucial to personal relationships (Davies and Rogers, 1985). Impairment of social skill is indicated through inappropriate facial expression and body contact, lack of verbal greetings and small talk, inappropriate comments and lack of empathy in responding to others. Social cognition is also impaired. For example, they are deficient in the understanding of others' perspectives and of social situations and social cues. Their general intellectual deficits interfere directly with the development of social competence. In turn, the inadequate social competence leads them to experiences which hinder social growth or increases problem behaviours.

Social adaptiveness of individuals with mental retardation is hindered by the various behaviour problems they exhibit. Some of these problems are sufficiently severe to meet criteria for clinical diagnoses. Bregman (1991) clearly demonstrated that between one-third and two-thirds of those with MR show significant psychopathology. Scott (1994) also noted that the retarded population shows three to four times more problems than the general population. In addition, behaviour problems increase as retardation becomes more severe (Harden, 1998). Aggression, anxiety, depression, attention problems, hyperactivity, obsessive-compulsive disorder, schizophrenia, autism, stereotypies and self-injury have all been reported among the mentally retarded youths (Bregman, 1991). But it is more difficult to identify some problems like depression, particularly when the retardation is severe.

CAUSES OF MENTAL RETARDATION

Mental retardation is associated with hundreds of specific medical and genetic conditions as well as with psychosocial disadvantage. Even then, causation is not clearly identified in an estimated 20 to 30 per cent of cases of severe retardation and in 50 to 60 per cent of mild retardation (Gilberg, 1997). However, it is often reported that both biological factors and psychosocial factors contribute to MR (Luckasson et al., 1992). Scott (1994) identified three kinds of influences, namely, organic risk factors, polygenic inheritance and psychosocial or cultural influences.

(a) Organic Risk Factors

Mental retardation is attributed to organic risk factors. This implies that biological conditions account for disordered brain function and intellectual deficiency. A variety of genetic aberrations, both inherited and non inherited, are associated with specific syndromes of mental retardation. Particularly the syndromes such as Down syndrome, Fragile X syndrome, and Williams syndrome are very closely associated with MR. Simonaff et al. (1996) suggested that aberrations in the number and structure of chromosomes are single most common cause of severe Retardation. Down syndrome, the most common single disorder of mental retardation, occurs in approximately one in a thousand births (Thapar et al., 1994). This condition accounts for an estimated

5 per cent of mild retardation and 30 per cent of more severe cases (Gilberg, 1997). Down syndrome is mainly formed due to trisomy condition of 21st chromosome. That is, the # 21 chromosome appears in a triplet instead of a pair and as a result such persons have 47 chromosomes instead of 46 chromosomes. The trisomy condition is said to occur due to non-disjunction of chromosome 21 during meiosis. Down syndrome was formerly called 'mangolism' and persons with this defect were called 'mangoloid idiots'. They also have multiple malformations like flattened face with fissures and increased space between the eyes. Nose is also flattened and the ears are malformed. The mouth remains constantly opened. The heart, hands and feet are also defective in condition.

Fragile X syndrome is another condition associated with mental retardation. It affects about 5 per cent of cases of more severe retardation and 5 per cent of cases of mild retardation (Gilberg, 1997). It acquired its name from an abnormal 'fragile' site on the X chromosome. The associated mental retardation in Fragile X syndrome are inherited in a similar manner as in Mendelian single- gene patterns. The Fragile X syndrome involves defective metabolism, which means the inability of the body to convert a common dietary substance. For example, the inability to convert phenylalanine (amino acid) to tyrosine (another amino acid) results in the accumulation of phenylalanine causing abnormal brain development. This clinical condition is known as 'phenylketonuria' (defective protein metabolism). Other clinical conditions like Maple Syrup Urine Disease (abnormal metabolism of leucine, isoleucine and valine), Schilder's Disease (decrease in fats in Central Nervous System resulting in demyelination of cerebral white matter) and Galactosemia (in ability to convert galactose, a carbohydrate to glucose) are also associated with mental retardation.

Fragile X syndrome involves abnormal repeats of a triplet of DNA nucleotides (cytosine, guanine, guanine) in the area of FMR -1 gene. Normal persons have between six and fifty of these repeats where as in the full-blown fragile X syndrome, it is over two hundred. The clinical symptoms in males are long faces, large ears and oversized testicles. In general, there is decline in IQ from about 10 to 15 years of age (State, King and Dykens, 1997) in both the sex. Weaknesses in short-term memory, Visual-motor co-ordination, sequential processing, mathematics and attention or also exhibited. Behavioural difficulties include hyperactivity, stereotypies and poor peer relations.

Williams Syndrome is associated with mild to moderate retardation with mean IQ being in the middle fifties. It is a rare disorder involving a gene deletion on chromosome 7. The characteristic features are 'elfinlike' face, growth deficiency, cardiac and kidney problems, abnormal calcium metabolism and deficiencies in mental abilities such as general knowledge, abstract conceptualizations and problem solving (Rossen et al., 1996). Performance IQ tends to be significantly lower than verbal IQ. Visual spatial skills are below the expected level on par with the children's mental age.

Prenatal, perinatal and postnatal factors also contribute to mental retardation. Prenatal exposure to disease, chemicals, drugs, radiation, poor nutrition, and Rh incompatibility may hinder the intellectual development of the child. Maternal use of toxic agents such as cocaine, heroine, tobacco, alcohol, caffeine and even food additives results in mental retardation of the child. Researchers have exposed 'fetal alcohol syndrome' (FAS) as a significant health problem for expectant mothers, who consume large quantities of alcohol and for their unborn children (Hetherington and Parke, 1986). Children with FAS are characterized by a variety of physical deformities as well as mental retardation. Research has linked some antibiotic, anticonvulsant and anticancer medications used by pregnant women to fetal malformations (Batshaw and Perret, 1986). In addition, medication prescribed to women during labour and delivery has also resulted in affecting the mental abilities of the child, in many cases. Retardation can occur because the expectant mother is malnourished or because the child, once born, does not have a proper diet (Hallahan and Cruickshank, 1973). Radiation is another hazardous condition to unborn fetus. Disorders due to an abnormal length of pregnancy, such as prematurity (if pregnancy is too short) and postmaturity (if pregnancy is too long) can also result in retardation. Low birth weight is often used as an index of prematurity. Both prematurity and low birth weight (below 5.5 pounds) can lead to a variety of physical and behavioural abnormalities, including retardation (Balckman, 1984b).

Complications during delivery such as improper positioning of baby's head in the uterus, head injury, seizures and anoxia (complete deprivation of oxygen) may cause a basis for mental retardation. MR may also be caused postnatally by a variety of variables including malnutrition, diseases, lead poisoning and head injuries from auto, bicycle and other accidents. These factors may interfere in many ways with nervous system functioning and development.

Brain damage can also result from infections that may lead to mental retardation. Infections can occur in the expectant mother or the infant or the young child after birth. Rubella (German measles), syphilis and herpes simplex in the mother can cause retardation in the child. The infections of the child that can affect mental development are meningitis (inflammation of meninges covering the brain) and encephalitis (an inflammation of the brain). Meningitis is caused by a variety of bacterial and viral agents, whereas encephalitis is caused by a group 'B-arbovirus' and transmitted by culicine mosquitoes. Encephalitis is a zoonotic disease (ie. infecting many animals and incidentally man). It affects at all ages but frequent among children between 2–15 years. It severely affects intelligence which results more often in MR.

'Paediatric AIDS' is the fastest growing infectious cause of mental retardation. The vast majority of children with paediatric AIDS do obtain their infection during birth from their mothers, who used intravenous drugs or where sexually active with infected men (Baumeister, Kupstas and Klindworth, 1990). Infections can also result in micro cephalus or hydrocephalus. 'Microcephalus' is a condition characterized by a small head with the sloping forehead. It may be caused by infections such as rubella or AIDS (Rubinstein, 1989) or by a genetic disorder. 'Microcephalus condition'-results in mental retardation ranging from severe to profound. Similarly, 'hydrocephalus' results from an accumulation of cerebrospinal fluid inside or outside the brain. Biocage of the circulation of the fluid, which results in a build up of excessive pressure on the brain and enlargement of skull, can occur for a variety of reasons such as encephalitis, meningitis, malformation of the spine or tumors. The degree of retardation depends on how early it is diagnosed and treated. Thus the organic influences are expected to cause mental retardation through abnormal brain development or brain damage. Hence, they are pathological.

(b) Polygenic Factors

Polygenic influences are non pathological and derive from multiple genes whose effects combine to produce variation in intelligence in normal individuals, resulting in mental retardation in limited number of cases. Few studies on individual with retardation bear implications for polygenic inheritance (Thompson, 1997). we have also research evidences for the fact that polygenic influences vary with the level of retardation. A family study revealed that the IQs of sibling of children with severe retardation averaged 103, hinting that severe retardation did not 'run in families' and that some specific organic factor caused retardation in the affected child. On the contrary, the IQs of siblings of children with mild retardation averaged 85, suggesting general family influence, particularly, polygenic inheritance (Scott, 1994).

(c) Psychosocial/Cultural Factors

There are a quite number of mentally retarded children who usually appear normal and have no identifiable organic etiology. Their IQ scores happen to be within the range between 50 and 70 and they possess relatively good adaptive skills. They are often first identified at the time of entering school. Such cases are associated with cultural-familiar retardation (Crnic, 1988) for which psychosocial and cultural factors are identified as causes.

Mild retardation seems to occur among the lower economic classes as well as in some minority groups. In these cases, mental retardation is caused by psychosocial/cultural disadvantage. Certain scheduled tribes and tribals in the Indian population are the best examples for this. According to Sameroff (1990), parental attitudes, social support and stressful events are the important psychosocial variables. They are highly correlated with social class and they put children at risk for mental retardation. Many research studies have demonstrated the specific association between home environment variables, social class and children's intellectual development. For example, Hart and Risley (1992) reported that IQ at age three was related to lower social class and parental practices, that is, interacting with the child, talking to the child and being actively interested in what the child did. As a matter of fact, educationally and economically deprived parents may lack skills or they may be unable to stimulate their children's language and cognitive development. On reaching school, the children of such parents may have low educational motivation, exposure and achievement, and as a result become school dropouts.

ASSESSMENT OF MENTAL RETARDATION

Assessment of MR children is essential for school placement and also for getting special services. Further, accurate assessments assist parents to have understanding of their children's functioning, to seek help in facilitating their development and above all to manage their children's behaviour. Professionals measure two major areas to determine whether individuals are mentally retarded or not: intelligence and adaptive behaviour. The assessment of these two areas mostly rely on standardized tests. Hence there is a general criticism that these tests do not provide adequate information for offering interventions (Dettermen and Thompson, 1997). Intellectual capability and adaptive ability are thought to be related to a moderate degree. Even then there is certainly difference between these two concepts, making it necessary to measure each one separately vide different techniques.

(1) Assessing Intelligence

There are many types of IQ tests. Generally, individually administrated tests are preferred due to their accuracy and predictive capabilities rather than group tests. Further, for placement in a special education programme, individual tests are essential. The most common individual IQ tests for children are the Stanford Binet and Wechsler Intelligence Scale for Children – Revised (WISC – R). Apart from these tests, Kaufman Assessment Battery for Children (K – ABC) is also a relative new test that has predictive validity similar to that of the Wechsler Child test.

(a) Stanford–Binet Test

Stanford–Binet test is now in its fourth edition. In this test, items are grouped into fifteen subtests (e.g. vocabulary, copying, memory for objects), with the items increasing in difficulty. Verbal reasoning, abstract/visual reasoning, quantitative reasoning and short-term memory are the four cognitive areas assessed for individuals from two to twenty- three years of age. Standard Age Score (SAS) for each of the four areas and the entire scale is obtained for each individual. The Standard Age Scores are then compared with performance of a standard norm group of the same chronological age. The average SAS is statistically set at 100. A person who scores higher than 100 is thought to be better than average for his/ her age . Similarly, if a person obtains SAS less than 100, then it means a less-than-average performance. These SAS are nothing but what we wall IQs.

(b) Wechsler Test

Wechsler Intelligence Scale for Children (WISC-III) for six-to-sixteen year- olds and the Wechsler Preschool and Primary Scale of Intelligence (WPPSI-R) for the age range 4 to 6 years are very popular for assessing mentally retarded children. They consist of different subtests such as vocabulary, puzzles and arithmetic problems. Each subtest contains items that become increasingly difficult. The subtests are either verbal or performance tasks. The verbal tests concentrate on verbal skills, knowledge of the environment and social understanding whereas the performance subtests emphasize perceptual motor skills, speed and non verbal abstraction. The Wechsler scale offers three deviation IQs: a verbal IQ, a performance IQ and a full-scale IQ that combines verbal and performance scores. The average performance being 100, the performance is compared with a norm group of similar age.

(c) Kaufman Test

Kaufman test is designed for children from age two-and-a-half to twelve-and-a half. The K-ABC evaluates two fundamental information processing abilities: sequential processing and simultaneous processing. Sequential processing is assessed with subtests that call forth step-by-step processing of verbal, numerical and other content. On the other hand, simultaneous processing is assessed through subtests that require integrating several pieces of visual- spatial information at the same time. Thus a child gets a scale for Sequential Processing, a score for Simultaneous Processing and a Mental Processing Composite score that is a based on non verbal subtests from the sequential and simultaneous processing tasks. An achievement score is also derived from performance on six subtests such as arithmetic and word knowledge. The average score for each of these four scales is 100.

(2) Assessing Adaptive Behaviour

Numerous measures are available for assessing adaptive behaviour. Interviews with families and caretakers, direct observation and self-report measures are generally used for assessment of adaptive behaviour. Several standardized scales are also available and attention should be given to reliability and validity. To be of much use, the adaptive behaviour scales must accurately reflect current functioning. At the same time, the success of scales highly depends on the accuracy of reports given by parents and caretakers. Some of the commonly used scales are the AAMD Adaptive Behaviour Scale – School Edition (Lambert and Windmiler, 1981), the Adaptive Behaviour Inventory for Children (ABIC) (Mercer and Lewis, 1977), the Vineland Adaptive Behaviour Scales and AAMR's Adaptive Behaviour Scales. The AAMD scale has two separate sections to measure daily living skills and personality-cum-behaviour. The ABIC assesses adaptive behaviour in six areas, namely, family, community, peer relations, non academic school roles, earner–consumer and self-maintenance. The latest revision of the Vineland Adaptive Behaviour Scale has 3 versions. Two versions are semi-structured interviews for parents and other care-takers and they can be used with youth from birth to age eighteen and with low-functioning adults. The third version consists of items for teachers of three-to twelve-year-old. All versions cover four major behavioural domains, namely, communication, daily living skills, socialization, and motor skills. In addition, there is an optional domain of maladaptive behaviour (except in the teacher's version). Scores from the separate domains and an over all score can be compared with scores earned by a normal standard group and also with the performance of smaller special groups such as mentally retarded, emotionally disturbed and hearing-impaired persons. Similarly, the recent revisions of AAMR's Adaptive Behaviour Scales (Adaptive Behaviour Scales–Residential and Community [ABS–RC: 2]) and Adaptive Behaviour Scales-School Edition [ABS–S: 2]) are of much use to assess adaptive behaviour. Many domains of functioning such as independent functioning, domestic activity, self-direction, rebellious behaviour, responsibility and socialization are assessed by ABS–RC: 2. It is designed for persons from age 3 to adulthood. The ABS–S: 2 is designed for children aged three to sixteen, primarily for students with mild and moderate levels of retardation.

Apart from intelligence tests and adaptive behaviour tests, functional assessment is also essential. Functional assessment provides hypotheses about how a targeted behaviour is presently functioning for the individual; that is, what variables are reinforcing or otherwise contributing to maintaining the behaviour. Functional assessment gathers information about why a person is engaging himself in a particular behaviour in a particular setting and at the particular time. Such information can then be used to construct effective intervention because knowing about what contributes to/maintains a certain behaviour can facilitate its modification. Several methods like interviews, rating scales, checklists and direct observations are useful for functional assessment. Functional analysis is a prominent type of functional assessment and it is widely used recently. It involves a demonstration of the events hypothesized as responsible for the behaviour's occurrence or non occurrence.

For severe and profound retardation curriculum-based assessment is increasingly employed. This is because norm-referenced intelligence tests lack sensitivity to developmental changes. Curriculum-based assessment should focus on the skill areas, such as self-help, social-emotional behaviour, language and motor functioning.

TREATMENT FOR MENTAL RETARDATION

The intellectual and adaptive functioning along with interpersonal and behavioural problems must be given due consideration while treating the mentally retarded. Medical conditions must also be attended when treatment is offered to severely retarded individuals. Hence the treatment of MR involves application of behavioural techniques as well as pharmacological medication along with psychotherapy.

(a) Behavioural Modification Techniques

Behaviour modification techniques aim at self-help programmes. Recently, training in social skills and self-control has become common, especially for mild and moderate retardation (Matson and Coe, 1991). Such training often includes cognitive components. Further, many researchers recognized the acquisition of daily living skills as crucial (Danforth and Drabman, 1990; Taras and Matese, 1990). 'Discrete-trial learning' and 'incidental learning' are the two different methods of skill training. Both these methods are guided by operant principles. In discrete- trial learning, the clinician selects the task to be learnt and provides simple clear directives, prompts, and consequences for appropriate behaviour. Teaching is usually conducted in a quite place, away from distractions. On the other hand, the incidental learning involves informal teaching situation which is less structured and more natural. The child initiates the learning situation amidst everyday contexts. For example, the child's asking for a toy is used as an opportunity for teaching. Both the above teaching-learning methods have been proved to be highly effective and particularly, the incidental learning is effective for generalization of learning.

The behavioural approach also aims to train caregivers in various settings like home, community and residential institutions. Training also focuses on general principles or on management of a specific child and it may be delivered to groups or to individual families. Training courses and curricula are designed to spread information to caregivers. Outcomes of such programmes are evaluated and as a result the value of programmes in terms of modification of everyday activities of the child are established. The parent training programmes have been proved highly effective. Parents can get utmost profit from on going contact with professionals (Handen, 1998). Though behavioural modification techniques are successful in serving the mentally retarded case loads, who were viewed as unable to learn in the past, the application of these techniques requires skill, effort and perseverance.

(b) Pharmacological Medication

Medication is of no use to strengthen intellectual functioning of the retarded. But it is widely employed for medical and behavioural symptoms. A wide range of medications are employed to treat behavioural problems that co-occur with mental retardation (Singh et al., 1998). Drug treatment increases as the number and severity of behavioural problems increase. Medication use is also higher for those living in institutions, particularly for those in institutions with restrictive environments. However, the management of medication for MR requires special consideration. Many cases with retardation have language impairments and hence accurate diagnosis of problems is difficult in many cases. Therefore, medication practices require careful supervision, which should include determining drug efficacy and possible side effects.

(c) Psychotherapy

Psychotherapies aim to reduce behavioural/psychological problems (Szymanski and Kaplan, 1991). Many children as well as adolescents with retardation benefit from these therapies. An important point to be noted here is that the psychotherapeutic techniques should be adapted to the developmental level of the child. The therapists must take care in setting specific goals. Language must be concrete and clear when using psychotherapeutic techniques. In addition, nonverbal techniques like play or other activities may also be used in cases who have communication difficulties. The treatment sessions should not be unduly long. Instead, short and frequent sessions serve the purpose well.

EDUCATIONAL PROVISIONS FOR MR CHILDREN

Handen (1998) felt that the most extensive and common interventions for mental retardation are educational services. In the United States, the educational provisions offered for MR children were subjected to change in accordance with the changing attitudes towards MR. During middle to late 1800s, there was a strong optimistic belief to offer education and 'moral training' in special schools so as to enable the MR to return to society as capable individuals. Then during the period upto early 1990s, focus was on neuropathology and retardation was seen as incurable defect and hence utmost efforts were taken to protect the retarded persons from the society. From early to middle 1990s, intelligence tests were introduced to, 'discover' the mild retardation and general assumptions to link MR with antisocial behaviour were prevalent. As a result of such assumptions, the custodial institutionalization of MR was advocated as a kind of 'sterilization'. Only after the middle 1900s, the rights of retarded persons to public education, treatment, and life in community were recognized. The concept of normalization was globally accepted and it is kept in abeyance until now. Even in the Indian context such awareness is gaining momentum. A letter from Mr. Saravanan (in THE HINDU, dated 6th.. May, 2004), a participant in the three-day course on mental retardation for the nursing staff confirms this. The course sessions reiterated many aspects, such as psychological assessment of a child, behaviour modification, management of the MR, speech therapy, maternal health and nutrition, special education, exercise therapy, yoga and occupational therapy. Experts came out with their opinion that more than the medicines, an extra dose of personal care and affection from the family members and other caregivers can work wonders in treating the ailments of the MR.

An Extract from 'THE HINDU' Dated, May 6th, 2004

An Extra Dose of Personal Care

Those who are afflicted with even minor ailments need extra care and affection from their kin for a speedy recovery. And imagine the plight of the mentally retarded. Experts feel that more then the medicines, care and affection of their families can do wonders for them.

Mental ailments are of various categories. Persons with psychological disorders may become mental patients, while some are born mentally retarded. Psychologists feel that it will be unwise to expect the family members to show more interest in the well being of such patients; it is also the duty of nurses, counsellors and teachers of special schools to equip themselves better to look after them.

"Persons suffering from other mental ailments can be cured by medicines, but not the mentally retarded. The only solution is prevention. That requires the pregnant women to undergo genetic tests and regular checks to prevent the birth of a mentally retarded child. We found that while the number of mentally retarded cases is on the rise over the years, the trained manpower to deal with such cases is not sufficient. Hence, we decided to organise a three-day course in mental retardation for the

nursing staff, in association with the Madurai Kamaraj University and the Development Association for Training and Technology Appropriation (DATA), an NGO, at the MKU NSS Coordinator's Office from April 28," said R. Ravikumar, Principal, Bethshan Special School.

On the first day, V. Neethi Arasu, a neurologist, delivered a lecture on the medical aspects of mental retardation with a focus on epilepsy. Paediatrician and neurologist D. Meikandan dealt with screening, identification and early intervention. The participants were exposed to expert views on psychological assessment of a child, behaviour modification, management of the mentally retarded, speech therapy, maternal health and nutrition, special education, exercise therapy, yoga and occupational therapy.

There was also a feedback session at the end of the course, attended by around 100 nursing staff.

From T. Saravanan in Madurai.

Due to the development of favourable attitudes towards the MR in the last few decades, many service models have been evolved. Those models include better diagnosis and intervention. A part and parcel of these models is the concept of normalization, which was first popularised in Scandinavia and this concept stresses that the treatment should aim at producing behaviours that are as normal as possible and should accomplish this goal by methods as culturally normal as possible (Mesibov, 1992). The philosophy of normalization has been widely applied to the lives of people with handicaps and has influenced educational services and living arrangements for persons with MR.

The growing social commitment during the last few decades to the rights of handicapped children to appropriate education finally resulted in a legal reform in the United States by passing the Public Law 94 – 142, the Education for All Handicapped Children Act of 1975. Subsequently, Public Law 99 – 457 amended the Education for All Handicapped Children Act by extending the provisions to developmentally delayed three-to-five-year olds and creating voluntary intervention for infants. Further, the Education for All Handicapped Children Act was expanded under the title the Individuals with Disabilities Education Act (IDEA). It ensured legally an access to free and public education to all students with handicaps. It assisted states and localities in providing education. It also took steps to assess and assure the effectiveness of educational efforts. IDEA has strengthened individualized programming. In furtherance, under the policy of mainstreaming, many children are integrated with their peers in the schools through a variety of placement programmes that are arranged in continuum of integration. For example, children with intermittent or limited supports were placed in regular class-based programmes, which ensured special materials, equipments, special consultation facilities and resource rooms with special education teacher. On the other hand, the children with pervasive support needs were placed in non-school-based programmes with either hospital instruction or homebound instruction.

The integration programmes have many advantages. First of all, placement in regular classrooms can avoid stigmatization. It can also encourage the modelling of academic and social skills. Integration in regular school settings enables the child to play a full role in society in adulthood. Polloway and his colleagues (1991) advocated that educational curriculum from elementary school onwards should be geared toward long- range planning for adult integration into the community.

The integration programmes at the early elementary level should be oriented towards providing mildly and moderately retarded children with 'readiness skills', that is, abilities which are prerequisites for later learning. Thus they must include things such as the ability to:

1. sit still and attend to the teacher;
2. discriminate auditory and visual stimuli;
3. follow directions;
4. develop language;
5. increase gross and fine motor co-ordination;
6. develop self-help skills; and
7. interact with peers in a group situation.

The teachers should provide instruction in language and concept development. Further, they should help the MR children in the rudiments of socialization. Readily designed programmes are available for training socially adaptive behaviours. For example, ACCEPTS (A Curriculum for Children's Effective Peer and Teacher Skills) developed by Walker et al. (1983) is one such programme, which is a tightly structured and sequenced set of activities. Its main objective is to teach children to get along with their peers.

Educational programmes for the MR during the later elementary years, should focus on academics, particularly functional academics, in order to do such things as reading a news paper, reading the telephone book, reading labels on goods at the store, making change and filling out job applications. Further, as Hasazi and Clark (1998) emphasized, they need to learn the rudiments of community and vocational living skills.

The educational programmes for severely and profoundly retarded students should include the following features:

1. age-appropriate curriculum and materials;
2. functional activities;
3. community- based instruction;
4. integrated therapy;
5. interaction with non-disabled students; and
6. family involvement.

In addition, applied behaviour analysis can be adapted to teach the mentally retarded children, especially those with severe learning problems. 'Applied behaviour analysis' refers to the application and evaluation of principles of learning theory in teaching situations. According to Wolery, Bailey and Sugai (1998), it consists of six steps. First, the teacher identifies the overall goal. This usually consists of a skill area in which the student needs more work in or an inappropriate behaviour that he/she needs to decrease. Second, further information is obtained on the identified skill area or behaviour by taking a baseline measurement. The baseline measurement shows that at what level the student is currently functioning. The teacher can later compare the student's performance after instruction with the original baseline performance. Third, the teacher decides on a specific learning objective, that is, he/she breaks down the over all goal in to specific skills, which the child is expected to learn. Fourth, the teacher implements an intervention designed to increase needed skills or decrease inappropriate behaviour. Fifth, the child's progress is monitored by way of frequent (or daily) measurements. Sixth, the teacher evaluates the effects of the intervention, usually by charting the student's performance during intervention and comparing it with the baseline performance. Based on this evaluation, the teacher makes a final decision as to whether to continue, modify or end the instruction.

For years, the traditional placement for the severely and profoundly retarded individuals was the institutions. With the increased sophistication in dealing with the special problems of severely retarded children and the growing public commitment to their education as well as the growth of the philosophy of normalization, the movement to deinstitutionalize the individuals with retardation is gaining momentum. The movement to deinstitutionalization sounds protest against the negative qualities observed in traditional institutions, such as social isolation, regimentation, fostering of dependency and lack of power of the residents (Lord and Pedlar, 1991). Hence there is a growing consensus towards alternative living arrangements, which provide more normal and more positive experiences.

SUMMARY

The mentally retarded children are those who are socially incapable and intellectually disabled with deviant mental functioning. Hence they become handicaps in the daily tasks of living. Earlier, the terms 'idiot', 'imbecile' and 'maron' were employed synonymously to denote the mental retardation. But later more positive labels such as 'intellectually challenged' are used. Sociologists held the view that the individual's social system determines the retardation.

AAMR defined MR to be characterized by significantly sub average intellectual functioning and limitations in two or more adaptive skill areas. In other words, an IQs score of 70 to 75 or below and deficit adaptive behaviour are the warranting characteristics of MR.

MR was earlier classified into different categories on the basis of variability that exits in abilities. But at present, it is classified based on the levels of the needed support. DSM-IV continues to classify MR by intelligence levels and thus it identifies four levels of MR: mild, moderate, severe, and profound. This classification coincides with the classification used by educators in the United States.

When prevalence of MR is examined, the variables such as socio economic group, gender, environment and physical disorders are to be considered. MR is more prevalent in some minority groups. Further, it is prevalent more among males than females. It is also associated with a high prevalence of physical disorders.

The MR children exhibit cognitive problems in the areas of attention, memory, language and academics. They naturally lag behind their non-retarded peers in all areas of achievement. Piagetians believed that the retarded children follow the same universal sequence of stages as other children but they advance more slowly and fall short of full mental growth. The MR children are also candidates for a variety of social and emotional problems. They have, in addition, motivational problems, deficits in crucial social skills, which are necessary for personal relationships and psychopathology.

MR is associated with hundreds of specific medical and genetic conditions as well as with psychosocial disadvantage. It is often believed that both biological factors and psychosocial factors contribute to MR. A variety of genetic aberrations, both inherited and non inherited are associated with specific syndromes of MR. Syndromes such as Down syndrome, Fragile X syndrome, and Williams syndrome are very clearly associated with MR. Prenatal, perinatal and postnatal factors too contribute to MR. Brain damage due to infections such as Rubella, Sypilis, Herpes, infections such as Meningitis, Encephalitis and Paediatric AIDS can give rise to MR.

The non-pathological or polygenic influences drive from multiple genes whose effects combine to produce variation in intelligence and result in mental retardation in a limited number of cases. Psychosocial and cultural factors such as low economic status, minority ethnic groups, and restricted home environments are the other causal factors.

Assessment of MR warrants the measurement of intelligence through intelligence test and of adaptive behaviour. Stanford - Binet test, Wechsler test and Kaufman test are some of the commonly used tests of intelligence. Similarly interviews, observations and self-report measures are used to evaluate the adaptive behaviour. In addition, readily designed adaptive behaviour scales are also available. Functional assessment is also necessary apart from intelligence and adaptive behaviour test. Curriculum based assessment is increasingly employed for severe and profound retardation and this kind of assessment should focus on the skill areas such as self-help, social-emotional behaviour, language, and motor functioning.

Treatment for the MR should take into consideration the intellectual and adaptive functioning along with interpersonal and behavioural problems. It should involve application of behavioural techniques, pharmacological medication and psychotherapy. Medication is widely employed to treat medical and behavioural symptoms that co-occur with MR. But medication practices require careful supervision. Psychotherapies aim to reduce behavioural/ psychological problems.

The most extensive and common interventions for MR are educational services. The concept of educating the MR has evolved through various beliefs across many eras. The latest favourable attitude toward MR advocates for normalization, deinstitutionalization and integration programmes for mainstream education. They should provide the MR children with 'readiness skills' to face life and to compete with normal peers. In addition, applied behaviour analysis can be adapted to teach the MR children. There is a growing consensus towards alternative living arrangements that offer more normal and more positive experiences rather than the restricted and traditional institutions, which are characterized by social isolation, regimentation and lack of power.

REFERENCES

Batshaw, M.L. and Perret, Y.M., (1986), *Children with Handicaps: A Medical Primer.* (2nd Ed.), Baltimore: Paul H. Brookes.

Baumeister, A.A., Kupstas, F. and Klindworth, I.M., (1990), 'New Morbidity: Implications for Prevention of Children's Disabilities'. *Exceptionality,* 1(1), 1-16.

Blackman, J.A., (1984b), 'Low Birth Weight'. In J.A. Blackman (Ed.), *Medical Aspects of Developmental Disabilities in Children Birth to Three.* (Rev. 1st ed. pp. 143-146). Rockville, MD: Aspen System Corp.

Borkowski, J. G. and Cavanaugh, J. C., (1979), 'Maintenance and Generalization of Skills and Strategies by the Retarded'. In N. R. Ellis (Ed). *Handbook of Mental Deficiency: Psychological Theory and Research.* (2nd Ed). Hillsdale, NJ: Lawrence Erlburm.

Borkowski, J. G. and Wanschura, P. B., (1974), 'Mediational Processes in the Retarded'. In N. R. Ellis (Ed). *Internation Review of Research in Mental Retardation.* Vol. 7. New York: Academic Press.

Bregman, J.D., (1991), 'Current Developments in the Understanding of Mental Retardation: Part II Psychopathology'. *Journal of the American Academy of Child and Adolescent Psychiatry,* 30, 861-872.

Brooks, P. H., and Ma Cauley, C., (1984), 'Cognitive Research in Mental Retardation'. *American Journal of Mental Deficiency,* 88, 479–486.

Brown, A. L., (1974), 'The Role of Strategic Behaviour in Retardate Memory'. In N. R. Ellis (Ed). *International Review of Research in Mental Retardation.* Vol. 7. New York: Academic Press.

Crnic, K.A., (1988), 'Mental Retardation'. In E.J. Mash & L.G. Terdal (Eds.), *Behavioural Assessment of Childhood Disorders Selected Core Problems'.* New York: Guilford.

Danforth, J.S. and Drabman, R.S., (1990), 'Community Living Skills'. In J.L. Matson (Ed.), *Handbook of Behaviour Modification with the Mentally Retarded.* New York: Plenum.

Davies, R. R. and Rogers, E. S., (1985), 'Social Skills Training with Persons Who are Mentally Retarded'. *Mental Retardation,* 23, 186–196.

Detterman, D.K. and Thompson, L.A., (1997), 'What is So Special About Special Education?' *American Psychologists,* 52, 1082-1090.

DSM–IV, (1994), 'Diagnostic and Statistical Manual of Mental Disorders' (4th Edition) Washington: *American Psychiatric Association.*

Gilberg. C., (1997), 'Practitioner Review: Physical Investigations in Mental Retardation'. *Journal of Child Psychology and Psychiatry,* 38, 889--897.

Glidden, L. M., (1985), 'Semantic Processing, Semantic Memory, and Recall'. In N. R. Ellis(Ed). *International Review of Research in Mental Retardation*. Vol. 13 (pp. 247-278). New York: Academic Press.

Hallahan, D. P. and Cruickshank, W. M., (1973), *Psycho Educational Foundations of Learning Disabilities*. Englewood Cliffs, NJ: Prentice Hall.

Handen, B. L., (1998), 'Mental Retardation'. In E. J. Mash and L.G.Terdal (Eds.), *Treatment of Childhood Disorders*. New York: Guilford Press.

Hart, B. and Risley, T.R., (1992), 'American Parenting of Language-learning Children: Persisting Differences in Family-child Interactions Observed in Natural Home Environment'. *Developmental Psychology*, 28, 1096-1105.

Hasazi, S.B. and Clark, G.M., (1988), 'Vocational Preparation for High School Students Labelled Mentally Retarded: Employment as a Graduation Goal'. *Mental Retardation*, 26,(6), 343-349.

Hetherington, E.M. and Parke, R.D., (1986), *'Child Psychology: A Contemporary Viewpoint*. (3rd Ed.), New York: McGraw Hill.

Hodapp, R. M. and Zigler, E., (1997), 'New Issues in the Developmental Approach to Mental Retardation'. In W. E. MacLean (Ed.), *Ellis's Handbook of Mental Deficiency, Psychological Theory and Research*. Mahwah, NJ: Lawrence Erlbaum.

Lambert, N. and Windmiller, M., (1981), *AAMD Adaptive Behaviour Scale–School Edition'*. Washington, DC: American Association of Mental Deficiency.

Leahy, R., Balla, D. and Zigler, E., (1982), 'Role Taking, Self-image, and Imitation in Retarded and Non-retarded Individuals'. *American Journal of Mental Retardation*, 92(5), 472–475.

Lord, J. and Pedlar, A., (1991), 'Life in Community Four Years after the Closure of an Institution'. *Mental Retardation*, 29, 213-221.

Luckasson, R., (1992), 'Mental Retardation: Definition, Classification and Systems of Supports'. Washington, DC: *American Association on Mental Retardation*.

Luftig, R. L., (1988), 'Assessment of the Perceived School Loneliness and Isolation of Mentally Retarded and Non-retarded Students'. *American Journal of Mental Retardation*, 92 (5), 472–475.

MacMillan, D. L, (1982), *Mental Retardation in School and Society*, (2nd Ed.), Boston: Little, Brown.

MacMillan, D. L., Keogh, B.K. and Jones, R. L., (1986), 'Special Educational Research on Mildly Handicapped Learners'. In M. C. Wittrock (Ed), *Handbook of Research*. New York: McMillan.

Maston, J.L. and Coe, D.A., (1991), 'Mentally Retarded Children'. In T.R. Kratochwill & R.J. Morris (Eds.), *The Practice of Child Therapy*, Boston: Allyn and Bacon.

Merce, J.R., (1973), *Labelling the Mentally Retarded*. Berkley: University of California Press.

Mercer, J.K. and Lewis, J.F., (1977), *Adaptive Behaviour Inventory for Children, Parent Interview Manual System of Multicultural Pluralistic Assessment*. New York: The Psychological Corporation.

Mesibov, G.B., (1992), 'Letters to the Editors'. Response to Thompson and McEvoy. *Journal of Autism and Developmental Disorders*, 22, 672-673.

Polloway, E.A., Patten, J.R., Smith, J.D. and Roderique, T.W., (1991), 'Issues in Programme Design for Elementary Students with Mild Retardation: Emphasis on Curriculum Development'. *Education and Training in Mental Retardation*, 26, 144-150.

Rossen, M., Klima, E. S., Bellugi, U., Bihrle, A. and Jones, W., (1996), 'Interaction Between Language and Cognition: Evidence from Williams Syndrome'. In J. H. Beitchman, N.J. Cohen, M.M. Konstantareas, and R. Tannock (Eds.), *Language, Learning and Behaviour Bisorders*. New York: Cambridge University Press.

Rubinstein, A., (1989), 'Background, Epidemiology, and Impact of HIV Infection in Children'. *Mental Retardation*, 27(4), 209-211.

Sameroff, A.J., (1990), 'Neo-environmental Perspectives on Developmental Theory'. In R.M. Hodapp, J./A. Burack, and E. Zigler (Eds.), *Issues in Developmental Approach to Mental Retardation*. New York: Cambridge University Press.

Schultz, E. E., Jr., (1983), 'Depth of Processing by Mentally Retarded and MA-matched Non Retarded Individuals'. *American Journal of Mental Deficiency*, 88, 307–313.

Scott, S., (1994), 'Mental Retardation'. In M. Rutter, E. Taylor, and L. Hersov (Eds.), *Child and Adolescent Psychiatry: Modern Approaches*. Cambridge, M. A: Blackwell.

Simonoff, E., Bolton, P. and Rutter, M., (1996), 'Mental Retardation: Genetic Findings, Clinical Implications and Research Agenda'. *Journal of Child Psychology and Psychiatry*, 37, 259–280.

Singh, N. N., Osward, D. P. and Ellis, C.R., (1998), 'Mental Retardation'. In T. H. Ollendick & M.Hersen (Eds). *Handbook of Child Psychopathology*, New York: Plenum Press.

State, M. W., King, B. H. and Dykens, E., (1997), 'Mental Retardation: A Review of the Past 10 years'. Part II. *Journal of the Academy of Child and Adolescent Psychiatry*, 36, 1664--1971.

Szymanski, L.S. and Kaplan, L.C., (1991), 'Mental Retardation'. In J.M. Weiner (Ed.), *Textbook of Child & Adolescent Psychiatry*, Washington, DC: American Psychiatric Association.

Taras, M.E. and Matese, M., (1990), 'Acquisition of Self-help Skills'. In J.L. Matson (Ed.), *Handbook of Behaviour Modification with the Mentally Retarded*. New York: Plenum.

Thaper, A., Gottesman, J. J, Owen, M. J., O' Donovan, M. and McGuffin, P., (1994), 'The Genetics of Mental Retardation'. *British Journal of Psychiatry*, 164, 747–758.

Thompson, L.A., (1997), 'Behavioural Genetics and the Classification of Mental Retardation'. In W.E. MacLean (Ed.), *Ellis' Handbook of Mental Deficiency, Psychological Theory and Research*. Mahwah, NJ: Lawrence Erlbaum.

Tomporowski, P. D. and Tinsley, V., (1997), 'Attention in Mentally Retarded Persons'. In W. E. MacLean (Ed), Ellis'. *Handbook of Mental Deficiency, Psychological Theory and Research*. Mahwah, NJ: Lawrence Erlbaum.

Walker, H.M., McConnell, S., Holmes, D., Todis, B., Walker, J. and Golden, N., (1983), *The Accepts Programme*. Autism, TX: Pro-Ed.

Woodward, W. M., (1979), 'Piaget's Theory and the Study of Mental Retardation'. In N. R. Ellis (Ed). *Handbook of Mental Deficiency*. Hillsdale, NJ: Erlburm.

Worley, M., Bailey, D.B. and Sugai, G.M., (1988), *Effective Teaching Principles and Procedures of Applied Behaviour Analysis with Exceptional Students*. Boston, Allyn & Bacon.

Zigler, E. and Balla, D., (1982), 'Introduction: The Developmental Approach to Mental Retardation'. In E. Zigler and D. Balla (Eds). *Mental Retardation: The Developmental Difference Controversy*. (pp. 3–8). Hillsdale, NJ: Erlbaum.

11

Language and Learning Disabilities

OBJECTIVES

This chapter describes the concept, meaning and importance of language and learning disabilities. It presents the classification of language disability and its prevalence. Further, it offers the general characteristics of LD children. In analyses the clinical characteristics with regard to deficits in reading, writing and mathematical abilities. It explains the psychological and behavioural problems of the language and learning disabled children. It delineates the various factors associated with LD. Finally, it presents assessment approaches, the treatment procedures and educational issues of language and learning disabilities. After reading this chapter, the readers must be able to:

(i) Define language and learning disabilities;

(ii) Understand the classification of language disability;

(iii) Know the general characteristics of language and learning disabled children;

(iv) Differentiate the clinical characteristics with regard to deficits in reading, writing and mathematical abilities;

(v) List out the psychological and behavioural problems of the language and learning disabled children;

(vi) Delineate various factors associated with LD;

(vii) Understand the assessment practices in LD field;

(viii) Know the various treatment approaches to LD; and

(xi) Present the educational issues of language and learning disabilities.

In the previous chapter, we have seen mental retardation, a developmental disorder, which affects intellectual functioning at various levels of severity. Very often these intellectual handicaps or impairments are not general. In other words, they appear in some specific areas and not in others. For instance, there are children who exhibit specific language and/or learning disabilities but otherwise look normal intellectuals with normal physical abilities. These children show developmental delay in speech and language facilities, problems in visual/auditory perception, problems in visual motor co-ordination and ultimately academic difficulties. Yet they have intact intelligence and absence of sensory handicaps, such as blindness or deafness. Hence, they do not fit into the existent categories of exceptionality. It was Kirk (1963) who coined the term 'learning disabilities' to focus on the learning difficulties of these children. These children with specific language and/or learning disabilities can vary from being very subtle to severe, with concomitant effects on academic performance. The specific language and learning disabilities, at large, can cast a shadow of failure over the child during school years. They may even interfere with innumerable daily activities that require speaking, reading, writing or dealing with numbers. As a result, peers may often respond negatively to a child's language and learning disability and parents and teachers may attribute such impairments to the child's laziness or lack of motivation. If not diagnosed and intervened during early years of childhood, these problems may adversely affect social relationships in adulthood and occupational success. Further, these language and learning disabilities have increasing impact on individual lives because of enhanced demands for certain kinds of learning in our day-to-day life in the industrially as well as technologically sophisticated world.

THE CONCEPT OF LEARNING DISABILITY

Historically, two major themes tried to explain 'language and learning disabilities' (Lyon, 1996a). One has medical orientation, which has been indebted to the physician Paul Broca's theory. Paul Broca traced the inability of some individuals to express themselves verbally while maintaining the ability to comprehend what others said to an area in the left hemisphere of the brain (which is now called 'Broca's area'). From then onwards, it was widely documented that brain injury or damage in adults led to a variety of behavioural symptoms, such as speech problems, learning difficulties and inattention (Hammill, 1993). Similar problems in children too were hypothesized to be caused by brain dysfunction of some sort, sometimes even too subtle to be identified.

The second major theme regarding language and learning disabilities sprang from the concern that a select group of children had educational needs that were not being met by the schools. Until the 1960's, the children whose school performance was below their general ability were called 'under achievers' (Kessler, 1988). Much attention was given to their psychosocial behaviour, motivation, anxiety and family functioning. Moreover, it was recognised that some of children had specific learning problems, such as reading and arithmetic. Many parents and professionals were very much concerned about the fact that the needs of these children were not properly satisfied. In the meantime, the behavioural scientists too had begun to recommend ways and means to remedy the problem of learning disorders (Lyon, 1996a). In 1963, in a symposium in New York City, sponsored by the Fund for Perceptually Handicapped Children, Samuel Kirk, a well respected educator, brought to the notice of the educators that the children of their concern exhibited a variety of deficiencies (that were assumed to be related to neurological dysfunction), especially learning difficulties, perceptual problems and hyperactivity. He suggested that the term 'learning disabilities' would be suitable for all these children and also would avoid the need to establish nervous system dysfunction in identifying such youngsters. Kirk's presentation marked the creation of a new field (Taylor, 1988a). The term gradually became widely accepted by professionals as well as parents. Thanks to Kirk, educators and parents henceforth started playing an important role in an area, which was earlier, dominated by physicians and psychologists. The children who might otherwise have been labelled 'mentally retarded' were given hope that the problem was only limited and could be treated.

DEFINING LEARNING DISABILITIES

The nature of the academic difficulties in Learning Disabled (LD) children is selective and specific. Unlike the general learning problems in retardants, the learning disabilities in LD children are located in a more limited/specific area. The source of a child's learning disability is psychological process problems. The process problems impede the LD child's normal development in reading, spelling, mathematics and writing (Kirk, 1972). The formal definition of National Advisory Committee on handicapped children (1968) of the United States included all the above aspects and it is probably the most commonly accepted definition.

"Specific learning disability means a disorder in one or more of the basic psychological processes involved in understanding or in using language spoken or written, which may manifest itself as an imperfect ability to listen, think, speak, read, write, spell or to do mathematical calculations. The term includes such conditions as perceptual handicaps, brain injury, minimal brain dysfunction, dyslexia and developmental aphasia. The term does not include children who have learning problems which are primarily the result of visual, hearing, or motor handicaps, of mental retardation, of emotional disturbance, or of environmental, cultural or economic disadvantage".

The above definition was later incorporated into the US Public Law 94-142 (1977) and it additionally stated a criteria for assessing the specific learning disability of a child.

"If the child does not achieve commensurate with his/her age and ability levels in one or more of seven specific areas: 1) oral expression; 2) listening comprehension; 3) written expression; 4) basic reading skill; 5) reading comprehension; 6) mathematics calculation; and 7) mathematics reasoning), when provided with learning experiences appropriate for the child's age and ability levels".

The definition of National Advisory Committee on Handicapped children has been widely criticised for two specific aspects. First, the definition states that learning disabilities cannot occur jointly with other handicaps or cultural or economic disadvantage. But research findings of Cravioto (1972) suggested that learning disabilities can occur in children from impoverished homes where they do not have balanced and nutritious diets. Second, the NACHC's definition includes a list of obscure conditions, that is, "perceptual handicaps, brain injury, minimal brain dysfunction, dyslexia and developmental aphasia", which give rise to concerns as to how and with what criteria these conditions are to be established. Hence the National Joint Committee for Learning Disability (NJCLD, 1981) has issued an alternative definition, redressing the criticisms.

"Learning disabilities is a generic term that refers to a heterogeneous group of disorders manifested by significant difficulties in the acquisition and use of listening, speaking, reading, writing, reasoning or mathematical abilities. These disorders are intrinsic to the individual, presumed to be due to central nervous system dysfunction, and may occur across the life span. Problems in self-regulatory behaviours, social perception and social interaction may exist with learning disabilities but do not by themselves constitute a learning disability. Although a learning disability may occur concomitantly with other handicapping conditions (e.g. sensory impairment, mental retardation, social and emotional disturbance) or environmental influences (e.g. cultural differences, insufficient/inappropriate instruction), it is not the direct result of those conditions or influences".

DEFINING LANGUAGE DISABILITIES

Historically, language disorders have been referred to as 'aphasia'. This means loss of language due to brain damage or dysfunction. But this term does not accurately fit developmental impairments in children. Hence, the terms 'the developmental aphasia' and 'developmental dysphasia' have been used. In the United States, the terms 'Specific Language Disorders' (SLD) or 'Specific Language Impairment' (SLI) are commonly used. Therefore it is understood that 'the language disorders' and 'language disabilities' are used interchangeably. Further, the term 'difficulty' is also used interchangeably with 'disability', 'disorder' or 'impairment'. Language disorder refers to deviance from the expected norm of a language skill. Similarly, 'language delay' means not reaching the expected age appropriate norm of a language skill at a particular age. On the other hand, 'language impairment' refers to language loss or distortion. Since all these conditions lead to language difficulties of some sort or the other, the term 'language difficulty' can be used interchangeably with 'language disorder', 'language impairment', 'language deficit' or 'language disability' (Reddy and Santhakumari, 2003). Many times, the language disorder in one or more psychological processes spoken or written in which the difficulty manifests itself as an imperfect ability to listen, think, speak, read or write (Martin and Miller, 1996). The American Speech – Language Hearing Association (ASHA, 1980) proposed a working definition for language disorder:

"A language disorder is the abnormal acquisition, comprehension, or expression of spoken or written language. The disorder may involve deficits in all or any one or some of the phonologic, morphologic, semantic syntactic or pragmatic components of the language disorders frequently have problems in sentence processing or in abstracting information meaningful for storage and retrieval from short and long-term memory".

The Diagnostic and Statistical Manual of Mental Disorders – Fourth Edition (DSM-IV, 1994) has also defined the language disability as 'phonological, expressive and receptive-cum-expressive disorder'.

NEED FOR UNDERSTANDING THE CONCEPT OF LANGUAGE AND LEARNING DISABILITIES

The language and learning disabilities, which refer to developmental problems in reading, writing and arithmetic (the 'three Rs' of the classroom that are essential to learning as well as every day functioning), are also termed 'dyslexia', 'dysphasia' and 'dyscalculia'. They exert concomitant effects on academic performance and their reflections will inevitably be felt in wider educational setting and interactive processes. In addition, these disabilities have both pervasive and cumulative effects not only on the academic growth and development but also on the career and civil life of the individual. Due to this, the individual may become a social wreck due to frustration and self-pity. Stevenson (1996) appropriately stated that psychological and behavioural problems have often been interpreted as a consequence of these disabilities. Grasham and Elliot (1980), Margalitt (1989) and Rourke (1988) came out with their findings that peers, teachers and parents tend to display negative attitude towards the children with language and learning disabilities. Bryan (1997) predicted the risk of social rejection for such children, whereas Ritter (1989) and Rourke and Fuerst (1995) found them to be lacking in social competence. They further added that these children might react to the academic failure and social rejection with frustration, anger and acting out behaviours. Above all, the children with language and learning disabilities constitute a considerable percentage of school going population (Reddy and Santhakumari, 2003). Hence a thorough understanding of the concept of language and learning disabilities is crucial for identification, prevention as well as for designing and implementation of intervention programmes.

CLASSIFICATION OF LANGUAGE DISABILITIES

There are two major approaches prevailing in practice that venture to classify language disabilities. They are Etiological-Categorical approach and Descriptive-Developmental approach. The former tries to categorise the language disorders or disabilities in terms of their causes/reasons. Each etiological category, therefore, summarizes a cluster of behaviours that differentiate the language disabled child form his normally developing peers. The use of etiological typologies dates back to the early works of McGinnis (1963) and Myklebust (1954). Later, the etiological classification done by McCormick and Schiefelbush (1984) included 5 categories of language disorders:

1. Language and communication disorders associated with motor disorders due to brain pathology;
2. Language and communication disorders associated with sensory deficits, which encompass hearing, visual and speech impairments;
3. Language and communication disorders associated with central nervous system damage. (When the damage is mild, the children are classified as learning

disabled. When it is severe, they are classified as developmental aphasics);

4. Language and communication disorders associated with severe emotional, social dysfunctions, which encompass the psychotic, the schizophrenic and the autistic. They exhibit a severe disruption in the development of their verbal and non-verbal interaction skills;

5. Language and communicative problems associated with cognitive disorder, which encompass children with mental retardation. The degree of the cognitive disabilities of these children varies on par with the level of retardation.

Kamhi (1990) added one more category to the above list, that is, culturally and socially deprived. Bloom and Lahey (1978) highlighted the limitations of the Etiological-categories approach. They pointed out that a particular diagnostic label does not delineate what exactly the child knows about the language and what it needs to know. Furthermore, it is rare to find a child who fits into one single category. For example, the same child may be mentally retarded and simultaneously he/she may possess autism.

As against the above model, the descriptive-developmental approach classifies the language disabilities by way of describing them. It does not classify based on causes. Instead, it aims to comparing the language disabled child's ability to comprehend and formulate language with that of the non-disabled child. The main assumption of this approach is that a child with a language disability needs to learn what the non-disabled child needs to learn at some point in development (Naremore, 1980). Bloom and Lahey (1978) followed this approach. They held the view that disruptions might occur in form, in use or in the interactions among them. Based on the nature of disruption, they identified 5 types of language disabilities:

1. Deficits in learning linguistic from which include the difficulties to internalise and use phonological, morphological and syntactic rules;

2. Deficits in conceptualising and formulating ideas about events and relations and these deficits encompass difficulties to deal with the semantic component of the language;
3. Difficulties in language use and in adjusting language to meet with the different communicative functions/ intentions;
4. Difficulties in integrating form, content and use which are known as association problems; and
5. Lagging far behind in language and communication skills expected from the level of a particular age. This kind of disability is known as 'delayed language development'.

The American Speech–Language Hearing Association (ASHA, 1980) identified the following types, according to its definition:

1. Impairment in language comprehension;
2. Impairment in language expression (formulation);
3. Combination of both;
4. Difficulties in listening and speaking or reading and writing;
5. Inability to process linguistic information, organize and store it or retrieve it from memory.

The DSM-IV (1994) classifies language disabilities as phonological, expressive and receptive-cum-expressive disorders. Phonological disability has to do with the misproduction of speech sounds. This type of disability includes deficits in producing age-appropriate speech sounds, using speech sound substitutions, distortions and omissions of speech sounds. Expressive language disability involves impairment in expressed language, production of speech with regard to vocabulary, sentence structure and other aspects of language output. For example, children with expressive disabilities may have a limited vocabulary and may speak in extremely short, simple sentences. The receptive-cum-expressive language disability involves problems in comprehending the communication of others. The students who have such a difficulty may not respond to speech or respond inappropriately. Single words, phrases, the multiple meanings of a word, tense conjugations and word order may also pose problems to them.

PREVALENCE OF LANGUAGE DISABILITY

Whitehurst and Fidchel (1994) consider that the expressive language disability is more common than the receptive type. Simple phonological probiems (misarticulations) increase throughout childhood and are uncommon in adolescence. However, milder impairments may not be evident until schoolwork places greater cognitive demands on the child. According to Miller and Tallal (1995), many language disabilities seem to be delays in the use of normal language. There is also considerable variation in the severity of disorder. Anyway, both receptive and expressive disabilities are frustrating. But the child with comprehension (expressive) problems is at much greater developmental risk. Similarly, Cohen (1996) found that in clinic populations, prevalence of specific language disability (SLD) is much great, running as high as 71 per cent. Whitehurst and Fischel (1994) reported that boys are having higher rates of SLD than girls. On the contrary, Lyon (1996a) found that there is no gender difference in phonological deficits.

GENERAL CHARACTERISTICS OF CHILDREN WITH LANGUAGE AND LEARNING DISABILITIES

The label 'learning disability' encompasses a heterogeneous group of learners with diverse characteristics. Some of the important characteristics are: 1) hyperactivity; 2) frequent shifts in emotional moods; 3) attention disorders; 4) impulsivity; 5) disorders of memory and thinking; 6) motor deficits which refer to general co-ordination problems that result in awkward or clumsy movements; 7) orientation and specific learning deficits and most importantly; and 8) deficits in metacognitive and meta linguistic abilities.

Children with SLD exhibit a variety of cognitive deficits. They have impairment in the processing of rapid or brief sounds and limited capacity to process information, which slows down the processing of large amounts of information. As information processing is slow, auditory information too is affected. Most of SLD children are basically and seriously deficient in areas of pragmatic social communicative functions as reported by McLean and Synder McLean (1978). Wigg and Semel (1984) found that the SLD children have problems in figurative language processing. Further, these children exhibit difficulty in generalizing the newly learnt language behaviours from one context to another. Normal language users have both flexibility and creativity to integrate and process component structural parts into a single whole and similarly to break a whole syntactic structure (e.g. a complete sentence) into component parts. On the contrary, the SLD children are neither flexible nor creative and hence exhibit serious limitations in language production and usage.

CLINICAL CHARACTERISTICS AND DEFICITS OF READING

According to Gathercole (1998), the children with language disability have deficits in short-term memory for sounds. That is, they are extremely poor in phonological short-term memory. As a result, they have reading problems and so they struggle to pronounce words correctly during oral reading. They read excessively slow and haltingly. Due to limited vocabulary, though they are able to read, they do not understand what they have read or do not remember what they have read. Good reading calls forth phonological processing ability, intact visual perception, phonological awareness, good short-term phonological store and sub vocal rehearsal. The language-disabled children are deficient in one or more of the above aspects. Often some of them are reported to have hyperlexis. That is, they have highly developed word recognition skills with little or no comprehension of words they recognise. In other words, their visual-verbal decoding ability is not integrated with semantic and reading comprehension. Moreover, they do not understand how words are functionally related in various syntactic structural patterns. As a result, they have difficulties in the use of verb endings and inflectional morphemes. They are not skilful in handling various syntactic structures like questions, negation, co-ordination, sequence and temporality to express a variety of ideas. The supra-segmental phonological features of rate, prosody, rhythm, stress and intonation are often found to be deviant in their speech. Fay and Shuler (1980) held that such deviant and deficient speech patterns may be the result of an inability to process, register and generate supra-segmental features within a linguistic message.

Deficits in metacognitive awareness and metacognitive strategic use, particularly deficits in executive functioning affect reading. In general, the children with LD lack knowledge about when, why and how to use the strategies that they possess (Pressley and Levin, 1987). The metaskills, involve the ability to revise reflect and repair language rules. Metalinguistic skills represent a higher conceptual understanding of linguistic production and comprehension, memory, information processing, reasoning and problem-solving (Brown, 1978). But the students with language and learning disabilities have pervasive deficits in strategic competence, which, inturn, limits the development of more abstract meta skills. In fact, Paris (1986) ascertained that the children who received the metacognitive programme have developed their awareness about reading. Salmon et al. (1989) reported that students who were exposed to metacognitive instruction in reading classrooms improved not only in their comprehension skills but also in their writing ability, which was assessed as a transfer task. Ryan (1980) asserted that metalinguistic ability is a prerequisite for learning to read. Ehri (1979) established considerable evidence linking the development of metalinguistic ability with the onset of literacy or learning to read. Palinscar (1982) improved reading comprehension in learning disabled children by teaching them specific cognitive and metacognitive strategies. Santhakumari (2003) ascertained the effectiveness of metacognitive strategies like task-orientation, task-planning, self-monitoring, self-regulation and self-evaluation in overcoming the language learning disabilities in receptive, phonological and expressive language areas.

CLINICAL CHARACTERISTICS AND DEFICITS IN WRITING

Problems in the mechanics of writing, which are most prevalent among language and learning disabled children, lead to the problem of dysgraphia. Normal children have a gradual development of smooth, rapid and clear handwriting. But in the presence of specific disabilities, the task of producing letters and words on paper goes very slowly and it is also laborious. Therefore, the children with dysgraphia are not able to submit or complete the written assignments within the stipulated time. Even after consuming a lot of time and effort, the quality of their written work in terms of clarity, legibility and neatness is poor. This is because of the lack of visual-motor coordination. Again, the disabled children involved in written work lack skill in understanding the goal of their writing, developing a plan, organizing the points to be written and linking ideals all of which demand the components of metacognition, that is analysed knowledge and cognitive control in which the disabled children are poor demonstrators. Mostly their written work demonstrates weakness in sentence construction, awkward phrasing, lack of paragraphing, poor punctuation and deficits in organization.

Linguistic competence necessitates knowledge of language, which, in turn, is of two types. The first one is 'declarative knowledge' which refers to our factual knowledge about language form and content with regard to phonology, morphology and semantics. The other one is 'procedural knowledge' that refers to the use of language in specific communicative contexts and this knowledge offers guidelines for selection of strategies for 'comprehension' and expression. Comprehension means making sense of what others say or write, whereas 'expression' means making ourselves understood to others either orally or in print. Normal learners synthesize both these knowledges and focus on meaning as well as form simultaneously. But the students with language disability have inadequacy either in declarative or in procedural knowledge and also are unable to integrate both these knowledges. This is known as schema level breakdown. Sometimes, their inability in organizing the information with ease leads to cognitive level breakdown. As a result, they are not able to cognisize and present linguistic concepts and principles. In addition, problems also occur in making inferences with regard to assuming roles of listener or speaker. This results in breakdown at discourse level. Further, their limited flexibility in using the linguistic strategies leads to breakdown at the semantic-syntactic levels. Due to such deficits in linguistic and communicative behaviours, the students with language disabilities present a number of challenges to their parents, teachers, peers and society as a whole.

CLINICAL CHARACTERISTICS AND MATHEMATICAL DISABILITIES

The children with mathematical disabilities (dyscalculia) exhibit an array of deficits including problems in accurately reading numbers, simple addition and subtraction, understanding arithmetic terms and symbols, paying attention to arithmetic signs, spatial organizations and memory for numerical facts. Visual-spatial, language and reading abilities play an important role in children's success in arithmetic. Further, the arithmetic ability also demands visual discrimination, memory for visual sequences, visual motor co-ordination, language skill and problem-solving ability all of which pose problems to the specific learning disabled children.

Metacognition is also a determining factor of academic success in mathematics. Bryant (1985) stressed the need for metacognitive training to children so as to enable them fare better in mathematics. Slife, Weiss and Bell (1985) found the mathematically disabled children to be less accurate in their problem solving skills (metacognition) as well as in their strategic behaviour of regulating their cognition, when they were doing mathematical problems. Kramarski et al. (2001) investigated the effects of multilevel (MMT) versus Unilevel Metacognitive Training (UMT) on mathematical reasoning and reported that MMT group significantly outperformed other groups involved in the investigation. Those children in MMT group were also able to transfer their metacognitive knowledge to a new situation.

VARIATIONS IN CLINICAL CHARACTERISTICS

Learning disabilities can be described as reading, writing or mathematical disorders, if they are 'pure' and exhibit difficulty in anyone area. But often deficits occur in combinations. For example, the children with reading problems also have learning difficulties. Similarly variation is also seen within a disorder. For instance, mathematical deficits may exist only in simple computing or reasoning and the child may be sound in other skills related to mathematics. Similarly in reading also, some are deficient in associating sound with symbols while some others may be deficient in visual processing. Hence, a clinical picture should have ample scope to include heterogeneity so that each child's disabilities must be carefully assessed to maximize the effectiveness of intervention.

PSYCHOSOCIAL AND BEHAVIOURAL PROBLEMS OF THE LANGUAGE AND LEARNING DISABLED

Psychological and behavioural problems have often been interpreted as a consequence of language and learning disabilities. Peers, teachers and parents tend to display negative attitude towards the children with language and learning disabilities because they associate learning disabilities with a variety of annoying problematic behaviours, such as anxiety, immaturity, disruptiveness and hyperactivity. These children receive lower rating in cooperation, coping, tactfulness, responsibility and other such attributes. Bryan (1997) also sounded caution against the risk of social rejection for these children. Ritter (1989) found them to be lacking in social competence. Beitchman et al. (1996) reported that there is a higher risk for a variety of behavioural disturbances, both internalizing and externalising problems for the learning disabled children. Associations with attention problems and hyperactivity are well established. Particularly, specific language impairment is found to be associated with overactivity and behavioural immaturity. Similarly, reading disorder has frequently been associated with conduct disorder. The children with learning disability are often reported to react to academic failure and social rejection with frustration, anger and acting-out behaviours.

Fergusson and Lynskey (1997) found antisocial behaviour to be correlated with concurrent and later reading difficulties. Rourke and Fuerst (1995) reported that Nonverbal Learning Disability (NVLD), a distinct subtype of learning disability, is associated with the development of internalizing behavioural problems.

There are evidences for the fact that some of the children with learning disabilities have lowered self-esteem with regard to their academic performance. Licht and Kistner (1986) found the learning disabled children to enter into a vicious cycle of academic failure and low motivation that works against them. Research evidences also reveal that children with learning disabilities tend to have lower expectations for success than other children. They tend to believe that their efforts will not improve the situation and that the situation is controlled by external variables (Allen and Drabman, 1991).

FACTORS ASSOCIATED WITH LEARNING DISABILITIES

Many factors are associated with learning handicaps. The critical causes of LD are biological, psychological and environmental factors.

1. *Biological Factors*

It has so long been held that neurological damage or dysfunction underlies language and learning disabilities. Early theorists linked brain disorder with average intelligence as well as with learning, perceptual, language and behavioural problems such as hyperactivity. There are many learning disabled children with histories of neurological disorders such as cerebral palsy, epilepsy, nervous system infection and head injury (Taylor, 1988a).

Genetic influence on learning disabilities is firmly established (De Fries and Gillis, 1993). Bishop (1992a) reported that language dysfunction 'run in families'. Hereditary influences have also been established by many research findings. For example, Beitchman and Young (1997) ascertained that most of first-degree relatives of reading disordered children have reading problems.

Specific chromosomes and mechanisms that might be responsible for reading disorders have been identified. Chromosomes 15 and 6 have been implicated in some cases. In other words, inheritance is linked to one of these genes. Both polygenic and single-gene effects are suspected.

Brain abnormalities too are thought to have influence on learning disabilities. Paul Broca demonstrated that a small area of left frontal lobe (now called Broca's area) was associated with language production. Recently, brain scans and other research methods have revealed the importance of several brain structures in language and reading functions. Studies regarding dyslexia revealed that visual information was processed by both the hemispheres of the brain and the right hemisphere held the visual stimuli in reverse form and order. For most children, this arrangement was not a problem because the left hemisphere became dominant over the right. But in dyslexia, left hemisphere dominance was considered flawed and so the right hemisphere gained some control and as a result its reverse patterns were expressed in many ways.

More recently, it was established that plenum temporale, a triangular-shaped region on the upper surface of the temporal lobe extending to the lower surface of the parietal lobe, is involved in phonological processing. Normally, the left side of planum temporal is larger than the right side. But in individuals with dyslexia this asymmetry is absent. Further, abnormal cell structure as well as abnormal activation and metabolism are found in the cases of dyslexia.

In 1998, Shaywitz and his colleagues studied using functional magnetic resonance imaging the brains of adult dyslexic and normal readers when they were engaged in highly demanding phonological tasks. The dyslexic readers revealed relative under activation in the visual cortex, angular gyrus and Wernicke's area (an area in the temporal lobe) and relative overactivation around Broca's area. This finding adds further evidence for phonological difficulties in reading disorder.

2. *Psychological and Environmental Factors*

The role of psychosocial and motivational effects on learning disability is well established. Of several variables that influence the development of language and learning, early vocabulary growth, which the child is indebted to its mother and other caretakers at home, plays an important role. In broken homes, the children may not have a congenial atmosphere for the vocabulary benefits. Similarly, the family interactions, parental attitudes towards learning, child management practices, parenting styles, social class and cultural values adopted by the family are some of the factors that can influence children's learning. Stevenson and Fredman (1990) confirmed that large family size and certain aspects of mother-child interaction were linked to reading problems. They also noted that family involvement in the child's learning may be especially influential in early reading acquisition. Bee (1997) considered that in families where the parents have low IQs, there is often serious family disorganization and cognitive or emotional deprivation (in the form of a lack of attention and reinforcement from others), along with poverty, inadequate health care, poor nutrition and a lack of education all of which can operate simultaneously with genetic factors to produce learning disabilities.

Strategic deficits and insufficient metacognitive skills contribute to LD. According to Flavell (1982), efficient learning depends upon the successful interaction among three categories of knowledge about cognition: person variables, task variables and strategy variables. Person variables refer to an individual's knowledge and beliefs concerning human beings (that is, his own self and others). Knowledge about task variables refers to one's learning from experience that different kinds of tasks exert different kinds of information processing demands. Strategy variables refer to those strategies for monitoring an individual's cognitive progress such as planning, checking, monitoring, testing, revising and evaluating. The learning disabled children are found by many researchers to be deficient in both knowledge about cognition and regulation of cognition. In short, they have deficits in metacognition. Researchers on metacognitive theory proposed that learning disabled children have strategic deficits and they viewed LD children as maladaptive learners, who do not participate actively in their own learning process, through the use of efficient strategies; who lack self-awareness and awareness of task demands; or who may use strategies inappropriately for the given task (Torgesen, 1977a). Santhakumari (2003) too ascertained that the children with language learning difficulties have metacognitive strategic deficits. As Torgesen (1977a) alluded, meta variables are the one of the underlying causes as well as explanatory mechanism of LD children's inability in learning. Wong (1982) found that LD children lacked self-checking skills. Wiig (1990) too held the perspective that many students with language disabilities show delays in metalinguistic maturation and strategic use. Warner et al. (1982) too hypothesized that individuals with learning disabilities either have delayed or deficit executive functioning.

Learning disabilities can also be the result of various other environmental factors occurring pre-natally, peri-natally or post-natally, although pre-natal factors account for by far the largest proportion of learning disabilities. The most important pre-natal influence is from consuming alcohol and drug like heroin by expectant mothers. Perinatal influence on learning disabilities includes birth trauma, prematurity (and associated low birth weight) and asphyxiation. Post-natal influences include exposure to various toxins (such as pesticides and lead form car exhaust fumes) and malnutrition. Similarly, it is a known fact most of the children belonging to culturally, economically and environmentally disadvantaged groups are more prone to exhibit learning disabilities.

Englemann (1977) named another environmental factor, which contributes to learning disability, that is, poor teaching. Many professionals believe that if teachers were better prepared to handle the special learning problems of children with appropriate instructional methods in the early years of schooling, most of the learning disabilities could be avoided or even set right.

ASSESSMENT OF LANGUAGE AND LEARNING DISABILITIES

Psychological and educational testing of the LD must be oriented towards providing relevant information for educational programming. Scores on a test can be translated into educational recommendations. This is known as 'diagnosis for teaching' and this diagnosis, sometimes called 'prescriptive teaching', is nothing but an educational prescription in the form of educational tasks on the basis of diagnostic information gained from testing and observation of the child. Four methods of tests are very popular in the field of learning disabilities: 1) standardized tests; 2) process tests; 3) informal reading inventories; and 4) formative evaluation methods.

In some cases, the child may be evaluated in mental health settings, and subsequently schools may make an assessment and then arrange a meeting among teachers, parents and other relevant individuals to discuss the evaluation and plan for intervention.

Appropriate assessment requires an interview with the parents and seeks information about the child's prenatal, developmental and medical history; the child's behavioural and social functioning; family background; and family functioning and concerns.

Psychological tests, which establish the child's academic achievement, general intelligence and specific language, cognitive, perceptual or motor skills also serve the purpose of identifying the learning disabilities. Curriculum-based assessment is also suggested by some researchers like Nelson (1994). Several studies indicate that students make more progress when their teachers use curriculum-based assessment: Santhakumari (2003) developed curriculum based diagnostic tests to identify the language difficulties of students in receptive, phonological and expressive language areas. The focus of academic assessment should be on reading, spelling and arithmetic skills. At the same time, it should also be noted that all components of an academic domain need to be tested. For example, evaluation of reading skill should include measures of sounding out phonemes, words, recognizing sounds for letters and comprehending written material.

Taylor (1988a) suggested for a comprehensive assessment of LD, which should include the child's psychological adjustment. It also takes into account environmental factors that can promote or have an adverse influence on the child's functioning. For instance, evaluation of parental attitudes, environmental stress and the match between the child's abilities and other' expectations are important aspects of assessment.

Satz and Fletcher (1988) suggested that assessment should be made at an appropriately early time. Reading problems can be predicted in kindergarten or first grade. If the learning disabilities are not identified and properly intervened in the early years, they may lead to severe problems, which may then become very difficult to overcome. They may even result in behaviour problems, which may culminate in a risk of social rejection for the child.

TREATMENT FOR LANGUAGE AND LEARNING DISABILITIES

There are several possible orientations for planning treatment programmes for learning disabled children. Interventions for LD has reflected the multidisciplinary nature of the field. Psychologists, physicians, educators, optometrists and communication therapists all have a hand in treatment. Many different approaches were employed in the late 1960s and 1970s. according to Lyon and Cutting (1998), those approaches reflected three models. The biological model proposed that treatment should focus on the underlying biological and learning disabilities. The psycho educational model, which is also known as the diagnostic-remedial model, assumes that treatments must relieve psycho neurological deficits that are underlying LD. The behavioural model directed treatment towards improving academic skills through learning principles and it made no assumptions about underlying etiology or deficits. The treatments based on the biological and psycho educational models have not been proved successful either in remediating academic performance or in reducing the proposed underlying deficits of LD. But the behavioural model has enjoyed more success and continues to play a role in the interventions that are favoured today (Lyon and Cutting, 1998).

Majority of the professionals recognize the following three categories as main approaches: 1) behaviour modification; 2) direct instruction; and 3) cognitive and metacognitive training.

1. *Behaviour Modification*

The behavioural approach aims at identifying academic or social skill deficits and modifying them through contingency management, feedback, and modelling. The goal of this approach is to increase the efficiency of LD children in terms of increased number of completed arithmetic problems, strengthened comprehension of written materials or improved handwriting. Reinforcement includes verbal praise, tokens or desired activities. In practice, these behavioural techniques are often combined with direct instruction and cognitive approaches.

2. Direct Instruction

Direct instruction pinpoints difficult or new academic learning tasks and teaches them. In other words, if a child has a disability in reading, then exercises and practices are given in letters, words and other literacy materials. The tasks are analysed into components. The direct instruction involves the steps such as selecting and stating goals, presenting the new (or the difficult) materials in small steps and with clear and detailed explanations, incorporating student practice, guiding them and monitoring their understanding with immediate feedback and reinforcement. The direct instruction focuses specifically on the instrumental process. A variety of direct instruction programmes are available for reading, arithmetic and language. These programmes consist of precisely sequenced, fast-paced lessons taught to small groups of four to ten. There is heavy emphasis on drill and practice. The direct instruction programmes not only result in immediate academic gains but also lead to long-term academic gains. These programmes have been proved effective with high-risk students (Morrell, 1998).

3. Cognitive Approaches

These approaches emphasize the remediation of deficits in metacognition and executive functions in information processing. The students are taught to understand better their own cognitive processes and to regulate their cognitive activity (Palinscar and Brown, 1986). They are encouraged to become active problem solvers. Instruction emphasizes increasing awareness of task demands, using appropriate awareness of task demands, using appropriate strategies, monitoring the success of the strategies and switching to another strategy when necessary. This approach has been proved successful in many areas like reading comprehension, mathematics, written expression, memory skills and study skills.

Santhakumari (2003) applied metacognitive approach to remediate language difficulties in receptive, phonological and expressive language areas by promoting the comprehensive metacognitive strategies: i) task-orientation; ii) task-planning; iii) self-monitoring; iv) self-regulation; and v) self-evaluation. She could arrive at a systematic procedure for metacognitive strategy adoption. The visual representation of the procedure is given below through a model:

SANTHAKUMARI'S (2003) MODEL FOR METACOGNITIVE STRATEGY ADOPTION

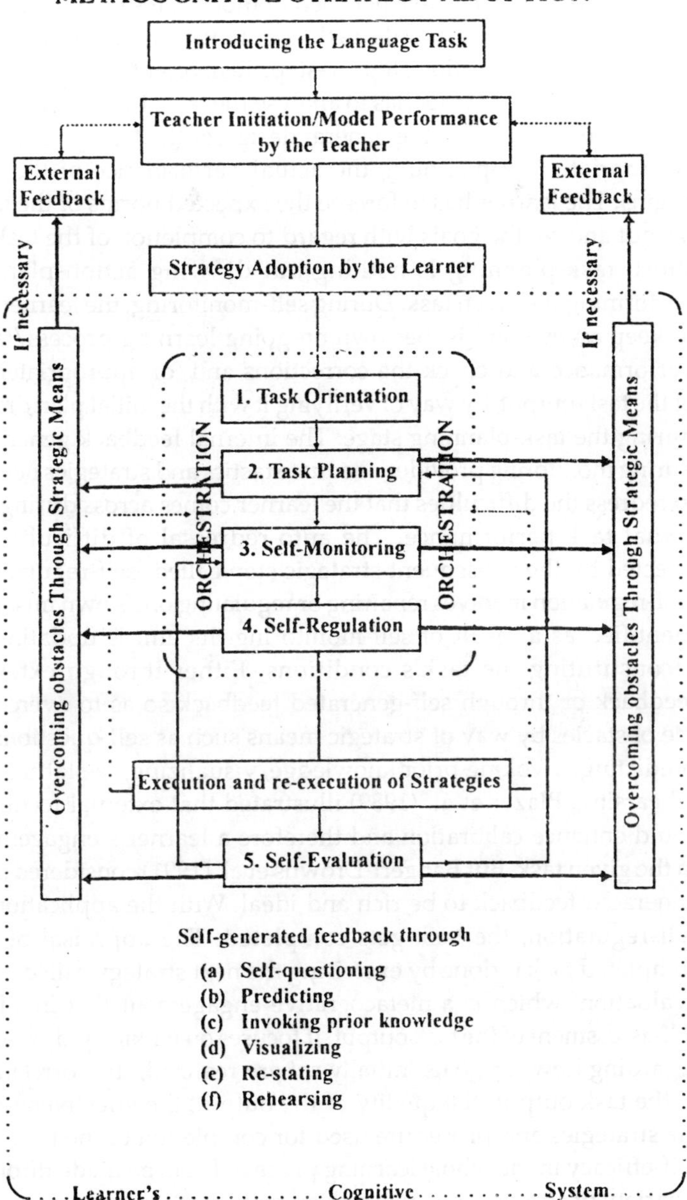

The teacher introduces the language task to be mastered, and explains its goals. The teacher then demonstrates through model performance of the whole task, explicitly manipulating the metacognitive operation step-by-step. Task orientation is the first step in which the learner has to analyse the task. In task-planning, the learner has to plan the general design of the task given. With appropriate task-planning, the actual performance of the task begins. The learner has to foresee the expected norms of the task-output and set the goals with regard to completion of the task. In short, task-planning is nothing but drawing action-plan for performing the given task. During self-monitoring, the learner has to keep an eye on his/her own on-going learning process/task-performance and check the corrections and/or appropriateness of the task-output, by way of verifying it with the initial plan drawn during the task-planning stage. The internal feedback generated during monitoring provides adequate tactics and strategies needed to redress the difficulties that the learner comes across during the actual task-performance. The auto-redressal of difficulties is effected by the subsequent strategic step called 'self-regulation'. Self-regulation involves repairing or regulating one's own mistakes identified as a result of self-monitoring. Its aim is updating or reconstituting the task's conditions. Either through external feedback or through self-generated feedback so as to overcome the obstacles by way of strategic means such as self-questioning, predicting, invoking prior knowledge, visualizing, re-stating and rehearsing. Blazer et al. (1989) illustrated that external feedback could enhance calibration and therefore a learner's engagement in the given task. But Bangert-Drowns et al. (1991) considered self-generated feedback to be rich and ideal. With the application of self-regulation, the task gets completed. The appraisal of the completed task is done by exercising the next strategy called 'self-evaluation' which is a metacognitive engagement that involves self-assessment of the task output. If focuses on making judgements regarding how far goals initially set are realized, the correctness of the task output, the quality of the output, the effectiveness of the strategies and procedure used for completion of the task and self-efficacy in the whole learning process. It can be made through a variety of strategic means, such as, self-questioning, comparing and verifying the output with a set standard, seeking suggestions from others, analysing the reasons for the correctness/incorrectness of the task output and identifying the gap between one's own performance and the set standard.

The impact of the metacognitive theory and research on the learning disabilities field is also evident from many research findings. Alley and Deshler (1979) designed a remedial procedure called COPS, an error-monitoring strategy to teach LD students to monitor errors in their written assignment and they found this approach highly successful. Palinscar (1982) improved reading comprehension in LD students by teaching them specific cognitive and metacognitive strategies. There were also strategic intervention studies by Hallahan et al. (1979), which focus on training of self-monitoring skills among LD students. The above research findings bring to limelight that metacognition has generated a new orientation in remedial instruction of LD students in which there is an emphasis on the basic tenet of cognitive psychology, namely, the centrality of the students' active participation in and responsibility for his/her own learning (Brown, 1980).

EDUCATIONAL ISSUES OF LANGUAGE AND LEARNING DISABILITIES

Most students with learning and language disabilities are in regular classrooms. If the regular classroom teacher has no training in learning disabilities, a special education teacher may act as a consultant. If resource room facilities are arranged, then it is important to note that experiences in the resource room should be integrated with those of the regular classroom. The most severely handicapped in learning can be advised to self-contained special classrooms. Both the resource room and special classrooms teachers should have ample training in special education. In special classrooms, the class size should be small (may be within ten) so that instruction can be better individualized.

For LD students with mild disabilities who can easily fit into regular classroom, the Regular Education Initiative (REI) has substantial implications. REI is a movement to advance the idea that most children with disabilities can be best served in the regular classroom setting (Carnine and Kameenui, 1990). It is part of the broader movement to integrate people with handicaps into regular education and society in general (Hammill, 1993) and thus synonymous to the concept of inclusive education.

The following principles of instruction are likely to enhance learning in a variety of settings and particularly with students who have learning disabilities (Taylor, 1989):

1. Academic competence is related to the amount of time devoted to students' being engaged in academic work;
2. Academic competence is also related to the teacher's active instruction, modelling, directing and guiding learning in structured steps and feedback;
3. Some degree of individualized instruction is helpful. This principle is related to the idea of mastery learning. In other words, a fixed minimum level of achievement can be set and the child can be provided with instruction and practice to reach that level;
4. Generalization of learning across tasks and time usually must be deliberately built into instruction. For instance, after a child learns a particular arithmetic technique, practice in using the technique on slightly different problems can be given;
5. Incentives are helpful and they should be tied to specific goals;
6. Training is best focussed on remediating all deficiencies rather than focussing on a single deficit because improvement in one skill often is not related to improvement in another. In addition mastery of lower-order skills and knowledge is necessary for higher-order abilities.

Apart from following the above principles, the teacher, when offering remediation to LD, should give scope for promotion of cognitive and metacognitive strategic competence among the LD children so as to enable them attain cognitive self-management.

SUMMARY

Deficits in psychological processes manifested in language, reading, writing, listening, thinking and arithmetic are referred to as learning disabilities (LD). The children with LD can vary from being very suitable to severe, with concomitant effects on academic performance and at large, they cast a shadow of failure over the child during school years.

Historically, two major themes tried to explain 'language and the other disabilities'. One has medical orientation and the other sprang from the concern that a select group of children had educational needs that were not being met by the schools. In 1963, in a symposium in New York city, Samuel Kirk suggested the term 'learning difficulties' to refer these children with leaning difficulties in specific area/s. Unlike the general learning problem in the retardates, the LD children with learning problem in the retardates, the LD children have specific problems in a more limited area. NJCLD has issued a definition of LD and suggested that LD can occur jointly with other handicaps too. At the same time, it stressed that LD is not the direct result of handicapping conditions like sensory impairment or environmental influences.

Language disability is a specific learning disability and it is defined as an abnormal acquisition, comprehension or expression of spoken or written language. The DSM-IV classifies language disability into three categories such as phonological, expressive and receptive-cum-expressive disorders. The etiological-categorical approach tries to categories the language disorders in terms of their causes. The descriptive-developmental approach classifies the language disabilities by way of describing them.

The children with language and learning disabilities exhibit heterogeneous characteristics. Generally they are deficit in areas of pragmatic social communicative functions. Some of them are hyperactive, have frequent shifts in moods, attention disorders, impulsivity and disorders of memory and thinking.

The clinical characteristics of children with reading deficits are poor phonological short-term memory, lack of phonological processing, defective visual perception, poor visual-verbal decoding and lack of metacognitive awareness and sophistication.

The children with writing problems or dysgraphia exhibit problems in the mechanics of writing. They have deficits in analysed knowledge and cognitive control. The children with mathematical disabilities reveal an array of deficits, such as inadequate visual discrimination, lack of visual motor co-ordination and problem-solving ability.

Learning disability can occur in any one specific area like reading, writing, or mathematics. Often, it can occur in combinations. Variations are also seen within a single disorder.

Psychological and behavioural problems have often been interpreted as a consequence of language and learning disabilities. Associations between LD and attention problems as well as hyperactivity are well established. Children with LD often react to academic failure and social rejection with frustration, anger and acting-out behaviours. They have lowered self-esteem, low motivation and low expectation for success.

Biological, psychosocial and environmental factors are associated with LD. There are research evidences for neurological disorders, genetic factors, hereditary influences and brain abnormalities contributing toward LD. The psychosocial factors are related to the family interactions, parental attitudes, child management practices, social class, cultural values, deficient meta abilities and metacognitive strategic competence. Environmental factors occurring pre, peri and post-natally account for by far the largest proportion of LD. Another important environmental factor is poor teaching.

Assessment of language and learning disabilities is normally done through measures such as standardized tests, process tests, informal reading inventories and formative evaluation methods. Appropriate assessment requires an interview with the parents and other caregivers. It also calls forth curriculum-based diagnostic analysis. Assessment should be made at an appropriately early time. If not identified and intervened in the early years, learning problems may culminate in severe behavioural problems as well as social risk.

Treatment measures and interventions for LD has reflected the multidisciplinary nature of the field. Psychologists, physicians, educators, optometrists and communication therapists all have a hand in treatment. The three important models of treatment are biological model, psycho-educational model and behavioural model. The major approaches in vogue to treat LD currently are behaviour modification, direct instruction and cognitive approaches. The cognitive approach emphasizes the remediation for metacognitive deficits and insufficient executive functions in information processing. The impact of the metacognitive theory and research on LD field has generated a new orientation in remedial interventions.

The educational needs of the most of the LD children should be met with in regular classrooms. If resource room facilities are provided, care should be entrusted to make children's experiences in resource room to be integrated with these of the regular classrooms. The most severely handicapped in learning can be directed to special classrooms. Both the resource room and special classroom teachers should have ample training in special education. For LD students with mild disabilities, who can easily fit into regular classroom, Regular Education Initiative (REI) has substantial implications. The concept of REI is synonymous to the concept of inclusive education.

REFERENCES

Allen, J.S. and Drabman, R.S., (1991), 'Attributions of Children with Learning Disabilities Who are Treated with Psycho Stimulants'. *Learning Disability Quarterly*, 14, 75-79.

Alley, G. and Deshler, D., (1979), *Teaching the Learning-disabled Adolescent: Strategies and Methods*. Love Publishing Company.

Bangert-Drowns, R.L., Kulik, C.C., Kulik, J.A. and Morgan, M.T., (1991), 'The Instructional Effect of Feedback in Test-like Events'. *Review of Educational Research*, 61, pp. 213-238.

Bee, H., (1997), *The Developing Child*, (8th. Ed.). New York: Longman.

Beitchman, J.H. and Young, A.R., (1997), 'Learning Disorders with a Special Emphasis on Reading Disorders'. A Review of the Past 10 Years. *Journal of American Academy of Child and Adolescent Psychiatry*, 36, 1020-1032.

Beitchman, J.H. Wlson, B. Brownlie, E.B., Walters, H., Inglis, A. and Lancee, W., (1996), 'Long-term Consistency in Speech/language Profiles: II. Behavioural, Emotional, and Social Outcomes. *Journal of the American Academy of Child and Adolescent Psychiatry*, 35, 815-85.

Bishop, D.V.M., (1992a), 'The Biological Basis of Specific Language Impairment '. In P. Fletcher & D. Hall (Eds.) Specific Speech and Language Disorders in Children: Correlates, Characteristics and Outcome.

Blazer, W.K., Doherty, M.E. and O'Conner, R., (1989), 'Effects of Cognitive Feedback on Performance'. *Psychological Bulletin*, 106, pp. 410-433.

Bloom, L. and Lahey, M., (1978), 'Language Development and Language Disorders'. New York: Macmillan.

Brown, A.L., (1978), 'Knowing When, Where and How to Remember: A Problem in Metacognition'. In R. Glaser (Ed.), *Advances in Instructional Psychology*, Hillsdale, NJ: Lawrence Erlbaum Associates.

Brown, A.L., (1980), 'Metacognitive Development and Reading'. In R.J. Spiro, B. Bruce & W.F. Brewer (Eds.), *Theoretical Issues in Reading Comprehension*. Hillsdale, NJ: Erlbaum.

Bryan, T., (1997), 'Assessing the Personal and Social Status of Students with Learning Disabilities'. *Learning Disabilities Research and Practice*, 12, pp. 63-76.

Bryant, P.E., (1985), 'The Distinction Between Knowing When to Do a Sum and Knowing How to Do It'. *Educational Psychology*, 5, pp. 207-215.

Carnine, D.W. and Kameenui, E.J., (1990), 'The General Education Initiative and Children with Special Needs: A False Dilemma in the Face of True Problems'. *Journal of Learning Disabilities*, 23, 141-144, 148.

Cohen, N.J., (1996), 'Unsuspected Language Impairments in Psychiatrically Disturbed Children: Developmental Conditions and Associated Conditions'. In J.H. Beitchman, N.J. Coghen, M.M. Konstantareas & R. Tannock (Eds.), *Language, Learning and Behaviour Disorders*, New York: Cambridge University Press.

Cravioto, J., (1972), 'Nutrition and Learning in Children'. In N.S. Springer (Ed.), *Nutrition and Mental Retardation*, Ann Arbor, MJ: Institute for the Study of Mental Retardation and Related Disability, 25-44.

De Fries, J.C. and Gillis, J.J., (1993), 'Genetics of Reading Disability'. In R. Plomin & G.E. McClear (Eds.), *Nature, Nature & Psychology*. Washington, DC: American Psychological Association.

Ehri, L.C., (1979), 'Linguistic Insight: Threshold of Reading Acquisition'. In T.G. Waller and G.E. MacKinnom (Eds.), *Reading Research: Advances in Theory and Practice*,: Academic Press, New Town.

Engelman, S.E., (1977), 'Sequencing Cognitive and Academic Tasks'. In R.D. Kneedler & S.G. Tarver (Eds.), *Changing Perspectives in Special Education*. Columbus. OH: Chas E. Merrill.

Fay, W. and Schuler, A., (1980), *Emerging Language in Autistic Children: Language Intervention Series*. Baltimore, University Park Press.

Ferguson, D.M. and Lynskey, M.T., (1997), 'Early Reading Difficulties and Later Conduct Problems'. *Journal of Child Psychology and Psychiatry*, 38, 899-907.

Flavell, J.H., (1982), 'Speculations About the Nature and Development of Metacognition'. In F.E. Weinert & R.H. Kluwe (Eds.), *Learning by Thinking,* West Germany: Kuhlhammer.

Gathercole, S.E., (1998), 'The Development of Memory'. *Journal of Child Psychology and Psychiatry,* 39, pp. 3-27.

Grasham, F.M. and Elliott, S.N., (1989), 'Social Skills Deficits as a Primary Learning Disability'. *Journal of Learning Disabilities,* 22, pp. 120-124.

Hallahan, D.P., Llyod, J., Kosiewicz, M.M. and Kneedler, R.A., (1979), 'A Comparison of the Effects of Self-recording and Self-assessment on the On-task Behaviour and Academic Productivity of a Learning Disabled Boy (Technical Report 13)'. Charlottesville, VA: University of Virginia Learning Disabilities Research Institute.

Hammill, D.D., (1993), 'A Brief Look at the Learning Disabilities Movement in the United States'. *Journal of Learning Disabilities,* 26, 295-310.

Kamhi, A., (1990), 'Language Disorders in Children'. In M. Leahy (Ed.), *Disorders of Communication.* London: Whur.

Kessler, J.W., (1988), *Psychopathology of Childhood.* Englewood Cliffs, NJ: Prentice Hall.

Kirk, S.A., (1963), 'Behavioural Diagnosis and Remediation of Learning Disabilities'. In Proceeding of the Conferences on Exploration into the Problems of the Perceptually Handicapped Child, First Annual Meeting. (Vol. 1), Chicago.

Kirk, S.A., (1972), *Educating Exceptional Children,* (2nd Ed.): Houghton–Mifflin.

Kramarski, B., Mevarech, Z.R. and Lieberman, A., (2001), 'Effects of Multilevel Versus Unilevel Metacognitive Training on Mathematical Reasoning'. *The Journal of Educational Research,* 94, pp. 293-300.

Licht and Kistner, J.A., (1986), 'Motivational Problems of Learning-disabled Children: Individual Differences and Their Implications for Treatment'. In T.K. Torgesen & B.Y.L. Wong (Eds.), *Psychological and Educational Perspectives on Learning Disabilities,* New York: Academic Press.

Lyon, G.R., (1996a), 'Learning Disabilities'. In E.J. Mash & R.A. Barkley (Eds.), *Child Psychopathology,* New York, Guilford Press.

Lyon, G.R. and Cutting, L.E., (1998), 'Learning Disabilities'. In E.J. Mash & R.A. Barkley (Eds.). *Treatment of Childhood Disorders.* New York: Guilford Press.

Margalit, M., (1989), 'Academic Competence and Social Adjustment of Boys with Learning Disabilities and Boys with Behaviour Disorders'. *Journal of Learning Disabilities,* 22, pp. 41-45.

Martin, D. and Miller, C., (1996), *Speech and Language Difficulties in the Classroom.* David Fulton Publishers, London.

McCinnis, M., (1963), *Aphasic Children: Identification and Education by Association Method*. Washington, DC: Alexander Graham Bell Association for the Deaf.

McCormick, L. and Schiefelbusch, R.L., (1984), *Early Language Intervention*, Columbus, OH: Merill/Macmillan.

McLean, J. and Snyder-McLean, L., (1978), *A Transactional Approach to Early Language Training*, Columbus, OH: Merill/Macmillan.

Miller, S.L. and Tallal, P., (1995), 'A Behavioural Neuro-science Approach to Developmental Language Disorders: Evidence for a Rapid Temporal Processing Deficit'. In D. Cicchetti & D.J. Cohen (Eds.), *Developmental Psychopathology*, Vol. 2, New York: John Wiley.

Morrell, R., (1998), 'Project Fellow Through: Still Ignored'. *American Psychologist*, 53, 318.

Myklebust, H., (1954), *Auditory Disorders in Children: A Manual for Differential Diagnosis*, New York: Grune & Stratton.

Naremore, R., (1980), 'Language Disorders in Children'. In T. Hixon, L. Schriberg & J. Saxman (Eds.), *Introduction to Communication Disorders*. Englewood Cliffs, NJ: Prentice Hall.

National Joint Committee for Learning Disabilities (NJCLD), (1981), 'Issues on Definition'. Unpublished Manuscript, (Available from the Orion Dyslexia Society, 724, York Road, Baltimore, MD21204).

Nelson, N.W., (1994), 'Curriculum-based Assessment and Intervention'. Language, Speech and Hearing Services in Schools, 2, pp. 170-184.

Palinscar, A.S., (1982), 'Improving the Reading Comprehension of Junior High Students Through Reciprocal Teaching of Comprehension-monitoring Strategies'. Unpublished Doctoral Dissertation, University of Illinois.

Palinscar, A.S. and Brown, A.L., (1986), 'Interactive Teaching to Promote Independent Learning from Text'. *The Reading Teacher*, 39 (8), pp. 771-777.

Presley, M. and Levin, J.R., (1987), 'Elaborative Learning Strategies for the Inefficient Learners'. In S.J. Ceci (Ed.), *Handbook of Cognitive, Social and Neuropsychological Aspects of Learning Disabilities*, Hillsdale, NJ: Erlbaum.

Reddy, G.L., Santhakumari, P. and Kusuma, A., (2003), *Language Disorders and Intervention Strategies: A Practical Guide to the Teachers*. Discovery Publishers, New Delhi.

Ritter, D.R., (1989), 'Social Competence and Problem Behaviour of Adolescent Girls with Learning Disabilities'. *Journal of Learning Disabilities*, 22, 460-461.

Rourke, B.P., (1988), 'Socio-emotional Disturbances of Learning Disabled Children'. *Journal of Consulting and Clinical Psychology*, 56, pp. 801-810

Rourke, B.P. and Fuerst, D.R., (1995), 'Cognitive Processing, Academic Achievement and Psychological Functioning: A Neuro Developmental Perspective'. In D. Cicchetti and D.J. Cohen (Eds.), *Developmental Psychology*, New York, John Wiley.

Ryan, E.B., (1980), 'Metalinguistic Development and Reading'. In L.H. Waterhouse, K.M. Fischer and E.B. Ryan (Eds.), *Language Awareness and Reading*. New York, DE: International Reading Association.

Salmon, G., Globerson, T. and Guterman, E., (1989), 'The Computer as a Zone of Prominal Development'. Internalizing Reading Related Metacognition from a Reading Partner'. *Journal of Educational Psychology* 81, pp. 620-627.

Santhakumari, P., (2003), 'Effectiveness of Metacognitive Strategies in Overcoming Language Learning Difficulties Among Higher Secondary Students'. Unpublished Doctoral Dissertation, Alagappa University Karaikudi, Tamil Nadu, India.

Satz, P. and Fletcher, J.M., (1988), 'Early Identification of Learning Disabled Children: An Old Problem Revised'. *Journal of Consulting and Clinical Psychology*, 56, 824-329.

Slife, B.D., Weiss, J. and Bell, T., (1985), 'Separability of Metacognition and Cognition: Problem Solving in Learning Disabled and Regular Students'. *Journal of Educational Psychology*, 77, pp. 437-445.

Stevenson, J., (1996), 'Developmental Changes in the Mechanisms Linking Language Disabilities and Behaviour Disorders'. In J.H. Beitchman, N.J. Cohen, M.M. Konstantareas & R. Tannock (Eds.), *Language Learning and Behaviour Disorders*. New York: Cambridge University Press.

Stevenson, J. and Fredman, G., (1990), 'The Social Environmental Correlate of Reading Ability'. *Journal of Child Psychology and Psychiatry*, 31 681-698.

Taylor, H.G., (1988a), Learning Disabilities'. In E.J. Mash & L.G. Terdal (Eds.) *Behavioural Assessment of Childhood Disorders*, 2nd Ed., New York Guilford.

Taylor, H.G., (1989), 'Learning Disabilities'. In E.J. Mash & R.A. Barkley (Eds.) *Journal of Childhood Disorders*, New York: Guilford.

The ASHA Committee on Language, Speech and Hearing Services in the Schools, (1980), 'Definitions for Communicative Disorders or Differences', *ASHA*, 22, 317-318.

Torgesen, J.K., (1977a), 'The Role of Non-specific Factors in the Task Performance of Learning Disables Children: A Theoretical Assessment' *Journal of Learning Disabilities*, 10, 27-34

Warner, M.M., Schumaker, J.B., Alley, G.R. and Deshler, D.D., (1982), 'An Epidemiological Study of Learning Disabled Adolescents in Secondary Schools: Performance on a Serial Recall Task and the Role of Executive Function'. (Research Report No. 55): Lawrence KS: University of Kansa, Centre of Research on Learning.

Whitehurst, G.J. and Fischel, J.E., (1994), 'Early Developmental Language Delay: What, If Anything, Should the Clinician Do About It?' *Journal of Child Psychology and Psychiatry,* 35, 613-648.

Wiig, E.H., (1990), 'Linguistic Transitions and Learning Disabilities: A Strategic Learning Perspective'. *Learning Disability Quarterly,* 13, pp. 128-140.

Wiig, E.H. and Semel, E.M., (1984), *Language Assessment and Intervention for the Learning Disables,* (2nd Ed.), Boston, Allyn and Bacon.

Wong, B., (1982), 'Strategic Behaviour in Selecting Retrieval Cues in Gifted, Normal Achieving and Learning Disabled Children'. *Journal of Learning Disabilities,* 15, pp. 33-37.

12

Autism and Schizophrenia

OBJECTIVES

This chapter describes the nature, classification and diagnosis of autism and schizophrenia. It vividly portrays the characteristics of autistic schizophrenic children and delves into analysing the causes of autism as well as schizophrenia. It delineates the assessment procedures of autism and schizophrenia. Ultimately, it presents the various measures of treating both autism and schizophrenia. After reading this chapter, this readers must be able to:

(i) Define autism and schizophrenia;

(ii) Present their nature, classification and diagnosis;

(iii) Draw the characteristics of autistic and schizophrenic children;

(iv) Analyse the various factors causing autism and schizophrenia;

(v) Differentiate autism from other disorders;

(vi) Understand the various assessment practices available to evaluate autism and schizophrenia; and

(vii) Know different types of interventions for treating both autism and schizophrenia.

Autism and Schizophrenia have a history of being intricately connected. But now these disorders are widely considered independent from each other. Both the disorders involve pervasive problems in social, emotional and cognitive functioning. Both have developmental lag and have been considered as associated with adult psychoses, involving disruptive disturbances, which imply abnormal perceptions of reality and need for supervision and protection (Volkmar, 1996). Kraepelin (1913) set the basis for modern classification, calling a group of psychotic disturbances 'dementia praecox' (senility of youth). He believed that these disturbances reflect a progressive deterioration and that they began early in life. Blueler later applied the term 'Schizophrenia' to the disorders and argued that deterioration was not inevitable and that the time of origin was more varied. Both Kraepelin and Blueler agreed that a small number of cases had begun in childhood also. Till 1930s, various diagnostic terms such as 'disintegrative psychoses' and 'childhood psychoses' were applied. Sometime later, 'childhood schizophrenia' served as a general label. In 1943, Leo Kanner described it as the 'early infantile autism'. He argued that it was different from other cases of severe disturbance, which often had later onset. Many research findings from various countries indicated a large number of cases before age three, remarkably low prevalence in childhood and increased prevalence in adolescence (Rutter, 1978). Subsequent investigations led to different conceptualizations of what once was considered 'psychoses of youth'. Today autism and schizophrenia are viewed as distinct disorders and hence these two disorders are dealt with separately one by one in this chapter.

AUTISM-NATURE, CLASSIFICATION AND DIAGNOSIS

Kanner (1943) found some severely affected children with communicative deficits, good but atypical cognitive potential and behavioural problems such as obsessiveness, repetitious actions and unimaginative play. Their fundamental disturbance was an inability to relate to people and situations from the beginning of life. Their parents referred to them as 'self-sufficient', 'like in a shell', 'happiest when left alone' and 'acting as if people were not there'. Kanner applied the term 'autism', which means an absorption in the self or subjective mental activity, to refer to the extreme condition of disturbance in emotional contact with others.

Subsequently, autism was recognized as a distinct syndrome of severe disturbance that arises in infancy or early life.

DSM has recognized autism as a subcategory of Pervasive Developmental Disorders (PDD), which are characterized by early occurring, severe impairments that are qualitatively deviant compared to the person's developmental level. DSM–IV (1994) describes the diagnostic features of autism as follows:

Diagnostic Features of Autistic Disorder (DSM–IV)

1. Qualitative impairment in social interaction manifested by:
   - *(a)* impaired nonverbal behaviours
   - *(b)* failure to develop age–appropriate peer relations
   - *(c)* lack of spontaneous sharing of interests
   - *(d)* lack of social or emotional reciprocity
2. Qualitative impairment in communication manifested by:
   - *(a)* delay or lack of spoken language
   - *(b)* impairment in initiating or sustaining conversation
   - *(c)* stereotyped, receptive or idiosyncratic language
   - *(d)* lack of age–appropriate, spontaneous make–believe or imitative play
3. Restrictive, repetitive, stereotyped behaviour, interests or activities manifested by:
   - *(a)* preoccupation with stereotyped restrictive interests
   - *(b)* inflexible adherence or non-functional routines or rituals
   - *(c)* stereotyped repetitive motor mannerisms
   - *(d)* persistent preoccupation with parents of objects

Diagnosis requires a total of six items or more with all three features present and with social interaction impairments more heavily weighted. Onset must occur prior to age three. Subgroups of autism are proposed by some investigations based on characteristics such as language problems, social functioning or nervous system dysfunction (Volkmar et al., 1997b). Another widely accepted distinction is between higher and lower functioning autism. The higher functioning autism is defined by an IQ of 70 or above and the individuals with higher functioning autism have less severe symptoms, distinct educational needs and better prognosis (Wing, 1997).

Many children display disorders that appear similar but not identical to autism. The major classification systems include them all with autism under the general category PDD. Three of such major syndromes are Rett's Disorder (found only in females), Childhood Disintegrative Disorder and Asperger's Disorder (which is viewed as mild form of autism).

PREVALENCE ON AUTISM

The population study of Lotter (1966) indicated the frequency of autism to be 4.5 per 10,000 children. But a recent review of epidemiological studies conducted over thirty years in several countries reveals that autism is very rare and its median prevalence is 4.8 per 10,000 (Fombonne et al., 1997). Boys consistently display autism more often than girls, with the ratio 3:1 (Klinger and Dawson, 1996).

CHARACTERISTICS OF AUTISTIC CHILDREN

The children with autistic disorder reveal three primary difficulties, which are called 'the triad'. First, they exhibit problems in social interaction that begins very early. Many of them are socially unresponsive, fail to track people visually, avoid eye contact, exhibit an 'empty' gaze and fail to respond to others with emotional expression and positive effect. During childhood, aloofness and disinterest are noticed. They ignore others, fail to engage in co-operative play or seem overly content to be alone (Volkmar et al., 1997a).

Secondly, the autistic children have disturbed communication, both verbal and nonverbal. Eventhough these deficits are subtle, they strongly suggest a specific problem in understanding social and emotional stimuli, such as emotional expressions on the faces of other people. These children use fewer nonverbal signals and project an 'expressionless woodenness' (Attwood, Frith and Hermelin, 1988). Deficits in 'joint attention interactions' are also noted. Both comprehensive and expression of spoken language are problematic. The comprehension of language is sometimes found to be delayed and sometimes it is short of specific language disorder. They remain mute or rarely say more than words or simple phrases. Their babbling and verbalizations are abnormal in tone, pitch and rhythm. These deficits may persist into adolescence and adulthood. The use of odd words or phrases is common. Echolalia and pronouns reversal are also common. The most notable impairment of language is in pragmatics, that is, the social use of language. The autistic children include irrelevant details in conversations, interrupt, shift inappropriately to another topic and fail to develop conversation. In higher-functioning autism, children can do better; able to tell story; and able to read. But the comprehension of what they read is below normal (Lord and Paul, 1997).

The third primary difficulty of autistic children is a typical and bizarre behaviours which are described as restricted, rigid, obsessive, repetitive or stereotyped activities or interests. Some stereotyped motor behaviours often reported are rocking, toe-walking, whirling, and arm, hand or finger flapping (Klinger and Dawson, 1996). These children may hoard worthless objects or may talk ceaselessly about an object and be upset if it is lost. Further, play behaviours are often rigid and lacking in social imitation and imagination. They adapt rigid routines. Changes in the environment may cause them to react with considerable upset.

Though the sensory organs are intact in autistic children, abnormal responses to stimuli are common and hence lead to the conclusion that they have sensory and perceptual deficits. Both over sensitivity and under sensitivity are reported. In case of over sensitivity, the child may respond even to moderate stimuli. Where as in under sensitivity, the child may fail to respond to verbal communications, sounds or other such stimuli and this is reflected in many ways. For instance, they may not react the sight of other; may walk into object; or may let objects fall from their hands.

Intelligence is not a diagnostic criterion for autism. Eventhen, it is important in clinical descriptions. Originally, Kanner described the children with autism as of average intelligence and some of them with specific disabilities. Many research findings reveal that at least 75 per cent of autistic children show mental retardation. They exhibit greater deficits on tasks involve abstract and conceptual thinking, language and social development.

A small minority of autistic population exhibits cognitive skills (splinter skills), which are inconsistent with their general intelligence. Some of them show amazing savant abilities. Pring and Hermelin (1993) reported that spectacular memory, mathematics, calendar calculations, work knowledge and music and art talents are displayed by some autistic children. These abilities often emerge early in life, with out training and without obvious inheritance.

Autistic children often display various behaviour problems, such as, aggression, outbursts, temper tantrums and hyperactivity. Their mood often changes unpredictably and inappropriate or excessive fears and anxiety are very common. Self-injurious behaviour (SIB) like head banging, biting of the hands, scratching, eye grouping and hair pulling are commonly reported among the children with autism (Schreibman and Charlop-Christy, 1998). It should be mentioned here that these behaviours are not specific to autism. But they interfere with learning and adaptation and hence require good management.

Apart from behavioural problems, the children with autism also exhibit psychological deficits. They have affective-social deficits. In other words, they have impairments in recognizing, comprehending and responding to socio emotional stimuli. Normal development requires children to understand that persons exist and that they themselves are both like and different from others. Such knowledge arises out of interactions with others. Hobson (1993) emphasizes that affect places a crucial role in interpersonal understanding and it is very important for human functioning. In autism, affect is disturbed and hence social processing is defective. As a result, the children with autism do not understand how others and think about the world and their social behaviour, communication skill and symbolic thinking are adversely influenced.

The individuals with autism are lacking in 'the theory of mind'. In other words, their social cognition is deficient. Theory of mind enables human beings understand the existence of mental states like desires, intentions, beliefs, feelings and the like and these mental states are connected to action. In other words theory of mind is the ability to read others' mind, which guides our interaction with others. For example, if we infer that someone is sad, we may try to be kind towards that person. The theory of mind typically develops gradually and by three to four years is fairly well under way (Wellman, 1993). This theory of mind is either delayed or lacking in autism. The impairment in theory of mind underlies many of the social and language deficits of autism (Baron-Cohen et al., 1997).

The children with autism have deficits in executive functioning also (Ozonoff, 1997). Many of them perform poorly in tests of executive functions. Executive functions involve many underlying operations. For instance, attention is an important component. Many research studies report that the children with autism are deficient in attention.

Individuals with autism are considered to be weak in central coherence. That means, they tend to focus on the parts of stimuli and fail to integrate information in to wholes. Many problems arise due to weak central coherence, particularly problems in reading tasks in which it is important to consider the whole context. For instance, the correct pronunciation of 'live' depends upon the context. In the sentence 'They live in a hut', the word 'live' should be pronounced as/liv/. On the otherhand, in the following sentence 'They saw a live rattlesnake', the word 'live' should be pronounced as/laiv/. The autistic children do not fare well in such tasks because these tasks demand the skill of extracting global meaning (Happe, 1996).

The children with autism have neurological abnormalities such as motor clumsiness, tremor and abnormalities of gait, posture and reflexes (Minshew et al., 1997). In many cases, higher than average head circumference and brain volume have been found (Piven et al., 1996 a) Many studies indicate that increased volumes of the parietal, temporal and occipital lobes are associated with autism (Minshew et al., 1997). Abnormalities are also noted in various other locations of the brain. For example, much research evidences are established for microscopic abnormalities of the cerebellum and limbic system structures (Pennington and Welsh, 1997). These tend to show reduced number of cells and/or reduced cell density. Some other findings suggest that malformations may develop during the prenatal period.

In brain functioning, the association of autism with epilepsy and abnormal EEGs was one of the earliest in the indications of biological dysfunction (Minshew et al., 1997). Epilepsy can develop at any age but onset is more common in childhood and in adolescent than earlier. This relatively late onset is different from what occurs in mental retardation (Bailey et al., 1996). Brain dysfunction is also suggested by abnormal EEGs in about 50 per cent of cases. Epilepsy and abnormal EEGs may be more common in severe cases.

Extensive biochemical analyses reveal that blood levels of serotonin are high in 20 to 50 per cent of autistic children (Anderson and Hoshino, 1997). At present attention has also been given to the opiates (endorphins) because they are suspected of being involved in symptoms such as decreased pain and self-injurious behaviour, repetitive behaviour, and poor social relationship. The diverse neurological investigations bring to limelight the fact that a highly localized abnormality will not account for autism. Rather it is more likely that abnormalities exist at the neural system level or in multiple brain parts, with the cortex being involved (Minshew et al., 1997). It appears that brain development characterized by abnormal growth of neurons, excessive tissue in some areas, and too little tissue in other areas, affects several cognitive functions including those involved in emotional and social interaction.

CAUSES OF AUTISM

There is little support for psychosocial or other environmental factors causing autism. But there is increased evidence for the association of biological factors with autism. The biological factors include medical conditions, inheritance and prenatal and birth complications.

(i) Medical Conditions

Several medical conditions have associations with autism. Well known genetic disorders are linked with this disorder. Fragile x syndrome (about which we have seen in Chapter X) is found in an estimated 2.5 per cent of cases of autism (Rutter et al., 1997).

Another genetic disorder called 'tuberous sclerosis' is expected to cause 0.4 to 2.8 per cent of cases of autism (Dykens and Volkamar, 1997). This disorder occurs from spontaneous mutations and is transmitted through dominant genes, with the gene on chromosome 9 and on chromosome 16 having been identified (Harrison and Bolton, 1997). The affected individuals have variable phenotypes involving benign tumors of the brain and many other organs, which were described as 'potato–like tubers' and hence they gave rise to the name 'tuberous sclerosis'. Seizure disorders are common and between 50 to 60 per cent of all cases who show mental retardation. When autism and tuberous sclerosis are linked, most cases are associated with mental retardation and seizures. This suggests that autism stems from brain pathology accompanying tuberous sclerosis (Bailey et al., 1996).

Some other medical conditions associated with autism are phenylketonuria (PKU) and other genetic abnormalities, cerebral palsy, infections such as meningitis, hearing impairment and epilepsy. Gilberg (1992) came to the conclusion, based on the study conducted in Sweden, that 37 per cent of cases were linked to identifiable medical conditions. But, it is still unclear whether medical conditions should be viewed as direct causal factors of autism or as coexisting factors of autism.

(ii) Inheritance

Genetic transmission is thought to be more influential. Folstein and Rutter (1978) established for the first time that autism could be a severe manifestation of a broader cognitive/linguistic/ social inherited disturbance. Family studies of autism (Bailey et al., 1996 and Newsom, 1998) also confirm this view. But the mode of transmission is still unknown. Some investigators favour several interacting genes, whereas others see evidence of autosomal and sex-linked inheritance. This suggests that different modes of transmission may operate in different cases. Genetic heterogeneity may also cause autism. For example, different genes may influence different features like language deficits, social deficits etc. Other wise different mixtures of genes may produce variations in the clinical picture (Le Couteur et al., 1996).

(iii) Prenatal and Birth Complications

Tsai and Ghaziuddin (1991) suggest prenatal and perinatal stress causing damages of brain may result in autism, especially when autism occurs extremely early in life. Prenatal Rubella and influenza, low birth weight and prematurity, older age of mothers, breech delivery, respiratory distress and maternal bleeding or some of birth variables identified to have links with autism. But these conditions account for a small minority of cases.

The above-mentioned biological causal factors may work alone or in combination to adversely affect the developing brain. What parts of the brain are involved, how brain functioning is disturbed and how brain abnormalities bring about the psychological deficits and symptoms of autism are not yet established.

DIFFERENTIATING AUTISM FROM OTHER DISORDERS

Autism has many characteristics in common with other disorders. However, differential diagnoses can be made according to certain criteria. First of all, the autistic children are different from the mental retarded mainly on the factor relating to the uneven developmental delay. The retarded children show relatively even deficits in all functioning areas, where as the autistic children may evidence isolated, 'splinter' aptitudes for high level functioning in areas such as mechanical, mathematical or musical abilities (Rimland, 1978).

Autism is typically differentiated from childhood schizophrenia on two bases: 1) Childhood schizophrenia usually has an older age of onset (5–12 years), where as the autistic syndrome appears to be present from both and is readily apparent prior to 30 months of age; and 2) Schizophrenic individuals commonly show higher levels of language ability characterized by thought disorder or word salad, while the autistic children exhibit a very limited use of language (typically mutism or echolalia).

In differentiating autism from central disorders of language processing (aphasia), we have to look for language delays, which are accompanied by disturbances in response to sensori stimuli and/or inappropriate relations to people and objects (Ritvo and Freeman, 1978).

ASSESSMENT OF AUTISM

The variability among cases and the need to evaluate several areas of functioning make assessment of autism demanding. Medical and neurological assessments are normally used because they are helpful in identifying autism, investigating its causation and treating associated conditions like seizures. The neurological exam, neuropsychological battery, visual and hearing examination, brain scans, EEGs and other tests are appropriate measures of assessment. But the extent of such assessments can be expected to vary with individual cases. Hence psychological and behavioural assessment is necessary for diagnosis as well as for treatment. The psychological and behavioural assessment includes interview with parents and other caretakers and also testing and behavioural observation of the affected child.

Many interview formats, checklists, and behavioural procedures have been designed for assessment. These instruments focus on child's behaviour and they mostly inquire into prenatal, family and other variables. Ratings are done based on actual observation of the child, impressions of the child's past or present behaviour or records.

The frequently used instruments are Childhood Autism Rating Scale (CARS), Autism Behaviour Checklist (ABC) and Autism Diagnostic Observation Schedule (ADOS).

Childhood Autism Rating Scale (CARS)

CARS is the most widely used instrument and it consists of 15 items on which the child is rated during or immediately after observation, usually by trained professionals. The items cover the areas of functioning such as emotional response, imitation, social relations, communication perception and intelligence (Schopler, Reichler and Renner, 1988). Directions are provided to create situations for observation of specific behaviours. Each item is rated on a seven-point scale based on the observation and reports from parents and others. The scores obtained from rating reveal extent of deviance from the normal behaviour. Based on the scores, the children are categorized as severely autistic, mild to moderately autistic or non autistic.

Autism Behaviour Checklist (ABC)

ABC is also a widely used instrument. It consists of 57 items placed in 5 categories: sensory, relating, body and object use, language, social and self-help skills (Krug, Arick and Almond, 1978). It was constructed to identify severely handicapped persons who exhibit severe autistic behaviours and it is part of a larger assessment instrument aimed at educational planning. (Newsom and Hovanitz, 1997). It is most useful in screening young children who are autistic and require further evaluation.

Autism Diagnostic Observation Schedule (ADOS)

The instrument consists of eight semi-structured tasks to assess children of six to eighteen years with a mental age of at least three years (Lord et al., 1989). It is based on formal observation and its administration requires twenty to thirty minutes. This is constructed mainly for higher functioning, verbal autistic persons. It emphasizes social behaviour and language. Most of the tasks have two sets of materials so that children with different developmental levels can be evaluated. Performance in each task is rated and ratings are given in four domains, namely, social interaction, communication, stereotyped behaviour and mood and non-specific abnormal behaviour. The ratings are made on a three-point scale, from normal to autism.

Intelligence Tests

This use of intelligence tests helps to obtain scores, which are moderately stable over time and is helpful in several ways (Newsome and Havanitz, 1997). These tests are helpful to predict academic achievement and classroom placement, especially for higher-functioning children. They are also helpful in evaluating the outcome of intervention. The widely used tests of intelligence are the Stanford-Binet and the Wechsler scales. With autistic persons who are mute, deaf or minimally verbal, Leiter International Performance Scale and the Raven's Coloured Progressive Matrices are employed. Developmental scales such as the Bayley Scales of Infant Development are used to assess young or low-functioning children.

Adaptive Behaviour Scales

They are helpful in differentiating autism as well as planning treatment. These scales are very often employed among older children and adolescents (Newsom and Hovanitz, 1997). For identifying deficits in many practical domains and for evaluating educational outcomes, AAMR's Adaptive Behaviour Scale is very useful. Vineland Adaptive Behaviour Scales indicate greater social deficits with autism than with other developmental disabilities (Newsom and Hovanitz, 1997).

Behaviour and Skill Analysis Technique

This technique emphasizes the needs of the children in particular environmental settings and the shaping of behaviour to meet those needs. This is usually employed when behavioural and educational treatments are predicted. This procedure calls forth much time as well as observation and implementation; it is very useful for selecting and monitoring intervention.

Behavioural assessment determines the specific behaviours that require modification and also identifies variables which guide and influence behaviours. In autism, it is necessary to assess behaviours, which interfere with child's being productive, such as self-stimulation, self-injury, and high activity level. Schreibman (1997) considers functional assessment, which examines how problem behaviour functions for the child, to be highly beneficial.

Assessment of Family

The social emotional isolation of autistic children may make them difficult for families to cope (Siegel, 1997). The families of autistic children experience many of the stresses of parents of other developmental disordered children. As major caregivers for autistic children, the parents always become a critical part of therapeutic team. Hence their well being ensures better therapeutic effects. In this aspect, family assessment is a basic need for facilitating the treatment of autism. Family assessment depends mostly on interviews and questionnaires that evaluate stress, child management, attitudes, coping, conflict, financial as well as educational status, motivation, and skills for participation in treatment. The most widely employed tools for family assessment are Family Environment Scale (Moos and Moos, 1986) and the Parenting Stress Index (Abidin, 1995).

TREATMENT FOR AUTISM

Early treatment efforts were frequently based on the influence of psychoanalytic theory, which emphasized that childhood problems might be rooted in parental behaviour. This theory proposes that failed parenting causes autism. By the course of time this assumption became suspicious and hence clinicians resorted to other interventions focusing on changing specific behaviours or meeting specific needs of the children with autism. Some interventionists aimed at more comprehensive improvement in the functioning of the children with autism (Rogers, 1998).

At present, many kinds of treatment are offered and some of them are unconventional approaches, which include megavitamins, hugging therapy, auditory training, visual training, physical exercise, allergy desensitisation and psychomotor skills patterning. Klin and Cohen (1997) recognize that many unconventional treatments for autism have not been adequately studied or proved effective. Most of unconventional approaches are inappropriate interventions, though they make excessive therapeutic claims (Klin and Cohen, 1997). Noteworthy cures have been achieved by pharmacological behavioural and educational interventions.

(a) Pharmacological Interventions

Many kinds of medications have been explored and very often they are recognized as adjuncts in the treatment of autism. Antipsychotic medications are of first choice. Haloperidol (Haldol), a dopamine antagonist, is one of the best studied and most effective

(Campbell et al., 1996). Generally, anti psychotic medications can reduce agitation, aggressiveness, stereotypies, social withdrawal, emotional instability and self-injurious behaviour (Dawson and Castelloe, 1992). Care should be allocated to study side effects because in many cases adverse side effects may occur over time. Particularly motor problems, including tardive dyskinesia (involuntary repetitive movements of the tongue, mouth and jaw) might arise. Campbell et al. (1997) found that such side effects occur in 33 per cent of patients in a single study.

Risperidone, another atypical anti-psychotic medication is found to reduce aggression, over activity and stereotypies across all ages (Nicolson, Awad and Sloman, 1998). Importantly, it avoids the adverse motor side effects of the typical anti-psychotic medications. In some cases, weight gain and sedation are reported. Abnormal liver functioning is also noted in some children.

25 to 50 per cent of autistic children show high blood serotonin levels. Such high levels of serotonin are associated with greater intellectual and stereotypic impairments. Hence substances, which reduce brain serotonin, are often recommended. For example, fenfluramine is reported to effect various benefits. But later studies (Aman and Kern, 1989) reveal that there is concern about anoxeria, weight loss, sedation, impaired learning ability, irritability and toxic effects on the brain. Hence, at present, fenfluramine is not widely recommended.

Summarily, many medications, though they show efficacy in reducing problem behaviours and in facilitating behavioural and educational interventions, are yet to be studied thoroughly. In pharmacological treatment, dosage level and age of the affected children are the important variables to be taken care of. When the pharmacological medications are prescribed to very young children, continuous monitoring of effects should be warranted.

(b) Behavioural Interventions

Behavioural approach is aiming at teaching specific positive behaviours related to language, social interaction, and self-care and thus reduce specific undesirable behaviours such as aggression self-stimulation and self-injury. The frequently used behavioural techniques are reinforcement, punishment, extinction, shaping, fading and generalization techniques. The behavioural techniques have a strong motive to train parents and other caregivers also.

It is obvious that intensive, comprehensive behavioural programmes are necessary to bring about substantial improvement in the lives of autistic individuals. Some of the behavioural interventions, which have been proved successful, are listed below. These interventions focus on specific behaviours.

(i) Acquisition of Language/Desirable Behaviour

Lovaas, Young and Newsom (1978) conceptualised acquisition as the learning of receptive and expressive speech. They considered the teaching of speech to autistic children is of foremost importance.

(ii) Receptive Labelling

This is another effective step. In this type of intervention, the autistic child is presented with preferred food or an object. The therapist verbally refers to the food in some way and the child is expected to respond nonverbally. If the child successfully responds, a reward is ensured. If the child does not respond, a prompt is given. The prompt is then faded. Generalization of learning is also built by providing training through different people in different settings. Speech sounds, words and phrases are generally programmed so that the child acquires a repertoire of language through modelling and reinforcement. In due course, when language itself becomes reinforcing, external rewards and prompts are faded. More advanced forms of language, such as pronouns, adjective, verb tenses and plurals are gradually taught. Over considerable time and effort, many children are able to generate sentences and to respond to an array of verbalizations. Operant learning can be supplemented and strengthened by more effective procedures to promote generalization and to encourage more natural communication (Koegel et al., 1998). Schreibman (1997) suggested that incidental learning can also be employed so that the child's behaviour comes more under the control of the natural environment.

(iii) Reducing Maladaptive Behaviour

The maladaptive behaviours such as bizarre speech, tantrums, aggression and self-injury interfere with social relationships, learning and educational placement. They even harm directly the individuals with autism. These behaviours can be reduced through many techniques. Many interventional programmes aimed at reducing one of the important maladaptive behaviours-self-injurious behaviour (SIB). When medications as well as behavioural interventions fail to be successful in reducing SIB, punishments are employed. Punishments include squirting lemon juice into the mouth and contingent electric shock. The aversive treatment may be effective sometimes. But they raise serious ethical questions (Shopler, 1994). They are also seen as inhumane and painful. They may cause serious physical side effects, stress and even death. Many health institutes recommend aversive treatment only in brief interventions for severe cases. More over, aversive treatment should be decided upon only after review and consent (Bergman and Gerdtz, 1997).

Another alternative procedure, which is more effective and acceptable is comprehensive analysis of variables which can influence problem behaviours like self-injury. Newsom (1998) presented schema for organizing such influences.

Schema of Variables Influencing Problem Behaviours

(Adapted from Newsom, 1998)

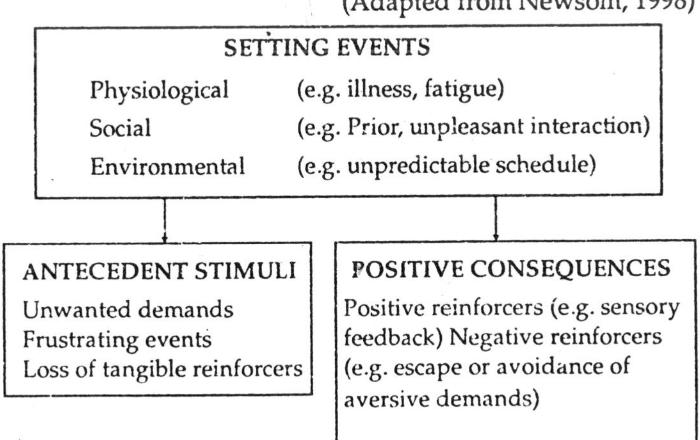

What Newsom emphasized is treatment can focus on any of the three classes of variables shown in the schema or on some combinations of them. Such analysis of self-injury provides a general guide to intervention. Modification of setting events and antecedent stimuli can prevent SIB from occurring at all. Modification of reinforcement contingencies can reduce already occurring behaviour. But functional assessment of variable that influence SIB is crucial. Naturalistic observations of the child, interviews with caregivers and ratings scales are helpful in functional assessment of variables. Further, functional analysis can be conducted, in which the disordered individual is exposed to different conditions. The rate of SIB is observed in order to determine the variables that are influencing the behaviour.

Durrand (1990) and his colleagues followed an approach called 'Functional Communication Training'. They have shown that SIB and other maladaptive behaviours are often used intentionally as a way to communicate needs or desires. They analyzed how SIB is functioning and then train more adaptive communication that can substitute self-injury. Durrand believed that Functional Communication Training is not only effective but also results in generalizations to other situations. Further, it sustains overtime. It is successful in the home, residential settings and schools.

COMPREHENSIVE TREATMENT PROGRAMMES

The techniques/approaches discussed above have emphasized treatment of specific targeted behaviours. On the other hand, the comprehensive treatment programme is an intensive behavioural procedure that aims at generating multiple positive outcomes for children with autism. Lovaac's UCLA project (1970) is the best example for comprehensive treatment programme. TEACCH (Treatment and Education of Autistic and related Communication handicapped CHildren) is another comprehensive educational treatment programme in which priority was given to three areas: home adjustment, education and community adaptation. This programme aimed at providing services, research and training for autism and related disorders. TEACCH has evolved as an alternative to psychoanalytic based approach in the university of North Carolina. The shared values of TEACCH Programme are as follows:

- characteristics of autism are understood from observation;
- parent-professional collaboration is vital;
- the child's adoption is improved through teaching new skills and making environmental accommodations to deficits;
- assessment for individual treatment occurs through formal instruments or informal observation;
- priority is given to cognitive and behaviour therapy;
- enhancement of skill and acceptance of deficits go hand-in-hand;
- a holistic orientation deals with the whole situation and ultimately;
- life long community-based services are crucial.

Any comprehensive treatment programme should aim at realizing the above values so as to attain success in terms of effectiveness.

EDUCATIONAL PROVISIONS FOR AUTISTIC CHILDREN

In America, autism is among the disabilities included in the Individuals with Disabilities Education Act (IDEA) and thus states and school districts are obliged to identify children with autism, provide services from birth, include families in evaluation and intervention and deliver appropriate educational programmes. In the absence of such a legal mandate in India, the commitments to the least restrictive alternative, to the concept of normalization and also to the integration of autistic children (at least the children who fall with in the range of mild to moderate) in the mainstream education should be realized. Parents, educators and professionals must go in for inclusive education with increased educational opportunities and there by minimize the chances for institutionalisation. Research investigations indicate that some autistic children can benefit academically and socially from classroom interaction with normal peers (Peck et al., 1978). At the same time we must also realize the fact that inclusion without support is likely to fail. Factors such as adaptation of curricula, social skill training, teacher attitude and encouragement of peer interaction should be allocated due consideration. However, the marked differences in abilities of the autistic children also suggest the need for alternative educational settings.

Educational opportunities provided to autistic individuals should bring about improvement in their functioning. The educational environments that are designed to prepare the autistic youth for future employment should hold promise for independent living and increased quality of life. Experiences that stress the aspects, such as task-completion, metacognitive sophistication, self-management, and specific vocational training can be helpful. Grandin (1997) considered that making a gradual transition from school to the work environment and building on the interests and talents of the individual to create job skills should be crucial.

As Shyamala (2004) suggested, yoga practices and pranayama to the autistic youth might take them a long way by providing them inner strength and cognitive soundness. Improvement in the lives as well as in the personalities of individuals with autism should be the result of all-rigorous research and commitment and advocacy of professionals and the families themselves. It should also be recognized that the improvements effected through interventions should be maintained throughout life. The maintenance of improvements in terms of behaviour change does not occur automatically (except in few cases). The implication is that improvement maintenance must be systematically programmed.

SCHIZOPHRENIA-DEFINITION, DIAGNOSIS AND CLASSIFICATION

(a) Definition

Schizophrenia is the most serious of all the disorders identified in ICD-10 and DSM-IV. Blueler (1911) coined the term 'schizophreninia' to refer to a 'splitting' of the mind's various functions in which the personality loses its unity. It should not be confused with 'multiple personality disorder', in which personality splits into two or more separate identities. The confusion probably arises because the word 'schizophrenia' derives from the Greek words 'schizein' (to split) and 'phren' (the mind). As it is noted in many cases, schizophrenia is a 'splitting' between thoughts and feelings, the consequences being bizarre and maladaptive behaviour. In a small percentage of cases of schizophrenia, as identified by both Kraepelin and Blueler, the onset occurs in childhood. The youth, who were classified with childhood schizophrenia varied a great deal from each other, attempts have been made for the past few decades to identify subgroups and syndromes. Further, the essential features of schizophrenia hold across age and hence the same basic diagnostic criteria can be applied to individuals of all ages. Even then, in tune with the clinical and research literature, distinctions are often made among childhood schizophrenia (with onset by age twelve or so) and schizophrenia that first occurs during adolescence or during adulthood.

(b) Diagnosis

The following major diagnostic symptoms of schizophrenia are identified by DSM-IV: 1) delusions; 2) hallucinations; 3) disorganized speech; 4) disorganized or catatonic behaviour and 5) negative symptoms of diminished affect, speech content and goal-directed activities. Of these features, delusions, hallucinations and disorganized speech are considered typical features of psychosis to indicate a break with reality. Delusions are erroneous beliefs and hallucinations are erroneous perceptions. Both these features are considered to be the hallmarks of schizophrenia. The feature—'disorganized speech'—indicates disordered thinking of the individual. Similarly the disordered behaviour is manifested through many ways such as inappropriate silliness, unexpected agitation and aggression, lack of self-care and so on. 'Catatonic behaviours' are motor disturbances like decreased or excessive motor reactivity and rigid and strange bodily postures. All these symptoms are considered to be positive symptoms. The individuals with schizophrenia also exhibit negative symptoms. In other words, they lack normally occurring behaviours. They may exhibit little emotion and their speech may consist of brief replies that do not seem to convey much information (alogia), or they may not initiate/maintain goal-directed actions (avolition). All of the above mentioned schizophrenic behaviours disrupt normal adaptation and relationships. Diagnosis requires continuous disturbance for at least six months.

Youth can be successfully diagnosed by the above symptoms. But strong reliance on positive psychotic symptoms for diagnosis has implication for very young children. Early developmental levels may not furnish these psychotic symptoms. Hence the current diagnostic system cannot identify schizophrenia if it exists very early. Gooding and Iacono (1995) consider that it is difficult to diagnose it until age seven or eight.

In Britain, schizophrenia's diagnosis relies on three 'first-rank symptoms', namely: i) 'passivity experiences and thought disturbances'; (ii) 'hallucinations '; and (iii) 'primary delusions'. The presence of one or more of these, in the absence of brain disease, is likely to result in schizophrenia. The first symptom includes 'thought insertion', 'thought withdrawal' and 'thought broadcasting'. 'Thought insertion' refers to thoughts being inserted into the mind from outside, under the control of external forces, whereas 'thought withdrawal' refers to thought being removed from the mind under the control of external forces. 'Thought broadcasting', means thoughts being made known to others. Similarly, hallucinations (perceptions of stimuli not actually present) may occur in any sense modality. The most common are auditory hallucinations. Voices are supposed to be heard from outside the individual's head and offer a 'running commentary' on behaviour in the third person (such as "He is washing his hands. Now he'll go and dry them"). 'Somatosensory' hallucinations involve changes in how body feels. It is often described either as 'burning' or as 'numb'. 'Depersonalization' is a type of hallucination in which the person reports feeling separated from the body. The third feature, that is, 'delusions' (false beliefs) persist even in the presence of disconfirming evidence. Delusions are of many kinds: delusion of grandeur (believing that a person is important or powerful), delusion of persecution (believing that one is being plotted or conspired against), delusion of reference (believing that objects, events and so on have a personal significance) and delusion of nibilism (believing that nothing really exists and that all things are simply shadows). All delusions are held with extraordinary conviction. The above-mentioned first-rank symptoms are subjective experiences and hence they can only be inferred on the basis of the individual's verbal reports.

(c) Classification

The DSM-IV subcategorises schizophrenia as paranoid and disorganized schizophrenia. The other classification systems include the following subcategories of schizophrenia: hebephrenic schizophrenia, simple schizophrenia, catatonic schizophrenia, paranoid schizophrenia, undifferentiated (or atypical) schizophrenia and other disorders.

(1) Hebephrenic Schizophrenia

This is the most severe type of schizophrenia. It is often diagnosed in adolescence and young adulthood. It is also progressive and irreversible. Its main characteristics are incoherence of language, disorganized behaviour, disorganized delusions, vivid hallucinations and a loosening of associations. It is also characterized by flattened or inappropriate affect and by extreme social withdrawal and impairments.

(2) Simple Schizophrenia

This usually appears during late adolescence and it has a slow, gradual onset. Mainly, the individual withdraws from reality; has difficulty in making or maintaining friends; is aimless and lacks drive; and shows a decline in academic or occupational performance.

(3) Catatonic Schizophrenia

It is a striking impairment of motor activity. Individuals may hold unusual and difficult positions until their limbs grow swollen, stiff and blue from lack of movement. Catatonic schizophrenics may engage in 'agitated catatonia', that is, bouts of wild, excited movement and thus they may become dangerous and unpredictable. Some of them are 'mute' and be totally unresponsive to external stimuli. Another characteristic is 'negativism' in which the individual sits either motionless and resistant to instructions or does the opposite of what has been requested.

(4) Paranoid Schizophrenia

Its dominant characteristic is the presence of well-organised, delusional thoughts. It shows the highest of awareness and least impairment in the ability to carry out daily functions. Language and behaviour appear relatively normal. The delusions are usually accompanied by hallucinations, which are typically consistent with them. It tends to have a later onset than the other types and is the most homogenous type.

(5) Undifferentiated or Atypical Schizophrenia

This is a 'catch-all' category for individuals who are either fit the criteria for more than one type. For instance, disorders of thought, perception and emotion, without the features particular to the types described above, would result in the label undifferentiated being applied.

(6) Other Disorders

These include 'schizophreniform psychosis' (similar to schizophrenia, but lasting for less than 6 months), 'schizotypal disorder' (eccentric behaviour and unusual thoughts and emotions resembling those of schizophrenia, but without characteristic schizophrenia abnormalities), and 'schizo affective disorder' (cases in which both schizophrenia and affective characteristics are prominent, but which do not justify a diagnosis of either schizophrenia or an affective disorder).

The reliability and validity of the subcategories are debated with regard to adult cases and subgroups have not been systematically applied to children.

PREVALENCE OF SCHIZOPHRENIA

Prevalence data of childhood schizophrenia are limited because of the low frequency of the disorder in youth. Prevalence is therefore age-related. According to a review, childhood prevalence estimates are twenty or fewer cases per ten thousand (that is 0.2 per cent or less), compared with the adulthood rate of 1 per cent (Gooding and Iacono, 1995). Further, prevalence is thought to be extremely low before age five or six, to increase somewhat during childhood and then to rise rapidly during adolescent to reach the adult rate (McClellan and Werry, 1997). Asarnow and Asarnow (1996) reported that at early ages, schizophrenia has often been reported as more frequent in males than in females. Volkmar (1991) reported that schizophrenia in children may occur at higher rates in less educated and less professionally successful families. In adulthood, schizophrenia is more prevalent in the lower social classes. It is also observed invariably in all cultures throughout the world.

CHARACTERISTICS OF CHILDHOOD SCHIZOPHRENIA

The core psychotic characteristics are striking. But the associated characteristics are very important considerations. The psychotic characteristics are hallucinations, delusions and thought disorder. Children experiencing hallucinations report hearing, seeing, or smelling things that others do not hear, see or small. Such perceptual abnormalities can vary in content and in complexity. For instance, hallucinations are simple when the individual sees indistinct shapes or sounds, whereas they are complex when the individual's perceptions are more organized such as identifiable figures or voices (Volkmar et al., 1995). The studies of Kolvin (1971), Green et al. (1992), Russell et al. (1989) and Volkmar et al. (1988) confirm that childhood characteristics of schizophrenia are auditory hallucinations, visual hallucinations, delusions and thought disorder. Further, these studies indicate the delusions occur relatively frequently and with consistency the schizophrenic children maintain the divisions or false beliefs even in the face of realistic contradiction. For instance, they believe that some harm is impending from some one. Russell, Bott and Sammons (1989) listed the different types of hallucinations and delusions prominent among children. They also bring out the percentage of children experiencing those various types of disturbances.

Types of Hallucinations and Delusions and the Percentage of Children Experiencing them

Types of Hallucinations	Per Cent	Types of Delusions	Per Cent
Non affective auditory	80	Persecutory	20
Command	69	Somatic	20
Visual	37	Bizarre	17
Conversing voices	34	Reference	14
Religious	34	Grandoise	11
Persecutory	26	Thought insertion	11
Commenting voices	23	Control/influence	9
Tactile	17	Mind reading	9
Olfactory	6	Thought broadcasting	6
Somatic	6	Thought Control Religious	3

Other associated characteristics of childhood schizophrenia are motor abnormalities, which include awkwardness, delayed milestones, poor coordination, and peculiar posture (Cantor, 1988). Emotional and social disturbances also occur. The children often exhibit lack of emotion. They laugh, cry or show anger, when the situation does not warrant such a response (Green et al., 1992). Coldness, moodiness, anxiety and depression have been reported (Prior and Werry, 1986). The schizophrenic children also experience social withdrawal and isolation, inability to initiate social interaction and ineptness (Watkins et al., 1988).

The schizophrenic children are not as deficient as autistic children in basic language skills. But their communication is found to be impaired in childhood and adolescence (Watkins et al., 1988). Caplan et al. (1996) found that their speech to be obviously reflecting thought disorder and many atypical features, such as echolalia, neologisms and decreased use of conjunctions to connect ideas.

The childhood schizophrenics perform somewhat deficiently in intelligence tests. Most of them score at borderline to average levels. Ten to twenty percent of cases show low IQ scores (McClellan and Werry, 1997). Green et al. (1992) found that relative deficits may exist on verbal tasks and tasks requiring short-term information processing. Jacobsen and Rapoport (1998) reported that intelligence declines during at least the first few years after psychotic symptoms appear.

Normal children are able to selectively attend to some information and exclude the rest, when they are constantly bombarded by sensory information. But this ability is impaired in schizophrenia and leads to overwhelming and unitegrated ideas and sensations, which affect concentration. Thus, schizophrenics are easily distracted. This failure to maintain an attentional focus is reflected in the inability to maintain a focus of thought. This, in turn, is reflected in the inability to maintain a focus on language.

CAUSES OF SCHIZOPHRENIA

Schizophrenia is caused by multiple factors. The most important factors are neurological abnormalities, genetic abnormalities pregnancy and birth complications and social and psychological factors, which are dealt here one by one.

(1) Neurological Factors

Later-occurring schizophrenia involves neurological abnormalities. Neurological dysfunction is suggested by general characteristics of children with schizophrenia, such as perceptual deviations, motor delay, coordination problems and others of neurological signs (Jacobson and Rapoport, 1998). Neurological signs have also been reported as childhood symptoms of persons diagnosed in adulthood.

Structural abnormalities of the brain have been the reason for schizophrenia. Brain imaging methods clearly identify structural abnormalities of brain. The most common finding is slight enlargement of the ventricles (fluid-filled spaces), which suggests under development or loss of brain tissue. Indeed, gray matter of the brain appears reduced. Reduced volume is found in the temporal-limbic area and the frontal area, and this finding has been associated with poor adjustment before diagnosis and neuropsychological deficits (Gur et al., 1998). Weinberger (1994) reported that neurons in the brain of schizophrenics are abnormal and in abnormal locations.

Disturbances are demonstrated in the frontal and temporal-limbic areas. Some adults with schizophrenia have difficulty in visually tracking a continuously moving stimulus. Data also show the same in adolescents and children. These tracking problems may be related frontal lobe dysfunction. Neuropsychological tests indicate that various deficits in attention and information processing, such as verbal memory, abstraction, language and executive functions. The frontal and temporal lobes are involved in such functions. PET scans reveal that the prefrontal area of the brain is under-active when engaged in processing tasks (Gershon and Rieder, 1992). Further, low reactivity of the autonomic nervous system, which might involve the hippocampus, has been widely reported for a subgroup of adults with schizophrenia (Ohman and Hultman, 1998). A study on child patients also reveals abnormalities in autonomic functioning that resemble anomalies seen in chronic adult patients (Jacobson and Rapoport, 1998).

(2) Genetic Factors

There is higher occurrence of schizophrenia or schizophrenic-like disorders in the first-degree relatives of children with schizophrenia (Jacobsen and Rapoport, 1998). Chromosome abnormalities have also been revealed in a few children.

The risk for adult schizophrenia rises as one's genetic relationship to schizophrenic person increases (Gottesman, 1993). For example, risk is about 13 per cent for children of a schizophrenic parent but only 2 per cent for first cousins. Similarly, identical twins have greater concordance than fraternal twins. Estimates of heritability are reported to be high (Canon et al., 1998). Researches are also going on to determine the genes and modes of genetic transmission causing schizophrenia.

(3) Pregnancy and Birth Complications

Structural brain deficit are often associated with variables such as early birth, low birth weight, multiple births, infections, physical trauma, lack of oxygen and convulsions (Gooding and Iacono, 1995). Prenatal infections have also association with schizophrenia. Canon and his colleagues (1993) studied high-risk Danish children and came out with the finding that pregnancy/

birth complications and genetic risk were independently associated with adult-onset schizophrenia. They also found that these variables acted together to contribute to the development of schizophrenia.

(4) Social and Psychological Factors

Life events such as adverse happenings or demands for changes that are stressful are the possible environmental factors having influence on adult-onset schizophrenia. Acute stress is the sole cause of symptoms of schizophrenia in many cases. Stress also interacts with other factors to contribute to etiology.

Family characteristics are also supposed to cause schizophrenia. Earlier, it was hypothesized that childhood schizophrenia was caused by family factors such as immature mothering and passive fathering, inability of the child to separate from the mother and reactions to pathological family dimensions (Goldfarb, 1970). Renewed interest in the family examines communication deviance (CD), which is defined as vague and distorted communication that indicates dysfunction in thinking and attention (Asarnow, 1994). Research findings reveal that CD was higher in parents of children with schizophrenia or a related condition that it was in parents of children showing depression or a related condition.

Family disturbance played a role in etiology. The possible influence of family climate is investigated in the Finnish Adoption study, which followed adopted children of mothers with schizophrenia (Tienari et al., 1990). The findings clearly indicated that the adopted offspring of schizophrenic parents had high rates of schizophrenia. Many other family research studies suggested that vulnerable compact who experience certain kinds of disturbed family interactions are especially stressed and that this combination of variables increases the risk for schizophrenia.

ASSESSMENT OF SCHIZOPHRENIA

Assessment of a child or an adolescent suspected of schizophrenia needs to be broad involving several sessions and multiple informants. McClellan and Werry (1997) suggested for the following categories of information as a guide for comprehensive assessment:

1. Historical information, including pregnancy complications, early development, age of onset, medical and family history;
2. Information with regard to positive and negative symptoms of schizophrenia and associated features;
3. Psychological assessment, including intelligence, communication, and adaptive skills testing;
4. Physical and neurological test formations, EEG, brain scan and other medical tests for the cases in which medical etiology is suspected;
5. Information acquired from consultations with the school and social services as necessary.

Professionals express concern about evaluating the psychological manifestations of childhood schizophrenia. Standardized rating scales and semi-structured interviews are helpful. The Schedule for Affective Disorders and Schizophrenia for Kiddies and for School-aged Children (Asarnow, 1994 and Kaufman et al., 1997) are such scales. Yet, the emphasis on psychotic symptoms in diagnosing the disorder in young children is problematic because psychosis tends to occur only after non-psychotic symptoms. Further, it is sometimes difficult to identify true hallucinations and delusions in young children less than five or six years of age, who are still limited in thinking logically and in distinguishing reality from fantasy.

Developmental level influences the identification of thought disorder. Language skills are crucial in assessing thought disorder and evaluation might be affected by the level of these skills. Further, it is reasonable to assume that what is considered abnormal thinking might vary with development level. In this regard, Caplan (1994) made a distinguishing study on children's thinking. She employed both a standardized test and an interview to elicit children's responses to stories. She found that loose associations are rare in normal children past age seven and then onwards illogical thinking decreases. She confirmed that loose associations may be a particularly strong indicator of childhood schizophrenia.

On the other hand, assessment of adolescents and older adolescents appears less problematic than that of children. Since psychotic symptoms appear more similar to those observed in adult- onset schizophrenia, assessment scales and procedures for adults are more useful. It should be mentioned here that psychotic symptoms in adolescents or adults do not always indicate full-blown schizophrenia. Research findings of Altman, Collins and Mundy (1997) reveal that 2 to 30 per cent of youth, either at risk or in clinical groups, report hallucinations and delusions that are not severe enough for the diagnosis of schizophrenia. Hence a comprehensive assessment should be invested with high care and caution.

TREATMENT FOR SCHIZOPHRENIA

There is a lack of systematic research on treatment of childhood schizophrenia. Hence, to some extent we must generalize from what is known about treatment of adults. The treatment for schizophrenia has got a long history that has undergone many changes in attitudes. On par with the attitudinal changes, treatment approaches too changed. They ranged from pessimistic, negligent and abusive methods to optimistic and sympathetic interventions. During the last several decades, thanks to the advent of anti psychotic medications as well as the philosophy of normalization, community living increased. Treatment also varies on the basis of severity of the cases, the phase the case is in, opportunity for treatment, community/family support and the perspective of the therapist. Early intervention is desirable, since it is associated with fewer symptoms in the immediate future. In addition the treatment procedure is considered as the best only when it employs multiple methods such as pharmacological, psychoanalytic, behavioural and family approaches so as to alleviate the frequently encountered multiple problems.

(a) Pharmacological Treatment

The schizophrenic adults were once treated with electro convulsive shock (ECS) therapy. But this therapy induces seizures and as a result brain damage may occur and hence it is rarely used with children and adolescents. In the United States, a few states have legally banned the ECS therapy with youth.

At present, the medical treatment of prescribing antipsychotic medications that reduce dopamine is preferred for schizophrenic patients of all ages. These medications can alleviate hallucinations, delusions, thought disturbance and other symptoms in adults. But they do not help to relieve negative symptoms. Research findings reveal that only modest improvement is possible among children and adolescents (McKenna, Gordon and Rapoport, 1994). Further, these medications have adverse side effects such as dyskinesia and other motor abnormalities. So they are less effective for youth than adults.

Recently, interest in the newer, atypical antipsychotic drugs has developed. Research findings indicate that risperidone and especially clozapine may be effective for youth (Kumra et al., 1997). These medications, which affect serotonin and dopamine, do not have the adverse side effects of the typical antipsychotics. Further, they relieve both positive and negative symptoms. But some researchers came out with their findings that clozapine is associated with side effects such as seizures and impairment of immune system. Hence, even newer antipsychotic medications like olanzapine are being tested for children (Kumra et al., 1998).

(b) Psychoanalytic Therapy

Psychoanalytic therapy proposes that schizophrenia results from an ego, which has difficulty in distinguishing between the self and the external world. Another account attributes it to a 'regression' to a infantile stage of functioning. Freud believed that schizophrenia occurred when a person's ego either became overwhelmed by the demands of the id, or was besieged by unbearable guilt from the super ego. Rather than resolving the intense 'intra-psychic conflict', the ego retreats to the oral stage of psychosexual development, where the infant has not yet learned that it (that is, the infant) and the world are separate. The role of therapist is, therefore, to help the child establish a separate self, interpret the world, distinguish reality from fantasy, develop a sense of mastery and find more adaptive defences (Cantor and Kestenbaum, 1986). For adolescents, there is a focus on the developmental tasks. Regardless of age, an intense, warm and trusting relationship is critical. But now a days, this approach has been de-emphasised (King and Noshpitz, 1991).

(c) Behavioural Treatment

Behavioural model proposes that schizophrenia can be explained in terms of conditioning and observational learning. Hence behavioural treatment too relied on operant and cognitive-behavioural techniques for treating later-onset schizophrenia. Operant treatment has been employed for many years in hospitals and other institutions to encourage self-care and other daily living habits. The main aim is to develop the clients into active agents in their own lives and to facilitate them to leave the hospitals for less restrictive environments. Behavioural approach is applied in many different settings and most often it is a component of family interventions.

Behavioural therapy targets to reduce both maladaptive and bizarre behaviours, which interfere with functioning and adaptive behaviours. Social interaction skills are modelled and reinforced. 'Behaviour shaping' and 'token economies' are the most frequently used therapy techniques, which focus on positive reinforcement to change behaviour. These methods are effective in eliciting and maintaining desired behaviours. However, they are limited by a lack of generalization beyond the therapeutic setting. To avoid this, therapists need to work in environments that are as representative of real life as possible.

(d) Family Involvement Therapy

Appropriate family involvement and support is critical to clients. The family members themselves can benefit from counselling and training. Family treatment approach is, therefore, a very familiar as well as effective technique. Its aim is to reduce the levels of hostile emotional involvement among the family members. In this mode, the family is informed of the biological nature of schizophrenia and of the importance of compliance with medication treatment. The family members are provided with behavioural and cognitive training on how best they can express feelings at home and also on how best they can solve problems. Falloon and his colleagues (1985), cited in Davison and Neale (1998) have made an attempt in family intervention and reported that family intervention was more beneficial than individual psychotherapy.

Generally, the need for a comprehensive approach along with supportive environment involving the combination of multi-measures such as pharmacotherapy, psychosocial treatment, behavioural intervention, family therapy, individual therapy, the teaching of specific academic or developmental skills and occupational considerations, is felt for treating later-onset schizophrenia. Among young people, medications are somewhat effective and the other components of adult treatment apply well. But more and more researches are needed to arrive at effective treatment measures for children.

SUMMARY

Autism and schizophrenia were once considered 'psychoses of youth'. Now they are viewed as distinct disorders. Autism is recognized as a sub-category of Pervasive Development Disorder and it is diagnosed by impaired social interaction, impaired communication and restricted preoccupations and stereotyped behaviours. DSM-IV diagnosis requires the occurrence of symptoms by age three. Autism is a very rare disorder and occurs more in boys than girls. Sensory organs are intact in autistic children. Even then, abnormal responses to stimuli are common. At least 75 per cent of the autistic children show mental retardation. Most of the autistic children exhibit behaviour problems as well as psychological deficits. They have affective-social deficit too. They have deficit executive functioning and are weak in central coherence.

Medical conditions have associations with autism. Fragile x syndrome and tuberous sclerosis are expected to cause autism in some cases. Other medical conditions linked with autism are phenylketonuria, cerebral palsy and meningitis. Genetic factors are also suspected to cause autism. Apart from that the prenatal and perinatal stress causing brain damages may result in autism.

Medical and neurological assessments are normally used for identification as well as treatment. Interviews, checklists and behavioural procedures have been designed for assessment. Intelligence tests as well as adaptive behaviour scales also do much help in assessment. In addition, behaviour and skill-analysis technique is useful when educational and behavioural treatments are predicted. Family assessment is a basic need for facilitating appropriate treatment.

Early treatment efforts were based on the psychoanalytic perspective. According to this theory, failed parenting causes autism. But recent treatment procedures aim at more comprehensive improvement in the functioning of the children with autism. Note worthy cures have been achieved by pharmacological, behavioural and educational interventions. More recently, comprehensive treatment programmes aiming at generating multiple positive outcomes have been developed. The absence of legal treatment mandate in India, commitments to least restrictive alternative, the concept of normalization and integration of autistic children under the mainstream education should be realized.

The educational provisions offered to autistic children should hold promise for independent living and increased quality of life. Yoga practices and pranayama may provide them ample inner strength and cognitive soundness. Further, improvement maintenance should be ensured through out life vide systematic programmes.

Schizophrenia refers to splitting of the mind's various functions in which the personality loses its unity. It is a splitting between thoughts and feelings. Its onset occurs in childhood in a limited number of cases. The major diagnostic symptoms of schizophrenia are identified by DSM-IV as delusions, hallucinations, disorganized speech and behaviour as well as negative symptoms of diminished affect, speech content and goal-directed activities. DSM-IV also sub categorizes schizophrenia as paranoid and disorganized schizophrenia.

Prevalence of schizophrenia is age related. According to a review, the prevalence rate is 20 cases per 10,000 for childhood schizophrenia compared to the adulthood rate of 1 per cent. Prevalence is extremely low before age five or six. It increases during childhood and rises rapidly in adolescence as well as in adulthood. Schizophrenia is reported more in males than in females. It is more prevalent in lower social classes and also observable in all cultures through out the world.

The psychotic characteristics of schizophrenics are hallucinations, delusions and thought disorder. Other associated characteristics of childhood schizophrenia are motor abnormalities, emotional and social disturbances. But they are not as deficient as autistic children in basic language skills. However, their communication is found to be impaired in childhood and adolescence. They perform somewhat deficiently in intelligence tests and fail to maintain an attentional focus.

Schizophrenia is caused by multiple factors such as neurological abnormalities, genetic abnormalities, pregnancy and birth complications and social and psychological factors.

Assessment of schizophrenia needs to be comprehensive involving several sessions and multiple informants. Evaluation of psychotic symptoms in very young children gives rise to concern. Developmental level influences the identification of thought disorder. For instance, lose association is very rare in normal children. Hence lose associations may be treated as a strong indicator of childhood schizophrenia. But assessment of adolescents and adults appears less problematic.

There is a lack of systematic research on treatment of childhood schizophrenia. Hence, the treatment of adults is generalized to treatment for all ages. A treatment procedure is considered best only when it employs multiple methods such as pharmacological, psychoanalytic, behavioural and family approaches to alleviate multiple problems. Medications can alleviate positive symptoms but they do not relieve negative symptoms. Further, medications effect only modest improvement among children and adolescents. Adverse effects are also reported as consequences of medication. The psychoanalytic treatment enables the child to establish a separate self and to distinguish reality from fantasy. But this approach is de-emphasized now-a-days. The behavioural treatment relies on operant and cognitive-behavioural techniques to reduce maladaptive and bizarre behaviours. 'Behaviour shaping' and 'token economies' are the commonly used behaviour techniques.

Family involvement as well as support is critical. Family members too need to be provided with behavioural and cognitive training. Research findings reveal that family interventions are more beneficial than individual psychotherapy.

REFERENCES

Abidin, R.R., (1995), *Parenting Stress Index: Professional Manual (3rd Ed.)*. Odessa, F.L.: Psychological Assessment Resources.

Altman, H., Collins, M. and Mundy, P., (1997), 'Sub Clinical Hallucinations and Delusions in Non-psychotic Adolescents'. *Journal of Child Psychology and Psychiatry*, 38, 413-420.

Aman, M.G. and Kern, R.A., (1989), 'Review of Fen-fluamine in the Treatment of the Developmental Disabilities'. *Journal of American Academy of Child and Adolescent Psychiatry*, 28, 549-565.

American Psychiatric Association, (1994), *Diagnostic and Statistical Manual of Mental Disorders*. Washington, DC.

Anderson, G.M. and Hoshino, Y., (1997), 'Neurochemical Studies of Autism'. In D.J. Cohen & F.R. Volkmar (Eds.), *Handbook of Autism and Pervasive Developmental Disorders*. New York: John Wiley.

Asarnow, J.R., (1992), 'Childhood-onset Schizophrenia'. *Journal of Child Psychology and Psychiatry*, 35,1345-1371.

Asarnow, J.R. and Asarnow, R.F., (1996), 'Childhood Onset Schizophrenia'. In E.J. Mash & R.A. Barkley (Eds.), *Child Psychopathology*. New York: Guilford Press.

Attwood, A., Firth, U. and Hermelin, B., (1998), 'The Understanding and Use of Interpersonal Gestures by Autistic and Down's Syndrome Children'. *Journal of Autism and Developmental Disorders*, 18, 241-257.

Bailey, A., Philips, W. and Rutter, M., (1996), 'Autism: Towards an Integration of Clinical, Genetic, Neuropsychological and Neurobiological Perspectives'. *Journal of Child Psychology and Psychiatry*, 37, 89-126.

Baron-Cohen, S., Jolliffe, T., Mortimore, C. and Robertson, M., (1997), 'Another Advanced Test of Theory of Mind: Evidence from Very High Functioning Adults with Autism or Asperger Syndrome'. *Journal of Child Psychology and Psychiatry*, 38, 813-822.

Bleuler, E., (1911), *Dementia Praecox or the Group of Schizophrenias*. New York: International University Press.

Campbell, M. Armenteros, J.L., Maone, R.P., Adams, P.B., Eisenberg, Z.W. and Overall, J.E., (1997), 'Neuroleptic-related Dyskinesias in Autistic Children: A Prospective Longitudinal Study'. Journal of the American Academy of Child and Adolescent Psychiatry, 36, 835-843.

Campbell, M., Schopler, E., Cueva, J. E. and Hallin, A., (1996), 'Treatment of Autistic Disorder'. *American Academy of Child and Adolescent Psychiatry*, 35, 134-143.

Cannon, T.D., Mednick, S.A., Parnas, J., Schulsinger, F., Praestholm, J. and Vestergaad, A., (1993), 'Developmental Brain Abnormalities in the Offspring of Schizophrenic Mothers'. *Archives of General Psychiatry,* 50, 551-564.

Cantor, S., (1988), *Childhood Schizophrenia.* New York: Guilford.

Caplan, R., (1994), 'Thought Disorder in Childhood'. *Journal of the American Academy of Child and Adolescent Psychiatry,* 33,605-615.

Caplan, R., Guthrie, D. and Komo, S., (1996), 'Conversational Repair in Schizophrenic and Normal Children'. *Journal of American Academy of Child and Adolescent Psychiatry,* 35, 941-949.

Davison, G.C. and Neale, J.M., (1998), *Abnormal Psychology.* New York: Wiley.

Dawson, G. and Castelloe, P., (1992), 'Autism'. In C.E. Walker & M.C. Roberts (Eds.), *Handbook of Clinical Child Psychology.* New York: Wiley.

Durrand, V.M., (1990), *Severe Behaviour Problems: A Functional Communication Training Approach.* New York: Guilford.

Dykens, E.M. and Volkmar, F.R., (1997), 'Medical Conditions Associated with Autism'. In D.J. Cohen & F.R. Volkmar (Eds.), *Handbook of Autism and Developmental Disorders.* New York: John Wiley.

Folstein, S. and Rutter, M., (1978), 'A Twin Study of Individuals with Infantile Autism'. In M. Rutter & E. Schopler (Eds.), *Autism: A Reappraisal of Concepts and Treatment.* New York: Plenum.

Fombonne, E., du Mazaubrun, C., Cans, C. and Grandjean, H., (1997), 'Autism and Associated Medical Disorders in a French Epidemiological Survey'. *Journal of the American Academy of Child and Adolescent Psychiatry,* 36,15861-1569.

Gershon, E.S. and Rieder, R.O., (1992), 'Major Disorders of Mind and Brain'. *Scientific American,* 127-133.

Gilberg, C. L., (1992), 'The Emmanuel Miller Memorial Lecture 1991. Autism and Autistic -like Conditions: Subclasses among Disorder of Empathy'. *Journal of Child Psychology and Psychiatry,* 33, 813-842.

Goldfarb, W., (1970), 'Childhood Psychosis'. In P.H. Mussen (Ed.), *Carmichael's Manual of Child Psychology,* Vol.2. New York: Wiley.

Gooding, D.C. and Iacono, W.G., (1995), 'Schizophrenia Through the Lens of a Developmental Psychopathology Perspective'. In D. Cicchetti & D.J. Cohen (Eds.), *Developmental Psychology* (Vol.2). New York: John Wiley Interscience.

Gottesman, I.I., (1993), 'Origins of Schizophrenia: Past as Prologue'. In R. Plomin & G.E. McClean (Eds.), *Nature and Nurture Psychology.* Washington, DC; American Psychological Association.

Grandin, T., (1997), 'A Personal Perspective on Autism'. In D.J. Cohen & F.R. Volkmar (Eds.), *Handbook of Autism and Pervasive Developmental Disorders*. New York: John Wiley.

Green, W.H., Padron-Gayol, M., Hardesty, A.S. and Bassiri, M., (1992), 'Schizophrenia with Childhood Onset: A Phenomenological Study of 38 Cases'. *Journal of the American Academy of Child and Adolescent Psychiatry*, 31, 968-976.

Gur, R.E., Cowell, P., Turetsky, B.I. Gallacher, F., Cannon, T., Bilker, W. and Gur, R.C., (1998), 'A Follow-up Magnetic Resonance Imaging Study of Schizophrenia'. *Archives of General Psychiatry*, 55, 145-152.

Happe, F.G.E., (1996), 'Studying Weak Central Coherence at Low Levels: Children with Autism do not Succumb to Visual Illusions'. *Journal of Child Psychology and Psychiatry*, 37, 873-878.

Harrison, J. E. and Bolton, P.F., (1997), 'Tuberous Sclerosis'. *Journal of Child Psychology and Psychiatry*, 38, 603-614.

Hobson, P., (1993), 'Understanding Persons: The Role of Affect'. In S. Baron-Cohen, H. Tager -Flusberg & D.J. Cohen (Eds.), *Under Standing other Minds*. New York: Oxford Press.

Jocobsen, L.K. and Rapoport, J.L., (1998), 'Research Update: Childhood-onset Schizophrenia: Implications of Clinical and Neurological Research'. *Journal of Child Psychology and Psychiatry*, 39, 101-113.

Kanner, L., (1943), 'Autistic Disturbances of Affective Contact'. *Nervous Child*, 2, 217-250.

Kaufman, J., Birmacher, B., Brent, D., Rao, U., Flynn, C., Moreci, P., Williamson, D. and Ryan, N., (1997), 'Schedule for Affective Disorders and Schizophrenia for School-age Children-Present and Lifetime Versions (K-SDAS- PL): Initial Reliability and Validity Data'. *Journal of the American Academy of Child and Adolescent Psychiatry*, 36, 980-988.

King, R.A. and Noshpitz, J.D., (1991), *Pathways of Growth: Essentials of Child Psychiatry*, Vol. 2. New York: John Wiley & Sons.

Klin, A. and Cohen, D.J., (1997), 'Ethical Issues in Research and Treatment'. In D.J. Cohen & F.R. Volkmar (Eds.), *Handbook of Autism and Pervasive Developmental Disorder*. New York: John Wiley.

Klinger, L.G. and Dawson, G., (1996), 'Autistic Disorder'. In E.J. Mash & R.A. Barkley (Eds.). *Child Psychopathology*. New York: Guilford Press.

Koegel, R.L., Camarata, S., Koegel, L.K., Ban-Tall, A. and Smith, A.E., (1998), 'Increasing Speech Intelligibility in Children with Autism'. *Journal of Autism and Developmental Disorders*, 28, 241-251.

Kolvin, I., (1971), 'Psychoses in Childhood—A Comparative Study'. In M. Rutter (Ed)., *Infantile Autism: Concepts, Characteristics and Treatment*. London: Churchill-Living stone.

Kraepelin, E., (1913), *Clinical Psychiatry: A Textbook for Physicians.* (Translated by A. Diffendorf). New York: Macmillan.

Krug, D.A., Arick, J. and Almond, P., (1978), *Autism Screening Instrument for Educational Planning.* Portland, OR: ASIEP Education.

Kumra, S., Herion, D., Jacobsen, L. K., Briguglia, S. and Grothe, D., (1997), 'Case Study: Risperidone Induced Hepatotoxicity in Paediatric Patients'. *Journal of the American Academy of Child and Adolescent Psychiatry,* 36, 701-705.

Kumra, S., Jacobson, L. K., Lenane, M., Smith, A., Lee, P., Malanga, C. J., Karp, B.I., Hamburger, S. and Rapoport, J. L., (1998), 'Case Series: Spectrum of Neuroleptic-induced Movement Disorders and Extra Pyramidal Side Effects in Childhood Onset Schizophrenia'. *Journal of the American Academy of Child and Adolescent Psychiatry,* 37, 221-227.

Le Couteur, A., Bailey, A., Goods, S., Pickles, A., Robertson, S., Gottesman, I. and Rutter, M., (1996), 'A Broader Phenotype of Autism: The Clinical Spectrum of Twins'. *Journal of Child Psychology and Psychiatry,* 37, 785-802.

Lord, C. and Paul, R., (1997), 'Language and Communication in Autism'. In D.J. Cohen and F.R. Volkmar (Eds.), *Handbook of Autism and Pervasive Developmental Disorders.* New York: John Wiley.

Lord, C., Rutter, M., Goode, S., Heemsbergen, J., Jordan, H. Mawhood, L. and Schopler, E., (1989), 'Autism Diagnostic Observation Schedule: A Standardized Observation of Communicative and Social Behaviour'. *Journal of Autism and Developmental Disorders,* 19, 185-212.

Lotter, V., (1996), 'Epidemiology of Autistic Conditions in Young Children. I. Prevalence'. *Social Psychiatry,* 1, 124-137.

Lovaas, O.I., Young, D.B. and Newsom, C.D., (1978), 'Childhood Psychosis: Behavioural Treatment'. In B.B. Wolman (Ed.), *Handbook of Treatment of Mental Disorders in Childhood and Adolescence.* Englewood Cliffs, NJ: Prentice Hall.

McClellan, J. and Werry, J., (1997), 'Practice Parameters for the Assessment and Treatment of Children and Adolescents with Schizophrenia'. *Journal of the American Academy of Child and Adolescent Psychiatry,* 33, 616-635.

McKenna, K., Gordon, C.T., Lenane, M., Kaysen, D., Fahey, K. and Rapoport, J.L., (1994), 'Looking for Childhood-onset Schizophrenia: The first 71 Cases Screened'. *Journal of American Academy of Child and Adolescent Psychiatry,* 33, 636-644.

Minshew, N.J., Sweeney, J.A. and Bauman, M.L., (1997), 'Neurological Aspects of Autism. In D.J. Cohen and F.R. Volkmar (Eds.)., *Handbook of Autism and Pervasive Developmental Disorders.* New York: John Wiley.

Moos, R.H. and Moos, B.S., (1986), *Family Environment Scale Manual (2nd Ed).* Palo Alto, CA: Consulting Psychologists Press.

Newsom, C., (1998), 'Autistic Disorder'. In E.J. Mash & R.A. Barkley (Eds.), *Treatment of Childhood Disorders*. New York: Guilford Press.

Newsom, C. and Hovanitz, C.A., (1997), 'Autistic Disorder'. In E.J. Mash & L.G. Terdal (Eds.), *Assessment of Childhood Disorders*. New York: Guilford Press.

Nicolson, R., Awad, G. and Sloman, L., (1998), 'An Open Trial of Risperidone in Young Autistic Children'. *Journal of the American Academy of Child and Adolescent Psychiatry,* 37, 372-376.

Ohman, A. and Hultman, C.M., (1998), 'Electro Dermal Activity and Obstetric Complications in Schizophrenia'. *Journal of Abnormal Psychology*. 107, 228-237.

Ozonoff, S., (1997), 'Casual Mechanism of Autism: Unifying Perspectives from an Information Processing Framework'. In D.J. Cohen, F.R. Volkmar (Eds.)., *Handbook of Autism and Pervasive Developmental Disorders*. New York: John Wiley.

Peck. C.H., Apolloni, T., Cooke, T.P. and Raver, S.A., (1978). 'Teaching Retarded Preschoolers to Imitate the Free-play Behaviour of Non-retarded Classmates: Training and Generalized Effects'. *Journal of Special Education*, 12, 195-207.

Pennington, B.F. and Welsh, M., (1997), 'Neuropsychology and Developmental Psychopathology'. In D. Cicchetti & D.J. Cohen (Eds.), *Developmental Psychopathology*, New York: John Wiley.

Piven, J., Arndt, S., Bailey, J. and Andreasen, N., (1996a), 'Regional Brain Enlargement in Autism: A Magnetic Resonance Imaging Study'. *Journal of the American Academy of Child and Adolescent Psychiatry,* 35, 530-536.

Pring, L. and Hermelin, B., (1993), 'Bottle, Tulip and Wineglass: Semantic and Structural Picture Processing by Savant Artists'. *Journal of Child Psychology and Psychiatry*, 34,1365-1385.

Prior, M. and Werry J.S., (1986), 'Autism, Schizophrenia and Allied Disorders'. In H.C. Quay and J.S. Werry (Eds.), *Psychological Disorders of Childhood*. New York: Wiley.

Rimland, B., (1978), 'Inside the Mind of An Autistic Savant'. *Psychology Today,* 12, 68-80.

Ritvo, E.R. and Freeman, B.J., (1978), 'National Society for Autistic Children Definition of the Syndrome of Autism'. *Journal of Autism and Childhood Schizophrenia*, 8, 162-167.

Rogers, S., (1998), 'Empirically Supported Comprehensive Treatments for Young Children with Autism'. *Journal of Clinical Child Psychology*, 27, 168-179.

Russell, A.T., Bott, L. and Sammons, C., (1989), 'The Phenomenology of Schizophrenia Occurring in Childhood'. *Journal of American Academy of Child and Adolescent Psychiatry*, 28, 399-407.

Rutter, M., (1978), 'Diagnosis and Definition'. In M. Rutter and E. Schopler (Eds.) *Autism: A Reappraisal of Concepts and Treatments*. New York: Plenum.

Rutter, M., Bailey, A., Simonoff, E. and Pickles, A., (1997), 'Genetic Influences and Autism'. In D.J. Cohen & F.R. Volkmar (Eds.), *Handbook of Autism and Pervasive Developmental Disorders*. New York: John Wiley.

Schopler, E., (1994), 'Behavioural Priorities for Autism and Related Developmental Disorders'. In E. Schopler & G.B. Mesibov (Eds.), *Behavioural Issues in Autism*. New York: Plenum.

Schopler, E., Reicher, R.J. and Renner, B.R., (1988), *The Childhood Autism Rating Scale (CARS)*. Los Angels: Western Psychological Services.

Schreibman, L., (1997), 'Theoretical Perspectives on Behavioural Intervention for Individuals with Autism'. In D.J. Cohen & F.R. Volkmar (Eds.), *Handbook of Autism and Pervasive Developmental Disorders*, New York: John Wiley.

Schreibman, L. and Charlop-Christy, M.J., (1998), 'Autistic Disorder'. In T.H. Ollendick & M. Hersen (Eds.). *Handbook of Child Psychopathology*. New York: Plenum.

Shyamala, V., (2004), 'Effectiveness of Certain Strategies in Overcoming Antisocial Behaviour Among High School Students'. Unpublished Doctoral Thesis, Alagappa University, Karaikudi.

Siegel, B., (1997), 'Coping with the Diagnosis of Autism'. In D.J. Cohen & F.R. Volkmar (Eds.), *Handbook of Autism and Pervasive Developmental Disorders*, New York: John Wiley.

Tienari, P., Lahti, I., Sorri, A., Naarala, M., Moring. J., Kaleva, M., Wahlberg, K.E. and Wynne, L.C., (1990), 'Adopted-away Offspring of Schizophrenics and Controls: The Finnish Adoptive Family Study of Schizophrenia'. In L.N. Robins & M. Rutter (Eds.), *Straight and Pathways from Childhood to Adulthood*. New York: Cambridge University Press.

Tsai, L.Y. and Ghaziuddin, M., (1991), 'Autistic Disorder'. In J.M. Wiener (Ed.), *Textbook of Child & Adolescent Psychiatry*. Washington, DC: American Psychiatric Press.

Volkmar, F.R., (1996), 'Childhood and Adolescent Psychosis: A Review of the Past 10 Years'. *Journal of the American of Child and Adolescent Psychiatry*, 35, 843-851.

Volkmar, F.R., (1991), 'Childhood Schizophrenia'. In M. Lewis (Ed.), *Child and Adolescent Psychiatry: A Comprehensive Textbook*. Baltimore: Williams and Wilkins.

Volkmar, F.R., Becker, D.F., King, R.A. and McGlashan, T.H., (1995), 'Psychotic Processes'. In D. Cicchetti & D.J. Cohen (Eds.)., *Developmental Psychopathology*, New York: John Wiley.

Volkmar, F.R., Cicchetti, D.V., Dykens, E., Sparrow, S.S., Leckman, J.F. and Cohen, D.J., (1988), 'An Evaluation of the Autism Behaviour Checklist'. *Journal of Autism and Developmental Disorders*, 18,81-97.

Volkmar, F.R., Klin, A. and Cohen, D.J., (1997b), 'Diagnosis and Classification of Autism and Related Conditions: Consensus and Issues'. In D.J. Cohen & F.R. Volkmar (Eds)., *Handbook of Autism and Pervasive Developmental Disorders*. New York: John Wiley.

Watkins, J.M., Asarnow, R.F. and Tanguay, P.E., (1988), 'Symptom Development in Childhood Onset Schizophrenia'. *Journal of Child Psychology and Psychiatry*, 29, 865-878.

Weinberger, D.R., (1994), 'Biological Basis of Schizophrenia: Structural/ Functional Considerations Relevant to Potential for Anti Psychotic Drug Response'. *Journal of Clinical Psychiatry Monograph*, 12:2, 4-8.

Wellman, H.M., (1993), 'Early Understanding of Mind: The Normal Case'. In S. Baron-Cohen, H. Tager-Flusberg & D.J. Cohen (Eds.). *Understanding Other Minds*. New York: Oxford Press.

Wing, L., (1997), 'Syndromes of Autism and Atypical Development'. In D.J. Cohen & F.R. Volkmar (Eds.), *Handbook of Autism and Pervasive Developmental Disorders*. New York: John Wiley.

13

Disorders of Basic Physical Functions

OBJECTIVES

This chapter deals with problems in basic physical functioning such as eating, elimination and sleep disorders. It presents different types of eating disorders and the various treatment measures. Similarly, the major elimination disorders like enuresis and encopresis, the factors causing these disorders and their respective treatment procedures are presented. Ultimately, the chapter describes the categories of sleep disorders, such as dyssomnias and parasommias along with the treatment methods. After reading this chapter, the readers must be able to:

(i) Know the various eating disorders, their causal factors and different treatment methods;

(ii) Present the different types of elimination disorder, factors causing each and treatment measures to cure them;

(iii) Define sleep disorders;

(iv) Differentiate dyssomnias from parasomnias;

(v) Analyse the context for the development as well as onset of sleep disorders; and

(vi) Describe the treatment for sleep disorders.

Children often exhibit problems of physical functioning and health, which represent the interface between psychology and paediatrics and hence require collaboration between psychologists and physicians. For example, early problems with the feeding of infants and toddlers, problems in managing toilet training and difficulties in getting children to sleep are some of them. For many of these problems, parents often turn to paediatrician. Both the child's ability to master the relevant tasks of basic physical functioning and the parents' ability to train the child are important to the well being of both. Negligence either on the part of parents or on the part of the child may lead to severe problems like eating, elimination and sleep disorders and pose a high risk to the child's social functioning. In this chapter, the commonly encountered problems, namely, eating disorders, elimination disorders and sleep disorders that are part of normal development, are dealt with.

EATING DISORDERS

Eating disorders are characterised by physically and/or psychologically harmful eating patterns. In ICD-10, they are categorised as "behavioural syndromes associated with physical disturbances and physical factors". A wide range of problems such as under eating, finicky eating, overeating, problems in chewing and swallowing, bizarre eating habits, annoying mealtime behaviours and delays in self-feeding are reported. O'Brien (1996) found that approximately 30 per cent of a sample of parents of infants and toddlers reported that their children refuse to eat the food presented to them. Restricted eating is often accompanied by other behavioural problems like tantrums, spitting and gagging. Severe cases of food refusal are also associated with even more difficult social and psychological problems and ultimately result in medical complaints and malnourishment due to life-threatening weight loss and failure to gain weight. Thus some eating disorders may endanger the physical health of the child.

Different Types of Eating Disorders, Their Causes and Remedial Measures

The most common clinical disorders of eating that have attracted attention of researchers and clinicians are rumination, pica, obesity, anorexia nervosa and bulimia nervosa.

Rumination

Rumination or mercyism is a syndrome with a long history (Kanner, 1972) and it is characterized by the voluntary and repeated regurgitation of food or liquid in the absence of an organic cause. When infants ruminate, they appear deliberately to initiate regurgitation. The child's head is thrown back, and chewing and swallowing movements are made until food is brought up. In most of the cases, the child initiates rumination by placing his/her fingers down the throat or by chewing on objects. The child exhibits little distress. Instead, pleasure appears to result from the activity. If rumination continues, serious medical complications can result, with death being the outcome in extreme cases (American Psychiatric Association, 1994).

Rumination is observed in normal infants as well as in individuals with mental retardation. Among normal children, it usually appears during the first year of life whereas in the mentally retarded individuals, a later onset is observed. The incidence increases with greater degrees of mental retardation. Kerwin and Berkowitz (1996) reported that in both the groups (i.e. normal infants and mental retarded individuals), rumination is more prevalent in males.

According to Mayes (1992), rumination in infants can be attributed to a disturbance in the mother-infant relationship. The mother sometimes may have psychological difficulties of her own which may prevent her from providing the infant with a nurturant relationship. Or she may be experiencing significant life stress which interferes with her ability to attend to the infant. As a result, the infant attempts to provide this missing gratification. In some cases, rumination also occurs as a habit. Further, in individuals diagnosed as mental retarded, rumination develops as a learned habit.

Rumination is treated with a variety of treatment procedures like satiation and aversive technique. In satiation procedure, the individual is fed large quantities of food. The aversive procedure involves the administration of unpleasant-tasting substances or a mild shock contigent on the child's initiating behaviours that lead to ruminate. But the aversive procedures are generally avoided by parents and professionals. They prefer to find non-aversive alternatives. Treatment procedures that emphasize contingent use of social attention have been found successful. There are also suggestions for non-contingent stimulation and attention to be tried with infant ruminators (Mayes, 1992). These procedures are doubly blessed in the sense they are acceptable to parents and also easy to be implemented at home by the parents. To attain higher degrees of effectiveness, sufficiently controlled evaluations of interventions, particularly with infants, are suggested.

2. Pica

'Pica' type of eating disorder is characterized by the habitual eating of substances, which are usually considered inedible, such as, paint, paper, fabric, hair, bugs and dirt. ('Pica' is the Latin word that denotes a bird, which is known for the diversity of objects it eats). Most infants develop a habit, during the first year of life, of putting a variety objects into their mouths, which, as a developmental milestone, is partly a way of exploring the environment. The infant then typically learns within the next year to explore the discrimination between edible and inedible materials. Only when infants persistently eat inedible materials beyond this age, the diagnosis of pica is usually made. This disorder is most common among the infants of two-and three-year-old. This is reported highly among mentally retarded individuals (McAlpine and Singh, 1986). This disorder leads to various other damages like parasitic infection and intestinal obstruction due to the accumulation of hair and other materials. Furthermore, pica also appears to be related to accidental poisoning (American Psychiatric Association, 1994).

Kerwin and Berkowitz (1996) have postulated a number of causes for pica type of eating disorder. There is one proposition that views pica as an attempt to satisfy nutritional deficits. In other words, youngsters start eating strange substances, when food becomes unavailable to them. Other causes are parental inattention, lack of supervision, and lack of adequate stimulation. Research findings also suggested cultural influences.

Millican and Lourie (1970) studied the black children who belonged to the families who had migrated from the southeastern

United States. The pregnant women in those families have a custom of eating of earth containing clay and laundry starch. This behaviour is governed by some superstitious beliefs. Millican and Lourie (1970) reported an interesting observation that the mothers of children with pica were found to have a higher frequency of the behaviour than mothers of children without pica.

The mothers as well as children following pica should be properly educated and informed to dispense with such behaviours. Some cases may also need more intensive therapeutic endeavours. Bell and Stein (1992) suggested for behavioural interventions. Such behavioural procedures range from less intrusive aversive techniques, such as contingent squirts of water to the child's face and restraining the child from repeating pica. These procedures are normally combined with reinforcement of appropriate behaviour and increased attention to the child. Professionals advocate that less intrusive procedures should be tried prior to employing more aversive techniques.

3. *Obesity*

Obesity is one of the most prevalent nutritional diseases in children and adolescents. It is a significant health problem. Prevalence of obesity increases with age (Aristimuno et al., 1984). Research evidence also indicates that there is an increase in the percentage of obese children who will become obese adults (Rolland-Cachera et al., 1987). Another interesting finding is the prevalence of childhood obesity is increasing (Campaign et al., 1994).

Childhood obesity is associated with innumerable physical health problems, particularly those related to risk of heart disease (Dietz, 1995). Further, social and psychological problems too accompany obesity (Pierce and Wardle, 1993). Obesity is supposed to create an enormous psychological burden, which may have more adverse effects than the disorder itself, in terms of suffering. Israel and Shapiro (1985) studied the psychological problems associated with obesity. They found that the behaviour problem scores of obese children were significantly higher than the scores of general population. In addition, obese children's social interactions are adversely affected by negative evaluations. Generally children hold negative views regarding obesity and hence over-weight children are ranked as less liked. Normally they are described as 'lazy', and 'stupid' by other children. Further, obesity is accompanied by reduction of activity and dexterity and as a result, the obese children are subjected to the feelings of social isolation and rejection. Dietz (1995) reported that the above effects appear to continue throughout life. He also found that college acceptance rates were lower for obese adolescent girls than for non-obese girls with comparable academic credentials.

Obesity is supposed to be caused by multiple and complex influences, such as biological, psychological and social/cultural influences (Leibel and Hirsch, 1995). Biological causes involve both genetic factors and the metabolic effects of dieting and exercise. Montague et al. (1997) found that the severely obese children have leptin deficiencies. Leptin is a protein, which is considered to be involved in signalling the brain to end eating. Experiments using mice were helpful to identify a gene that appears to control the production of leptin. However, genetic contributions in man are very complex and hence need rigorous investigations.

Biological influences are not independent. They interact with environmental influences to cause obesity. Environmental conditions at school as well as at home, food habits followed by families, natures of occupations are the major environmental factors having impact on obesity. Many research investigations also bring out the effect of psychological factors on the development of obesity. Most of the obese children have food intake and activity behaviours, which are in need of change (Schlicker, Borra and Regan, 1994). Problematic food consumptions as well as inactivity are considered to be affected by environmental influences. They are also learned in the same manner as any other behaviour disorder is learned. For instance, children watch and imitate the eating behaviour of their parents and others around them. In many families, children are reinforced for engaging in the style in which their parents eat (Klesges and Hanson, 1988). Physical and social stimuli also influence eating and inactivity, which become almost automatic in some circumstances. In addition, people learn to use food to overcome stress and negative mood states, such as boredom, and anxiety. Social learning perspective seeks to break such learned patterns and to develop more desirable as well as adaptive patterns of behaviour.

An important cultural influence on obesity is society's view of it. Television viewing is one of the major influences that suggest that the larger society might contribute to the development of weight problems in children. Mostly, children watch television on average about two to three hours a day and such perennial television viewing gives rise to the negative effects of inactivity. Television watching has also an adverse influence on children's diets (Jeffrey et al., 1979). Dietz and Gortmaker (1995) confirmed a significant association between time spent on television watching and the prevalence of obesity.

Most effective treatment effects can be attained by multifaceted programmes, which emphasize behavioural interventions and education that aim at behaviour modification. Such educative behavioural intervention programmes, in the opinion of Israel et al. (1994), should address four areas: i) intake, which includes nutritional information, caloric restriction, changes in actual eating and food preparation behaviours; ii) activity, which includes both specific exercise programmes and increasing the energy expended in daily activities; iii) cues, which identify the external and internal stimuli associated with excessive eating or inactivity; and iv) rewards, which provide positive consequences for progress by both the child and the parent. Israel et al. (1985) have also emphasized the inclusion of parental involvement as an important treatment component. They suggest to parents a brief course in the general principles of child management as well as in a behavioural weight-reduction programme during which the application of general parenting skills to weight reduction should be emphasized. Changing family lifestyles is also important to maintain the treatment effects. The child's self-regulatory skills should also be enhanced (Israel et al., 1994). A combination of multidimensional treatment programme with enhanced training in comprehensive self-management skills can work wonders in treating the problem of obesity. A regular and systematic practice of yogasanas and pranayama helps to reduce weight. In addition, intake of raw sprouted grams and raw vegetables may help to reduce appetite and thereby reduce the great quantities of food consumed, which in turn gives room for weight reduction.

4. *Anorexia Nervosa and Bulimia Nervosa*

These are eating disorders, which involve maladaptive attempts to control body weight, significant disturbances in eating behaviour and abnormal attitudes about body shape and weight. Until recent times, these disorders were thought to exist very rarely. But due to the increasing awareness of beauty concept in the modern times, there is a tremendous increase in the number of cases reporting anorexia nervosa and bulimia nervosa. Even great celebrities like Princess Diana was said to have these disorders.

When attempts to sub-categorize a particular disorder are made, several dimensions are considered. Similarly, when we try to sub-categorize the eating disorder, we consider the dimensions, such as weight status (that is, whether the person concerned is over weight or under weight), the presence or absence of binge-eating (binge is usually defined by person's eating a larger amount of food during a discrete period of time) and the method employed to control one's weight (such as restricting and purging strategies). Now, we will consider how these dimensions are involved in describing the above-mentioned two disorders.

(a) *Anorexia Nervosa*

Literally, anorexia nervosa means 'nervous loss of appetite'. It is characterized by prolonged refusal to eat adequate amounts of food, which results in deliberate weight loss. Body weight loss is often accompanied by the cessation of menstruation in females (amenorrhoea). For a diagnosis of anorexia nervosa to be considered the individual must weigh less than 85 per cent of normal or expected weight for height, age and sex. As a result of their significant weight loss, anorectics look emaciated. They also show a decline in general health, which is accompanied by many physical problem (Sharp and Freeman, 1993). These include low blood pressure and body temperature, constipation and dehydration. In many cases of AN, the extremeness of weight loss leads to significant medical complications, such as, anaemia, hormonal changes, cardio vascular problems and dental problems.

In five to 15 per cent of cases, anorexia nervosa (AN) is fatal (Hsu, 1990). For instance, Karen Carpenter, Grammy award singer, died at the age of thirty-two of heart failure, which was the result of her suffering from the effects of AN for many years. The seriousness of the extreme weight loss in anorectics is illustrated by Bruch's (1979) classic description of one of her clients: "She (Alma) looked like a walking skeleton, with her legs sticking out like broomsticks, every rib showing, and her shoulder blades standing up like little wings. Her arms and legs were covered with soft hair.... Her face was hollow like that of a shriveled-up old woman with disease".

Anorectics will avoid most calorie-rich foods such as meat, milk products, sweets and other desserts. They will often limit their consumption to little more than a lettuce leaf and carrot. They show reduced pleasure in eating. Even though they do not experience deficiencies in taste, they do have a low hedonic responsiveness to taste and an aversion to the oral sensation of fat (Sunday and Halmi, 1990).

One other characteristic of anorectics is a 'distorted body image' in which the individual does not recognize the body's thinness. Though their bones appear protruding, many anorectics still see themselves as being fat and deny that they are 'wasting away'. As Bruch (1978) observed, they vigorously defend gruesome emaciation as not being too thin.

DSM-IV distinguishes between two sub-types of AN. This distinction is based on whether or not the person binges. Binge-eating/purging anorectics exhibit a persistent pattern of binge eating and purging. On the other hand, restricting anorectics achieve their weight loss by fasting and /or exercise and do not binge-eat. These sub-groups have been found in large clinical samples and they are reported to differ on a number of individual and family characteristics (Dacosta and Halmi, 1992).

AN occurs primarily in females and female anorectics outnumber males by a factor of 15: 1 (Hartley, 1997). This disorder usually has its onset in adolescence, the period between 14 and 16 being most common (Hsu, 1990). However, the onset occurs later in adult life or before adolescence. Lask and Bryant-Waugh (1992), for example, have reported cases of the disorder in children as young as eight. Estimates of AN's incidence vary. American data suggest that one in 250 females may experience the disorder (Lewinshon et al., 1993). But in Britain, the figure is somewhat higher, ranging from one in 100 to four in 100 (Sahakian, 1987), with around 70,000 people recognised as anorectic (Brooke, 1996).

It has been suggested that AN has a biological basis. It has been proposed that dysfunction in the hypothalamus leads to the disorder. The hypothalamus plays an important role in the regulation of eating. Kaplan and Woodside (1987) showed that when nor-adrenaline acts on part of the hypothalamus, non-humans begin eating and show a marked preference for carbohydrates. Serotonin, by contrast, apparently includes satiation and suppresses appetite, especially for carbohydrates. Any condition, which increased serotonin's effects, would decrease eating. However, there is not yet sufficient evidence to indicate whether hypothalamic dysfunction and changes in neurotransmitter levels are causes of AN, effects of it or merely correlates (Kaye et al., 1993).

AN may also have a genetic basis. There is a tendency for the disorder to run in families, with first-and second-degree relatives of anorectic individuals being significantly more likely to develop the disorder compared with first-and second-degree relatives of a control-group of non- anorectic (Strober and Katz, 1987).

Twin studies have also been used to investigate the role of genetic factors. Askerold and Heiberg (1979) reported a 50 per cent concordance rate for MZs brought up in the same environment, which they see as strong evidence that genes play an important role. However, in the absence of concordance rates for DZs and MZs reared apart, this claim is difficult to evaluate. Holland et al. (1984) reported a concordance rate of 55 per cent for MZs brought up in the same environment and seven per cent for DZs. Although this difference hints at genetic involvement, the concordance rate suggests that if genes do play a role, it is likely to be a small one (Treasure and Holland, 1991).

The psychodynamic model proposes that AN represents an unconscious effort by a girl to remain pre-pubescent. On the other hand, the behavioural model sees AN as a phobia concerning the possibility of gaining weight. Indeed, AN might be appropriately called 'weight phobia' (Crisp, 1967). This phobia is assumed to be the result of the impact of social norms, values and roles. The 'cultural idealization' of the slender females (as represented by 'supermodels') may be one cause of the fear of being fat (Petkova, 1997).

(b) Bulimia Nervosa

Literally, bulimia comes from the Greek 'bous' meaning 'ox' and 'limos' meaning 'hunger'. Russell (1979) saw bulimia nervosa as 'an ominous variant' of anorexia nervosa. Bulimia nervosa (BN) is characterized by periodic episodes of 'compulsive' or 'binge' eating, the rapid and seemingly uncontrolled consumption of food, especially that rich in carbohydrates. A persistent over concern with body shape and weight is also exhibited. This of course means that the bulimic individual needs to employ some method of compensating for eating binges. The most frequently cited method is purging by vomiting or the use of laxatives.

DSM–IV uses the following criteria to diagnosis BN:

1. recurrent episodes of binge-eating;
2. recurrent inappropriate compensatory behaviour to prevent weight gain;
3. occurrence of items 1 and 2 at least twice a week for three months; and
4. self-evaluation unduly influenced by body shape and weight.

In order to receive the diagnosis of BN, the above symptoms must not occur exclusively during episodes of Anorexia Nervosa. In other words, a person who displayed these symptoms as part of AN would not receive both diagnosis.

There are two sub-types of BN, based on the principal consideration of whether or not purging is employed to compensate for binge eating. They are a purging type, in which the person regularly induces vomiting or misuses laxatives, diuretics or enemas and a non purging type in which the person fasts and/or exercises but does not regularly purge.

One of the issues that is faced in diagnosing BN as a disorder is the high frequency of bulimic behaviour reported in the general population of late adolescents and young adults and the high prevalence of concern about body shape and weight. The frequency of bulimic behaviour is at an average rate of two to three times a week and sometimes as often as 30 times a week.

Most bulimics are women, with fewer than five per cent of cases presenting for treatment being men (Cooper, 1995). BN typically begins in adolescence or early adulthood and generally appears later than in AN. Bulimia nervosa is also more frequent than AN and may affect as many as five per cent of the population. Like anorectics, bulimics too have 'an intrusive fear of fatness' and they are unduly concerned with their body and shape and hence they take drastic steps to control their weight. Clearly, bulimics recognise their eating behaviour is abnormal and feel frustrated by it. However, they are unable to control the behaviour voluntarily. Because of the guilty feelings bingeing and purging are usually carried out in secret and consequently, many bulimics go unrecognised even to close friends and family.

Purging produces some effects that might be noticeable to others. One of these is a 'puffy' facial appearance, which is a consequence of swollen parotid glands caused by vomiting. Another is deterioration in tooth enamel caused by the stomach acid produced when vomiting occurs. A third is the development of calluses over the back of the hand, caused by rubbing the hand against the upper teeth when the fingers are pushed into throat to induce vomiting. Other associated physiological effects include digestive tract damage, dehydration and nutritional imbalances. Psychological effects include anxiety, sleep disturbances and depression. Associations between 'self-mutilative' and BN have also been reported (Parry-Jones & Parry-Jones, 1993). One such unusual form of self-mutilative behaviour is blood letting.

Noradrenaline, serotonin, hormones and endorphins may all play mediating roles in BN. For example, elevated plasma endorphin levels have been found in bulimics, although whether these are a cause, or a consequence or a correlate of the disorder is still unknown. Reports based on clinical cases have also suggested early sexual abuse as a cause of eating disorders, particularly, bulimia nervosa. However, empirical support is lacking for this suggestion too.

TREATMENT FOR ANOREXIA NERVOSA AND BULIMIA NERVOSA

Both AN and BN are proved to be complex and difficult to treat. These disorders derive from and are maintained by a variety of influences. Hence there is considerable heterogeneity among individuals exhibiting these eating disorders. Some of the treatment approaches are pharmacological measures, family therapy and cognitive-behavioural therapy.

(a) Pharmacological Treatment

Many case reports suggest that different pharmacological treatments can be successful. But controlled research regarding children and adolescents sounds care and caution (Walsh, 1995). There seems to be little support available for the effectiveness of pharmacological approaches to the treatment of AN. In controlled studies with adults, antidepressant medication is reported to be effective for treating BN (Werry and Aman, 1999). But this effectiveness may be limited to a minority of patients. Further, the role of antidepressants in treating BN in youngsters still remains unclear. When pharmacological medications are used, cautions regarding side effects should be taken care of.

(b) Family Therapy

Family therapy is derived from the perspective that the families are intimately involved in the maintenance of the disordered eating behaviours. In clinical practice, the use of family therapy is widespread in treating of eating disorders. There is some research support for the effectiveness of family interventions for adolescence with AN (Steiner and Lock, 1998). There are a variety of approaches to therapy with families of eating-disordered young women. The family systems approach, represented by Minuchin and his colleagues (1978), is a well-known approach. This approach views the family context as central to many disorders involving somatic symptoms, including Anorexia Nervosa. These researchers, therefore, insisted that the entire family system must be treated. When they administrated family therapy, they found that 86 per cent of the fifty-three cases recovered from both AN and its psychosocial components.

(c) Cognitive-Behavioural Treatment

This type of treatment is widely accepted to treat Bulimia Nervosa. This treatment involves a multifaceted programme that is based on the rationale that cognitive distortions and a loss of control over eating are at the core of the disorder (Fairburn, 1997). According to this view, cognition regarding shape and weight are the primary features of the disorder and other features of the disorder, such as dieting and self-induced vomiting are secondary expressions of these concerns. In the initial stage of treatment, the patient is educated regarding BN and the cognitive view of the disorder is made clear. During this stage, behavioural techniques are also used to reduce bingeing and compensatory behaviours like vomiting and to establish control over eating patterns. These techniques are supplemented with cognitive restructuring techniques, and as treatment progresses, there is an increasing cognitive focus on targeting inappropriate weight-gain concerns and on training self-control strategies for binge eating. Finally, a maintenance strategy to sustain improvements and to prevent relapses is also included.

Treatments of AN from a cognitive – behavioural perspective involves two phrases: intervention to restore body weight and to save the patient's life; and subsequent extended interventions to ameliorate longstanding adjustment and family difficulties and to maintain normal weight. Many of these interventions have effectively treated hospitalized patients at a critical point in their illness.

ELIMINATION DISORDERS

Control of elimination is viewed as a developmental milestone for a child. Toilet training is an important concern for parents of young children (Schroeder and Gordon, 1991). The usual sequence of acquisition of control over elimination is nighttime bowel control, daytime bowel control, daytime bladder control and finally, nighttime bladder control. Usually, bowel and daytime bladder training are completed between the age of eighteen and thirty-six months. But there is considerable variation among children. Parents also differ in their opinion about toilet control. This opinion of parents is related to cultural values, attitudes and real-life pressures on the parent, such as day-care requirements and other siblings. Ready availability of disposable diapers reduces the inclinations of many parents towards the desirability of starting training early. Most important elimination disorders, which give rise to concern are enuresis (inability to control bladder) and encopresis (inability to control bowel).

1. Enuresis

The term 'enuresis' comes from the Greek word meaning 'I make water'. It refers to the repeated voiding of urine during the day or night into bed or clothes when such voiding is not due to a physical disorder, such as diabetics or urinary tract infection. The lack of urinary control is not usually diagnosed as enuresis prior to the age of five (Doyles, 1989). In addition, a certain frequency of lack of control of bladder is required to be diagnosed as an enuresis. This frequency varies with the age of the child. Normally, at least two frequencies per month is the criterion for children of five or six years of age, with less frequency of wetting required for the diagnosis of enuresis in older children. Mostly daytime bladder control is achieved earlier. But nighttime bladder control is achieved more slowly.

Enuresis may be nocturnal (night time bedwetting) or diurnal (daytime). It is referred to as 'primary', if the child has never demonstrated bladder control and as 'secondary', when the problem is preceded by a period of urinary continence. Walker et al. (1989) found that about 85 per cent of all cases of enuresis are of the primary type. Estimates of the prevalence of nocturnal enuresis generally indicate that approximately 15 to 20 per cent of five-year-old children have episodes at least once per month and that by seven years of age, approximately 7 to 15 per cent of children are enuretic at that frequency. By the midteens, the prevalence of enuresis decreases to about 1 per cent (Ondersma and Walker, 1998).

Factors Causing Enuresis

A number of factors are considered to cause enuresis. But no definitive factor has been established. Gerard (1939) viewed that enuresis was the result of emotional disturbances. It is also suggested that sleep abnormalities contribute to the development of enuresis. It is believed, for example, that nocturnal enuresis occurs because the child is an unusually deep sleeper. Another biological proposition views that a lack of normal nocturnal increases in Anti Diuretic Hormone (ADH). A lack of normal nocturnal increase in ADH might lead to a higher production of urine. Further, family histories of enuresis frequently reveal a number of relatives with the same problem (Christophersen and Edwards, 1992). The behavioural theories believe that wetting results from a failure to learn control over reflexive wetting, which inturn can result from either faulty training or other environmental influences that interface with learning, such as a chaotic or stressful home environment.

Treatment for Enuresis

Before starting any treatment, first the child should be assessed by a physician to find out whether there is any medical reason for the urinary difficulties. In addition, careful preparation and ensuring of parental co-operation are necessary for initiating the treatment. A variety of pharmacological agents have been used in the treatment of enuresis. Imipramine hydrochloride (Tofranil), a tricyclic antedepressant is most commonly employed medication. But there is reason for concern regarding side effects (Ondersma and Walker, 1998). Another medication, desmopressin may have less risk of side effects. It has the ability to control high urine output during sleep. Behavioural treatment methods such as urine-alarm or bell-and-pad system have received considerable research attention to treat nocturnal enuresis.

2. Encopresis

Encopresis refers to passing faeces into the clothing or other unacceptable area when this is not due to physical disorder. The diagnosis is made when this event occurs at least once a month in a child of at least four years of age (American Psychiatric

Association, 1994). Distinction is made among the sub-types of encopresis based on the presence or absence of constipation. Most of encopretic children are chronically constipated and are classified as having constipation with overflow incontinence (or retentive encopresis). Estimates of the prevalence of encopresis average about 2 to 3 per cent among seven-to eight-year old children. Percentages appear to decrease with age, being very rare by adolescence and the problem occurs more frequently in males (Ondersma and Walker, 1998). Encopresis carries a social stigma. It is a source of distress to both parents and children. Hence, it is associated with more behavioural problems. For example, Young et al. (1996) studied the children with encopresis and reported that they have higher Total Behaviour Problem and lower social competence scores on the Child Behaviour Checklist. In addition, encopresis has associated psychological difficulties, that may be a consequence rather than an antecedent of encopresis, or both may be related to common environmental factors like stressful family circumstances.

Factors Causing Encopresis

A variety of causes are suggested. Initial constipation may be influenced by factors such as diet, fluid intake, medications, environmental stresses or inappropriate toilet training. The rectum and colon may become distended by the hard faeces. The bowel then becomes incapable of responding with a normal defecation reflex to normal amounts of faecal matter. Further, encopresis is more likely to occur in the presence of developmental inadequacies in the structure and functioning of the physiological and anatomical mechanisms required for bowel control. But these organic inadequacies are viewed as temporary. The behavioural perspective focuses on faulty toilet training procedures.

Treatment for Encopresis

The treatment efforts for encopresis combine both medical and behavioural management modes. First, both the parent and the child are educated about encopresis. Then, the next step usually consists of an initial cleanout phase using enemas or high fiber intake to eliminate faecel impactions. After that, parents are asked to schedule regular toilet times and to use suppositions if defecation does not occur. Modification in diet, laxatives and stool softeners are employed to facilitate defecation. Positive consequences, such as a shared activity chosen by the child, are used to reward unassisted bowel movements in the toilet, as well as clean pants. If soiling occurs, the children may instructed to clean themselves and their clothes. Research suggests that such treatment is highly effective, with success rates up to 100 per cent and low relapse rates (Onsersma and Walker, 1998).

SLEEP DISORDERS

Children often have problems involving sleep. They may suffer difficulties in going to sleep and to sleep through the night. They are often troubled by nightmares. To understand these common problems as well as to overcome them, it is necessary to understand the variations in normal sleep. At all ages, there is considerable variability in normal sleep patterns. Further, the patterns of sleep change with development. For instance, the newborn infant sleeps for about 16 hours per day. By the time the child is one year old, the average amount of sleep has fallen to 12 hours. The typical 10 or 11-year-old child sleeps about 8 hours a day. In addition, there are two broad phases of sleep: rapid eye movement (REM) sleep and non rapid eye movement (NREM) sleep. NREM sleeps is divided into four stages of which third and fourth are the deepest stages of sleep, characterized by very slow waves in EEG and are thus referred to as slow wave sleep (SWS). The brain cycles through these stages of sleep throughout the night. The time spent in different stages of sleep also varies and changes with development. For instance, in the first year of life, active REM sleep changes from about eight hours to about half this amount, thus also reducing the proportion of time spent in REM relative to other phase of sleep. The sequencing, or patterns in which the various stages of sleep occur also changes. The phases of sleep are intermixed in irregular patterns in infants. However, as the child develops, regular patterns of light NREM, deep NREM, and REM sleep are gradually established. Stores (1996) illustrated the pattern of sleep stages that may be characteristic for an older child or an adolescent and also pinpointed the stages of sleep during which some of the sleep disorders would occur.

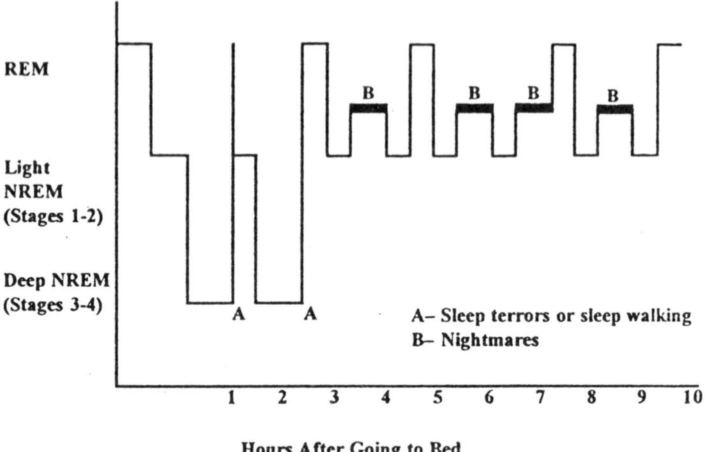

Sleep stage patterns typical of an older child and the points at which sleep disorders might occur. (Adapted from Stores, 1996)

In relation to the above context, most of the sleep disorders are defined. During the first year of life, many children do not sleep and nightmares often occur during the second year, and the three-to-five-year-old presents a variety of problems, including difficulty in going to sleep, nighttime awakenings, and nightmares. Mindell's (1993) survey suggests that approximately 25 per cent of one-to-five-year-olds experience some form of sleep disturbance. Even in adolescence, complaints regarding sleep are common, particularly the need for more sleep and difficulty in falling asleep.

Sleep problems are generally experienced by many children. But these problems are not necessarily associated with other psychological or behavioural difficulties. In fact, if a sleep problem does not cause the child significant distress or result in impairment in social, educational or other important areas of functioning, then it would not be considered a diagnosable mental disorder (DSM – IV). However, in some cases, sleep problems may be associated with or predictors of other behavioural problems.

Types of Sleep Disorders

There are many types of sleep disorders, which are of great concern to parents, clinicians, children and adolescents (Anders and Eiben, 1997). The sleep disorders which are of primary concern are usually classified into two major categories: dyssomnias (problems in initiating and maintaining sleep or of excessive sleepiness) and parasomnias (disorders of arousal, partial arousal or sleep-stage transitions) (American Sleep Disorders Association, 1990).

1. Dyssomnias

If the children face problems in going to/initiating sleep and maintaining sleep through the night, and if these problems become severe and chronic enough, then they fall under this category. The problems of sleep and waking are very common and often occur together. They are often viewed as manifestations of the child's neuro physiological development and therefore they are expected finally to clear up. Hence, parents should often ensure whether it is caused by some breathing difficulties or real fears on the child's part. Sometimes, the sleep difficulties of infants and very young children are associated with feeding practices. For example, milk intolerance may also account for some sleep difficulties. In such cases, removal of milk products from the diet should result in normalization of sleep after a relatively short period of time (Horne, 1992).

Cognitive development is also an important factor to recognize a sleep problem by the child. The child must be able to cognisize that it can neither initiate nor maintain sleep. The older children experience worrisome cognitions about school or peers, ruminations about past or anticipated fears with regard to studies, which may give rise to sleep problems. Hence assessment should include all these factors in addition to medical and dietary issues, the child's functioning in various other domains, family environment and parental expectation (Durand et al., 1998).

The treatment for dyssomnia includes pharmacological agents and behavioural interventions. When pharmacological medications are used, adequate concern regarding negative side effects is an important aspect. The behavioural treatment should include various procedures, which focus on the consequences applied to the child's behaviours and on techniques of stimuli control (Bootzin and Chambers, 1990).

2. *Parasomnias*

Sleep disorders, such as sleepwalking, sleep terrors and nightmares are included in this category.

Sleepwalking is otherwise known 'somnambulism'. Shakespeare's Lady Macbeth is a well-known fictitious character, which had somnambulism. Initially, sleepwalking begins with the child's sitting upright in bed. The eyes, though they are open, appear 'unseeing'. Usually, the child leaves the bed and walks around and such an episode may last for a few seconds at a minimum. Sometimes it may even last for thirty minutes or longer. The most important aspect in sleepwalking is that the whole episode is not at all recorded in memory. Long episodes may result in physical injury sometimes.

Almost 15 per cent of children between the age of five and twelve have experiences of sleepwalking. It is estimated that one to six per cent of the population seems to have persistent sleepwalking. The vast majority of sleepwalking episodes occurs in the first one to three hours following sleep onset (refer stores' figure that illustrates sleep patterns). Unlike the case for adults, the presence of sleep walking in children has not been found to be associated with psychological disturbance (Stores, 1996). Research findings also reveal that central nervous system immaturity is of significance in sleepwalking. Further, frequency of sleepwalking has been reported to be influenced by the specific setting, stress, fatigue and physical illness (American Psychiatric Association). The family patterns of sleepwalking insist the role of heredity as an important casual factor. Further, greater concordance rates for sleepwalking among monozygotic twins than among dizygotic twins bring out the contribution of genetic component to the disorder.

The sleep terrors and nightmares are fright reactions, which occur during sleep. The sleep terrors are also termed 'night terrors' or 'pavor nocturnus' and they are experienced by one to 6 per cent of children. They are more common in males. They typically occur between the ages of four and twelve. Both nightmares and sleep terrors are often confused but they differ in a number of ways (refer Stores' figure). As seen in the figure, sleep terrors occur during deep, slow-wave sleep and at a fairly constant time, usually about two hours into sleep. When the child is in still-sleep, all of a sudden, it sits upright in bed and screams, as a result of sleep terror. The face shows obvious distress and there are signs of automatic arousal, such as rapid breathing and dilated pupils. Further, repetitive motor movements may occur. The child totally appears disoriented and confused. Attempts to comfort the child remain largely unsuccessful. Most often, the child returns to sleep without full awakening and has little or no memory of this event the next morning. The conceptualization of the cause of sleep terrors is similar to that previously described for sleepwalking. Both of them occur in the same part of the sleep cycle. Wilson and Haynes (1985) clearly differentiated the characteristics of Nightmares and Sleep terrors.

Characteristics Differentiating Nightmares and Sleep Terrors

(Adapted from Wilson and Haynes, 1985)

Nightmares	Sleep Terror
Occur during REM sleep.	Occur during Non-REM sleep
During middle and later portions of the night.	During first third of night
Verbalizations, if any, are submitted.	Child wakes with cry or scream and verbalizations usually present.
Only moderate physiological arousal.	Intense physiological arousal (increased heart rate, sweating)
Slight or no movements	Motor activity, agitation.
Easy to arouse and responsive to environment.	Difficult to arouse and unresponsive to environment.
Episodes frequently remembered.	Very limited or no memory of the episode.
Quite common.	Somewhat rare (1 to 6 per cent).

TREATMENT FOR SLEEP DISORDERS

Both sleep terror and sleepwalking episodes usually disappear spontaneously in many cases. So education and support are sufficient for most of the cases. Even then, some treatment measures are suggested usually, which include response interruption, contigency management, instructional procedures and anxiety reduction procedures (Dollinger, 1986). Medical treatments are also in practice but they give rise to concern for side effects.

Nightmares, a fright reaction occurring during sleep, are common in children between the age of three and six years (American Sleep Disorders Association, 1990). They are often the direct manifestations of fear, anxiety and dreadful imaginations, which the child faces. Theoretical explanations suggest for multiple causes, such as developmental physiological and environmental factors for nightmares. But anxiety is consistently viewed as the basis for nightmares and hence majority of treatments focus on anxiety reduction.

SUMMARY

Children often exhibit problems of physical functioning and health, which represent the interface between psychology and paediatrics and hence require collaboration between psychologists and physicians. The commonly encountered problems are eating disorders, elimination disorders and sleep disorders.

Eating disorders are characterised by physically and/or psychologically harmful eating patterns. Some eating disorders may endanger the physical health of the child. The most common clinical disorders of eating are rumination, pica, obesity, anorexia nervosa and bulimia nervosa. Rumination or mercyism is a syndrome characterized by the voluntary and repeated regurgitation of food or liquid in the absence of an organic cause. If rumination continues, serious medical complications can result, with death being the outcome in extreme cases. It is treated with a variety of treatment procedures like satiation and aversive technique.

Pica type of eating disorder is characterized by the habitual eating of substances, which are usually considered inedible, such as, paint, paper, fabric, hair, bugs and dirt. This disorder leads to various other damages like parasitic infection and intestinal obstruction. A number of causes are postulated for pica. First, it is viewed as an attempt to satisfy nutritional deficits. Parental inattention, lack of supervision, lack of adequate stimulation and cultural influences are the other causes.

Obesity is one of the most prevalent nutritional diseases in children and adolescents. It is a significant health problem. It is caused by multiple and complex influences, such as biological, psychological and social/cultural influences.

Anorexia Nervosa (AN) and Bulimia Nervosa (BN) are eating disorders, which involve maladaptive attempts to control body weight, disturbances in eating behaviour and abnormal attitudes about body shape and weight. AN refers to 'nervous loss of appetite' and is characterized by prolonged refusal to eat adequate amounts of food. AN is sub-categorized into binge eating/purging anorectics and restricting anorectics. AN occurs primarily in females.

Bulimia Nervosa is an 'ominous variant' of Anorexia Nervosa. BN is characterized by binge eating, persistent over concern for body shape and weight and purges or vomiting. The two sub-types of BN are purging and non-purging types. Most bulimics are women. BN typically begins in adolescence or early adulthood. Both BN and AN can be treated with pharmacological measures, family therapy and cognitive-behavioural therapy.

Control of elimination is viewed as a developmental milestone for a child. Most important elimination disorders are enuresis and encopresis. Enuresis refers to the repeated voiding of urine during the day or night into bed or clothes, when such voiding is not due to a physical disorder, such as diabetics or urinary tract infection. Enuresis may be nocturnal (night time) or diurnal (daytime). Encopresis refers to passing faeces into the clothing or other unacceptable area when this is not due to physical disorder. Since it bears a social stigma, it is a source of distress to both parents and children. Encopresis is more likely to occur in the presence of developmental inadequacies in the structure and functioning of the physiological and anatomical mechanisms required for bowel control. The treatment efforts for encopresis combine both medical and behavioural management modes.

Children often have problems involving sleep. The sleep disorders which are of primary concern are usually classified into two major categories: dyssomnias and parasomnias. Dyssomnias involve problems in initiating and maintaining sleep through the night. Parasomnias involve sleep disorders, such as sleepwalking, sleep terrors and nightmares. The treatment measures are suggested for sleep disorders include response interruption, contigency management, instructional procedures and anxiety reduction procedures. Medical treatments are also in practice but they give rise to concern for side effects.

REFERENCES

American Psychiatric Association, (1994), *Diagnostic and Statistical Manual of Mental Disorders*. Washington, DC: American Psychiatric Association.

American Sleep Disorders Association, Diagnostic Classification Steering Committee, (1990), *The International Classification of Sleep Disorders: Diagnostic and Coding Manual*. Rochester, MN: American Sleep Disorders Association.

Anders, T. F. and Eiber, L.A., (1997), 'Paediatric Sleep Disorders: A Review of the Past 10 Years'. *Journal of the American Academy of Child Adolescent Psychiatry*, 36, 9-20.

Aristimuno, G.G., Foster, T.A., Voors, A.W. , Srinivasan, S.R. and Brenson, G.S., (1984), 'Influence of Persistent Obesity in Children on Cardiovascular Risk Factors'. The Bogalusa Heart Study. *Circulation*, 69, 895-904.

Askevold, F. and Heiberg, A., 1979, Anorexia Nervosa: Two Cases in Disordant MZ Twins, Psychological Monograph, 70, 1-70.

Bell, K.E. and Stein, D.M., (1992), 'Behavioural Treatments for Pica: A Review of Empirical Studies'. *International Journal of Eating Disorders*, 11, 377-389.

Bootzin, R. R. and Champers, M. J., (1990), 'Childhood Sleep Disorders'. In A.M.Gross & R.S. Drabman (Eds.)., *Handbook of Clinical Behavioural Paediatrics*. New York: Plenum.

Brooke, S., (1996), 'The Anorexia Man'. *The Sunday Times* (Style Section), 11, February, 17.

Bruch, H., (1979), *The Golden Cage: The Enigma of Anorexia Nervosa*, New York: Vintage Books.

Bruch, H., (1978), *Eating Disorders: Obesity, Anorexia Nervosa and the Person Within*. New York: Basic Books.

Campaigne, B.N., Morrison, J.A., Schumann, B.C., Faulkner, F., Lakatos, E., Sprecher, D. and Schreiber, G.B., (1994), 'Indexes of Obesity and Comparisons with Previous National Survey Data in 9-and 10-year old Black and White Girls: The National Heart, Lung, and Blood Institute Growth and Health Survey'. *Journal of Paediatrics*, 124, 675-680.

Christophersen, E.R. and Edwards, K.J, (1992), 'Treatment of Elimination Disorders: State of the Art 1991'. *Applied and Preventive Psychology*, 1, 15-22.

Cooper, J.E., (1995), 'On the Publication of the Diagnostic and Statistical Manual of Mental Disorders (4th Edition)', *British Journal of Psychiatry*, 166, 4-8.

Crisp, A.H., (1967), 'Anorexia Nervosa'. *Hospital Medicine*, 1, 713-718.

Dacosta, M. and Halmi, K.A., (1992), 'Classifications of Anorexia Nervosa: Question of Subtypes'. *International Journal of Eating Disorders*, 11, 305-313.

Dietz, W.H., (1995), 'Childhood Obesity: Prevalence and Effects'. In K.D. Bronwell & C.G. Fairburn (Eds.), *Eating Disorders and Obesity: A Comprehensive Handbook*. New York: Guilford Press.

Dietz, W.H., Jr. and Gortmaker, S.L., (1985), 'Do We Fasten Our Children at the Television Set? Obesity and Television Viewing in Children and Adolescents'. *Paediatrics*, 75, 807-812.

Doleys, D.M., (1989), 'Enuresis and Encopresis'. In T.H. Ollendick & M. Hersen (Eds.), *Handbook of Child Psychopathology*, 2nd Ed. New York: Plenum.

Dollinger, S.J., (1986), 'Childhood Sleep Disturbances'. In B.B.Lahey & A.E. Kazdin (Eds.), *Advances in Clinical Child Psychology*, Vol. 9. New York: Plenum.

Durrand, V.M., Mindell, J., Mapstone, E. and Gernet-Dott, P., (1998), 'Sleep Problems'. In T.S. Watson & F.M. Gresham (Eds.). *Handbook of Child Behaviour Therapy*. New York: Plenum Press.

Fairburn, C.G., (1997), 'Eating Disorders'. In D.M. Clark & C.G. Fairburn (Eds.)., *Science and Practice of Cognitive Behaviour Therapy*, Oxford: Oxford University Press.

Gerard, M.W., (1939), 'Enuresis: A Study in Etiology'. *American Journal of Orthopsychiatry*, 9, 48-58.

Hartley, P., (1997), 'Eating Disorders: Myths and Misconceptions'. *Biological Science Review*, 9, 25-27.

Holland, A.J., Hall, A., Murray, R., Russell, G.F.M. and Crisp, A.H., (1984), 'Anorexia Nervosa: A Study of 34 Twin Pairs and One Set of Triplets'. *British Journal of Psychiatry*, 145, 414-418.

Horne, J., (1992), 'Sleep and Its Disorders in Children'. *Journal of Child Psychology and Psychiatry*, 33. 473-487.

Hsu, L.K., (1990), *Eating Disorders*, New York: Guilford.

Israel, A.C. and Shapiro, L.S., (1985), 'Behaviour Problems of Obese Children Enrolling in a Weight Reduction Programme'. *Journal of Paediatric Psychology*, 10, 449-460.

Israel, A.C., Guile, C.A., Baker, J.E. and Silverman, W.K., (1994), 'An Evaluation of Enhanced Self-regulation Training in the Treatment of Childhood Obesity'. *Journal of Paediatric Psychology*, 19, 737-749.

Jeffrey, D.B., Lemnitzer, N.B., Hess, J.M., Hickey, J.S., Mc Lellarn, R.W. and Stroud, J., (1979), *Children's Responses to Television Food Advertising: Experimental Evidence of Actual Food Consumption*. Paper Presented at a Meeting of the American Psychological Association, New York City, September.

Kanner, L., (1972), *Child Psychiatry*, 4th Ed. Springfield, IL: Chas. C. Thomas.

Kaplan, A. and Woodside, D., (1987), 'Biological Aspects of Anorexia Nervosa and Bulimia Nervosa'. *Journal of Consulting and Clinical Psychology*, 55, 645-653.

Kaye, W.H., Weltzin, T.E. and Hsu, L.G., (1993), 'Relationship Between Anorexia Nervosa and Obsessive and Compulsive Behaviours'. *Psychiatric Annals*, 23, 365-373.

Kerwin, M. E. and Berkowitz, R.I., (1996), 'Feeding and Eating Disorders: Ingestive Problems of Infancy, Childhood and Adolescence'. *School Psychology Review*, 25, 316-328.

Kerwin, M.E. and Berkowitz , R.I., (1996), 'Feeding and Eating Disorders: Ingestive Problems of Infancy, Childhood and Adolescence'. *School Psychology Review*, 25, 316-328.

Klesges, R.C. and Hanson, C.L., (1988), 'Determining the Environmental Causes and Correlates of Childhood Obesity, Methodological Issues and Future Research Directions'. In N.A. Krasnegor, G.D. Grave & N. Kretchmer (Eds.), Childhood Obesity: A Bio-behavioural Perspective. Caldwell, NJ: The Telford Press.

Lask, B. and Bryant-Waugh, R., (1992), 'Early-onset Anorexia Nervosa and Related Eating Disorders'. *Journal of Child Psychology and Psychiatry*, 33, 281-300.

Lewinsohn, P.M., Hops, H. Roberts, R.E., Seeley, J.R. and Andrews, J.A., (1993), 'Adolescent Psychopathology: I. Prevalence and Incidence of Depression and Other DSM-III-R Disorders in High School Students'. *Journal of Abnormal Psychology*, 102, 133-144.

Mayes, S.D., (1992), 'Rumination Disorder: Diagnosis, Complications, Mediating Variables and Treatment'. In B.B. Lahey & A.E. Kazdin (Eds.), *Advances in Clinical Child Psychology*, Vol.14. New York: Plenum.

Mc Alpine, C. and Singh, N.N., (1986), 'Pica in Institutionalized Mentally Retarded Persons'. *Journal of Mental Deficiency Research*, 30, 171-178.

Millican F.K. and Lourie, R.S., (1970), 'The Child with Pica and His Family'. In E.J. Anthony and C.Koupernik (Eds.), *The Child in His Family*, Vol. 1, New York: Wiley- Interscience.

Mindell, J.A., (1993), 'Sleep Disorders in Children'. *Health Psychology*, 12, 151-162.

Minuchin, S., Rosman, B.L. and Baker, L., (1978), *Psycho-somatic Families: Anorexia Nervosa in Context*. Cambridge, MA: Harvard University Press.

Montague, C.T., Farooqui, I.S., Whitehead, J.P., (1997), 'Congenital Leptin Deficiency is Associated with Severe Early–onset Obesity in Humans'. *Nature*, 387, 903-907.

O'Brien, M., (1996), 'Child-rearing Difficulties Reported by Parents of Infants and Toddlers'. *Journal of Paediatric Psychology*, 21, 433-446.

Ondersma, S.J. and Walker, E., (1998), 'Elimination Disorders'. In T.H. Ollendick & M. Hersen (Eds.), *Handbook of Child Psychopathology*, (3rd Ed.), New York: Plenum Press.

Parry-Jones, W.L.I. and Parry-Jones, B., (1993), 'Self Mutilation in Four Historical Cases of Bulimia'. *British Journal of Psychiatry*, 163, 394-402.

Petkova, B., (1997), 'Understanding Eating Disorders: A Perspective From Feminist Psychology'. *Psychology Review*, 4, 2-7.

Pierce, J.W. and Wardle, J., (1993), 'Self-esteem, Parental Appraisal and Body Size in Children'. *Journal of Child Psychology and Psychiatry*, 34, 1125-1136.

Rolland-Cachera,M.F., Deheeger,M., Guilloud- Bataille,M., Avons,P., Patois, E. and Sempe, M., (1987), 'Tracking the Development of Adiposity from One Month of Age to Adulthood'. *Annals of Human Biology*, 14, 219-229.

Russel, G.F.M., (1979), 'Bulimia Nervosa: An Ominous Variant of Anorexia Nervosa'. *Psychological Medicine*, 9, 429-448.

Sahakian, B., (1987), 'Anorexia Nervosa and Blumia Nervosa'. In R.L. Gregory (Ed.). *The Oxford Companion to the Mind*. Oxford: Oxford University Press.

Schlicker, S.A., Borra, S.T. and Regan, C., (1994), 'The Weight and Fitness Status of United States Children'. Nutrition Reviews, 52, 11-17.

Schroeder, C.S. and Gordon, B.N., (1991), *Assessment and Treatment of Childhood Problems: A Clinician's Guide*, New York: Guilford.

Sharp, C.W. and Freeman, C.P.L., (1993), 'The Medical Complications of Anorexia Nervosa'. *British Journal of Psychiatry*, 162, 452-462.

Steiner, H. and Lock. I., (1998), 'Anorexia Nervosa and Bulimia Nervosa in Children and Adolescents: A Review of the Past 10 Years'. *Journal of the American Academy of Child and Adolescent Psychiatry*, 37, 352-359.

Stores, G., (1996), 'Assessment and Treatment of Sleep Disorders in Children and Adolescents'. *Journal of Child Psychology and Psychiatry*, 37, 907-925.

Strober, M. and Katz, J.L., (1987), 'Do Eating Disorders and Affective Disorders Share a Common Aetiology?' *International Journal of Eating Disorders*, 6, 171-180.

Sunday, S.R. and Halmi, K.A., (1990), 'Taste Perception and Hedonics in Eating Disorders'. *Physiology and Behaviour*, 48, 587-594.

Treasure, J.L. and Holland, A.J., (1991), 'Genes and the Actiology of Eating Disorders'. In P. Mc Guffin & R. Murray (Eds.). *The New Genetics of Mental Illness*. Oxford: Butterworth.

Walker, C.E., Kenning, M., and Faust-Companile, J., (1989), 'Enuresis and Encopresis'. In E.J. Mash & R.A. Barkley (Eds.), *Treatments of Childhood Behaviour Disorders*. New York: Guilford

Walsh, B.T., (1995), 'Pharmacotherapy of Eating Disorders'. In K.D. Brownell & C.G. Fairburn (Eds.), *Eating Disorders and Obesity: A Comprehensive Handbook*. New York ; Guilford Press.

Werry, J.S. and Aman, M.G., (1999), *Practitioner's Guide to Psychoactive Drugs for Children and Adolescents*. (2nd Ed.), New York: Plenum Medical Book Company.

Wilson, C.C. and Haynes, S.N., (1985), 'Sleep Disorders'. In P.H. Bornstein & A.E. Kazdin (Eds.), *Handbook of Clinical Behaviour Therapy with Children*. Homewood, IL: Dorsey.

Young, M.H., Brennan, L.C. and Baker, S.S., (1996), 'Functional Encopresis'. In R.S. Feldman (Ed.), *The Psychology of Adversity*, Amberst: University of Massachusetts Press.

14

Changing Problem Behaviour

OBJECTIVES

This chapter deals with the different therapeutic claims to treat problem behaviours. It presents psychotherapy, focal psychotherapy, and different techniques in behaviour therapy. It also describes the behaviour modification therapies. It delineates the therapeutic measures based on behaviour shaping and token-economy system. Cognitive therapy model along with its variations are also presented. Ultimately, the chapter ends with an analysis of cognitive behaviour modification therapy and its association with meta-cognition. After reading this chapter, the readers must be able to:

(i) Know about psychotherapy and focal psychotherapies;

(ii) Define the behaviour therapy and explain various behaviour therapies;

(iii) Present the two broad categories of behaviour modification therapy;

(iv) Describe behaviour shaping and token-economy;

(v) Analyse the cognitive and metacognitive strategic orientation in therapies;

(vi) Delineate the different cognitive-behavioural therapies;

(vii) Understand the cognitive behaviour modification therapy and its association with metacognition; and

(viii) Realize the need for multidisciplinary concerns in changing problem behaviours.

Problem behaviour, by its very nature, leaves its mark on society in the sense that it results in social disapproval because it is harmful to maintaining social order. Problem behaviours are endemic and pervasive. Behavioural problems in children and adolescents are associated with serious negative consequences for both the children and those around them. Hence changing behaviours, which are problematic, is a major concern for psychologists, clinicians, psychopathologists, and parents. As there are many perspectives with regard to viewing causal factors of problem behaviours, there are a variety of therapeutic claims too in treating behaviour problems. The most important therapeutic claims are made by psychotherapy, behaviour therapy and cognitive-cum-metacognitive therapy, which are dealt here in this chapter.

FREUD AND PSYCHOTHERAPY

Freud (1933) and other psychotherapeutic models following Freudian perspective see problem behaviours as stemming from the demands of the id and/or the superego. If the ego is too weak to cope with these, it defends itself by representing them into the unconscious. However, the conflicts do not appear but find expression through behaviour and this is the 'disorder' a person experiences. Freud believed that by a process called 'psychoanalysis', the unconscious conflicts responsible for a person's disordered behaviour can be uncovered and thus they can be made conscious. By providing insight into these conflicts, the ego is made capable to deal more effectively with them. Through a 'therapeutic regression', (Winnicott, 1958) the person receiving psychoanalysis directed to experience 'repressed' or deeply buried unconscious feelings and wishes frustrated in childhood. This takes place in the 'safe' context of the psychoanalyst's consulting room, and the person (the analysand) is encouraged to experience the feelings and wishes in a more appropriate way with a 'new ending' (Alexander, 1946). Providing disturbed people with 'insight' (self-knowledge and self-understanding) enables them to adjust successfully to their deep-rooted conflicts and deal with them in a more 'mature' way. Thus, in Freud's words, psychoanalysis aims to 'drain the psychic abscess' and 'make the unconscious conscious'.

Normally, the ego's defence mechanisms repress certain thoughts. As a result, bringing the unconscious into consciousness is very difficult. Freud used a variety of techniques to breakdown an analysand's (the person undergoing psychoanalysis) defences, such as hypnosis, dream interpretation, parapraxes (Feudian slips), the interpretation of physiological cues and free-association. Hypnosis allows analysands to break through to things they were otherwise unaware of. But Freud later abandoned hypnosis because some of his analysands denied the accuracy of what they had revealed during hypnosis and some others found their revelations to be premature and painful. Similarly, Freud believed that unconscious impulses are expressed in dreams as a form of wish fulfilment. In addition, the interpretation of faulty actions (parapraxes) and the interpretation of physiological cues are also helpful to uncover the unconscious.

The most widely used technique in psychoanalysis is free association. In this, the analysand lies on a comfortable couch so that the analyst cannot be seen. The analysand is encouraged to say whatever comes to mind, no matter how trivial or frivolous it might seem. Freud called this 'the basic rule' of psychoanalysis. He believed that the ego ordinarily acts as a censor, preventing and threatening the unconscious impulses from entering consciousness. By free-associating, the censor could be 'by-passed'. Though it is the most widely used technique, it takes several sessions before analysands 'open up'. During analysis, the analyst remains 'anonymous' and does not express emotion or evaluate the analysand's attitudes. The analyst does not reveal information about him-or herself, since he needs to learn a great deal about the analysand. This form of interaction ensures that the analysand does not form a close, personal relationship with the analyst but views him or her purely as an 'anonymous and ambiguous stimulus'. While the analysand free-associates, the analyst acts as a sort of 'sounding-board', often repeating and clarifying what the analysand has said. Thus, the analysand tells his story of the past and the analyst helps to interpret it in terms of repressed conflicts and feelings.

Once interpretation is complete and the unconscious conflict has been brought into consciousness, the analyst and the analysand repeat and 'live out' the conflict. The associated feelings, which have been repressed for so long then become available for 'manipulation' by the analyst. Freud called this process 'transference' or 'transference neurosis'. In it, the original source of the conflict is displaced onto the analyst who now becomes the object of the analysand's emotional responses.

As therapy continues, the analyst may try to explain the analysand's behaviour in a way, which is new to him/her. For example, the analysands may be informed that their anger does not come from where they think it does, but rather that they are angry because the analyst reminds them of someone. In 'confrontation', the analyst tells the analysand exactly what is being revealed in the free association. In 'reconstruction', the analyst provides hypothetical historical statements of hitherto buried fragments of the analysand's past. For example, the analysand may be told that the anger is a repetition of feelings experienced as a child and that the analyst stands for the objects of that anger.

Once the analysand consciously understands the roots of the conflict, 'insight' has been achieved and the analysand must be helped to deal with the conflict in a mature and rational way. Freud believed that the analysands gained insight through a gradual increase in self-knowledge, which is called a process of 're-education'. This increase often involves repetitive consideration of all aspects of the conflict allowing the individual to face reality and deal with it effectively rather than deny and distort it. This is called 'working through'.

To breakdown the complex ego defences which have been developed to cope with the conflict, and to bring about a lasting personality change, the analysand and analyst need to work through every implication of the problem with complete understanding by the analysand. This is necessary to prevent the conflict from being repressed into the unconscious again. As a result, the individual is strengthened and therefore becomes capable of handling different aspects of the conflict without having to resort to 'defence mechanisms'. The ultimate goal of psychoanalysis is thus a deep-seated modification of personality so as to allow the affected persons to deal with problems on a realistic basis.

FOCAL PSYCHOTHERAPIES

Classical psychoanalysis is both intense, time-consuming and expensive involving perhaps three to six sessions per week over several years. Although some psychoanalysts still rigidly adhere to Freud's protracted techniques, some are flexible in fitting the therapeutic sessions to a person's needs. These analysts are known as psychoanalytically oriented psychotherapists. Most psychoanalytically oriented psychotherapies involve briefer treatment and use face-to-face interaction and hence they are called focal psychotherapies. No doubt, they also emphasize restructuring the entire personality. But they pay more attention to the analysand's current life and relationships than to early childhood. Important revisions of Freudian approaches have been made by ego psychologists/ego analysts. They focus on the ego rather than the id. Personality is seen as being shaped as much by the external environment as inner conflicts. This second generation includes Erikson, Horney, Anna Freud, Klein and Mahler.

BEHAVIOUR THERAPY

The psychotherapy attempts to produce insight into the causes of maladaptive behaviour. Such insights do not necessarily result in behavioural changes. Hence the behaviour therapy focuses on the behaviour-giving rise to a problem rather than the historical reasons for its development. Walker (1984) suggested that the term 'behaviour therapy' be confined to those therapies based on 'classical conditioning'. Those techniques based on 'operant conditioning' are described as ' behaviour modification techniques'. Behaviour therapies based on classical conditioning concentrate on stimuli that elicit new responses, which are contrary to the old maladaptive ones. Three therapeutic behaviour approaches were designed to treat phobic behaviours and they are Implosion therapy, Flooding and Systematic desentisation. Two more behaviour therapies were designed to treat other disorders by creating phobias and they are Aversion therapy and Covert sensitisation.

(a) Implosion Therapy

Both implosion therapy and flooding work on the principle that if the stimulus evoking a fear response is repeatedly presented without the unpleasant experience that accompanies it, its power to elicit the fear response will be lost. In implosion therapy, the therapist repeatedly exposes the person to vivid mental images of the feared stimulus in the safe therapeutic setting. This is achieved by the therapist getting the person to imagine the most terrifying form of contact with the feared object using 'stimulus augmentation' (vivid verbal descriptions of the feared stimulus, to supplement the person's imagery). After repeated trials, the stimulus eventually loses its anxiety-producing power and so the anxiety extinguishes (or implodes) because no harm comes to the individual in the safe setting of the therapist's room.

(b) Flooding

In flooding, the individual is forced to 'confront' the object or situation eliciting the fear response. For instance, a person with a fear of heights might be taken to the top of a tall building and physically prevented from leaving. By preventing avoidance of, or escape from, the feared objects or situation, the fear response is eventually extinguished. Wolpe (1973) describes a case in which an adolescent girl afraid of cars was forced into the back of one. She was then driven around continuously for four hours. Initially, her fear reached historical heights. But finally, it receded and by the end of the journey it had disappeared completely. Emmelkamp et al. (1992) reported that both implosion therapy and flooding are effective with certain types of phobia. However, for some people, both lead to increased anxiety and the procedures are too traumatic. Hence, they are to be used with considerable caution.

(c) Systematic Desentisation

Both implosion therapy and flooding use extinction to alter behaviour. But none of them trains people to substitute the maladaptive behaviour, such as fear an adaptive and 'desirable' response. Jones (1924) showed that fear responses could be eliminated if children were given candy and other incentives in the presence of the feared object. Her method involved 'gradually' introducing the feared object, bringing it closer and closer to the children, while at the same time giving them candy, until no anxiety was elicited in its presence. Wolpe (1958) popularised and refined it under the name 'systematic desentisation' (SD).

The therapy requires that an individual initially constructs an 'anxiety hierarchy' (a series of scenes or events rated from lowest to highest in terms of the amount of anxiety they elicit). Once the hierarchy has been constructed, 'relaxation training' is given. This will be the adaptive substitute response, which the most therapists use. Training aims to achieve complete relaxation, the essential task being to respond quickly to suggestions to feel relaxed and peaceful. After relaxation training, the person is asked to imagine, as vividly as possible, the scene at the bottom of the hierarchy, and is simultaneously told to remain calm and relaxed.

One problem with SD is its dependence on a person's ability to conjure up vivid images of encounters with a phobic object or situation A way of overcoming this is to use photographs or slides displaying the feared object or situation. Another approach involves live (in vivo) encounters. For instance, the person fearing spide s (an archnophobic) may be desensitised by gradually approaching spiders. Jones (1924) used this method. Wilson and O'Leary (1978) reported that 'in vivo' desensitization is almost always more effective and longer lasting than other desentisation techniques.

(d) Aversion Therapy

The above-mentioned three therapies are appropriate in the treatment of phobias occuring in specific situations. Aversion therapy, on the contrary, is used with persons who want to 'extinguish' the 'pleasant' feelings associated with socially undesirable behaviours. SD tries to substitute a pleasurable response for an aversive one. Aversion therapy reverses this and pairs an unpleasant event with a desired (for the person) but socially undesirable behaviour. If this unpleasant event and desired behaviour are repeatedly paired, the 'desired' behaviour should eventually elicit negative responses.

Aversion therapy has been used with some success in the treatment of alcohol abuse, smoking, over eating and children's self-injurious behaviours. Whatever its use, aversion therapy is unpleasant and hence it is appropriate only when the individual's consent is acquired. Moreover, the aversion therapy becomes inappropriate, if the individual does not learn an 'adaptive' response. For this reason, most behaviour therapists try to 'shape' new adaptive behaviours at the same time as extinguishing existing maladaptive ones.

(e) Covert Sensitisation

It has been argued by many therapists that aversion therapy is unethical and has the potential for misuse and abuse as Silverstein (1972) has reported. Hence, some therapists use covert sensitisation (CS) as an alternative and 'milder' form of aversion therapy. CS is a mixture of aversion therapy and SD. In CS, people are trained to punish themselves using their 'imaginations' and hence the term 'covert' is used. 'Sensitisation' is achieved by associating the undesirable behaviour with an exceedingly disagreeable consequence. For instance, a heavy drinker might be asked to imagine being violently sick all over himself/herself on entering a bar, and feeling better only after leaving and breathing fresh air. The individual is also instructed to rehearse an alternative 'relief' scene in which the decision not to drink is accompanied by pleasurable sensations. Cautela (1967) suggested that CS can be helpful in controlling overeating and cigarette smoking as well as excessive drinking.

BEHAVIOUR MODIFICATION THERAPY

Behaviour therapies based on operant conditioning are called behaviour modification techniques. They aim 'directly' at observable behaviours and they follow the perspective that behaviours under voluntary control are strongly influenced by their consequences. In other words, actions producing positive outcomes tend to be repeated whereas those producing negative outcomes tend to be suppressed.

Behaviour modification therapy techniques based on operant conditioning generally involve three main steps: 1) to identify the undesirable or maladaptive behaviour; 2) to identify the reinforcers that maintain such behaviour; and 3) to restructure the environment so that the maladaptive behaviour is no longer reinforced. One way to eliminate undesirable behaviours is to 'remove' the reinforcers that maintain them, the idea being that their removal will extinguish the behaviour they reinforce. Another way is to use aversive stimuli to 'punish' voluntary maladaptive behaviours. On the basis of the way in which the elimination of undesirable behaviours are made, the behavioural modification therapies are classified as therapies based on extinction and therapies based on punishment.

(a) Therapies Based on Extinction

The behavioural model proposes that individuals learn to behave in abnormal ways when they are unintentionally reinforced by others for doing so. For instance, a child, who receives parental attention when he or she shouts, is likely to engage in this behaviour in the future, attention is reinforcing. If abnormal behaviours can be 'acquired' through operant conditioning, they can also be eliminated through it. With a disruptive child, parents might be instructed to ignore the behaviour so that it is extinguished from the child's behavioural repertoire. Thus undesirable behaviours can be extinguished by removing the reinforcers that maintain them.

(b) Therapies Based on Punishment

In aversion therapy, an aversive stimulus, such as an electric shock, is used to classically condition a negative response to a desired but undesirable stimulus. Aversive stimuli can also be used to punish voluntary maladaptive behaviours. Cowart and Whaley (1971) studied an emotionally disturbed infant who was hospitalised because he persistently engaged in self-mutilating behaviour to such an extent that he had to be restrained in his crib. Electrodes were attached to the infant's leg and he was placed in a room with a padded floor (the self-mutilation involved violently banging his head against the floor). When the infant began the self-mutilating behaviour, he was given an electric shock. Initially, he was startled, but continued self-mutilating, at which point another shock was given. There were very few repetitions before self-mutilation stopped, and the infant could be safely let out of his crib.

It is generally regarded that therapies using punishment are not as effective as those employing positive reinforcement in brining about behaviour change. Further, punishment tends to produce only a temporary suppression of undesirable behaviour and unless another reinforcement inducing behaviour pattern is substituted for the punished behaviour, it will resurface. In addition, there are also ethical issues surrounding punishment's use, particularly with very young children. In Cowart and Whaley's study, however, the infant was engaging in a behaviour which was clearly very harmful, and with these sorts of behaviour, punishment is actually extremely effective.

BEHAVIOUR SHAPING AND TOKEN-ECONOMY

Apart from eliminating undesirable behaviours, operant conditioning can be used to shape and increase desirable behaviours. This can be done by providing 'positive reinforcement', when a behaviour is performed and making the reinforcement 'contingent' on the behaviour being manifested voluntarily. Behaviour shaping technique and token economy system use positive reinforcement to change behaviour. These therapeutic methods are effective in eliciting and maintaining desired behaviours. Isaacs et al. (1960) cured schizophrenic using positive reinforcement. Similarly, anorexia nervosa was also treated successfully by behaviour shaping therapy offering positive reinforcement. Ayllon and Haughton (1962) treated schizophrenics with a sort of token economy system and reported successful effects. Ayllon and Haughton's approach was further refined by Ayllon and Azrin (1968), who gave token to chronically disturbed individuals in exchange for desirable behaviour. In this system, the therapist first identifies what patients like (such as watching television or smoking cigarettes). When a productive activity occurs (such as making a bed or socialising with other patients), the patient is given tokens that can be exchanged for 'privileges'. The tokens therefore become conditioned reinforcers for desirable and appropriate behaviours. Ayllon and Azrin showed that tokens were effective in eliciting and maintaining desired behaviours.

Token economies have also been used in programmes designed to modify the behaviour of children with conduct disorders. Schneider and Byrne (1987) awarded tokens to children who engaged in helpful behaviours and removed the tokens for inappropriate behaviours, such as arguing or not paying attention.

COGNITIVE AND METACOGNITIVE STRATEGIC ORIENTATION IN THERAPIES

Most of the mental disorders/problem behaviours result from distortions in individual's cognition. The aim of cognitively/meta cognitively based therapies is to show the affected individuals that their distorted or irrational thoughts are the main contributes to their difficulties. If faulty modes of thinking are modified or changed, then disorders can also be alleviated. Cognitive therapies are also called cognitive-behavioural therapies since they have the goal of changing maladaptive behaviour by changing the way in which the individual thinks. Further, like psychodynamic therapies, cognitive therapies too aim to produce insight. However, rather than focusing on the past, they try to produce insight into current cognitions. Bandura's (1969) cognitive-behavioural therapy, Ellis' (1958) rational-emotive therapy, Beck's (1967) cognitive restructuring therapy, attributional therapy and Meichenbaum's (1985) stress inoculation therapy are some examples for cognitively based applications.

(a) *Bandura's Cognitive-Behaviour Therapy*

According to Bandura and other social learning theorists, humans and non-humans can learn directly without experiencing an event, and can acquire new forms of behaviour from others simply by observing them. This is called observational learning. Our observation of whether other people being rewarded or punished can strengthen or reduce our own inhibitions against behaving in similar ways. If we see a positive outcome for behaviour, our restraint against performing it is lowered. This is known as 'response disinhibition'. Similarly, if we see a negative outcome, our restraint is heightened, which is called 'response inhibition'. Bandura argues that behaviours can be altered by exposing those demonstrating appropriate 'models'. Modelling is nothing but performing the actions which the disordered individual is afraid to perform. Apart from changing problem behaviours, this kind of therapy aims to change thoughts and perceptions.

In participant modelling, the individual observes the therapist's behaviour and then imitates it. This method is more effective than having individuals watch filmed or videotaped models, which is otherwise known as 'symbolic modelling'. Modelling has been successfully used with a variety a phobias and to eliminate undesirable behaviours. It has also been used to establish new and more appropriate behaviours. For example, to do away with ophidiophobia (fear of snakes), the therapist performs the behaviour (touching the snake) fearlessly and gradually leads the participant (that is the phobic) into touching, stroking and then holding the snake's body with gloved hands first and then with bare hands while the therapist holds the snake securely by the head and tail. If the participant is unable to touch the snake following ample demonstration, he/she is asked to place her hands on the therapist's and move them down gradually until they touch the snake's body. If the participant no longer feels any apprehension about touching the snake under these conditions, anxieties about contact with the snake's head area and entwining tail are extinguished. The therapist then repeatedly performs the tasks fearlessly and the participant too joins him to perform the responses jointly. As the participant becomes less fearful, the therapist gradually reduces his participation and control over the snake, until eventually, the participant is able to hold the snake in his/her lap without assistance.

In 'assertive training', individuals with difficulty in asserting themselves in interpersonal situations are required to perform in the presence of a group who provide feedback about the adequacy of performance. Then, the therapist assumes the individual's role and models the appropriate assertive behaviour. The individual is asked to try again, this time imitating the therapist. The alternation between 'behavioural rehearsal' and modelling continues until the assertive behaviour has been mastered. When this occurs, the skills are tried out in real life situations. This approach is widely used in social skills training, in which the individuals who lack the ability to function effectively in certain situations observe others performing the desired behaviours and then attempt to imitate them. Bandura (1977) believes that the effectiveness of modelling is the resultant of the improved 'self-efficacy'.

(b) Ellis' Rational-Emotive Therapy (RET)

Ellis developed the Rational-Emotive Therapy in the 1950s. Ellis was basically a trained psychoanalyst. But he was dissatisfied with the 'passivity of psychoanalysis'. Hence he developed his own therapeutic approach. Even now RET is practised by a large number of therapists particularly in the USA. The aim of RET is to help individuals find flaws in their thinking and to make 'mincemeat' of these maladaptive cognitions by creating D, a dispute belief system which has no severe emotional consequences.

Ellis proposes that two of the most common maladaptive cognitions people hold are: 1) they are worthless unless they are perfectly competent at everything they try; and 2) they must be approved of and loved by everyone they meet. Because such beliefs make impossible demands on people who hold them, they lead to anxiety, failure and frequently, abnormal behaviour. Once the irrational beliefs have been identified, therapy continues by guiding the person to substitute more logical or realistic thoughts for the maladaptive ones, a task, which Ellis believes can be accomplished by any therapist. He sees the rational-emotive therapist as an 'exposing and nonsense-annihilating scientist'.

The first stage in RET is to enable the individual to recognise and question their irrational beliefs. The therapist will show the person how to ask questions like *"where is the evidence that I am a worthless person if I am not universally approved?"*, *"who says I must be perfect?"* and *"why must things go exactly the way I would like them to go?"*. Once the individual has thus recognised and analysed his beliefs, he is taught to substitute more realistic alternatives to arrive at 'full acceptance'. Further, a rational-emotive therapist emphasizes that failures should not be viewed as 'disastrous', confirming a lack of self-worth. Instead, they should be merely seen as 'unfortunate' events. RET is very successful in minimising self-defeating beliefs.

(c) Beck's Cognitive Restructuring Therapy

Beck (1967) was originally trained as a psychoanalyst. Beck's therapy assumes that disorders stem primarily from irrational beliefs that cause people to behave in maladaptive ways. Beck's therapy is specifically designed to treat depressed people. Depressed people suffer from a 'cognitive triad' of negative belief of themselves, their futures and their experiences (Beck et al., 1979). Such beliefs are seen as arising from faulty information-processing and faulty logic. Several types of faulty-thinking that can contribute to depression were identified by Beck (1974):

1. Magnification and minimisation: some people magnify difficulties and failures while minimizing their accomplishments and success;
2. Selective abstraction: some people arrive at conclusions based on only one rather than several factors that could have made a contribution;
3. Arbitrary inference: some people arrive at conclusions about themselves, despite the absence of any supporting evidence;
4. Overgeneralization: some persons arrive at a sweeping conclusion based on a single and sometimes trivial event.

Beck's therapy aims to alter such illogical thoughts of depressed persons about their situations and challenge beliefs about their worthlessness, inadequacy and inability to change their circumstances. Hence it identifies first the implicit and self-defeating assumptions depressed people make about themselves, change their validity and substitute more adaptive assumptions. An illustration of Beck's cognitive therapy is given below: It is an exchange between the therapist (who uses Beck's cognitive approach) and a student who believed that she would not get into the college she had applied to:

Beck's Approach to Cognitive Therapy in Action

Therapist: Why do you think you won't be able to get into the university of your choice?

Student: Because my grades were not really so hot.

Therapist:	Well, what was your grade average?
Student:	Well, pretty good up until the last semester in high school.
Therapist:	What was your grade average in general?
Student:	A's and B's.
Therapist:	Well, how many of each?
Student:	Well, I guess, almost all of my grades were A's but I got terrible grades my last semester.
Therapist:	What were your grades then?
Student:	I got two As and two Bs.
Therapist:	Since your grade average would seem to come out to almost all As, why do you think you won't be able to get into the university?
Student:	Because competition being so tough.
Therapist:	Have you found out what the average grades are for admissions to the college?
Student:	Well, somebody told me that a B+ average would suffice.
Therapist:	Isn't your average better than that?
Student:	I guess so.

(Adapted from Beck et al., 1979).

Thus, the therapist attempts to reverse the 'catastrophising beliefs' held by the student concerning herself, her situation and her future. The above exchange illustrates the strategy of identifying a person's misguided self-impressions. Once the self-impressions have been identified, the therapist's role is to attempt to disprove rather than confirm the negative self-image (Williams, 1992). As a result, the person undergoing the therapy may understand the origins of the disorder and ultimately develop skills to restructure his/her own misguided cognitions. Beck's cognitive restructuring therapy is most successful in treating depression (Andrews, 1991), and eating disorders (Fairburn et al., 1993).

(d) Attributional Therapy

Attributions are our beliefs about the causes of our own and other people's behaviours. Attributional therapists hold that, in some cases, depressed people make unrealistic or faulty attributions concerning their own behaviours and that these can cause considerable distress. When asked to explain successful or unsuccessful outcomes, most people show the 'self-serving bias'. However, this is reversed in depressed people, who attribute failures to internal causes even when there is no evidence to support such an attribution. Successful outcomes, by contrast, tend to be attributed to external causes. For example, a depressed individual who passes an examination may attribute the success to ' an easy examination paper that anybody could pass', when in fact it was the individual's own ability that produced the positive outcome. Attributional therapists attempt to break the vicious circle that people low in self-esteem experience. This involves training them to perceive success as resulting from internal factors and at least some failures from external factors beyond their control. Changing attributions can result in increased self-esteem, greater confidence and better performance. Moreover, beneficial changes can occur after only a small number of therapy sessions, which is clearly advantageous (Brockner and Guare, 1983).

(e) Meichenbaum's Stress-Inoculation Therapy

Meichenbaum's (1976) stress inoculation therapy assumes that people sometimes find situations stressful because they think about them in catastrophising ways. Stress inoculation therapy aims to train people cope more effectively with potentially stressful situations. The therapy consists of three stages. The first stages 'cognitive preparation or conceptualization'. This stage involves the therapist and person exploring the way in which stressful situations are thought about. Typically people react to stress by offering negative self-statements like 'I can't handle this'. This exacerbates an already stressful situation. The second stage, 'skill acquisition and rehearsal, attempts to replace negative self-statements with incompatible positive coping statements. These are then learned and practised. Meichenbaum (1976) listed out some of the coping and reinforcing self-statements used in stress inoculation therapy.

Coping and Reinforcing Self-Statements Used in Stress Inoculation Therapy

Preparing for a stressful situation.

- *What is it you have to do?*

- *You can develop a plan to deal with it.*
- *Just think about what you can do about it; that's better than getting anxious.*
- *No negative self-statements; just think rationally.*
- *Don't worry; worry won't help anything.*
- *May be what you think is anxiety is eagerness to confront it.*

Confronting and handling a stressful situation

- *Just 'psych' yourself up-you can meet this challenge.*
- *One step at a time; you can handle the situation.*
- *Don't think about fear; just think about what you have to do. Stay relevant.*
- *This anxiety is what the therapist said you would feel. It's a reminder to use your coping exercises.*
- *This tenseness can be an ally, a cue to cope.*
- *Relax; you're in control. Take a slow deep breath.*
- *Ah, good.*

Coping with the feeling of being overwhelmed

- *When fear comes, just pause.*
- *Keep the focus on the present; what is it that you have to do?*
- *Label your fear from 0 to 10 and watch it change.*
- *You should expect your fear to rise.*
- *Don't try to eliminate fear totally; just keep it manageable.*
- *You can convince yourself to do it. you can reason fear away.*
- *It will be over shortly.*
- *It's not the worst thing that can happen.*
- *Just think about something else.*
- *Do something that will prevent you from thinking about fear.*
- *Describe what is around you. That way you won't think about worrying.*

Reinforcing self-statements

- *It worked; you did it.*
- *Wait until you tell your therapist about this.*
- *It wasn't as bad as you expected.*
- *You made more out of the fear that it was worth.*
- *You damn ideas- that's the problem. When you control them, you control your fear.*
- *It's getting better each time you use the procedures.*
- *You can be pleased with the progress you're making.*
- *You did it!.*

(Adopted from Meichenbaum, 1976).

In the final stage of the (stress inoculation) therapy, which is called 'application and follow-through stage', the therapist guides the person through progressively more threatening situations that have been rehearsed in actual stress-producing situations. Initially, the person is placed in a situation that is moderately easy to cope with. Once this has been mastered, a more difficult situation is presented. According to Meichenbaum et al. (1982), the 'power of positive thinking' approach advocated by stress inoculation therapy can be successful in bringing about effective behaviour change, particularly in relation to anxiety and pain.

COGNITIVE BEHAVIOUR MODIFICATION THERAPY AND ITS ASSOCIATION WITH METACOGNITION

Cognitive behaviour modification is an executive control strategy that is allied closely to metacognition. This kind of therapy focuses on facilitating behavioural self-control, social problem solving skills and self-instructional training. It evolves as a result of the difficulties incurred by children in maintaining and generalizing socially appropriate behaviours and learning strategies. Metacognitive training assists children to control their own social and learning behaviours through self-treatment techniques, such as self-assessment, self-verbalization, self-instruction, self-guidance, self-monitoring, self-regulation, self-evaluation and self- reinforcement.

Jayaprabha's (2003) study established that metacognitive and cognitive strategies are effective in overcoming behaviour difficulties in children. Further, she found that narrative descriptions, pictorial representations, role-play and interaction with non-problematic peer through the means of guided questions are very helpful in generating the metacognitive and cognitive awareness. Multivarious researchers like Kazdin (1995), Osborne (2001), Schoenbrodt-Myers Lisa (2000) and Walker (1984) too successfully tried on behaviour modification through cognitive and metacognitive therapies. SanthaKumari (2003) reported that the comprehensive metacognitive strategies, such as task-orientation, task-planning, self-monitoring, self-regulation and self-evaluation are of immense value in overcoming language learning difficulties in receptive, phonological and expressive language areas and thus assist in cognitive behavioural modification.

Reddy and Shyamala (2003) highlighted to need to use cognitive and metacognitive strategies to overcome antisocial behaviours and to promote positive thinking and constructivism in students. Constructivism develops thinking skills, communication and social skills, encourages alternative methods of assessment, helps students transfer skills to the real world and promotes intrinsic motivation to learn. Thinking and constructivism are big ideas in education. Their implications for how teachers teach and learn to teach are enormous. Rather than receiving knowledge from the experts in training sessions, teachers and administrators will have to collaborate with peers, researchers and their own students to make sense of thinking and constructivism. Only then we can transform our nation, through education, with a thoughtful, critical scientific community, imbued with the passion for truth and for total human welfare.

Shyamala (2004) also made a landmark attempt on cognitive behaviour modification to overcome antisocial behaviour among high school students. She promoted a new thinking pattern among behaviourally disordered children through metacognitive strategies like 'stressing relevance', 'making predictions' and 'stressing consistency'. In her opinion, such metacognitive strategies remedy the inconsistencies in the disordered children's thinking and provide techniques for controlling or changing these habits of thinking. In addition, she suggested that thinking skills involving moral reasoning and anger management should be developed for changing problem behaviours. Moral reasoning has been devised by the use of role taking, 'self-control' and 'self-instruction', whereas anger-management has involved measures, such as cognitive preparation, skill acquisition and application training. Further, the development of inter-personal cognitive problem-solving skills was also promoted among unpopular and rejected children (excessive aggression and social withdrawal). The skills, which were given much focus are: 1) problem-sensitivity; 2) alternate solution thinking; 3) brainstorming; 4) means-ends thinking; 5) consequential thinking; and 6) causal thinking. Ultimately, she concluded that all sorts of problem behaviours prevalent among students can be overcome with the help of comprehensive interventions which emphasise orientation towards cognitive and metacognitive strategic competence among the behaviourally disordered population.

Reddy and Shyamala's (2004) research advocated the need to teach to develop thinking to overcome antisocial behaviour. There is an urgent need to teach thinking skills at all levels of education to prevent antisocial behaviour. The constructive teacher should draw attention to inconsistencies in student's thinking and provide techniques such as stressing relevance, making predictions and stressing in consistency (Watson, Bruce and Kopnicek, 1990). Constructive strategies that encourage cooperation, collaboration, critical thinking, problem solving, role playing and class discussions foster positive social interactions between students. Educationists, as constructivists, have a great role to play in guiding the students to rectify their thinking errors, to be more responsible for their emotions and reactions and to have a better tomorrow.

NEED FOR MULTIDISCIPLINARY CONCERNS

Therapeutic service as well as professional care to children and adolescents having problem behaviours calls forth multidisciplinary concerns. They involve scientific efforts of psychologists, psychiatrists, social workers, educational specialists, parents and several other professionals. Parents' participation in the treatment of their children is often crucial. The parents' needs, motivations and abilities cannot be ignored. When families drop out from treatment, the reasons for dropout give rise to concern for family matters and parents' perception of therapy. Moreover, the therapy provided to young people having problem behaviours requires special consideration of their motivation for treatment and their level of development. Consideration must be given to children's rights to have privacy, to assent to the kind of therapy selected to be given and to participate in decisions. Therapeutic care of the young clients also raises ethical and legal dilemmas.

SUMMARY

Problem behaviour results in social disapproval and hence leaves its mark on society. It is endemic and pervasive. As there are many perspectives with regard to viewing causal factors of problem behaviours, there are a variety of therapeutic claims too in treating problem behaviours. The most important as well as effective claims are made by psychotherapy, behaviour therapy and cognitive-behavioural modification therapy.

Psychotherapy is based on Freudian perspectives, which view problem behaviours as stemming from the demands of the id and/or the superego. Through a process called 'psychoanalysis', unconscious conflicts responsible for a person's disordered behaviour are uncovered. By providing insight into these unconscious conflicts, the ego can deal more effectively with them. Freud used a variety of techniques to break down the analysand's defences, including hypnosis, dream interpretation, parapraxes (Freudian slips) and interpretation of physiological cues. However, the most widely used technique is free association. Classical psychoanalysis is both intense, time-consuming and expensive. Hence psychoanalytically oriented psychotherapists go for briefer treatment and the use of face-to-face interaction. Their therapy is known as focal psychotherapy.

Behaviour therapy focuses on the behaviour which gives rise to a problem. 'Behaviour therapy' is confined to those therapies based on 'classical conditioning'. The techniques based on operant condition are described as behaviour modification therapy techniques. Implosion therapy, Flooding and Systematic Desensitisation are the behaviour therapy measures designed to treat phobic behaviours. Similarly, aversion therapy and covert sensitisation are behaviour therapies to treat other disorders by creating phobias.

Behaviour modification therapies based on operant conditioning aim directly at observable behaviours and they follow the perspective that behaviour under voluntary control are strongly influenced by their consequences. These therapies are widely classified as therapies based on extinction and therapies based on punishment.

Apart from eliminating undesirable behaviours, operant conditioning can also be used to shape and increase desirable behaviours. This can be done by providing positive reinforcement, and tokens. These behaviour shaping techniques and token economies are helpful to treat schizophrenia, eating disorders and conduct disorders.

Most of the problem behaviours result from distortions in individual's cognition. The aim of cognitively/metacognitively based therapies is to show the affected individuals that their distorted or irrational thoughts are the main contributors to their problem behaviours. These therapies are also called cognitive therapies or sometimes cognitive-behavioural therapy. Bandura's cognitive-behavioural therapy lays emphasis on modelling to develop assertiveness and social-skills among the individuals having problem behaviours. Ellis' Rational-Emotive Therapy too helps the disordered individuals to find flaws in their thinking by creating a dispute belief system. Beck's cognitive restructuring therapy, which is specifically designed to treat depression, also sees disorders stemming from irrational beliefs. Similarly, attributional therapists try to break down the vicious circles, which are mostly experienced by low self-esteem individuals. Meichenbaum's stress inoculation therapy assumes that people sometimes find situations stressful because of their misconceptions about them. This therapy, therefore, trains people to cope more effectively with potentially stressful situations through cognitive preparation, skill acquisition and rehearsal and application and practice. Cognitively based therapies are particularly helpful in treating panic disorders.

In the Indian context, Reddy and Shyamala highlighted the need for cognitive and metacognitive strategies to overcome antisocial behaviour and develop constructivism in students.

Santhakumari, Shyamala and Jayaprabha made successful efforts toward cognitive behaviour modification through cognitive as metacognitive strategic means. The metacognitive strategies, like task-orientation, task-planning, self-monitoring, self-regulation and self-evaluation and self-reinforcement are very helpful in changing problem behaviours as well as in modifying, shaping and maintaining appropriate cognitive behaviours.

Therapeutic service along with professional care to children and adolescents having problem behaviours calls forth multidisciplinary concerns. They involve scientific efforts of psychologists, psychiatrists, social workers, educational specialists, parents and several other professionals. Therapeutic care of the young clients also raises ethical and legal dilemmas.

REFERENCES

Alexander, F., (1946), 'Individual Psychotherapy'. *Psychosomatic Medicine*, 8, 110-115.

Andrews, G., (1991), 'The Evaluation of Psychotherapy'. *Current Opinions of Psychotherapy*, 4, 379-383.

Ayllon, T. and Azrin, N.H., (1968), *The Token Economy: A Motivational System for Therapy and Rehabilitation*. New York: Appleton Century Crofts.

Ayllon, T. and Haughton, E., (1962), 'Control of the Behaviour of Scizophrenic Patients by Food'. *Journal of the Experimental Analysis of Behaviour*, 5, 343-352.

Bandura, A., (1969), *Principles of Behaviour Modification*. New York: Rinehart & Winston.

Beck, A.T., (1967), *Depression Causes and Treatment*. Philadelphia: University of Philadelphia Press.

Beck, A.T., Rush, A.J., Shaw, B.F. and Emory, G., (1979), *Cognitive Therapy of Depression*. New York: Guilford Press.

Brockner, J. and Guare, J., (1983), 'Improving the Performance of Low Self-esteem Individuals: An Attribution Approach'. *Academy of Management Journal*, 29, 373-384.

Cautela, J.R., (1967), 'Covert Sensitisation'. *Psychology Reports*, 20, 459-468.

Cowart, J. and Whalley, D.L., (1971), 'Punishment of Self-mutilation Behaviour'. Cited in D.L. Whalley & R.W. Malott. *Elementary Principles of Behaviour*. New York: Appleton Century Crofts.

Ellis, A., (1958), *Rational Psychotherapy*. California: Institute for Rational Emotive Therapy.

Emmelkamp, P.M.G., Bouman, T.K. and Scholing, A., (1992), *Anxiety Disorders: A Practitioner's Guide*. New York: Plenum.

Fairburn, C.G., Jones, R. and Peveler, R.C., (1993), 'Psychotherapy and Bulimia Nervosa: The Long-term Effects of Interpersonal Psychotherapy, Behaviour Therapy and Cognitive Behaviour Therapy'. *Archives of General Psychiatry*, 50, 419-428.

Freud, S., (1933), *New Introductory Lectures on Psychoanalysis*. New York: Norton.

Issacs, W., Thomas, J. and Goldiamond, I., (1960), 'Application of Operant Conditioning to Reinstate Verbal Behaviour in Psychotics'. *Journal of Speech and Hearing Disorders*, 25, 8-12.

Jayaprabha, R., (2003), 'Metacognitive and Cognitive Strategies to Overcome Behaviour Difficulties in Children'. Ph.D. Thesis in Education, Alagappa University, Karaikudi.

Jones, M.C., (1924), 'The Elimination of Children's Fears'. *Journal of Experimental Psychology*, 7, 382-390.

Kazdin, A.E., (1995), 'Cognitive Behavioural Interventions Applied to Children Age Seven Through Thirteen with Antisocial Behaviour'. Ph.D. Thesis Submitted to Central University of Israel, Israel.

Kazdin, A.E., (1995), *Conduct Disorders in Childhood and Adolescence*. London: Sage.

Meichenbaum, D.H., (1976), 'Towards a Cognitive Therapy of Self-control of Self-control'. In G. Schawrtz & D. Shapiro (Eds.), *Consciousness and self-regulation: Advances in Research*. New York; Plenum Publishing Co.

Meichenbaum, D.H., Henshaw, D. and Himmel, N., (1982), 'Coping with Stress as a Problem-solving Process'. In W. Krohne & L. Laux (Eds.) *Achievement, Stress and Anxiety*. Washington, DC: Hemisphere.

Meichenbaum, D.H., (1985), *Stress Inoculation Training*. New York: Pergamon.

Osborne, (2001), 'Modelling and Coaching of Relevant Meta Cognitive Strategies for Enhancing Children's Behaviour'. University of Pennsylvania, Pennsylvania.

Reddy, G.L. and Shyamala, V., (2003), 'Thinking and Constructivism: Class Room Approaches'. University News, Vol. 41, No.17, April 28-May 04.

Reddy, G.L. and Shyamala, V., (2004), 'Thinking Errors and Antisocial Behaviour'. *Research and Reflections on Education*, Vol.2, No.2, April-June.

Santhakumari, P., (2003), 'Effectiveness of Metacognitive and Strategies in Overcoming Language Learning Difficulties Among Higher Secondary Students'. Ph.D. Thesis in Education, Alagappa University, Karaikudi.

Schneider, B.H. and Byrne, B.M., (1987), 'Individualising Social Skills Training for Behaviour-disordered Children'. *Journal of Counselling and Clinical Psychology*, 55, 444-445.

Schoenbrodt-Myers Lisa, (2000), 'Parent training on the Generalization and Maintenance of Clinically Developed Self-control Skills with Children Who have Attention Deficit Hyperactivity Disorder'. University of Pennsylvania, Pennsylvania.

Shyamala, V., (2004), 'Effectiveness of Certain Strategies in Overcoming Antisocial Behaviour Among High School Students'. Ph.D. Thesis in Education, Alagappa University, Karaikudi.

Silverstein, C., (1972), 'Behaviour Modification and the Gay Community'. Paper Presented at the Annual Conference of the Association for the Advancement of Behaviour Therapy, New York.

Walker, S., (1984), *Learning Theory and Behaviour Modification*. London: Methuen.

Watson, S. and Samenow, S., (1995), *'The Criminal Personality: A Profile for Change*. Jason Aroson.

Williams, J.M.G., (1992), *The Psychological Treatment of Depression*. London: Routledge.

Wilson, G.T. and O'Leary, K.D., (1978), *Principles of Behaviour Therapy*. Englewood Cliffs, NJ: Prentice Hall.

Winnicott, D.W., (1958), *Through Paediatrics to Psychoanalysis*. London: The Hogarth Press.

Wolpe, J., (1973), *The Practice of Behaviour Therapy*. New York: Pergamon Press.

Wolpe, J., (1958), *Psychotherapy by Reciprocal Inhibition*. Stanford, CA: Stanford University Press.

15

Research on Behaviour Disorders

OBJECTIVES

This chapter explains the nature of science. It describes the different basic methods of research, such as case study, systematic naturalistic observation, correlational methods, experimental methods and mixed designs. It further analyses the qualitative research method. In addition, cross-sectional, longitudinal and sequential research strategies are distinguished. The different designs in risk research are also analysed. The chapter explains in detail the epidemiological research and finally brings out the ethical issues in research on behaviour disorders. After reading this chapter, the readers must be able to:

(i) Understand the nature of science;

(ii) Explain the different basic methods of research;

(iii) Describe the qualitative research method;

(iv) Distinguish cross-sectional, longitudinal and sequential research strategies;

(v) Define risk research and comprehend the different risk research designs;

(vi) Delineate epidemiological research; and

(vii) Present the ethical issues in research on behaviour disorders.

The different theoretical perspectives of psychopathology provide frameworks for the investigation of behaviour disorders. Abundant researches are being conducted to test various hypotheses regarding multivarious dysfunctions in youth and adolescence. This chapter analyses the various research methods that are prevalent in the field of psychopathology. It describes the basic research designs and strategies and it also provides the examples of their applications. In all the research designs, objective and reliable knowledge of human behaviour is gained through some scientific methods. Hence the aim of the different research methods is the same, though they vary along several dimensions, such as settings, procedures, methods and purpose.

NATURE OF SCIENCE

The word 'science' is derived from the Latin word for 'knowledge' and it refers to knowledge gained by a particular method of inquiry. An important recent historic event is the application of scientific methods to human behaviour. Earlier, it was conceived that humans are complicated, mysterious and special creatures who cannot be subjected to scientific study. But now there is a tremendous change in the perspectives on humans and human behaviour. As a result, psychology and other related disciplines are committed to the view that scientific method can provide the most valid information about human mind, human functioning, behaviour and development.

The ultimate aim of science is to describe various phenomena and to offer explanations for them. Similarly, the investigators who are involved in the scientific study of behavioural disturbances too ask innumerable questions about normal and deviant/problem behaviours such as:

1. How many/what proportion of children are at risk for developing problem behaviours/behaviour disorder?
2. Is the type of parenting style related to the development of childhood/adolescent behaviour disorders?
3. Is there any way to find solutions in the regular classrooms for the learning disabilities as well as the behaviour disorders of children?

4. What are the causes of children's emotional disturbances, anxiety, depression and at large the conduct disorders?
5. Does child abuse have anything to do with internalizing and externalizing behavioural problems?
6. Do the children vary in the level of psychopathology on the basis of their gender?

The investigators most often attempt to arrive at answers for such questions. Otherwise, then try to determine the exact conditions under which a phenomenon occurs, and its relationship to other variables. Or else, they want to make decisions with regard to cause-and-effect relationships to understand better and to be able to predict behaviour.

It is not possible to pose and try to answer research questions in an intellectual vacuum. Hence the researchers rely on theories for guidance of their research endeavours. A theory can be defined as an integrated set of propositions to explain a phenomenon. Theoretical concepts and assumptions, therefore, guide research goals, choice of variables, procedures, analyses and conclusions. Initially the theoretical concepts may be little more than hunches or guesses based on informal observations. But, when the research work progresses, the theoretical concepts become more developed and specific. Subjectively as well as creativity is involved in generating research questions and making decisions with regard to those questions.

Specific hypothesis are derived from theories. Hypotheses are tentative assumptions and generally specific hypotheses are tested in a scientific manner. Hypothesis testing is essential in that it tends to build knowledge systematically rather than haphazardly. A research investigation rarely proves that a hypothesis is either correct or incorrect. On the other hand, it provides evidence for or against the hypothesis. As a result, a hypothesis that is supported serves as evidence for the underlying theory. A failed hypothesis, in contrast, serves to disprove, limit or redirect a theoretical phenomenon or proposition. The observations and theoretical proposition of the investigator thus go hand-in-hand to advance towards scientific understanding.

Researchers work in different settings, which range from the natural environments of the home or school to the more rigid and controlled laboratory surrounds. Similarly, they use different research methods and designs, depending on the purpose of the research. However, observation and measurement, reliability and validity are very important consideration in all cases.

Observation and measurement are considered to be the heart of a scientific endeavour. But they remain challenging aspects to behavioural scientists. because it is simple to observe and to measure overt action. On the other hand, thought and emotion, which are intricately entwined with action, cannot be easily measured because they are elusive in nature. In such cases, the scientists have to operationalize the behaviour or concept being studied. In other words, some observable and measurable operation must be selected to define the behaviour or concept. For instance, aggression might be operationalized as the frequency with which children actually push or strike some objects or persons. Similarly, depression might be operationalized by the degree to which an individual reports feelings of sadness or hopelessness. To obtain all sorts of information, the behavioural scientists make use of different kinds of observations and measurements. Sometimes, they directly observe overt behaviour with or without special apparatus. Sometimes, they record physiological functioning of the heart, brain or sense organs. They may even ask people to report or rate their own behaviour, feelings and thoughts. Or they may collect reports of others about the subject of investigation. Such efforts may either be conducted in a laboratory or in a natural setting.

Apart from assuming that knowledge can be gained through observation, the scientific endeavours also assume that actions and events repeat themselves under given identical conditions. In other words, information obtained through observation remains the some, even if the observation is made by different persons in different times If not, the original finding is considered *unreliable* or *inconsistent*. Hence, the scientific method poses the need for *reliability* of results. This need for reliability places a burden on researchers to conceptualize clearly and concisely, observe, measure and report their findings to others in such a way that other may replicate such studies and judge them correct. Scientific method, thus, calls forth openness to scunity and evaluation of others.

Scientific method also poses a need for validity of the findings. Reliability refers to consistency or repeatability of results. On the hand, validity refers to the correctness, soundness or appropriateness of scientific findings. Generally, validity is judged in terms of the purpose of the research and the way the results are used. In addition, research findings should have both internal and external validity. Internal validity refers to the extent (degree) to which alternative explanations can be ruled out (Campbell & Stanley, 1963). Internal validity is closely tied to the notion of control in research. It is maximized by research designs and procedures, which build control over the variables that could affect the findings of the investigation. 'External validity' asks the question of generalizability. To what populations and situations can the results of an investigation be generalized? (Campbell & Stanley, 1963). Researchers are always virtually interested in this question.

BASIC METHODS OF RESEARCH

Several research methods are used in investigations of behaviour disorders. Some of the basic and commonly used methods of research in the field of behaviour disorders are case study method, systematic naturalistic observation method, correlational methods, experimental methods and methods using controlled observations and mixed designs. These research methods vary from one another in several ways and each has its own strengths and weaknesses. Further, each method may be more suitable in some situations than in others.

(a) Case Study Method

This is the most commonly used method in researches on behaviour disorder. It focuses on an individual, describing the background, present and past life circumstances and characteristics of the person. Generally, case studies tell us about the nature, course, causes, correlates and outcomes of behaviour problems. The following case of a fifteen-year-old depressed boy, Nick, described by Compas (1997) is the best illustration for case study:

"Nick lives with his mother. His father left before Nick was born. Nick was born with a curvature of the spine as a result of which he walks awkwardly and is limited in his physical abilities...He is irritable and sullen much of the time that they (Nick and his mother) are constantly fighting and arguing. Even the slightest thing seems to send him into a fit of anger...he throws things and punches holes in walls and doors...He seems unhappy and is withdrawn, spending much time at home and alone...Nick is sullen and aloof and shows little emotion...feels hopeless. He is self-conscious about his appearance, his peers tease him and he feels that he is disliked and he hates himself. Nick's typical day is: He wakes up early in the morning after having stayed up late the night before watching T.V, but he lies in bed until 9.00 or 10.00 A.M. He then spends much of the day at home alone playing videogames or watching T.V...He eats and snacks junk food all day long. His mother returns home from work late in the afternoon. They often argue about his having missed another day of school. They eat dinner together silently while watching T.V. The rest of the evening is filled with arguments about Nick's homework, school attendance problems, about his refusal to go to bed before midnight".

The primary goal of such case study is to illustrate the nature of ailment. One of the strengths of case study is its power to illustrate. A case study can richly describe phenomena, even phenomena that are so rare that they would be difficult to study in other ways. A case study can provide hypotheses to be tested and clinically examine results produced by other methods.

The weaknesses of the case studies are concerning their reliability and validity. Sometimes, the case study descriptions go back in time. The accuracy and completeness of such retrospective data are often suspected and thus reliability of the data is in question. When case studies go beyond description to interpretations, there are few guidelines to judge the validity of the interpretations. External validity also is weak in case study method because only one person is examined and so the findings cannot be generalized confidently to others.

Inspite of their shortcomings, case studies have played an important role in the development of clinical psychology and psychiatry (Chess, 1988). Most of the clinicians consider case studies 'do-able' and relevant to their concerns.

(b) Systematic Naturalistic Method

This method consists of direct observation of individuals in their 'real world' so as to describe naturally occurring behaviours, to answer specific questions or to test hypotheses. Dadds and Colleagues (1992) made systematic naturalistic observation to investigate on the development or maintenance of childhood depression. They used this method for hypotheses testing. The degree to which naturalistic observations can be generalized depends on the way in which the subjects are selected and several other factors.

(c) Correlational Methods

These methods determine whether relationships exist between or among variables. The variables may be measured in the natural environment or in the laboratory in a variety of ways. The investigations then calculate a correlation coefficient, which is a quantitative measure of the existence, direction, and strength of the relationships.

(d) The Experimental Methods

This method meets the rigorous standards of the scientific method. It is characterized by the following major principles:

- an explicitly stated hypothesis;
- approximately selected subjects assigned to groups which are exposed to different conditions or manipulations;
- two or more conditions/manipulations are selected by the investigator as independent variables;
- observation and measurement of dependent variable;
- control of the procedures by the researcher; and
- comparison of the effects of conditions/ manipulations.

In the experimental method, control is of crucial importance. When different groups are exposed to different conditions, the experiences undergone by the subjects are observed, measured and meticulously presented. The totally controlled procedure allows final judgement about the causes of the findings of the study.

Experiments might be conducted with many groups of people. Sometimes they might be conducted in the laboratory. Similarly, selection of subjects too can be made in different ways. Statistical analyses might also vary in accordance with the number of groups. But the purpose of the statistical analyses remains the same. In other words, the aim of statistical analyses is to determine whether group differences go beyond what might be expected by chance. When a significant statistical difference is found, a causal connection between the independent and dependent variables can be assumed. The experimental method is thus a powerful tool for explanation.

It is also possible to conduct an experiment with a single individual or a few individuals. This approach is single-case design (single-subject experiment) or as time-series studies because measurements are taken across some particular time periods. In such an approach, internal validity is possible with careful control. But external validity is not strong because generalizations cannot be made with enough confidence. Indeed, external validity can be enhanced by repeating the experiment with different subjects. Single-subject designs are frequently used to evaluate the influence of a clinical intervention.

(e) Controlled Observations and Mixed Designs

When researchers study behaviour disorders, they often use designs, which involve classificatory variables. That is, subjects who differ in some characteristics (classification) are selected and compared. For instance, individuals who are delinquent and non-delinquent are measured under controlled conditions and compared. There may or may not be manipulations of other factors. It should be stressed here that when research participants are selected on the basis of a classificatory variable, interpretation of the findings must be made cautiously.

Researchers should also be cautious when they interpret the results of mixed designs. In this design, research groups are chosen on the basis of classificatory factors and then a manipulation occurs (Davison and Neale, 1996). For instance, think of the investigation in which both boys of ADHD and normal boys (the classificatory factor) are given two kinds of attention tasks (a manipulation).

Consider the situations that the ADHD group does well with one task but not the other, whereas the normal group does well in both the tasks. The problem of interpretation still exists despite the manipulation. It is not clear whether hyperactivity itself rather than some associated feature caused the results.

Thus the methods of research presented above vary in several ways. Each has its own strength and weakness. As manipulation occurs in controlled situation in the experiment and single-subject experiment methods, they meet the standards of internal validity in the best manner. They also permit causal inferences to be drawn in the best possible way. But the choice of research method purely depends on the purpose of the investigation, as well as practical and ethical considerations.

QUALITATIVE RESEARCH METHOD

The latest commitment in the field of psychology is the belief that truth or scientific knowledge must be grounded in direct observation (Krahn, Hohn and Kime, 1995). There is also increased commitment towards *qualitative measurement* obtained by *objective investigators in controlled situations*. Hence much interest has been invested in qualitative methods of research, which include in-depth interview, life histories, memoirs, some case descriptions and ethnographies (narrative of cultures). Diaries, letters and other written records may be examined. In addition, naturalistic observation is very important with situations being recorded initially in narration rather than with a restrictive coding of different categories of behaviour. Further, the data is viewed as more credible when the observer becomes a participant in the setting and thereby optimizes understanding. This is known as participant observation. Ely (1991) lists the following as the characteristics of qualitative research:

1. Qualitative research assumes that events can be adequately understood only when they are observed in the appropriate context;
2. The contexts of inquiry are not contrived. Instead they are natural;

3. It assumes that human behaviour and development are best understood from a personal frame of reference. Hence, individuals are given enough opportunity to speak for themselves about their beliefs, attitudes and experiences;
4. Qualitative research makes an attempt to understand the reported experience as a unified whole rather than in terms of separate variables.

In qualitative research, it is also usual to collect large amounts of written data. The collected narrative data, are then conceptualised, analysed and interpreted (Strauss and Corbin, 1990). This process includes coding or categorizing statements or written observations. What is coded, how the coding is done and how the data are interpreted vary with the approach selected and the aims of the study. Qualitative research method can also be used to create hypotheses and theories. Recent qualitative researches in psychology have examined life satisfaction in the elderly, stress related to loss of jobs, parents' perception of child psychotherapy, parents' adjustment to the birth of a handicapped child, and parents' experiences with regard to their child's threatening illness (Fiese and Bickman, 1998).

The shortcomings of qualitative research methods are:

- they often have small sample size;
- they gather a huge amount of data and it is difficult as well as costly to analyse them;
- they create a need for guidelines for analysis of data;
- the data have the subjective nature;
- their reliability and validity are under the threat of questioning.

It is suggested that validity can be increased by combining qualitative and quantitative approaches. Most of the investigators find the qualitative research methods to be flexible and broadly scoped.

CROSS-SECTIONAL RESEARCH STRATEGY

In this type of research method, different groups of subjects are observed at one point in time. For instance, the peer relations of fourth, sixth, and ninth-grade children can be compared. The cross-sectional strategy is relatively inexpensive. At the same time, it is very efficient. It also provides much information. But it is difficult to trace developmental changes using cross-sectional strategy.

LONGITUDINAL RESEARCH STRATEGY

In longitudinal research method, the same subjects are evaluated over time, with repeated observations or tests. This method sees development as it occurs. Lewis Terman's research on intellectually gifted children (Cravens, 1992) was of this type. He tested the gifted children several times over many decades. Terman's study was then followed by other investigators who traced the growth of intellectual, social and physical abilities.

The uniqueness of the longitudinal strategy lies in its capacity to answer questions about the nature and course of development. Verhulst and Koot (1991) reported that the longitudinal research is extremely helpful in answering the questions like: 1) Does an early traumatic event, such as the death of a parent, play a role in the origin of childhood pathology? 2) To what extent does adolescent aggression carry over into adulthood? 3) Can early interventions prevent later problems in infants who experience prenatal difficulties?

The longitudinal research has also certain shortcomings.

- It is time-consuming in the sense that it requires the investigators to commit themselves to a project for many years;
- It is extremely expensive;
- It is difficult to retain subjects over long periods of time;
- The loss of participants can bias the subject sample;
- The repeated testing of participants gives rise to problems;
- Efforts to change or improve the research tools make it difficult to compare earlier and later findings.

- Subjects are not the only ones who change over the years but also the society changes due to the influence of historical variables.

In other words, possible generational or cohort effects need to be carefully considered when interpretations are made in longitudinal research studies.

SEQUENTIAL RESEARCH STRATEGY

A combination of cross-sectional and longitudinal strategies is known as sequential strategy. To overcome the weaknesses in the cross-sectional as well as longitudinal strategies, sequential strategy is used by the researchers interested in developmental change (Farrington, 1991). Consider a hypothetical study, for example, in which groups of children of different ages are studied over a relatively short time span. At Time I, children aged 3, 6, and 9 years are examined in a cross-sectional study. Similar examination of the same groups of children occurs again three years later at Time II. Again anther study is made another three years later at Time III. Then cross-sectional comparisons are made at three different times as shown in the figure given below.

Schema of a Sequential Research Design

Age Group	TIME		
	I (2000)	II (2003)	III (2006)
A	3	6	9
B	6	9	12
C	9	12	15

Thus, the children (A, B, C) are studied longitudinally over a six-year period (2000-2006). The age range in the investigation is twelve years (from 3 to 15 years), although the study is completed in six years.

Such sequential designs provide a wealth of information through various sorts of comparison. For instance, if aggression is hypothesized to be increasing with age at Time I, II and III (cross-sectional analyses) and also across time for each group of children (the longitudinal analyses), evidences would be strong for developmental change over the entire age range. Moreover by comparing aggression at the age six, or nine, or twelve (as crossed in the figure), the impact of societal conditions could also be valued. It might be found, for instance, that aggression at age nine increased from the year 2000 to 2003 to 2006. Since only one age is involved, this increase is not developmental and likely indicates a change in societal conditions during the years under study. In this way, sequential designs become very powerful in separating age differences and developmental changes, while taking generational effects into consideration.

RISK RESEARCH

Concept of risk is very important in understanding, predicting and potentially reducing behaviour problems. The cross-sectional strategy can help identify possible risk factors. For instance, we could study children with learning disabilities at one point in time to determine whether parental discord acts as a correlate. Let us frame the hypothesis that parental discord plays children at risk. At this juncture, we may need to decide whether the parental discord operated earlier so as to affect the child. We can approach this task in two ways: 1) retrospective; and 2) prospective research designs.

1. *Retrospective Research Design*

The purpose of this design is to seek hypotheses about the relationship of early variables and the later-observed characteristics. Hence this design is known as follow-back method. But this design has an obvious weakness regarding the reliability of the data. Moreover, old records and memories of the past may be sketchy, biased or mistaken. This design has another shortcoming too. That is, the discovery of relationships between the past and the present does not necessarily establish causation. Inspite of the above mentioned drawbacks, this method is comparatively easy to conduct and helps best to form hypotheses about risk factors.

2. *Prospective Research Design*

In this type of research design, risk factors are investigated longitudinally, observing subjects at certain time intervals. When longitudinal observations are made, if subjects reveal problem behaviours, the researcher can examine the data to determine what variables are linked to the occurrence of that particular problem behaviour. But this design has to meet the drawbacks, such as lot of expenses and time as well as loss of subjects. Further, when researchers begin their investigations, they have to select variables that will be observed along the way. Selection is often based on educated guesses. While doing so, some important and relevant variables may be missed. Though this design has such shortcomings, it is invaluable in identifying risk factors and is commonly employed (Kopp, 1994).

3. *High-Risk Research Method*

This method entails selecting subjects who are known to be at risk because of a factor already associated with the disorder. For instance, children who are at high risk for developing schizophrenia because of their having a parent with schizophrenia, may be considered as subjects for a study. Mednick and Schslinger (1968) were the first to use this strategy. Marcus et al. (1993), and Parnas et al. (1993) too used this design.

EPIDEMIOLOGICAL RESEARCH

Epidemiological research focused initially on infectious diseases and hence it has its basis in medicine. This kind of research assumes that disease or disorder can best be understood and dealt with by viewing individuals in the context of the physical and social environments in which disorder develops (Costello et al., 1993). This method entails the collection of data from large general populations or representative samples of the populations. One of the main goals of epidemiological research is to establish the prevalence or incidence of disorders in a population. Epidemiological research method also seeks to understand how a disorder is distributed in the population, what factors are correlated with a disorder, what are the causes and modes of transmission, what groups of people are at high risk, and how the disorder can be remedied or reduced. Within this framework, the epidemiological researchers interested in behavioural disorders of youth normally apply the developmental perspective. They are particularly interested in the continuity and discontinuity of disorders, in the processes, which link early and later behaviours and in the risk factors that might operate at different ages.

An important issue in epidemiology is an extensive assessment of behaviour so as to determine disorder. To avoid both expenses and time limitations involved in extensive assessments, standardized-structured or semi structured interviews have been increasingly employed in epidemiology. Such standard instruments are very efficient and designed with the goal of diagnosis in mind. The development of such assessment techniques for epidemiology is an ongoing effort. Further, correlational methods are often used in epidemiological studies to determine relationships among variables. The cross-sectional strategy is also useful for epidemiological studies. However, longitudinal data are also needed to understand developmental patterns of disorders (Costello et al., 1993).

Epidemiological researches provide valuable information. Numerous epidemiological studies provide valuable data on the rates of disorders are distributed in populations with regard to variables such as sex, social class race etc., Such knowledge is very crucial for prevention as well as for the delivery of optimum interventional and mental health services. Further, epidemiological studies are very helpful in the identification of correlates which inturn makes possible the formulation of hypotheses about risk and causation. At present, epidemiological studies have become more advanced and hence increased benefits will be reaped from these studies.

ETHICAL ISSUES IN RESEARCH BEHAVIOUR DISORDERS

There is no doubt regarding the benefits reaped from scientific researches and enquiries. At the same time, the scientific researches sound concerns about the welfare and the rights of participants. One such concern is sensitivity to individual rights, which are of both legal and ethical in nature. Some of the past researches were found to document abuse of research subjects. For instance, children with mental retardation who resided in Willowbrook school in the state of New York were deliberately infected with hepatitis in order to study the disease (Glantz, 1996). Probably abuse in social science research may not be so drastic as in biochemical research. Eventhen, concerns for ethical issues constantly arise in the researches on behaviour disorders. The American Psychological Association has published a manual of ethical guidelines for research. Similarly, the Society for Research in Child Development has published guidelines, which specifically address research with children. Those ethical standards/guidelines are given below:

ETHICAL STANDARDS FOR RESEARCH WITH CHILDREN

1. *Non-harmful Procedure*

No research operation, which may physically or psychologically harm child should be used. The least stressful operation should be used. Doubts about harmfulness should be discussed with consultants.

2. *Informed Consent*

The child's consent should be obtained. The child should be informed of features of the research that may affect his/her willingness to participate. When working with infants, the parents should be informed.

3. *Parental Consent*

Informed consent of parents, guardians and those acting in loci of parents (e.g. school superintendent) should be obtained, preferably in writing.

4. *Additional Consent*

Informed consent should be obtained from persons, such as teachers, whose interaction with the child is the subject of the research.

5. *Incentives*

Incentives to participate in the research must be fair and they should not unduly exceed the ones, which the child normally experiences.

6. *Deception*

If deception or withholding information is considered essential, colleagues must agree with this judgement. Participants should be told later of the reason for the deception. Effort should be made to employ deception methods that have no known.

7. *Anonymity*

Permission should be obtained for access to institutional records and anonymity of information should be preserved.

8. *Mutual Responsibilities*

There should be clear agreement as to responsibilities of all parties in the research. The investigator must honour all promises and commitments.

9. *Jeopardy*

When information comes to the investigator's attention that may jeopardise the child's welfare, the information must be discussed with parents or guardians and experts who can arrange for assistance to the child.

10. *Unforeseen Consequences*

When research procedures result in unforeseen, undesirable consequences should be corrected and the procedures redesigned.

11. *Confidentiality*

The identity of subjects and all information about them should be kept confidential. When there is a threat for confidentiality, this possibility and methods to prevent it should be explained as part of the procedures of obtaining informed consent.

12. *Informing the Participants*

Immediately after data collection, any misconceptions that might have arisen should be clarified. General findings should be given to the participants, appropriate to their understanding. When scientific or human reasons justify withholding information, efforts should be made so that withholding has no damaging consequences.

13. *Reporting Results*

Investigators' words may carry unintended weight, thus, caution should be used in reporting results, giving advice, making evaluative statements.

14. *Implications of Findings*

Investigations should be mindful of the social, political and human implications of the research, and especially careful in the presentations of findings.

Following the above guidelines is a must for all researchers. The ethical concerns are often very complex and hence the researchers must be very careful. Special consideration should be given to cases involving young subjects, who need special protection. The basic ethical principle should be that no serious harm (either physical or psychological) should be done to participants. There are some procedures in the research process in which the children may feel very uncomfortable. Similarly, research on the effects of medication which can entail complex ethical dilemmas or serious side-effects must be conducted very cautiously. Particularly, in non-therapeutic research, the child's consent should be considered of utmost importance. For instance, when risk is greater than minimal and the research is unlikely to benefit the child directly, the child should be properly informed of that and only then the child's consent should be obtained. The prevailing emphasis on human rights and the recognition of abuses in the research investigations conducted in the past have led to quite stringent surveillance and guidelines.

SUMMARY

Different research methods and designs are useful to gain the knowledge of human behaviour. These methods vary along several dimensions, such as settings, procedures, methods and purpose.

An important historic event is the application of scientific methods to human behaviour. The investigators who are involved in the scientific study of behavioural disturbances ask many questions regarding normal and deviant/problem behaviours and they try to seek answers in some of them. Or else they try to determine the conditions under which a phenomenon occurs, and its relationship to other variables. Researchers rely on theories for guidance of their research endeavours. Specific hypothesis are derived from theories. Observation and measurement, reliability and validity are very important consideration in all types of research methods and designs.

Some of the basic and commonly used research methods in the investigations of behaviour disorders are case study method, systematic naturalistic observation method, correlational method, experimental methods and methods using controlled observations and mixed designs. They vary from one another in several ways. Each of these methods has its own strengths and weaknesses. Further, each method may be more suitable in some situations than in others.

The latest commitment in the field of psychology is the belief that truth or scientific knowledge must be grounded in direct observations and also there is increased commitment towards qualitative measurement. Hence much interest has been aroused in qualitative methods of research, which include in-depth interview, life histories, memories, some case descriptions and ethnographies (narrative of cultures). Reliability and validity can be problematic in these methods.

Research can also vary regarding whether a cross-sectional or a longitudinal is adopted. Cross-sectional studies ex mine groups of subjects at onetime. They are efficient and economical. They can establish age differences. The longitudinal strategy is more useful in tracing development. It is expensive in terms of cost and time. It may suffer from subject loss and repeated measurement. Further, longitudinal data may reflect general, or cohort, efforts.

Sequential research strategy combines both cross-sectional and longitudinal strategies so as to avoid shortcomings of both these strategies. This strategy is helpful in examining developmental changes, age differences and the influence of generational (historical) variables.

The concept of risk is very important in understanding, predicting and potentially reducing behaviour problems. The cross-sectional strategy can help identify certain possible risk factors. Both retrospective (follow-back) methods and prospective longitudinal methods are useful in identifying risk and possible causal factors. High-risk research method entails selecting subjects who are known to be at risk because of a factor already associated with the disorder.

Epidemiological research focused initially on infectitious diseases and hence it has its basis in medicine. Its aim is to establish the rates and disturbances of disorders in a population, the factors correlated with disorders, and risk and causal factors. It is also interested in the prevention and the treatment of disorders.

Concerns for ethical issues constantly arise in the researches on behaviour disorders. The American Psychological Association has published a manual of ethical guidelines for research. Similarly, the Society for Research in Child Development has also published guidelines, which specifically address research with children. Some of the guidelines insist the principles of non-harmful procedure, informed consent, anonymity, and confidentiality. Following such basic guidelines is a must for all investigators. The ethical concerns are often very complex and hence the researchers must be very careful. The prevailing emphasis on human rights and the recognition of abuses in the research investigations conducted in the immediate past have led to quite stringent surveillance and guidelines.

REFERENCES

Campbell, D.T. and Stanley, J.C., (1963), *Experimental and Quasi-experimental Designs for Research*. Chicago: Rand McNally.

Chess, S., (1998), 'Child and Adolescent Psychiatry Come of Age: A Fifty-Year Perspective'. *Journal of the American Academy of Child and Adolescent Psychiatry*, 27,1-7.

Compas, B.E., (1997), 'Depression in Children and Adolescents'. In E. J. Mash & L.G. Terdal (Eds.), *Assessment of Childhood Disorders*, (3rd Ed.) New York: Guilford Press.

Costello, E.J., Burns, B.J., Angold, A. and Leaf, P.J., (1993), 'How Can Epidemiology Improve Mental Health Services of Children and Adolescents?' *Journal of the American Academy of Child and Adolescent Psychiatry*, 32, 1106-1117.

Cravens, H., (1992), 'A Scientific Project Locked in Time: The Terman Genetic Studies of Genius, 1920s-1950s'. *American Psychologist*, 47, 183-189.

Dadds, M.R. Sanders, M.R., Morrison, M. and Rebgetz, M., (1992), 'Childhood Depression and Conduct Disorder: II. An Analysis of Family Interaction Patterns in the Home'. *Journal of Abnormal Psychology,* 101, 505-513.

Davison, G.C., and Neale, J.M., (1996), *Abnormal Psychology,* New York: Wiley

Ely, M., (1991), *Doing Qualitative Research: Circles Within Circles.* New York: The Falmer Press.

Farrington, D.P., (1991), 'Longitudinal Research Strategies: Advantages, Problems, and Prospects'. *Journal of the American Academy of Child and Adolescent Psychiatry,* 30,369-374.

Fiese, B.H. and Bickman, N.L., (1998), 'Qualitative Inquiry: An Overview for Paediatric Psychology'. *Journal of Paediatric Psychology,* 23,79-86.

Glantz, L.H., (1996), 'Conducting Research with Children: Legal and Ethical Issues'. *Journal of the American Academy of Child and Adolescent Psychiatry,* 35, 1283-1291.

Kopp, C.B., (1994), 'Trends and Directions in Studies of Developmental Risk'. In C.A. Nelson (Ed). *Threats to Optimal Development: Integrating Biological, Psychological, Social Risk Factors. the Minnesota Symposium on Child Psychology,* Vol.27. Hillsdale, NJ: Erlbaum.

Krahn, G.L. Hohn, M.F. and Kime, C., (1995), 'Incorporating Qualitative Approaches into Clinical Child Psychology Research'. *Journal of Clinical Child Psychology,* 24, 204-213.

Marcus, J., Hans, S.L., Auerbach, J.G. and Auerbach, A.G., (1993), 'Children at Risk for Schizophrenia: The Jerusalem Infant Development Study'. *Archives of General Psychiatry,* 50, 797-809.

Mednick, S.A. and Schulsinger, F., (1968), 'Some Pre-morbid Characteristics Related to Breakdown in Children with Schizophrenic Mothers'. In D. Rosenthal and S.S. Kety (Eds), *The Transmission of Schizophrenia Elmsford,* NY: Pergamon Press.

Parnas, J., Cannon, T.D., Jacobsen, B., Schulsinger, H., Schulsinger, F. and Mednic, S.A., (1993), 'Lifetime DSM-III-R Diagnostic Outcomes in the Offspring of Schizophrenic Mothers'. *Archives of General Psychiatry,* 50, 707-714.

Strauss, A., and Corbin J., (1990), *Basics of Qualitative Research.* Newbury Park, CA: Sage.

Verhurst, F.C. and Koot, H.M., (1991), 'Longitudinal Research in Child and Adolescent Psychiatry'. *Journal of the American Academy of Child Adolescent Psychiatry,* 30, 361-368.

Index

E

F